CONSTITUTIONALIZING THE PRIVATE SPHERE

Do private actors have constitutional duties? While traditionally only government actors are responsible for upholding constitutional rights, courts and constitution-makers increasingly do assign constitutional duties to private actors as well. Therefore, a landlord may have constitutional duties to their tenants, and a sports club may even have duties to its fans. This book argues that this phenomenon of applying rights "horizontally" can be understood through the lens of republican political theory. Themes echoing such concepts as the common good and civic duty from republican thought recur in discourses surrounding horizontal application. Christina R. Bambrick traces republican themes in debates from the United States, India, Germany, South Africa, and the European Union. While these contexts have vastly different histories and aspirations, constitutional actors in each place have considered the horizontal application of rights and, in doing so, made republican arguments.

CHRISTINA R. BAMBRICK is an assistant professor of political science at the University of Notre Dame. She studies constitutional theory and comparative constitutionalism. She previously taught at Clemson University and holds a PhD from the University of Texas at Austin.

CAMBRIDGE STUDIES IN CONSTITUTIONAL LAW

The aim of this series is to produce leading monographs in constitutional law. All areas of constitutional law and public law fall within the ambit of the series, including human rights and civil liberties law, administrative law, as well as constitutional theory and the history of constitutional law. A wide variety of scholarly approaches is encouraged, with the governing criterion being simply that the work is of interest to an international audience. Thus, works concerned with only one jurisdiction will be included in the series as appropriate, while, at the same time, the series will include works which are explicitly comparative or theoretical – or both. The series editors likewise welcome proposals that work at the intersection of constitutional and international law, or that seek to bridge the gaps between civil law systems, the US, and the common law jurisdictions of the Commonwealth.

Series Editors
David Dyzenhaus
Professor of Law and Philosophy, University of Toronto, Canada
Thomas Poole
Professor of Law, London School of Economics and Political Science

Books in the series

Constitutionalizing the Private Sphere: A Comparative Inquiry Christina R. Bambrick

Beyond Expropriation Without Compensation: Law, Land Reform and Redistributive Justice in South Africa Edited by Olaf Zenker, Cherryl Walker and Zsa-Zsa Boggenpoel

Trust, Courts and Social Rights: A Trust-Based Framework for Social Rights Enforcement David Vitale

The Collaborative Constitution Aileen Kavanagh

Non-Statutory Executive Powers and Judicial Review Jason Grant Allen

The Law as a Conversation among Equals Roberto Gargarella

Micronations and the Search for Sovereignty Harry Hobbs and George Williams

Fundamental Rights and the Legal Obligations of Business David Bilchitz

Courting Constitutionalism: The Politics of Public Law and Judicial Review in Pakistan Moeen Cheema

Ruling by Cheating: Governance in Illiberal Democracy András Sajó

Local Meanings of Proportionality Afroditi Marketou

Property Rights and Social Justice: Progressive Property in Action Rachael Walsh

Carl Schmitt's Early Legal-Theoretical Writings: Statute and Judgment and the Value of the State and the Significance of the Individual Lars Vinx and Samuel Garrett Zeitlin

Remedies for Human Rights Violations: A Two-Track Approach to Supranational and National Law Kent Roach

Europe's Second Constitution: Crisis, Courts and Community Markus W. Gehring

A.V. Dicey and the Common Law Constitutional Tradition: A Legal Turn of Mind Mark D. Walters

Administrative Competence: Reimagining Administrative Law Elizabeth Fisher and Sidney A. Shapiro

Legal Sabotage: Ernst Fraenkel in Hitler's Germany Douglas Morris

Proportionality in Action: Comparative and Empirical Perspectives on the Judicial Practice Edited by Mordechai Kremnitzer, Tayla Steiner and Andrej Lang

Constitutional Dialogue: Democracy, Rights, Institutions Edited by Geoffrey Sigalet, Grégoire Webber and Rosalind Dixon

The Veiled Sceptre: Reserve Powers of Heads of State in Westminster Systems Anne Twomey

Vigilance and Restraint in the Common Law of Judicial Review Dean Knight

The Alchemists: Questioning Our Faith in Courts as Democracy-Builders Tom Gerald Daly

Australia's Constitution after Whitlam Brendan Lim

Building the Constitution: The Practice of Constitutional Interpretation in Post-Apartheid South Africa James Fowkes

Dimensions of Dignity: The Theory and Practice of Modern Constitutional Law Jacob Weinrib

Reason of State: Law, Prerogative, Empire Thomas Poole

Bills of Rights in the Common Law Robert Leckey

The Guardian of the Constitution: Hans Kelsen and Carl Schmitt on the Limits of Constitutional Law Translated by Lars Vinx, with an introduction and notes by Lars Vinx

Parliamentary Bills of Rights: The Experiences of New Zealand and the United Kingdom Janet L. Hiebert and James B. Kelly

Lawyering for the Rule of Law: Government Lawyers and the Rise of Judicial Power in Israel Yoav Dotan

Balancing Constitutional Rights: The Origins and Meanings of Postwar Legal Discourse Jacco Bomhoff

Judges on Trial: The Independence and Accountability of the English Judiciary Shimon Shetreet and Sophie Turenne

Proportionality and Constitutional Culture Moshe Cohen-Eliya and Iddo Porat

The Politics of Principle: The First South African Constitutional Court, 1995–2005 Theunis Roux

The New Commonwealth Model of Constitutionalism: Theory and Practice
Stephen Gardbaum

Searching for the State in British Legal Thought: Competing Conceptions of the Public Sphere Janet McLean

Judging Social Rights Jeff King

Proportionality: Constitutional Rights and their Limitations Aharon Barak

Parliamentary Sovereignty: Contemporary Debates Jeffrey Goldsworthy

CONSTITUTIONALIZING THE PRIVATE SPHERE

A Comparative Inquiry

CHRISTINA R. BAMBRICK
University of Notre Dame

Shaftesbury Road, Cambridge CB2 8EA, United Kingdom

One Liberty Plaza, 20th Floor, New York, NY 10006, USA

477 Williamstown Road, Port Melbourne, VIC 3207, Australia

314–321, 3rd Floor, Plot 3, Splendor Forum, Jasola District Centre, New Delhi – 110025, India

103 Penang Road, #05–06/07, Visioncrest Commercial, Singapore 238467

Cambridge University Press is part of Cambridge University Press & Assessment, a department of the University of Cambridge.

We share the University's mission to contribute to society through the pursuit of education, learning and research at the highest international levels of excellence.

www.cambridge.org
Information on this title: www.cambridge.org/9781009293709

DOI: 10.1017/9781009293723

© Christina R. Bambrick 2024

This publication is in copyright. Subject to statutory exception and to the provisions of relevant collective licensing agreements, no reproduction of any part may take place without the written permission of Cambridge University Press & Assessment.

When citing this work, please include a reference to the DOI 10.1017/9781009293723

First published 2024
First paperback edition 2025

A catalogue record for this publication is available from the British Library

Library of Congress Cataloging-in-Publication data
Names: Bambrick, Christina R, author.
Title: Constitutionalizing the private sphere : a comparative inquiry / Christina R Bambrick, University of Notre Dame, Indiana.
Description: Cambridge, United Kingdom ; New York, NY : Cambridge University Press, 2024. | Includes bibliographical references and index.
Identifiers: LCCN 2024015836 (print) | LCCN 2024015837 (ebook) | ISBN 9781009293730 (hardback) | ISBN 9781009293709 (paperback) | ISBN 9781009293723 (epub)
Subjects: LCSH: Constitutional law–Philosophy. | Civil rights–Philosophy. | Equality before the law–Philosophy. | Republicanism–Philosophy. | Social change–Philosophy. | Local government. | Civil society.
Classification: LCC K3240 .B3595 2024 (print) | LCC K3240 (ebook) | DDC 342.08/501–dc23/eng/20240409
LC record available at https://lccn.loc.gov/2024015836
LC ebook record available at https://lccn.loc.gov/2024015837

ISBN 978-1-009-29373-0 Hardback
ISBN 978-1-009-29370-9 Paperback

Cambridge University Press & Assessment has no responsibility for the persistence or accuracy of URLs for external or third-party internet websites referred to in this publication and does not guarantee that any content on such websites is, or will remain, accurate or appropriate.

To the memory of
Irma and Joseph Noriega
Carmela and Vito Colonna

CONTENTS

Acknowledgments x

1 Introduction 1
2 A Republican Vein in Liberal Constitutionalism 16

Equality

3 The United States: Equality Along the Public–Private Divide 63
4 India: Citizens' Duties in Aspiring to Equality 101

Transformation

5 Germany: New Tensions Amid Radiating Values 148
6 South Africa: Toward Societal Transformation 188
7 The European Union: Republicanism in Supranational Context 243
8 Conclusion 271

Bibliography 279
Index 295

ACKNOWLEDGMENTS

Although writing is often a lonely endeavor, this book allowed me to cross paths with many exceptional, and exceptionally generous, people. I count these connections and dialogues among the most gratifying rewards of this project.

For insightful and often long conversations about the finer details of the contexts I study here, I am grateful to Gautam Bhatia, David Bilchitz, Sheila Camerer, Dennis Davis, Jackie Dugard, Holger Greve, Justice Dieter Grimm, Nicholas Haysom, Christoph Möllers, Ignatius Rautenbach, Christian Starck, Justice Leona Theron, Alexander Tischbirek, Johan van der Vyver, and Hoyt Webb.

For the opportunity to present my work and receive essential feedback, I am indebted to Ran Hirschl, Ayelet Shachar, the University of Göttingen, and the Max Planck Institute for the Study of Religious and Ethnic Diversity. Additionally, I am grateful to the Societas Aperta Feminarum in Iuris Theoria, the American Political Thought Journal Workshop, Justin Dyer and the Kinder Institute on Constitutional Democracy, the Penn State Law Working Paper Series, and various meetings of the American Political Science Association and Midwest Political Science Association for the opportunity to receive feedback on early versions of these chapters.

I am profoundly grateful to Stephen Gardbaum, Tarunabh Khaitan, Heinz Klug, Jud Mathews, Georg Vanberg, and Mariah Zeisberg for their participation in a manuscript workshop. To dedicate so much time to reading someone's work is a true gift, and this book is undoubtedly better as a result of their thoughtful engagement.

Support from the Institute for Humane Studies for a sabbatical semester and manuscript workshop was invaluable to completing this book, as was support from Notre Dame's Center for Citizenship and Constitutional Government and De Nicola Center for Ethics and Culture. I am grateful to Evelyn Behling and Bailey Baumbick for their superb research assistance, and to Rebecca Devine for truly excellent editing.

David Dyzenhaus, Tom Poole, and Marianne Nield at Cambridge University Press have supported this book with great enthusiasm and verve. I am thankful for their confidence in bringing this project to fruition. I am also grateful to the anonymous reviewers for their uncommonly helpful suggestions.

For friendship and solidarity in what otherwise would have been entirely solitary days of writing, I am deeply grateful to Katherine Bersch, Brookes Brown, Sarah Burns, Anna Fruhstorfer, Theresa MacArt, Abigail Moncrieff, Emma Planinc, and Jane Ryngaert. And for continual mentorship in navigating the writing and publishing process, I am grateful to Susan Collins, Mary Keys, Vincent Phillip Muñoz, Emilia Justyna Powell, and Stephen Wrinn.

In completing this and all future projects, I will always be indebted to the unmatched teachers from whom I learned at the University of Texas, chief among them Gary Jacobsohn, who took the ideas in this book seriously and made them better. I am also grateful to Daniel Brinks, J. Budziszewski, Victor Ferreres Comella, and Jeffrey Tulis for their generous mentorship.

To an even greater degree, I remain indebted to my family for loving and supporting me through every endeavor. I am thankful to Joshua for his constancy of love and confidence in me, to Daniel, who keeps me honest by asking almost daily if I did "big writing," and to Isabel, who was the most loyal of writing companions from her first days in the world.

A version of Chapter 2 appeared in "Horizontal Rights: A Republican Vein in Liberal Constitutionalism," *Polity* 52(3) (2020), 401–429.

1

Introduction

Facebook's right to monitor its platform conflicts with a user's right to post political opinions. A baker's right to religious liberty runs up against a same-sex couple's right to equal service. A private school administration's right to set health policies on its campus collides with a person's right not to wear a mask. Rights are invoked across a wide range of political disputes by a diverse set of actors – large corporations, small proprietors, and individual people, to name a few. These are all private parties, not state actors, and in a traditional model of constitutional rights, none could claim a constitutional right against the other. The constitution applies only to government action, whereas relationships among private companies or individuals fall under separate areas of law, often defined by ordinary legislative processes relating to antitrust, antidiscrimination, or public health initiatives, for example. The constitution simply is not at issue in these cases.

This traditional understanding of constitutionalism is often understood as a *vertical* model, whereby constitutional rights exist only between the government, above, and private actors, below. In other words, only the government is responsible for protecting, respecting, and fulfilling constitutional rights. In many ways, this conception of rights reflects a classical liberal ideology that would maintain a separate, private sphere of liberty unencumbered by the same constitutional duties that bind public actors. Since the mid twentieth century, however, some countries have adopted a *horizontal* model whereby private actors do have duties – specifically, duties to uphold the constitutional rights of others. Businesses, for-profit hospitals, independent schools, and even private individuals potentially hold some responsibility for constitutional rights, ranging from the freedom of speech to equal protection and nondiscrimination, and even such positive rights as health. In 2017, for example, South Africa's Constitutional Court decided that landlords had a constitutional duty to uphold their tenants' right to dignity in their living conditions. This case was not decided on the basis of housing codes or other statutory law, as it would be in the United States, but as a matter of constitutional rights. Thus, within this horizontal conception of rights, private actors live under a constitutional standard and have constitutional duties. The horizontal model – variously called horizontal application, horizontal effect, horizontal rights, or simply horizontality – allows people to articulate cases against other private actors using the language and moral weight of constitutional rights.

This book argues that the practice of horizontality deserves fuller treatment in the academy and beyond. This deeper understanding can be found through the lens of republican political theory – that is, the big-tent tradition of political thought from the classical republicanism of ancient Greece and Rome to the more recent instances of neorepublicanism. A republican theory of horizontality draws on concepts of the common good and duty as touchstones, marking horizontality's shift away from conventional liberal accounts of individual rights. Horizontality brings to the fore the necessity of limitations on rights, as private actors take on constitutional duties and as more rights come into conflict. As related to republicanism, horizontality can be understood as attempting a kind of democratization of the private sphere, wherein private actors become subject to the same values adopted by the proverbial "we the people" in the constitution. Political debates are unified under a constitutional rubric, and the republican conception of an encompassing common good supplants the ideal of individual liberties.

Rights-Centrism and the Horizontal Shift

In his philosophic investigation of the American Revolution, Morton White explores a revision that Thomas Jefferson made to one of the most famous lines in the Declaration of Independence. In his "original Rough draught," Jefferson wrote "that to secure these *ends*, Governments are instituted among Men."[1] This phrasing differs, of course, from the final, more familiar claim that governments are instituted to secure *rights*. Arguably, this change is not simply stylistic; instead, Jefferson redefines the very role of government as guardian of rights that people already

---

[1] Emphasis added. Morton White, *The Philosophy of the American Revolution* (New York: Oxford University Press, 1978), 249. See also Gary Jacobsohn and Yaniv Roznai, *Constitutional Revolution* (New Haven: Yale University Press, 2020), 171, fn. 95.

possess, rather than a means to attain ends not yet realized.² Later moments in American constitutional history evince similar understandings of constitutionalism, including interpretations of the Fourteenth Amendment that cemented an understanding of the constitution as governing state action only – not private action and perhaps not even state *inaction*.³ This partitioning of accountability between public and private actors tends to take background rules of private law as neutral; private actors are insulated from the commitments the state undertakes in the constitution. Indeed, government is seen as securing rights already acknowledged, and properly refraining from additional projects that risk running up against these rights.

As more countries adopted constitutions in the twentieth century, some followed the practice, at least initially, of limiting most provisions of their constitutions to bind only the actions of the state. After the adoption of the Basic Law in 1949, however, the German Federal Constitutional Court began to apply rights horizontally in its practice of *Drittwirkung*, or indirect third-party effect,⁴ despite some skepticism from some scholars and jurists. The concept of horizontality thus entered onto the scene of global constitutionalism, making it a real option that other courts and constitution-makers might adopt. In turn, legal scholars and practitioners expended much effort to understand horizontality's effects and limits, as well as to justify this shift in constitutionalism.

---

² White, *Philosophy of the American Revolution*, 249. Relatedly, Emily Zackin describes this kind of rights-centrism as inherently conservative in contrast with the more transformative tendencies that come of both positive rights and, this book would add, horizontal rights. She writes:

> Most accounts of rights' creation, both within and outside the United States, hold that dominant political coalitions write new rights into constitutions when (and precisely because) they are worried about losing their dominant positions. On this account, movements for new rights are fundamentally conservative projects, intended to maintain the status quo. However, the origins of positive rights in state constitutions are quite different.... [M]any positive-rights' advocates did not intend to crystallize existing political arrangements. Instead, these activists hoped to rewrite the rules of politics and transform their societies.

See Emily Zackin, *Looking for Rights in All the Wrong Places* (Princeton: Princeton University Press, 2013), 3–4, and Jamal Greene, *How Rights Went Wrong* (Boston: Houghton Mifflin Harcourt, 2021), 13.

³ See cases ranging from the *Civil Rights Cases*, 109 U.S. 3 (1883) to *DeShaney v. Winnebago County*, 489 U.S. 189 (1989).

⁴ Renáta Uitz, "Introduction," in *The Constitution in Private Relations*, ed. András Sajó and Renáta Uitz (Utrecht: Eleven, 2005).

With the introduction of horizontality, constitutions no longer aimed only to secure rights, but also to secure certain ends through extending the reach of rights. Robert Alexy elaborates a distinction between the kind of subjective rights that create obligations for particular actors, usually states actors, and objective rights that constitute values of the polity.[5] The rights-centrism that dominated previous conceptions of constitutionalism is thus qualified by the contention that, sometimes, the choices that individuals make under the auspices of private life bear on public commitments.[6] Of course, horizontality still operates in the context of liberal constitutionalism and employs the liberal language of rights. At the same time, it also entails an important shift – a kind of reversal of Jefferson's amendment to the Declaration – so that the constitution is no longer simply about protecting individual's rights from state interference, but now articulates public ends common to the polity. Whereas a rights-centric framework, as propounded by many of the social contract theorists of the modern era, tends to comprehend individual obligations merely in terms of what is necessary to secure one's own rights,[7] horizontality attempts to ground duties in the same substantive principles articulated in a constitution. The move from a vertical to horizontal model changes *who* is responsible – that is, the very orientation of rights relationships.

While acknowledging the ways in which horizontality runs up against traditional understandings of constitutionalism, constitutional scholarship (and even practice) in the past couple of decades has generally been sympathetic to horizontality. At the time of writing, no fewer than forty-eight national constitutions explicitly state that rights bind private actors.[8] This number does not include the other constitutions that point toward horizontality but depend on the courts to develop it more fully, such as in Germany, or those that provide it only for particular rights, such as in India. Even in the United States, the historic case *Shelley*

---

[5] Robert Alexy, *A Theory of Constitutional Rights* (Oxford: Oxford University Press, 2010).
[6] Prior to this development, the American Legal Realists made similar observations. In a sense, horizontal application thus represents a concrete doctrinal answer to their critique.
[7] Harry Jaffa, *Crisis of the House Divided* (Chicago: University of Chicago, 2009), 325; Pierre Manent, *Natural Law and Human Rights* (Notre Dame, IN: Notre Dame University Press, 2020), 8.
[8] Comparative Constitutions Project, "Binding Effect of Constitutional Rights," accessed September 13, 2023, https://www.constituteproject.org/constitutions?lang=en&key=binding&status=in_force.

v. Kraemer (1948)⁹ marks a decision approximating horizontality. In the context of the European Union, Eleni Frantziou maintains that the question of whether to apply rights horizontally ultimately speaks to what "kind of society the EU is setting itself out to be and the values that lie in its core."¹⁰ Since the UK's passing of the Human Rights Act (HRA), scholars have increasingly asked what rights obligations EU law entails for private entities, culminating in judgments by the European Court of Justice.¹¹

Scholars have also argued that horizontality is not a particularly novel innovation in constitutionalism. As Stephen Gardbaum observes, the statement in Article VI that the United States Constitution is the "Supreme Law of the Land" effectively establishes indirect horizontality insofar as the constitution must control the content of private law.¹² Moreover, in his book *Weak Courts, Strong Rights*, Mark Tushnet points out that countries maintain certain "background rules" of private law that necessarily confront – and so already answer – substantive questions about the limits of private action and how public law bears on private relations.¹³ In the German context, Mattias Kumm argues that horizontality is just another development in the larger move toward "total constitutionalism" in contemporary law and politics. Denying that horizontality is particularly novel, Kumm sees it almost as inevitable as countries adopt more ambitious socioeconomic rights in their constitutions.¹⁴ In light of the questions that horizontality raises for traditional

---

⁹ In this case, the US Supreme Court decided it could not enforce a racially restrictive covenant because of the requirements of the Equal Protection Clause of the Fourteenth Amendment.

¹⁰ Eleni Frantziou, "The Horizontal Effect of the Charter of Fundamental Rights of the EU: Rediscovering the Reasons for Horizontality," *European Law Journal* 21:5 (2015), 675.

¹¹ See, for example, Murray Hunt, "The 'Horizontal Effect' of the Human Rights Act," *Public Law*, 1998; Andrew Clapham, *Human Rights Obligations of Non-state Actors* (Oxford: Oxford University Press, 2006). See also the three edited volumes on the subject of horizontality published in the years following the HRA: Daniel Friedmann and Daphne Barak-Erez, eds., *Human Rights in Private Law* (Portland, OR: Hart, 2001); András Sajó and Renáta Uitz, eds., *The Constitution in Private Relations* (Utrecht: Eleven, 2005); Dawn Oliver and Jorg Fedtke, eds., *Human Rights in the Private Sphere* (Abingdon: Routledge-Cavendish, 2007).

¹² Stephen Gardbaum, "The 'Horizontal Effect' of Constitutional Rights," *Michigan Law Review* 102 (2003), 387–459.

¹³ Mark Tushnet, *Weak Courts, Strong Rights* (Princeton: Princeton University Press, 2008).

¹⁴ Mattias Kumm, "Who is Afraid of the Total Constitution? Constitutional Rights as Principles and the Constitutionalization of Private Law," *German Law Journal* 7:4 (2006), 341–369.

understandings, legal scholars have invested much energy in trying to explain how this phenomenon does or does not comport with the tradition of constitutionalism.

I argue that horizontality should be understood within the republican tradition, which expands the logic of rights to encompass ends and a broader set of citizens' duties. The constitutional ends that result from horizontality are *shared* ends – directed toward the common good, with both public and private actors beholden to certain duties. Constitutional actors may still use the language of rights, but horizontality calls for concepts beyond what conventional accounts of liberal constitutionalism typically provide. Indeed, as Kalyvas and Katznelson document, the development of liberalism in the eighteenth century was a reaction to the excesses of republicanism.[15] We can, in turn, think of horizontality as a kind of retrospective reaction to traditional accounts of constitutionalism, challenging the neutrality of the background rules of private law and reordering those rules according to public values.

Liberalism serves as a useful theoretical foil to elaborate a republican understanding of horizontality. Horizontality has, however, often been employed as an ameliorative mechanism in nonliberal circumstances – from postbellum America to post-Apartheid South Africa. Something like horizontality might sometimes seem provocative in a largely rights-respecting society that fears limiting rights unnecessarily, but applying constitutional duties to private actors may seem less controversial in an illiberal or more severely hierarchical society. In either case, by applying constitutional principles to create duties for private entities, constitutional agents aim to disrupt existing arrangements and narratives with the republican sensibility that private spaces or actors might somehow be corrected by public values.

Why Republicanism?

The republican interpretation offered here serves as a new lens through which to read and understand the discourses surrounding horizontality. As some of the most telling exchanges and arguments surrounding this topic have occurred in court cases, the main constitutional agents featured here are courts. Nevertheless, this is not primarily a doctrinal account of horizontality, but a theoretical account that builds on

---

[15] Andreas Kalyvas and Ira Katznelson, *Liberal Beginnings: Making a Republic for the Moderns* (Cambridge: Cambridge University Press, 2008).

constitutional histories. Put differently, the republican framework moves beyond the more common readings that, for example, emphasize doctrine, to uncover the profound questions of political theory that emerge from debates over horizontality: What is the relationship between the individual and the community? What is the nature of freedom? Answers often invoke republican themes that are explored in depth here.

While the argument itself is not normative, criteria and strategies for normative assessments emerge. Considering the history of race in the United States or South Africa, for example, it is not difficult to see the good that might come of applying some rights horizontally when such abuse occurs in private spaces. In such cases, the republican lens highlights more specifically how horizontality transcends rights-centrism in favor of ends of the community. At the same time, the republican lens may reveal a potential for the abuse of horizontality, as well. Authoritarian regimes have frequently invoked such concepts as the common good and civic duty in pursuit of centralized power. The possibility that horizontality might be employed in authoritarian contexts, or even to pass blame for society's ills onto nonstate actors, is corroborated in legal scholarship.[16]

Although horizontality reconceives the divide between public and private spheres, this practice generally has not amounted to a complete collapse of public and private, or a total turn to civic republicanism. Horizontality may be conceived as "a republican vein in liberal constitutionalism" in light of the way it operates in constitutional contexts and employs the classically liberal language of rights. Moreover, courts and other constitutional actors generally seek out limiting principles and preserve elements of conventional narratives in debates. In this way, arguments in favor of horizontality run up against other countervailing factors across time, place, and topic. Nevertheless, republican concepts travel in meaningful ways across very different contexts. Indeed, the arguments that diverse constitutional actors across time and place make in favor of horizontality reveal conceptions of community, duty, and freedom akin to those in republican political thought.

---

[16] See Ernest Caldwell, "Horizontal Rights and Chinese Constitutionalism: Judicialization through Labor Disputes," *Chicago-Kent Law Review* 88:1 (2012), 63–92; Ravi Nair, "Confronting the Violence Committed by Armed Opposition Groups," *Yale Human Rights and Development Law Journal* 1:1 (1998), 13–14; Nigel Rodley, "Can Armed Opposition Groups Violate Human Rights?" in *Human Rights in the Twenty-First Century: A Global Challenge*, ed. K. Mahoney and P. Mahoney (Dordrecht: Martinus Nijhoff, 1993), 297–318.

Theory and Practice: Plan for the Book

This book's republican account of horizontality begins first with a theoretical chapter, highlighting the distinction between the traditional vertical model of constitutionalism and the newer horizontal model. Typically, in constitutional theory, the vertical model is understood as rooted in an older liberalism, including stronger commitment to a separate private sphere. On the other hand, the horizontal model possesses affinities with republican thought, including a conception of the polity that is less tied to maintaining strict separation between spheres of life. The chapter connects constitutional practice with some of the core concepts and texts in the history of political thought. Even beyond the relationship between spheres, conversations in political theory about the nature of liberty and the relationship between the individual and community map onto debates about horizontality and its alternatives.

On the horizontal understanding, rights take on a new significance as they become more than mere limitations on government, but also posit prescriptive ends that implicate the polity as a whole. Two key concepts emerge from these observations. Specifically, horizontality gives rise to new calls for *parity* of public and private spaces according to constitutional values. This, in turn, amounts to a new source of *duties* for private actors in relation to their fellow citizens. Such concepts as the common good and duty, integral to republican thought, offer a baseline for conceptualizing the parity and duties to which horizontality gives rise.

Subsequent chapters illustrate how these concepts travel in meaningful ways and do similar work across different kinds of contexts, namely the United States, India, Germany, South Africa, and the European Union. Examining constitutional debates, founding documents, and political histories (including case law and statutory law), as well as interviews with practitioners and legal academics reveals how constitutional actors have discussed horizontality in diverse contexts and various areas of rights. While these contexts are different in myriad ways, constitutional actors in each of them have deliberated whether and how to adopt a horizontal model of rights. These deliberations occur across diverse histories and aspirations, institutions and interests, in these constitutional orders and display equally diverse positions in terms of horizontality.

These region-specific chapters are not meant to be "case studies" in the traditional sense of the term. Put differently, they are not included as countries "most different" from each other or "most similar" to each other, so as to control for particular factors in the analysis. These contextual chapters do not explain why courts decide questions of horizontality as they do, or why constitutionalism develops as it does in different countries. Rather, appropriate to this book as a work of constitutional theory, these chapters are illustrative in showing the variety of ends for which and ways in which horizontality has been employed. Likewise, these regions of study cover a range of political and legal circumstances that bolster or obstruct the practice of horizontality in each place. To borrow a turn of phrase from Kim Lane Scheppele, these chapters begin to construct different repertoires[17] for horizontality understood through a republican lens, as these diverse contexts are in different ways considered paradigmatic for the question of horizontality. Through these different paradigms, the book traces threads of republican discourses growing out of debates over horizontality. Republican themes take different forms and occur, to a greater or lesser extent, across issues and constitutional orders, so each context reveals something different about the republican potential of horizontality and the discourses surrounding this practice.

The first four examples may be understood as loose pairings, with the United States and India constituting one pair, and Germany and South Africa another. First, the constitutional experiences of the United States and India are brought into dialogue over the big question of *whether* their respective constitutions may be applied horizontally. As these countries have grappled with histories of racism and caste, the question of horizontality coheres around questions of equality and antidiscrimination. Republican themes relating to citizenship, fraternity, and the like emerge in arguments from those actors that would prefer something like a horizontal model of rights. In contrast, the experiences of Germany and South Africa are framed as centering around the question of *how far* the constitution applies horizontally. In particular, the common goal of societal transformation that both these constitutions undertake in one way or another raises questions about how far into private spaces, and to what kinds of issues, constitutional values ought to extend. Republican themes such as obligation to a common good or common morality, and even neighborliness, grow out of these debates.

The framers of the Indian Constitution pursued their practice of horizontality explicitly to avoid the discrimination black persons endured

---

[17] Kim Lane Scheppele, "Constitutional Ethnography," *Law and Society Review* 38:3 (2004), 389–406.

in the United States even after the ratification of the Fourteenth Amendment and its equal protection clause. Likewise, the South African framers pursued their more ambitious version of horizontality to transcend the traditional legal distinctions to which German jurists largely remained committed. Each of these countries had occasion to consider horizontality, and distinct approaches emerged out of the respective constitutional conversations. Taken together, these pairings tell a story of constitutional actors choosing (or not choosing) to transcend the traditional logic of constitutionalism in favor of something different, something more republican. This is not to argue that these entire constitutional orders are or are not republican, only that republicanism describes how people employ and discuss horizontality in what are otherwise complex, multifaceted constitutional contexts.[18] In this vein, the European Union serves as an important bookend to these chapters, offering an opportunity to consider horizontality in a supranational context where republican fundaments pertaining to community and citizenship are themselves in question.

The concluding chapter takes up contemporary issues such as the COVID-19 pandemic and Big Tech to consider the status of private actors in constitutional politics and the value of the republican framework in understanding these issues. The conclusion offers preliminary thoughts on the republican framework as a possible guide to determining when horizontality might be applied and how it may be supported, as both a practical and a normative matter. Specifically, constitution-makers and courts might make this constitutional practice more coherent by making it even more republican, perhaps through renewed emphasis on contestation or the legislative function in constitutional politics.[19]

The Clarity of the Republican Lens

Analyzing crucial constitutional moments – often founding moments when the question of horizontality was debated and, at least initially, decided – lays the groundwork to explore the relationships between these

---

[18] Rogers Smith's thesis that the United States' civic order develops out of "multiple traditions" could likely be applied in modified form to any of the contexts this book examines. See Rogers Smith, *Civic Ideals* (New Haven: Yale University Press, 1999).

[19] The chapter considers such arrangements as the "new commonwealth model," which Stephen Gardbaum describes in *The New Commonwealth Model of Constitutionalism* (Cambridge: Cambridge University Press, 2013).

constitutional moments and the governmental institutions that subsequently wrestle with the question of horizontality. Indeed, from these constitutional moments emerge additional questions that various governmental powers – particularly judicial and sometimes legislative – must address. A cluster of relations[20] among framing moments and these different powers illustrates how the republican features of horizontality ultimately hold different meanings for differently positioned agents. Challenges emerge in negotiations among institutions as they address questions about horizontality alongside various other considerations. The pull of traditional understandings often perseveres, as constitutional actors acknowledge that upholding rights will require preserving some private sphere. Differing understandings of freedom itself emerge in debates viewed through a theoretical lens of horizontality. Beyond these more theoretical questions, however, a wide range of interests and issues similarly countervail against horizontality across these chapters: persistent racism and the benefits some enjoy from old systems; fear of judicial overstep in policy matters; the financial expense for both private actors and the state; even sheer uncertainty about the practice of horizontality and what role it leaves for other nonconstitutional law and courts.

In light of these and other issues, jurists and other actors will often seek out limiting principles to horizontality or some kind of middle ground. One method is opting for what is called indirect horizontality. On the one hand, *direct* horizontality allows private actors to plead a cause of action directly against other actors on the basis of the constitution. Judges apply constitutional rights directly to private actors, creating duties to respect, protect, or fulfill the constitutional rights of other citizens. On the other hand, *indirect* horizontality entails that constitutional principles control the content and interpretation of all areas of law, from legislation to court judgments at common law. Indirect horizontality does not necessarily create obligations for private actors directly, but involves the constitution shaping the law that already regulates private spaces.[21] Recounting these and other arguments uncovers

---

[20] I am grateful to Mariah Zeisberg for this turn of phrase.
[21] Legal scholars debate how different direct and indirect horizontality are at a practical level (Mattias Kumm and Victor Ferreres Comella, "What Is So Special about Constitutional Rights in Private Litigation?" in *The Constitution in Private Relations*, ed. András Sajó and Renáta Uitz [Utrecht: Eleven, 2005]). However, most important for the purposes of the present book is the fact that constitutional actors have argued in debates as if the latter indirect approach occupies a desirable middle ground between strict verticality and horizontality, thus allowing them to navigate competing interests in play.

republican-inflected arguments within debates among differently situated agents about the question of horizontality.[22]

In either the direct or indirect variation, the consequence is that private entities accrue duties as a result of constitutional commitments to certain rights. To this extent, the republican framework speaks to both versions of horizontality. Nevertheless, constitutional framers and actors very often speak as if there were a difference between these approaches, and that the constitutional choice they adopt could lead to different outcomes. In the terms of this book, direct horizontality is taken to encompass a republican logic more fully – specifically in how public commitments bear on private entities directly, with less room for legislatures' discretion as to how duties are implemented in ordinary law. While important and interesting, the question of whether this distinction matters to case outcomes is beyond the scope of this book.[23] However, the chapters that follow demonstrate in the context of specific debates within and across countries how different constitutional discourses seem to adhere to these doctrinal variations. In short, indirect horizontality generally tracks a desire on the part of constitutional framers and other actors to maintain some separation between spheres, whereas direct horizontality tends to accompany a more thorough-going republican logic, an aspiration to shape the polity as a whole according to public principles. Arguably, subsequent chapters reveal the urgency (and resistance) accompanying the direct approach most strikingly in antidiscrimination initiatives across countries. That such doctrinal differences can track different substantive commitments is evinced in comparing, say,

---

[22] In her book *Public Rights, Private Relations*, Jean Thomas argues that an entirely new category of rights, which she calls "private law rights," is necessary to translate fully a relation of right and duty from public to private spaces. Such a new category would apply to the most essential constitutional commitments at stake and to private relationships involving the most power and dependency (Jean Thomas, *Public Rights, Private Relations* [Oxford: Oxford University Press, 2015]). In a sense, Thomas's proposal is even more republican than many actual horizontal arrangements. This is because she aims at a more robust concept of duty in private spaces than might result from indirect horizontality, which creates duties only through shaping private law. On the other hand, Thomas's proposal may be less republican in that she aims to bracket only the most crucial commitments as creating duties rather than the complete catalog of constitutional rights. This maintains some distance between the source of public duties and the source of private duties.

[23] Speaking to the distinction between direct and indirect horizontality, Mattias Kumm suggests that the results of these doctrines ultimately are not so different. See Kumm, "Who Is Afraid," 352.

the Indian and German constitutional projects, or even South Africa's Interim and Final Constitutions.

Even when horizontal rights obligations are mediated by private law, constitutional commitments are, in an important way, a source of duties of private actors. Hence, as in the republican tradition, individuals become accountable to the larger projects of the polity, regardless of whether they agree with those projects. In this way, horizontality constitutes something of an innovation of liberal constitutionalism in changing *who* is responsible for constitutional commitments and in designating the constitution as the source by which individuals are made responsible. This innovation may be justified to the extent that one finds compelling a republican conception of freedom as nondomination. While someone subscribing to the liberal conception of freedom as noninterference may be troubled by the degree and nature of interference in private relations that horizontality entails, one who maintains a republican conception of freedom as nondomination may be more inclined to recognize horizontality as leveraging the same constitutional principles that protect people from domination by public entities (imperium) to protect them also from domination by private entities (dominium).[24]

Some of the most heated debates occur around questions of equality and duties within the private sphere. Such matters are pressing in the United States and India, where debates about horizontality have focused on equality and antidiscrimination provisions.[25] Matters of equality and antidiscrimination figure into the German and, especially, South African practices of horizontality as well, raising questions about how far horizontality reaches into certain corners of private life, as both countries aim for transformation. Should equality itself apply horizontally, the German Federal Constitutional Court finally asked in the 2008

---

[24] Liberals like Mill recognize the threat of "dominium," such as in the social oppression that often accompanies public opinion. It is unclear, however, that his solution to this threat would accommodate the kind of centralized, state-initiated response that horizontality entails (John Stuart Mill, *On Liberty*, ed. Elizabeth Rapaport [Indianapolis: Hackett, 1978]).

[25] In an incisive article, Elisa Holmes argues that equality and antidiscrimination norms are conceptually distinct. This is because antidiscrimination norms do not necessarily require that everyone be treated alike. Moreover, the fact that some kind of equality exists among people does not by itself preclude the possibility of discrimination. For these and other reasons, Holmes concludes that equality per se is not the end sought by antidiscrimination norms. This argument is compelling on a philosophic level. Insofar as constitutional actors often conceive of and adopt equality and antidiscrimination norms to aim toward the same ends, however, this book typically treats them in such manner. Elisa Holmes, "Antidiscrimination Rights without Equality," *Modern Law Review* 68:2 (2005), 175–194.

Stadium Ban case?[26] Might private actors have duties with respect to positive rights that aim at a substantive form of status equality,[27] the South African Constitutional Court asked in *Daniels v. Scribante*?[28]

That the horizontality of rights related to equality would be contentious across contexts is not surprising. Rights related to equality are often conceived as part of a larger constitutional project and, thus, as demanding more of the duty-bearers, be they public or private actors. And when private actors are in fact the duty-bearers, the resultant limitations on rights and liberties enjoyed are felt more acutely in that they intervene more directly in private life.[29] In short, equality cases seem to be perceived as demanding more positive action of private actors. Thus, while the German *Lüth* case applying freedom of expression horizontally simply requires that an individual face what economic harm may arise from calls for a boycott,[30] the *Indian Medical Association* case applying affirmative action requirements to private actors actually involves revising existing systems and programs.[31]

Conclusion

Scholars across disciplines have long argued the interconnectedness of public projects and private decisions, specifically how private actions may bear on public projects – from Legal Realists and Critical Legal Studies scholars maintaining, in Mark Tushnet's words, "that 'private' property is actually a delegation of power from the state,"[32] to the famous feminist refrain that the personal is political.[33] Robust welfare states, antidiscrimination statutes, and an array of other arrangements implicitly concede

---

[26] *Stadium Ban*, 1 BvR, 2080/09, April 11, 2018.
[27] Philip Pettit, *On the People's Terms* (Cambridge: Cambridge University Press, 2012), 298.
[28] *Daniels v. Scribante and Another* (CCT50/16) [2017] ZACC 13.
[29] To the extent that some have found a tension between liberty and equality, such a tension promises to be only more acute when private actors are implicated (Laurie Ackermann, *Human Dignity: Lodestar for Equality in South Africa* [Cape Town: Juta, 2012], 326–327).
[30] *Lüth*, BVerfGE 7, 198 (1958).
[31] *Indian Medical Assn. v. Union of India*, (2011) 7 SCC 179.
[32] Tushnet, *Weak Courts, Strong Rights*, 169.
[33] Carol Hanisch, "The Personal Is Political: The Women's Liberation Movement Classic with a New Explanatory Introduction," in *Radical Feminism: A Documentary Reader*, ed. Barbara A. Crow (New York: New York University Press, 2000), 113–117. See also Nancy Isenberg, "The Personal Is Political: Gender, Feminism, and the Politics of Discourse Theory," *American Quarterly* 44:3 (1992), 449–458; Gila Stopler, "The Personal Is Political: The Feminist Critique of Liberalism and the Challenge of Right-Wing Populism," *International Journal of Constitutional Law* 19:2 (2021), 393–402.

CONCLUSION

this connection and suggest, on some level, that citizens have some obligation to public projects and to each other. With the introduction of horizontality in constitutionalism and attendant calls for parity among spheres and for citizens' duties to uphold constitutional commitments, this connection between private behavior and public projects becomes more explicit.

In horizontality, ideas from republican theory prove to be alive and quite relevant in constitutional politics. The claim is not that this tradition plays any significant role in these episodes from constitutional politics as a historical matter, nor is the goal to write off more conventional liberal narratives as irrelevant to horizontality. Rather the aim is to highlight the presence of republican elements in discourses surrounding horizontality. Whether or not particular arguments for horizontality prevail in law and politics, teasing out their republican themes imbues these debates with new significance and serves as a call to appreciate the full significance – in scholarship and practice – of horizontality. Moreover, the republican perspective offers new opportunities to assess institutional struggles pertaining to horizontality. Republican themes arise, for example, in considerations surrounding the role of courts, divisions of power in federal arrangements, the allocation of issues in a supranational union, and in constitutional assemblies aiming for transformation. Thus, while arguments for horizontality may sometimes seem new or surprising from a modern perspective emphasizing rights over duties, the republican lens reveals ways in which these discourses ultimately participate in conversations that are longstanding and not soon ending.

2

A Republican Vein in Liberal Constitutionalism

The classical liberal tradition has typically understood constitutions as protecting private individuals and entities from the encroachments of government. Of course, constitutions empower government, but they also seek to limit that power through checks and balances and, almost always, through enumerating a list of justiciable rights obligating the state.[1] At the time of writing, some 184 constitutions protect the freedom of expression against government action, for example.[2] Since the post–World War II era of constitution-making, an increasing number of countries have also included socioeconomic or positive rights in their constitutions. Hence, the right to healthcare now yields duties for the state in as many as 136 constitutions.[3] In each case, the constitution establishes a *vertical* relationship according to which government must respect, protect, and fulfill rights of the people.[4] Only state action is held to a constitutional standard. This vertical relationship leaves space for a separate private sphere in which private actors may pursue their own interests and projects, supported by government structures but unencumbered by those constitutional obligations that bind the state.

---

[1] Speaking of the purpose of the US Constitution in *Federalist* 51 Madison explains, "In framing a government which is to be administered by men over men, the great difficulty lies in this: you must first enable the government to control the governed; and in the next place oblige it to control itself." Alexander Hamilton, James Madison, and John Jay, *The Federalist Papers*, ed. Clinton Rossiter (New York: Signet, 2003), 319.

[2] Comparative Constitutions Project, "Freedom of Expression," accessed September 13, 2023, www.constituteproject.org/constitutions?lang=en&key=express&status=in_force.

[3] Comparative Constitutions Project, "Right to Healthcare," accessed September 13, 2023, www.constituteproject.org/constitutions?lang=en&key=health&status=in_force.

[4] "Maastricht Guidelines on Violations of Economic, Social and Cultural Rights," Human Rights Library, University of Minnesota, accessed September 3, 2022, http://hrlibrary.umn.edu/instree/Maastrichtguidelines_html; David Jason Karp, "What Is the Responsibility to Respect Human Rights? Reconsidering the 'Respect, Protect, and Fulfill' Framework," *International Theory* 12:1 (2020), 83–108, https://doi.org/10.1017/S1752971919000198.

Particular moments from American history demonstrate the crucial implications of working out which institutions belong to the public or private sphere, as well as the fact that these are not new questions by any means. Take for example the "white primary" cases. In *Grovey v. Townsend* (1935),[5] the Supreme Court's decision to classify the Democratic Party as a private organization perpetuated the continual disenfranchisement of African Americans. While the state of Texas's administration of elections constituted state action, the acts of the participating political parties did not. The state of Texas could thus authorize the Democratic Party in denying ballots to African American voters. While parties in some ways operate as nonstate actors, one cannot deny the essential ways in which they contribute to political processes. The Court in *Grovey* took advantage of this ambiguous status of parties and of the fact that it maintained full power to draw the line between public and private spheres. Not until *Smith v. Allwright* (1944),[6] a decade later, did the Court find that state permission to discriminate was in fact a violation of the Fifteenth Amendment insofar as it had the practical effect of excluding voter participation. Even in this case, however, the Court did not reverse course either in their initial decision to designate political parties as nonstate actors, or in the general practice of applying rights obligations only to state actors. Rather, the Court simply noted the extent to which the state of Texas was, in this particular situation, implicated in authorizing the decisions of the Democratic Party.

Many jurists and scholars have criticized this traditional modus operandi of courts, to determine which institutions are public and thus accountable to constitutional rights, versus those that are private and so insulated from constitutional obligations. The aforementioned US cases seem to hinge on mere semantic distinctions, for example. In this vein, the Legal Realists in the 1920s and 1930s argued that traditional boundaries between public and private were neither necessary nor self-evident, but contingent on social meanings. Feminist scholars have long noted that expansive definitions of "private" can have the pernicious effect of insulating personal harms such as domestic abuse occurring in private homes. The Critical Legal Studies movement would later build on many of these arguments. Following Robert Hale,[7] Mark Tushnet

---

[5] *Grovey v. Townsend*, 295 US 45 (1935).
[6] *Smith v. Allwright*, 321 US 649 (1944).
[7] Robert Hale, "Coercion and Distribution in a Supposedly Non-coercive State," *Political Science Quarterly* 38 (1923), 470–494.

maintains "the controversial proposition that 'private' property is actually a delegation of power from the state."[8] To him and other representatives of Critical Legal Studies, the state always acts when it codifies private law and designates private spaces. Although Tushnet acknowledges elsewhere that we may have reason not to abandon categories of "private" altogether,[9] the general critique made by this school of thought maintains that which institutions belong in which category is neither necessary nor self-evident and is, therefore, arbitrary and subject to abuse.

Perhaps these critiques are not insurmountable. Nevertheless, they do raise the possibility that jurists might enforce rights through a different method – that instead of redrawing boundaries between public and private, they might apply constitutional rights commitments to both public and private actors. Recent years have brought attention to the increasing power of society's private sectors.[10] Technology companies possess vast amounts of data. This has led European courts to consider whether such companies must honor a "right to be forgotten" of individuals who would not have their information available on the internet.[11] Moreover, media increasingly act as gatekeepers to popular fora, an issue which the US Supreme Court confronted in the 2019 decision of *Manhattan Community Access Corp v. Halleck*.[12] This particular case considered a public access television station's obligations with respect to the freedom of speech, a question with potential implications for such social media sites as Facebook and Twitter (now X). While not state actors, these companies enjoy resources and agency that rival the world's most powerful national governments. Such developments have given new salience to the question of whether rights relationships exist (or should be made to exist) between these private entities and the individuals that use their platforms.

---

[8] Mark Tushnet, *Weak Courts, Strong Rights: Judicial Review and Social Welfare Rights in Comparative Constitutional Law* (Princeton: Princeton University Press, 2009), 169.

[9] Louis Seidman and Mark Tushnet, "The State Action Paradox," in *Remnants of Disbelief: Contemporary Constitutional Issues* (Oxford: Oxford University Press, 1996), 49–71.

[10] Andrew Cockrell, "Private Law and the Bill of Rights: A Threshold Issue of Horizontality," in *Bill of Rights Compendium*, ed. Y. Mokgoro and P. Tlakula (Cape Town: LexisNexis), 3A4, para. 3A2.

[11] See Case C-131/12, *Google Spain v. AEPD and Mario Costeja González* [2014]; Case C-136/17 *GC et al. v. CNIL* [2019]; Case C-507/17, *CNIL v. Google* [2019]; *Right to Be Forgotten I*, BVerfGE 1 BvR 16/13 (2019); *Right to Be Forgotten II*, BVerfGE 1 BvR 276/17 (2019).

[12] *Manhattan Community Access Corp. v. Halleck*, 587 U.S. ___ (2019).

Some courts and constitution-makers now handle cases in exactly this way. Specifically, they give *horizontal application* to constitutional rights, interpreting them to create duties not only of the state but of private entities or nonstate actors as well. Such an approach does not necessarily abandon categories of public and private, but employs constitutional principles across the polity understood as a whole. According to the Indian Supreme Court, for example, the constitutional right to equality creates obligations of companies vis-à-vis workers.[13] According to the South African Constitutional Court, landlords have positive obligations to ensure their tenants live in conditions consonant with human dignity.[14] In these instances, courts have moved away from the liberal preoccupation of distinguishing public and private spheres in order to determine constitutional duties, toward a different logic that admits of duties across spheres. Jurists ask different questions about which public values and commitments ought to bind the polity as a whole, creating potential obligations of all actors regardless of their public or private status. In other words, increasingly, private actors may be called upon to protect, respect, and fulfill the same constitutional rights that obligate the state.

This practice of horizontal application has been employed to adjust the rules governing and behaviors within the private sphere. With horizontal application, the boundaries drawn between public and private become less rigid, as public values permeate traditionally private spaces. A constitutional commitment to freedom of expression may enjoy primacy in interchanges among individuals, even where the state is not involved at all, despite the fact that economic harm results from particular speech.[15] A horizontal constitutional commitment to equality may obligate private businesses not to deny access on the basis of race, caste, sex, or place of birth.[16] In this way, horizontal application pursues a kind of *parity* between private behavior and constitutional values when it might otherwise run counter to public projects, as was the situation in the "white primary" cases in the United States.[17]

Horizontal application departs from the traditional vertical model in the additional sense that it introduces a conception of citizens' *duties*, a

---

[13] *People's Union for Democratic Rights v. Union of India*, 3 SCC 235 AIR [1982] SC 1473.
[14] *Daniels v. Scribante and Another*, CCT50/16 [2017] ZACC 13.
[15] *Lüth*, BVerfGE 7, 198 (1958).
[16] Indian Constitution, Article 15.2.a.
[17] *Grovey v. Townsend*, 295 US 45 (1935); *Smith v. Allwright*, 321 US 649 (1944).

rarity in political cultures that prioritize rights and the individual. Many scholars, including Herbert Storing[18] and Mary Ann Glendon,[19] have emphasized the ill effects of individualism and the paucity of a sense of duty in contemporary America. Jamal Greene's recent book, *How Rights Went Wrong*, evinces how this sense persists, that something is lacking in American "rightsist" culture.[20] Greene's account, concerning the harms of absolutist understandings of rights common in the United States, does not explicitly mention but certainly points toward a need for something such as the limitations analysis underlying horizontal understandings of rights. Limitations analysis is the balancing that judges undertake when they limit a right in favor of some other constitutional end. With the introduction of horizontal application, private actors come to exist under a constitutional standard of scrutiny, thereby gaining duties in addition to the more commonly emphasized rights.

If the former vertical paradigm was characteristic of liberal constitutionalism, then, horizontal application introduces (or perhaps *re*introduces)[21] republican elements in the adjudication of private spaces. This is not to say that constitutional actors necessarily intend to wield horizontal application as a republican instrument but that, as a practical matter, horizontal application does function as such an instrument. Indeed, in applying rights horizontally, constitution-makers, courts, and other political actors deemphasize the differences between spheres, to conceive of the polity as more of a whole and to make constitutional projects the duty of public and private actors alike. This is also not to say that the specific duties of different actors become identical. Courts that apply horizontal application still understand the obligations of private actors differently

---

[18] Herbert Storing, "Slavery and the Moral Foundations of the American Republic," in *Toward a More Perfect Union: Writings of Herbert J. Storing*, ed. Joseph Bessette (Washington, DC: American Enterprise Institute, 1995), 142–144.

[19] Mary Ann Glendon, *Rights Talk: The Impoverishment of Political Discourse* (New York: Free Press, 1993).

[20] Jamal Greene, *How Rights Went Wrong* (Boston: Mariner Books, 2021).

[21] Certain natural law accounts do discuss explicitly the limitations on and duties growing out of rights. Hadley Arkes's book chapter "On the Danger of the Bill of Rights" argues for a return to discussing rights in the light of their moral foundations as opposed to the mere fact of their enumeration in such texts as the US Bill of Rights. This, he maintains, grounds rights more fully in their moral purposes and, by extension, equips us better to see the limits to rights as dictated by those same purposes. Arkes's account is not expressly republican but, in many ways, aligns better with republican thought than do many instantiations of contemporary liberalism because it does not shy away from such subjects as limits and even duties (Hadley Arkes, *Beyond the Constitution* [Princeton: Princeton University Press, 1992]).

from those of public actors, accounting for such factors as the importance of a right to the constitutional project and the resources available to private actors in comparison to the state.[22]

An additional consideration that becomes more important when rights are applied horizontally is the sheer fact that private persons do bear rights as persons, in contrast with state actors as such. Balancing rights among individuals, therefore, becomes an essential feature of horizontal application. While conventional liberal understandings might and do account for such balancing, the concern for civic duty built into republican theory offers conceptual resources to better understand the balancing of – and, by extension, limitations of – rights that horizontality entails. Even if private actors do not ultimately possess all of the responsibility accompanying the tripartite framework of human rights, to "respect, protect, and fulfill,"[23] the constitution still becomes a common source of obligation for all actors. This chapter demonstrates how certain features of horizontal application comprise a new republican logic, altering the terms and tenor of constitutional politics. Although this development may not constitute a complete turn to civic republicanism, it is a republican vein within liberal constitutionalism.

What purpose does this comparison with republican theory serve? Is it a mere academic curiosity, or does it offer analytic value as well? Republican theory's long tradition offers a trove of thought from which to draw in thinking about the relationship between community and the individual, between public and private. Per the conventional wisdom, civic republicanism prioritizes community or the common good, whereas liberalism tends to prioritize the individual. While both vertical and horizontal models involve balancing the rights of the individual with the good of the community, as stated earlier, the horizontal model signals a shift toward the goals of the community. No longer are constitutional rights simply about individuals; rather, rights are recast as public commitments that reach further and create duties for a wider range of actors.[24]

---

[22] See, for example, *Daniels v. Scribante*, para. 40.
[23] Karp, "What Is the Responsibility to Respect Human Rights?"
[24] Georg Sommeregger, "The Horizontalization of Equality: The German Attempt to Promote Non-discrimination in the Private Sphere via Legislation," in *The Constitution in Private Relations*, ed. András Sajó and Renáta Uitz (Utrecht: Eleven, 2005); Ulrich Preuss, "The German *Drittwirkung* Doctrine and Its Socio-political Background," in *The Constitution in Private Relations*, ed. András Sajó and Renáta Uitz (Utrecht: Eleven, 2005).

The contention here is that republicanism, liberalism, and their attendant differences offer existing frameworks within which to identify and understand corresponding differences between the horizontal and vertical models of constitutionalism. Put differently, the ways in which these traditions of political thought treat questions of the community and the individual, public and private, offer reference points to track the ways in which the horizontal and vertical models differ (or, perhaps, do not always differ) in their basic assumptions and discursive logics. To the extent that horizontal application marks a shift in the terrain of constitutional politics, republican theory (and its comparison with the liberal tradition) provides a framework by which to observe, and the language with which to describe, those changes that horizontality entails. To this end, this chapter leverages concepts from republican political thought to show how specific features of horizontal application do constitute an important shift. These features I call parity and duty. In these two features, the scope of rights changes so that they now form the content for common standards and duties for additional actors. In these changes, horizontal application approximates certain republican principles and diverges from certain liberal premises of the vertical model.

By *parity* I mean the way in which horizontal application alters the scope of constitutionalism, making the private sphere congruent with public values. In comparison with the vertical model, horizontal application distinguishes less between public and private, requiring that private entities act in a way that reflects parity with public commitments. Horizontal application therefore incorporates private actors into the constitutional project more directly. The vertical model might bring private actors closer to public values through ordinary legislation but, importantly, this would occur at the discretion of legislators and not as a result of the constitution's requirements. In other words, rights relationships remain unaltered in the vertical model even as private actors may be subject to new regulation and laws, because it is still the state acting to "respect, protect and fulfill" rights, albeit in new ways. In widening the scope of who is obligated to adhere to constitutional principles and projects, horizontal application reflects a new affinity with the republican conception of "the public thing" as a priority and, moreover, a priority for all citizens. This idea is clearly present in the commitment to the common good that recurs in republican thought. Horizontal application seems to require some analytic category of a common good in order to justify the introduction of individual duties, even at some cost to individual rights. As public or constitutional commitments gain new significance for nonstate actors, a more encompassing conception of political community emerges that approximates republican accounts of the common good.

This is not to say that the common good entails a static substance or settled consensus, however, either in my particular use of the term or in the republican tradition. Without wading into the extensive debates surrounding concepts of the common good or the public good, this book employs the idea of the common good simply to signal a new premise or point of reference in constitutional politics. Actors may continually debate the constitution's content;[25] indeed, contestation is another important republican concept. However, with horizontal application, these debates over constitutional meaning come to have greater reach as constitutional commitments apply across more spheres of life. The constitution remains as subject to debate as ever, through interpretation, construction, and ordinary political dispute. But the premises of rights shift from structuring the relationship between government and individuals, to constituting broader ends that, in various ways, apply to the community. The parity horizontal application entails thus involves thinking about constitutions in these new terms and as new communal referents, even as different parties continue to push their own preferred interpretations. Ultimately, rights remain protective of individuals but also pertain to broader ends and thus prescribe duties for a wider scope of actors.

Growing out of this parity is a second republican feature of horizontal application, and that is the new manifestation of *duty*. Positioning public and private actors under a common constitutional standard entails that private actors gain constitutional duties, tracking the republican understanding that people possess duties to one another by virtue of being equal citizens of a common polity. Of course, other traditions also call for certain dispositions of citizens. William Galston and Stephen Macedo have argued that even liberalism requires particular virtues to ensure a sufficient level of respect and tolerance among citizens.[26] However, these

---

[25] Gary Jacobsohn's concept of disharmony in constitutional identity is instructive to understand how constitutional politics may be comprised of both continuities with regard to certain concepts and discontinuities insofar as those concepts remain subject to interpretation (Gary Jacobsohn, *Constitutional Identity* [Cambridge, MA: Harvard University Press, 2010]). See also Jurgen Habermas's thinking on discourse and deliberation for another helpful account to understand the shapes of contestation in political community.

[26] Stephen Macedo, *Liberal Virtues* (Oxford: Oxford University Press, 1990); William Galston, "Liberal Virtues and the Formation of Civic Character," in *Seedbeds of Virtue*,

conceptions are more typically couched as boons for individuals' self-interest rather than as duties. And even when other theorists have employed the language of duty, as we see in Joseph Raz's work, the ultimate point of reference typically is still the individual, as I will discuss later, as opposed to public projects and a common good.[27] In these interconnected features of parity and duty, horizontal application departs from certain premises of liberal constitutionalism and finds affinity in a logic and values commonly associated with republicanism.

By making this descriptive argument that horizontal application tracks certain republican concepts, this chapter sets up the remainder of the book, showing the discourses that the practice of horizontal application brings about in constitutional politics. Moreover, the republican framework helps us see the upshots and stakes involved in this decision to think differently about the relationship between public and private spheres. The outcomes of this development may be positive, as constitutions address abuses in private spaces and introduce the kind of duty-mindedness that Glendon and Storing find lacking, at least in American political culture. Nevertheless, the republican framework can also uncover potential liabilities of horizontal application, if we attend to the critiques political thinkers have leveled against civic republicanism historically.[28] In light of this reflection, a natural question is whether horizontality's similarity with republicanism stops short of what some take to be republicanism's problematic features, insofar as horizontality still occurs in a liberal context. Though this chapter primarily concerns horizontality in the abstract, its conceptual work brings into sharp relief the weight of these theoretical questions, thereby laying groundwork to consider the constitutional politics of actual cases in the chapters that follow. Whether a country should adopt a vertical or horizontal model of

---

ed. Mary Ann Glendon and David Blankenhorn (Lanham: Madison, 1995); see also William Galston, *Liberal Pluralism* (Cambridge: Cambridge University Press, 2002); Iseult Honohan, "Educating Citizens: National-Building and Its Republican Limits," in *Republicanism in Theory and Practice*, ed. Iseult Honohan and Jeremy Jennings (Oxfordshire: Routledge, 2006), 199–213, at 203.

[27] Joseph Raz centers his theory around individual autonomy, for example. See his chapter "Freedom and Autonomy" in *The Morality of Freedom* (Oxford: Oxford University Press, 1986), 406–408.

[28] See Beau Breslin, *The Communitarian Constitution* (Baltimore: Johns Hopkins University Press, 2006), chap. 1; Gary Jacobsohn, *Apple of Gold* (Princeton: Princeton University Press, 1993), 46–47; Isaiah Berlin, "Two Concepts of Liberty" (1958), in *Four Essays on Liberty* (Oxford: Oxford University Press, 1969), 118–172; Linda K. Kerber, "Making Republicanism Useful," *Yale Law Journal* 97:8 (1998), 1663.

rights enforcement is not self-evident but contingent on the histories, challenges, and aspirations of the place.[29] In drawing from republican theory to better understand the logic of horizontal application, this book offers greater clarity about the nature of this choice that constitutional drafters and actors continue to face.

The remainder of this chapter proceeds with an overview of the liberal and republican traditions, in order to distinguish between them and their respective cores. It then turns to focus specifically on republican thought, expounding concepts such as the common good and duties among citizens. This discussion sets up the heart of the book's argument, that particular features of horizontal application (parity and duty) amount to new republican elements in constitutionalism. The final section raises potential republican concerns with the way horizontal application results from judicial action, weighing scholars' arguments that defend a role for courts on the very basis of republican liberty. The chapter concludes by suggesting that the concerns some scholars and jurists raise about horizontal application – namely about the way it increases judicial power – are contingent on context, depending at least in part on the conditions under which this practice is introduced. The following chapters delve into various contexts in detail to elucidate how horizontal application has been understood and debated in practice.

Distinguishing the Liberal and Republican Traditions

In arguing that horizontal application reflects republican principles more than the liberal principles commonly associated with constitutionalism, this chapter depends on a comparison between liberalism and republicanism. Vast bodies of scholarship examine the ways in which liberal and republican theories relate to each other in the history of political thought, as well as in the history of the American founding more specifically.[30]

---

[29] Jennifer Corrin, "From Horizontal and Vertical to Lateral: Extending the Effect of Human Rights in Post Colonial Legal Systems of the South Pacific," *International and Comparative Law Quarterly* 58:1 (2009), 31–71.

[30] On the liberal tradition in American political-constitutional history, see Louis Hartz, *The Liberal Tradition in America* (Orlando: Harcourt, 1955); Mary Ann Glendon, *Rights Talk* (New York: Free Press, 1991); Thomas Pangle, *The Spirit of Modern Republicanism* (Chicago: University of Chicago Press, 1990); Herbert Storing, "Slavery and the Moral Foundations of the American Republic," in *Toward a More Perfect Union*, ed. Joseph Bessette (Washington, DC: AEI Press, 1995). On the republican tradition, see Bernard Bailyn, *The Ideological Origins of the American Revolution* (Cambridge, MA: Belknap

Although this book's argument does not depend on any particular position in these broader debates, it does depend on liberalism and republicanism being different, which is not to say irreconcilable or entirely distinct. Rather, to claim that these traditions are distinguishable is fully compatible with subtle accounts arguing that liberalism is nested within republicanism or vice versa. Andreas Kalyvas and Ira Katznelson recount such a history.[31] These explanations demonstrate how republicanism and liberalism may be fundamentally tied to one another historically or theoretically, but also defined by different concepts and commitments.

How then do these traditions differ? This question may seem difficult to answer as the history of political thought has seen many versions of each. Liberal and republican scholars often converge on the proposition that the fundamental and encompassing difference consists in how each tradition understands liberty.[32] Hence, the tradition one finds most compelling may depend on which conception of liberty one thinks corresponds better to human nature and experience. Relatedly, crucial differences consist in how each tradition tends to conceive of the relationship between the individual and the community.

The conventional account holds that the liberal tradition grew out of various wars that plagued Europe in the years leading up to the Enlightenment.[33] Such political philosophers as Thomas Hobbes[34] and John Locke[35] sought a new basis on which to ground governmental

---

Press, 1992); Gordon Wood, *The Creation of the American Republic* (Chapel Hill: University of North Carolina Press, 1998); J. G. A. Pocock, *The Machiavellian Moment* (Princeton: Princeton University Press, 2003); and Rogers Smith, *Civic Ideals* (New Haven: Yale University Press, 1999). See also the concept of "republican synthesis" in "Toward a Republican Synthesis," *William and Mary Quarterly* 29:1 (1972), 49–80.

[31] Andreas Kalyvas and Ira Katznelson, *Liberal Beginnings: Making a Republic for the Moderns* (Cambridge: Cambridge University Press, 2008). On the American context see Joseph Postell, "Regulation during the American Founding: Achieving Liberalism and Republicanism," *American Political Thought* 5 (2016), 80–108, at 84.

[32] This, admittedly, opens up further debates about how properly to understand republican liberty. Contrast the accounts of liberal thinker Isaiah Berlin and republican thinker Philip Pettit in Isaiah Berlin, "Two Concepts of Liberty" (1958), in *Four Essays on Liberty* (Oxford: Oxford University Press, 1969), 118–172; Philip Pettit, *Republicanism: A Theory of Freedom and Government* (Oxford: Clarendon Press, 1997); and Philip Pettit, *On the People's Terms* (Cambridge: Cambridge University Press, 2012).

[33] For an alternative account, see Helena Rosenblatt, *The Lost History of Liberalism: From Ancient Rome to the Twenty-First Century* (Princeton: Princeton University Press, 2018).

[34] Thomas Hobbes, *Leviathan*, ed. Richard Tuck (Cambridge: Cambridge University Press, 1996).

[35] John Locke, *Second Treatise of Government*, ed. C. B. MacPherson (Indianapolis: Hackett, 1980).

authority, and so developed their theories of the state of nature. In each version, individuals exist in perfect freedom before the establishment of government, enjoying certain prepolitical natural rights. However, the state of nature ultimately proves inconvenient at best and dangerous at worst, as no institutions exist to enforce individual rights. Individuals thus contract with one another, ceding some of their natural rights to a governmental authority in exchange for order and protection. It is at this point that Hobbes and Locke part ways. While Hobbes thinks it necessary to empower an absolute sovereign simply to get people to live in relative peace, Locke develops the liberal premise that government can and ought to be limited, acting within certain constitutional boundaries to protect people's rights but no further. In Locke's telling, government exists for the sole purpose of protecting rights and so may not act beyond this designated purpose. Out of all this comes a common liberal understanding of freedom, sometimes identified as negative liberty,[36] freedom as noninterference,[37] or the right to be let alone.[38] Government exists so that people may be let alone and not face unwarranted interference in exercising their rights. Moreover, people adopt constitutions to ensure that government operates within these designated limits, purposely carving out a separate private sphere in which individuals may go about their lives with minimal government interference.

Liberty in republicanism has different origins. Classical republicanism finds its start in the Greco-Roman world with such philosophers as Aristotle, Polybius, and Cicero. In *The Politics*, Aristotle describes man as *zoon politikon*, a being that requires political community in order to flourish. Anyone who can flourish, let alone survive, without community must be either god or beast, he concludes.[39] Therefore, politics is natural in a way that it is not for liberal social contract theorists; indeed, political life is necessary for authentic freedom. For many republicans, freedom comes in the ability to engage in public life on an equal basis with one's fellow citizens, to debate the requirements of the common good, the laws

---

[36] Berlin, "Two Concepts."
[37] Pettit, *Republicanism*, 10, and his *People's Terms*, 11.
[38] Louis Brandeis and Samuel Warren, "The Right to Privacy," *Harvard Law Review* 4:5 (1890), 193–220, at 193.
[39] Aristotle, *The Politics*, ed. Stephen Everson (Cambridge: Cambridge University Press, 1996), I.1253a2–3.

under which citizens live, and the way forward for the polity.[40] From this common structure of republics, some conclude that republican freedom consists in "mastery over the self" or an ability to shape and control the polity's way of life.[41] On the other hand, others insist that there is a more fundamental core to republican freedom in the concept of freedom as nondomination.[42] Laborde and Maynor sum it up: "In the old republican adage, the people want not to be a master, but to have no master."[43] Thus, republican citizens are free insofar as they are equal among their fellow citizens and are not subject to arbitrary or alien rule. Moreover, insofar as the goal is nondomination, and domination is conceivable in both public and private life (*imperium* and *dominium*, respectively),[44] republican liberty requires that law be able to govern all spheres of life. Neorepublican scholars, as represented by Philip Pettit, claim to follow this more negative cadence of freedom as nondomination. Although they attempt through this formulation to carve out more space for liberty in private spaces, they also recognize the need for law to intervene in private life when necessary to prevent domination of some individuals by others.

As the republican tradition has evolved since its early formulations thanks to such theorists as Pettit, so too has liberalism developed since Hobbes and Locke. Now liberalism encompasses such philosophers as John Rawls[45] and Joseph Raz.[46] These later thinkers depart from a Lockean emphasis on limited government and noninterference toward more ambitious ends, such as those associated with modern welfare liberalism. Raz's perfectionist liberalism, for example, acknowledges a more positive role for government with the end of promoting autonomy among individuals. He explains that his principle of autonomy "yields duties which go far beyond the negative duties of noninterference,"[47] and that government should promote autonomy by incentivizing moral options that people may choose and discouraging immoral options that

---

[40] Iseult Honohan, "Educating Citizens: Nation-Building and Its Republican Limits," in *Republicanism in Theory and Practice*, ed. Iseult Honohan and Jeremy Jennings (Oxfordshire: Routledge, 2006), 199–213.
[41] Berlin, "Two Concepts."
[42] Pettit, *Republicanism* and *People's Terms*. Below I will illustrate how freedom as non-domination has been understood differently.
[43] Cecile Laborde and John Maynor, *Republicanism and Political Theory* (Hoboken: Wiley-Blackwell, 2008), 11.
[44] Pettit, *Republicanism*, 36.
[45] John Rawls, *A Theory of Justice* (Cambridge, MA: Harvard University Press, 1971).
[46] Joseph Raz, *The Morality of Freedom* (Oxford: Oxford University Press, 1988).
[47] Ibid., 408.

are not choiceworthy. He further discusses the importance of community, and even duties of private individuals, as crucial to promoting autonomy.[48] In his perfectionism, Raz thus departs from certain premises often associated with liberalism, namely, that government is limited and that freedom consists essentially in noninterference.

On this basis, some doubt Raz's liberal credentials altogether.[49] Indeed, in some ways his principle of autonomy seems to track republican conceptions of nondomination better. However, this fact need not undermine this book's argument that republicanism, as distinct from liberalism, offers an apt theoretical framework to describe horizontality. Raz's modified liberalism may well have the potential also to make sense of horizontal application.[50] However, the particular benefit of turning to another theoretical tradition – namely, republicanism – to describe horizontality is only underscored by the fact that one must turn to a kind of modified liberalism, say in Raz's thought, to begin to find a promising theoretical fit within liberalism itself.[51] Perhaps more importantly, and as will become clear in the chapters that follow, republican thought is helpful in understanding the discourses surrounding horizontal application for the particular way in which this tradition conceives of community and prioritizes the common good. This characteristic – in contrast with, say, the autonomy that forms the heart of even Raz's liberalism – proves valuable in illuminating how horizontality reorients constitutional politics and rights toward conceptions of the common good. On the other hand, it may be that this reorientation toward community ultimately serves liberal ends by expanding the scope of

---

[48] He explains how the nature of our community and the actions of those within that community fundamentally shape what choices we ultimately have in exercising our autonomy (ibid., 406).

[49] David A. J. Richards, "Kantian Ethics and the Harm Principle: A Reply to John Finnis," *Columbia Law Review* 87:3 (1987), 457–471; Wojciech Sadurski, "Joseph Raz on Liberal Neutrality and the Harm Principle," *Oxford Journal of Legal Studies* 10:1 (1990), 122–133; Jonathan Quong, "The Argument from Autonomy," in *Liberalism without Perfection* (Oxford: Oxford University Press, 2010), 45–72.

[50] See also Sonu Bedi, "The Scope of Formal Equality of Opportunity: The Horizontal Effect of Rights in a Liberal Constitution," *Political Theory* 42:6 (2014), 716–738.

[51] On a slightly different note, the claim in this chapter is that horizontality constitutes a republican vein *within* liberal constitutionalism. Perhaps, then, those theories that exist at a kind of intersection – whether Phillip Pettit's neorepublicanism or Joseph Raz's perfectionist liberalism – hold unique potential to describe this development that, on my account, also exists at a kind of intersection.

their reach.[52] Indeed, the extension of constitutional duties to private actors that defines horizontality may well comport with the way Razian autonomy may demand recognition from others. In this way, the republican forms of horizontality would seem to amount to a new extension of liberalism itself.

Scholarly discussions of liberty thus bear directly on republicanism's and liberalism's different understandings of the relationship between the individual and community. Longstanding debates over conceptions of the common good in early American political thought prove helpful here. In Gordon Wood's telling, Americans of the revolutionary era situated the community before the individual, maintaining the sort of thick conception of the common good associated with civic republicanism. He explains:

> In a republic ... each man must somehow be persuaded to submerge his personal wants into the greater good of the whole. This willingness of the individual to sacrifice his private interests for the good of the community – such patriotism or love of country – the eighteenth century termed "public virtue." A republic was such a delicate polity precisely because it demanded an extraordinary moral character in the people.[53]

Wood finds such a polity in early America.[54] In direct response to Wood's account, Gary Schmitt and Robert Webking,[55] as well as Herbert Storing,[56] argue that individual rights themselves formed the primary content of "the common good" in this period. They acknowledge that American political thinkers employed such republican terminology. However, they maintain, their conception of the common good located the individual and individual rights at the center, and so was not likely to require the submission of private interests to public causes in the same way as civic republicanism. Examining many of the quotes that Wood cites in his book, Schmitt and Webking conclude that the conception of the "common good" operative in the Early Republic was, in fact, "thoroughly modern."[57] They explain:

---

[52] I am grateful to Michael Giles for this insight.
[53] Gordon Wood, *The Creation of the American Republic* (Chapel Hill: University of North Carolina Press, 1998), 68.
[54] Ibid., 58–59.
[55] Gary Schmitt and Robert Webking, "Revolutionaries, Antifederalists, and Federalists: Comments on Gordon Wood's Understanding of the American Founding," *Political Science Reviewer* 9 (1979), 195–229.
[56] Herbert Storing, *What the Antifederalists Were For* (Chicago: University of Chicago Press, 1981).
[57] Schmitt and Webking, "Revolutionaries," 202.

> [T]he fact that one speaks of the public good does not mean that he understands the public good to be prior to individuals. Instead the public good can be precisely the protection of individual liberties against invasion by any individual or group. The common interest, according to his understanding, is to provide the conditions necessary for individuals to pursue their own interests.[58]

This is emphatically not the civic republicanism of ancient times. Indeed, this prioritization of individual rights better aligns with liberal premises and conceptions of liberty, arguably even Raz's prioritization of individual autonomy.[59] One could argue that this account simply represents another version of republicanism; however, this would still be a republicanism significantly adjusted according to liberal values.[60]

This crossroads in scholars' interpretations of early American political thought reveals core differences between republicanism and liberalism. Again, these traditions may not be irreconcilable; they may even share similar roots.[61] Nevertheless, they are different in how they order and understand the relationship between the individual and community. These different orderings in turn shape the way each understands such corollary concepts as the common good and duty, expounded in the next section. Schmitt and Webking's liberal account emphasizes the rights of individuals. Gordon Wood's more republican account finds something thicker, namely, a good or set of values distinct from individual rights, to which the polity is obligated and which may require putting community and fellow citizen before self.[62]

Neither tradition pretends that rights are absolute. Indeed, both sometimes call for balancing rights against what is variously called the common good, the general interest, or the public interest. Nevertheless, the purposes of and calculi behind balancing differ to the extent that their priorities and ends differ. Schmitt and Webking explain that "one can speak of a 'public good' without envisioning a good which has priority

---

[58] Ibid., 198.
[59] Raz, *Morality of Freedom*.
[60] This reading anticipates Kalyvas and Katznelson's argument discussed below (*Liberal Beginnings: Making a Republic for the Moderns* [Cambridge: Cambridge University Press, 2008]).
[61] Kalyvas and Katznelson, *Liberal Beginnings*.
[62] In a way, this seems to track the distinction that Robert Alexy elaborates between subjective and objective rights, with the liberal account mirroring subjective rights that may be claimed against particular entities and the republican account mirroring objective rights that amount to the values the polity maintains (*A Theory of Constitutional Rights* [Oxford: Oxford University Press, 2010]). I discuss this distinction at greater length below.

over individual rights; ... forms of government are means to ends, and not ends in themselves; and ... prudent men realize that individual rights sometimes must be restricted in order to maintain a civil society wherein individual rights can be respected."[63] This rationale behind restricting rights plainly differs from republican theories. Specifically, under the republican umbrella, rights may be restricted not simply to preserve the conditions that conduce to protecting one's own rights, as Schmidt and Webking explain. Rather, rights may be restricted for the sake of the community itself and for one's fellow citizens in themselves. Hopefully this serves to benefit the individual, too, as he or she lives in that community, but this may well be a byproduct rather than a fundamental end. Given all of this, it is perhaps unsurprising that almost every version of republicanism sets out some conception of citizens' duties, something we cannot always say about liberal thought.[64] Moreover, the execution of duty and the personal sacrifice it may involve is not the exception in republicanism but constitutive of political life as a citizen.

How does this discussion bear on horizontal application and what I call its republican nature? After all, the horizontal application of constitutional *rights* still involves a focus on individual rights. What remains of this chapter will show how features of horizontal application approximate the republican prioritization of the common good and duty, even while continually operating within a liberal constitutional framework. While constitutional actors still employ the language of rights, now attached to those rights are larger public values that yield obligations for public and private actors alike. The republican concepts of the common good and duty, therefore, describe the kind of constitutional moral landscape that we begin to see with horizontal application.

The Common Good and Duty in Republican Thought

In order to show how horizontal application may reflect republican understandings, it is necessary to exposit the particular principles of republicanism, such as freedom as nondomination, that can do this heavy lifting. This section elaborates the republican concepts of the common good and duty among citizens, showing how they emerge from

---

[63] Schmitt and Webking, "Revolutionaries," 212.

[64] On this point, Schmitt and Webking explain that the Antifederalists' "obvious concern for rights – not duties – makes it unlikely that they were the partisans of a tradition which in its normal practice subordinated the individual to the body politic" (ibid., 214).

a foundation of freedom as nondomination. This discussion lays the groundwork to connect these principles with horizontal application in the section that follows.

The very purpose of the polity, as Aristotle understands it, is to facilitate people's achievement of their human end of virtuous living.[65] More precisely, the purpose of the polity is to pursue the *common* good, or the good of the community taken as a whole, above any one person's individual good. He states, "For even if the good is the same for a city as for an individual, still the good of the city is apparently a greater and more complete good to acquire and preserve. For while it is satisfactory to acquire and preserve the good even for an individual, it is finer and more divine to acquire and preserve it for a people and for cities."[66] In this way one can see an early articulation of the republican idea that there exists a discernible good of the community, as well as the republican ideal that the promotion of this good is the primary function of politics. The common good may be understood to be distinct from, and sometimes counter to, private interests or even the aggregate of individual interests. Indeed, a republican conception of the common good refers to what is good for a community as such, the idea being that everyone ought to contribute to the good of the community and that the community will affect each individual's good in turn. This concept is so constitutive of Aristotle's understanding of a well-ordered polity that he employs it as *the* standard by which to distinguish good regimes from bad regimes, true forms of government from perversions.[67]

In Aristotle one can already see core concepts of what would develop into republican political theory. First, Aristotle gives an initial account of human beings as having a particular good that consists in virtue and in living the political life; second, Aristotle understands the common interest or common good as, in some ways, prior to the individual good. Even as republicanism has evolved, these points have been represented consistently in various iterations of the tradition. Some even argue that one can only be a republican philosopher or a republican statesman in a limited sense if one does not accept these premises.[68] For others, the

---

[65] Aristotle, *Politics*, I.1252a1–6.
[66] Aristotle, *The Nicomachean Ethics*, trans. Terence Irwin (Indianapolis: Hackett, 1999), I.2.1094b7–11; see also Aristotle, *Metaphysics*, trans. C. D. C. Reeve (Indianapolis: Hackett, 2016), Book VIII, 1045a8–10.
[67] Aristotle, *Politics*, III.1279a29–33.
[68] Stephen Gardbaum, "Law, Politics, and the Claims of Community," *Michigan Law Review* 90:4 (1992), 685–760.

republican understanding of the common good is less a matter of teleology and more a matter of what is necessary to achieve authentic freedom. Daly and Hickey associate the more teleological understanding with Aristotle, and the more liberty-centered interpretation with Roman thought, citing Pettit's conception of freedom as nondomination as an exemplar of this Roman republicanism.[69] Such differences in republican thought will reemerge below in considering precisely how republican understandings of the common good are reflected in the parity effected by horizontal application.

Unlike Aristotle, Machiavelli did not base his thought on any particular understanding of the human good. However, "the public thing" features prominently in his republicanism, as Machiavelli considers citizens' ability to debate the common good vigorously an essential feature of republican freedom.[70] S. M. Shumer explains:

> People have different values and different perspectives rooted in their individual lives, and, too, they compete for the same scarce values. To destroy that conflict, even to seek to destroy it, is to destroy politics. Machiavelli takes this a significant step further: it is active (even passionate) conflict that is the life force of public liberty, civic virtue, and even military courage.[71]

Amid this inevitable (and desirable) disagreement in public discourse, however, Machiavelli's ideal citizen will remain intent on pursuing the common good. Individual ambition and expression become "fused within the breast of each citizen" with the public good, and even with liberty.[72] On Machiavelli's telling, what made the Romans truly free was that, even after tempestuous debate, they pursued with unequivocal and united commitment the common good as dictated by the results of those debates.[73]

A few centuries later, Jean-Jacques Rousseau represents the republican tradition in his concepts of the social contract and the general will. Individuals can only be truly free, Rousseau argues, if they are not subject to alien or arbitrary rule, if each individual is self-governing. Given that

---

[69] Eoin Daly and Tom Hickey, *The Political Theory of the Irish Constitution* (Manchester: Manchester University Press, 2015), 42–44.
[70] Niccolo Machiavelli, *Discourses on Livy*, trans. Harvey C. Mansfield and Nathan Tarcov (Chicago: Chicago University Press, 1996).
[71] S. M. Shumer, "Machiavelli: Republican Politics and Its Corruption," *Political Theory* 7:1 (1979), 5–34, at 15.
[72] Ibid., 16.
[73] Ibid., 14–15.

we are bound, as a practical matter, to operate within the confines of civil society, the best chance we have of achieving the authentic freedom that comes with self-government is to enter into a social contract with others.[74] In this social contract, we surrender our rights and agree to comply with the general will. Since individuals have, in theory, consented and so vested their own will in the general will, they are obeying themselves in obeying the general will – they are, in fact, self-governing and free. Moreover, a community may "force to be free" those who would not comply with the decisions of the general will.[75] Thus, Rousseau's requirements for freedom lead to some limitation of the individual, and to a republican understanding of human freedom as consisting within the political life. Although this goes further than other versions of republican thought, Rousseau's emphasis on the public is characteristic of republicanism in general.[76]

From ancient republicanism to modern republicanism, one sees the privileged status of the common good, a prioritization of the "public thing." As Cicero explains in *On Duties*, "But when you have surveyed everything with reason and spirit, of all fellowships none is more serious, and none dearer, than that of each of us with the republic. Parents are dear, and children, relatives and acquaintances are dear, but our county has on its own embraced all the affections of all of us."[77] The *politeia* or *res publica* (the public thing) and its governing principles are all-encompassing and, therefore, require the citizen's devotion, even at some cost to private interests, but always with the ultimate result of securing one's freedom, understood as nondomination. Like liberals, republicans from Cicero to Pettit maintain a space for private interests and rights, such as those concerning property. However, in contrast with liberals, republicans of almost any stripe would ultimately understand their freedom as contingent upon, rather than infringed by, the larger commitments of the polity, understood as the common good.

In this idea of devotion to the common good, one begins to see the outlines of a republican sense of duty or solidarity. Many republican philosophers and statesmen have discussed the importance of inculcating

---

[74] Jean-Jacques Rousseau, *The Social Contract*, trans. Donald A. Cress (Indianapolis: Hackett, 2011), Book I, chap. 6.
[75] Ibid., chap. 7.
[76] Pettit further distinguishes Rousseau from other strands of republicanism; see Pettit, *Republicanism*, 30.
[77] Cicero, *On Duties*, ed. M. T. Griffin and E. M. Atikins (Cambridge: Cambridge University Press, 1991), I.57.

some connection and shared beliefs among citizens through civic education.[78] Aristotle explains that the young must be "trained by habit and education in the spirit of the constitution."[79] Inhering in a constitution is a kind of ethos, a particular shared life, in which people must be educated if the polis is to persist.[80] In her own account of education as a vehicle for a kind of solidarity among citizens, Iseault Honohan worries that "fostering solidarity has often been associated too closely with promoting cultural identity without taking sufficient account of the pluralist conditions of modern societies."[81] Honohan thus recognizes the value of a common culture, but insists that the sense of duty that education should foster is better understood as "willingness to acknowledge and assume the responsibilities entailed by interdependence; self-restraint in pursuing individual or sectional interests rather than the common good; and the inclination to engage open-mindedly with viewpoints of others in the public realm."[82] This contrasts with promoting a particular cultural identity. Aristotle, Cicero,[83] Rousseau,[84] the American Founders,[85] and contemporary theorists such as Honohan[86] all emphasize, albeit in different ways, the role of education in cultivating civic-mindedness and devotion to republican values and virtues. As Richard Bellamy states, "No constitution will itself survive long unless citizens identify with it."[87]

In this understanding, devotion to one's constitution entails devotion to one's *patria* (homeland) and, by extension, a sense of duty to one's fellow patriots. Maurizio Viroli explains how people only come to love liberty and virtue through the cultivation of such local bonds.[88] Again, we

---

[78] Honohan, "Educating Citizens."
[79] Aristotle, *Politics*, V.1310a17.
[80] For a more contemporary application of this idea, see Walter Murphy, *Constitutional Democracy* (Baltimore: Johns Hopkins University Press, 2007), 13. Moreover, Maurizio Viroli explains how local particulars such as "memories, places, heroes, hymns" serve as vehicles for cultivating a love of a common liberty. See Maurizio Viroli, "Which Patriotism for Europe?" *Eutopia Magazine*, August 5, 2014.
[81] Honohan, "Educating Citizens," 199.
[82] Ibid., 204.
[83] Cicero, *On Duties*, ed. M. T. Griffin and E. M. Atikins (Cambridge: Cambridge University Press, 1991).
[84] Jean-Jacques Rousseau, *Émile*, trans. Allan Bloom (New York: Basic Books, 1979).
[85] George Thomas, *The Founders and the Idea of a National University* (Cambridge: Cambridge University Press, 2014).
[86] Honohan, "Educating Citizens."
[87] Richard Bellamy, *Political Constitutionalism* (Cambridge: Cambridge University Press, 2007), 219.
[88] Maurizio Viroli, *For Love of Country* (Oxford: Oxford University Press, 1995).

see this idea as early in the republican tradition as Aristotle, who describes civic friendship as "the greatest good of states and what best preserves them against revolutions."[89] Later in *The Politics*, Aristotle further explains the value of such friendship:

> Such a community can only be established among those who live in the same place and intermarry. Hence there arise in cities family connexions, brotherhoods, common sacrifices, amusements which draw men together. But these are created by friendship, for to choose to live together is friendship.[90]

Thus, in Aristotle's understanding, friendship is requisite to community, including political community. This includes the sort of affection for one's neighbor that one might expect, but also a sort of proximity and sameness – shared blood to reinforce those affections. "To choose to live together," he states, "is friendship." Cicero further develops this idea of civic friendship in his account of duties. He states, "We are not born of ourselves alone,"[91] and suggests in his account of justice that we actually *owe* something to our country and fellow citizens. Not to give to our *patria* what we are able to give is nothing less than an injustice.[92]

In addition to the existential requirements of a polity and necessities of justice that Aristotle and Cicero, respectively, offer in support of civic bonds, fellow citizens must see each other as coequals and feel at least somewhat obliged to one another if they are to govern together. This need for meaningful and acknowledged equality among citizens has been present even when republics were not so egalitarian, as in Greece, Rome, and the United States during the slavery and Jim Crow periods.[93] Jack Balkin explains how "the historical tradition of republicanism ... insisted that economic self-sufficiency was central to participation in republican government," that one had to meet a threshold of leisure time and financial security in order to participate in politics, both as a practical matter and as a matter of being acknowledged as an equal.[94] "This demand," Balkin continues, "produced both conservative and egalitarian versions of republicanism."[95] It produced the conservatism of those

---

[89] Aristotle, *Politics*, 1262b7–8.
[90] Aristotle, *Politics*, 1280b35–1281a2.
[91] Cicero, *On Duties*, I.22.
[92] Ibid., I.23.
[93] Gordon Wood, *Empire of Liberty* (Oxford: Oxford University Press, 2011), 8.
[94] Jack Balkin, "Which Republican Constitution?" *Constitutional Commentary* 32 (2017), 31–59, at 33.
[95] Ibid.

republics that allowed only property-owning or noble members of society to be voting citizens. However, this same demand of economic self-sufficiency also gave rise to more modern versions of republicanism that have sought either to raise more individuals up to a certain level of independence and self-sufficiency, or to make material wealth less important so that a broader population may participate as equal members in politics and society. Arguably, this is the basic impulse behind the introduction of socioeconomic rights, which often serve as the backdrop for horizontal application.[96]

In a way, both the conservative and egalitarian versions of republicanism operate from the same premise: that a certain equality among citizens goes hand in hand with collective self-government and civic duty. The difference is that the conservative version identifies citizens from preexisting castes, whereas the latter, more egalitarian version makes a positive effort to equalize people and so bring them into the fold of citizenship.[97] In either case, one sees the necessity of shared responsibility and civic duty toward fellow citizens in a republican framework.

The Neorepublican Intervention

From the conservative versions of republicanism that Balkin discusses to the populist bent found in Rousseau, some scholars have worried about the broader implications and tendencies of republicanism. For example, Isaiah Berlin's famous characterization of the ancients' positive liberty is less than attractive in that their understanding of self-rule may be exercised to legitimate an oppressive communitarianism and even authoritarianism.[98] Against such apprehensions, Pettit argues that a consistent understanding of republicanism – that is, "freedom as non-domination," properly understood – is not susceptible to authoritarian perils. Rather, he argues, the fundamental core of republican thought may actually serve to critique other instantiations of republicanism as classist and homogenizing.[99] Similarly, Daly and Hickey explain that republicanism comes in different flavors, some of which are more palatable than others:

---

[96] Tushnet, *Weak Courts*.
[97] Pettit, *People's Terms*; Frank Michelman, "Law's Republic," *Yale Law Journal* 97:8 (1988), 1493–1537.
[98] Berlin, "Two Concepts."
[99] Pettit, *People's Terms*, 1–25.

THE NEOREPUBLICAN INTERVENTION   39

> The term [republicanism] is associated with the unitary and indivisible State advocated by Jean-Jacques Rousseau, but also the federalism and checks and balances promoted by Madison ... Some republicans have assumed that civic virtue can be realized only in a cohesive, austere and disciplined society, whereas more liberal-minded thinkers have argued that republican citizenship can occupy a more minimal domain and accommodate a range of co-existing private identities.[100]

Pettit attempts just this: he argues for "a minimal domain" of republican citizenship that can "accommodate a range of co-existing private identities."[101] Pettit juxtaposes republican freedom as nondomination with both the liberal conception of freedom as noninterference[102] and the more demanding accounts of republicanism sometimes identified with communitarian theories.[103] He follows Quentin Skinner[104] in arguing that republican freedom is properly understood "not as the positive benefit of participation in sovereign self-rule, but as a negative good that such participation might instrumentally serve: the good of escaping the imposition of others."[105] In this way, Pettit's theory may require the addition of another category in Berlin's framework, namely freedom not simply as self-rule but negatively conceived as nondomination.[106]

How, then, does Pettit's more moderate take on freedom as nondomination comport with a republican commitment to the common good and sense of duty among citizens? Although Pettit tends not to employ such language as "the common good" in the same way as classical republicans, the heart of his theory still reveals an essential kinship. First, he is very clear that nondomination *is* a common good, that is, a good that is good for all and can only be fully realized in common. He explains that

> there can be no hope of advancing the cause of freedom as nondomination among individuals who do not readily embrace both the

---

[100] Daly and Hickey, *Political Theory*, 9–10.
[101] Ibid., 10.
[102] Pettit, *People's Terms*, 8–11.
[103] Ibid., 11–18. See also Jose Marti and Philip Pettit, *A Political Philosophy in Public Life: Civic Republicanism in Zapatero's Spain* (Princeton: Princeton University Press, 2012), 32, 45–46.
[104] Quentin Skinner, "The Idea of Negative Liberty," in *Philosophy in History*, ed. Richard Rorty, Jerome B. Schneewind, and Quentin Skinner (Cambridge: Cambridge University Press, 1984), 193–222; Quentin Skinner, "The Paradoxes of Political Liberty," in *The Tanner Lectures on Human Values*, ed. Sterling McMurrin (Cambridge: Cambridge University Press, 1985), 227–250.
[105] Marti and Pettit, *Political Philosophy*, 32.
[106] Pettit, *Republicanism*, chap. 1.

prospect of substantial equality and the condition of communal solidarity. To want republican liberty, you have to want republican equality; to realize republican liberty, you have to realize republican community.[107]

In short, even republican liberty in its negative form of freedom as nondomination, as opposed to the more positive freedom as self-mastery, depends on a "republican community" dedicated to this conception of freedom and to its fruition for all members of the community. For Pettit, therefore, freedom is necessarily tied up with some understanding of a common good.

In the same way that freedom as nondomination requires republican community, so too might it be jeopardized by any sector of the community, by private and public entities alike. Pettit warns against the ways in which domination can occur in the private realm; one might think of the power of employers over their employees, or of large campaign donors in politics. For this reason, true freedom requires the cooperation of all spheres with respect to this public principle of freedom as nondomination. Hence, Pettit follows his republican predecessors in maintaining that both public and private spheres remain obligated to this common good, even as a matter of law. The fundamental requirement for preserving freedom is that interventions in private life occur "on the people's terms."[108] In other words, the public principle of nondomination may warrant interference in the private sphere so long as the people maintain meaningful control over the governing institutions that make these decisions.

Pettit also accounts for a republican sense of duty and requisite equality among fellow citizens. In *On the People's Terms*, he introduces the "eyeball test," the idea that freedom requires that an individual be able to "look others in the eye without reason for fear or deference."[109] In other words, freedom in a meaningful sense requires that fellow citizens be able to approach one another as equals. In contrast, we find domination in those instances when one evokes the kind of fear that would lead citizens to avert their eyes in deference before a fellow citizen. Pettit believes that this kind of domination, or arbitrary power, can be avoided if everyone enjoys a comparable standard of living. He explains: "Social justice, so interpreted, would require each citizen to enjoy the same free status, objective and subjective, as others. It would mandate *a substantive form of status equality*."[110] According to Pettit, the

---

[107] Ibid., 125–126.
[108] Pettit, *People's Terms*.
[109] Ibid., 298.
[110] Ibid., emphasis added.

securing of material factors, often controlled by the private realm, is necessary to achieve nondomination in a meaningful sense. Therefore, a polity must secure a certain level of material well-being in order for citizens to be able to "look others in the eye" and so view one another as coequals governing together. This concern over a degree of material equality, to which the "eyeball test" draws attention, echoes the emphasis of classical republicanism on material equality and self-sufficiency as prerequisites for participation in politics and society. Hence Pettit justifies intervention in the private sphere to secure such social and economic equality, as well as to prevent more direct forms of domination.

While republican thought is united by an understanding of freedom as nondomination, Pettit's theory proposes to focus on the more negative concern of not being subject to the arbitrary power of others, in contrast with other versions of republicanism that focus on the positive of self-rule. In some ways, this distinction is important to the task of demonstrating parallels between horizontality and republican thought insofar as one version may encompass more persuasive connections to horizontal application than the other. Indeed, horizontal application does seem to have an affinity to Pettit's negative formulation of nondomination as it addresses the threats to freedom that may occur in private spaces. In contrast, consider certain accounts of freedom as self-mastery, such as one finds in Rousseau's concept of the general will, that depend on a more complete subversion of one's individual will. Contemporary proponents of horizontal application, still operating within the framework of constitutionalism, likely would recoil from the implications of such Rousseauian theories and incline to more moderate neorepublicanism in order to ground horizontal application. Put differently, one might argue that it is in the context of neorepublicanism's negative conception of freedom that the practice of horizontal application is most accurately considered a republican vein within the tradition of liberal constitutionalism.

At the same time, neorepublicanism arguably is an heir of classical republican theories. In arguing that domination often occurs in the private sphere, Pettit follows classical theories in requiring governance of the polity taken as a whole – namely, that his republican conception of freedom must govern public and private spaces alike. This may not leave much room for accommodating differences in how individuals privately conceive of freedom. This is not to suggest that Pettit's theory of republicanism collapses into something like Rousseau's general will, but only to highlight that his account includes certain limits to what "the people's terms" may ultimately include.[111]

Regardless of how one comes down on such questions concerning positive and negative formulations of liberty in republican thought, the principle of freedom as nondomination forms the fundamental core of this tradition. Consequently, it illuminates the role of such concepts as the common good and duty that one finds in the practice of horizontal application.

Republicanism and Horizontality

What, then, is the connection between these principles of republican thought and horizontal application? More specifically, how do the principles of the common good and civic duty relate to this emerging practice in constitutionalism? And how does this comparison move us beyond technical legal issues to understand how horizontal application interacts with conventional understandings of constitutionalism? The parity and duty that characterize horizontal application make clear the relevance of this republican connection, which the remainder of this chapter will elaborate. It will consider these concepts separately to specify how exactly we find these republican features in the logic of horizontal application, as well as the discourses that emerge from its practice. However, parity and duty are fundamentally related, even two sides of the same coin. Therefore, subsequent chapters treat them together as comprising the unified republican character of horizontal application.

Parity in Horizontal Application

As republican thought holds up the common good as a binding standard for both public and private entities, so too does horizontal application charge both public and private actors with promoting constitutional values. This parity in the constitution's applicability to public and private entities shows some kinship with republicanism and, more specifically, with the concept of the common good that underlies the republican conception of freedom.

---

[111] For a compelling account of potential limits in Pettit's thought, such as the tension between substantive justice and procedural legitimacy, see David Dyzenhaus, "Critical Notice of *On the People's Terms: A Republican Theory and Model of Democracy*, by Philip Pettit, Cambridge University Press, 2012, xii + 333 pp.," *Canadian Journal of Philosophy* 43:4 (2013), 494–513.

For an example of how parity manifests in an actual instance of horizontal application and how it follows the logic of republican principles, one need not look further than the Federal Republic of Germany's famous *Lüth* case.[112] In 1951, pro-Nazi filmmaker Veit Harlan filed suit against Erich Lüth, arguing that Lüth had harmed Harlan's economic prospects by publicly calling for a boycott of his film. While the district court initially granted Harlan's injunction, the Federal Constitutional Court reversed the ruling seven years later, arguing that the German Basic Law committed the polity to an "order of objective moral and legal principles." Such principles have a "radiating effect" (*Ausstrahlungswirkung*), bearing on all areas of German law and life. For this reason, the Court argued that it would be remiss to pretend that Lüth's right to freedom of expression, guaranteed by the Basic Law, was irrelevant to the case (as the district court had ruled). Indeed, the Court ultimately sent the case back to the lower court with the instruction that it should consider how such principles of the Basic Law inform Germany's civil law.

In *Lüth*, the Federal Constitutional Court stated explicitly the importance of parity in certain foundational questions and constitutional commitments in public and private venues alike. In the same way that the framers of the Basic Law felt a sense of urgency to entrench commitments to human dignity and the inviolability of human personality just a few years after the conclusion of the Second World War, one senses a similar urgency in the Constitutional Court's *Lüth* decision to ensure that these defining constitutional commitments actually be constitutive of the polity as a whole. In speaking of the postwar German constitutional tradition, and the *Lüth* case in particular, Ulrich Preuss explains:

> [T]he right to free speech or to freedom of religion is not only a kind of concession of the society to individuals and their self-interest, but it equally serves the benefit of the society at large; a society in which each individual enjoys the fundamental rights of the Bill of Rights is *different and morally more advanced* than one in which these rights are lacking. Hence, it is in the interest of society itself to establish and sustain these rights. If this is so, *it cannot be tolerated that there are spheres of social life in which the spirit or the values of the fundamental rights are absent.*[113]

---

[112] *Lüth*, BVerfGE 7, 198 (1958).

[113] Ulrich Preuss, "The German *Drittwirkung* Doctrine and Its Socio-political Background," in *The Constitution in Private Relations*, ed. András Sajó and Renáta Uitz (Utrecht: Eleven, 2005), 23–32, at 26, emphasis added.

This interpretation of postwar German constitutionalism suggests that the horizontal application of rights is motivated by more than the sheer convenience of enlisting the private sphere, or even by the goal of protecting individual rights. Rather, Preuss describes an ethos of the polity, a moral position that may permit some degree of difference but that ultimately begs for, and demands, a united front in the polity's commitment to certain governing principles. Thus, the horizontal application of rights can serve to infuse the life of the polity with the "spirit or the values of the fundamental rights," in the same way that citizens of a republican polity are equally held to pursue the common good of the polity as their own. In this way, constitutional rights commitments may be just as much "about" that private entity charged with promoting rights as they are about the rights-bearer. In a sort of Dworkinian turn, horizontal application as a practice suggests an obligation to make each society the most attractive that it can be.[114]

One might object that parity between public and private spheres is different in some important ways from the principle of the common good associated with republicanism. Indeed, horizontality operates within a larger framework of rights that, on certain formulations, may exist in tension with the sort of civic-mindedness that republicanism requires.[115] The objection might continue that, in horizontal application, one employs the language of rights and thereby frames the issue as a conflict of rights, an essentially liberal formulation that does not leave much space for considerations of the common good.[116] Nevertheless, horizontal application still entails a privileging of the "public thing" above one's immediate private interests, and not simply as a result of the sort of refereeing or policing that virtually all political philosophers have understood as being part of the role of government.[117] Rather, horizontality requires the suspension of private interests in the explicit service of public ends, a notion difficult to find in the work of classical liberals. Indeed, horizontality will require that people yield their rights claims to other, perhaps more constitutive commitments of the polity.

---

[114] I am indebted to Daniel Brinks for this insight.
[115] Wood, *Creation*, 68.
[116] Duncan Ivison, "Republican Human Rights?" *European Journal of Political Theory* 9:1 (2010), 31–47.
[117] The point that humankind requires systems of government and policing is particularly emphasized in such state-of-nature theories as those advanced by Hobbes and Locke. The obvious exception to this broad claim is anarchical theory.

In the same spirit as Schmidt and Webking's argument, however, one might push back that the common good to which people yield their rights in horizontal application itself simply comprises rights. In other words, whatever common good that horizontal application may further amounts to simply the amalgamation of individual rights. In this telling, there is not anything external to the self or truly common of which to speak in horizontal application; this development is little more than an extension of the same rights protections of the traditional vertical model. While the rights to which the polity commits are not contentless or neutral, the objection may continue, they are also not qualitatively the same as a republican understanding of the common good. Robert Alexy's discussion of horizontal application and his treatment of subjective versus objective rights go some way to show how, in fact, horizontal application entails reconceiving rights so that they are more than claims to level against another.[118] While this "subjective" understanding of rights is still operative in horizontal application, it operates alongside an "objective" understanding of rights by which rights commitments become goods or values in themselves, independent of the claims they allow one to make against another. In this way, rights become principles in a way that brings them closer to resembling a thicker common good. Hence, Germany's Federal Constitutional Court ruled that the freedom of expression was a part of Germany's "order of objective moral and legal principles." It is because these principles have a "radiating effect" that they may sometimes necessitate the concession or sacrifice of others in both public and private spaces.[119]

At the same time, courts account for the burden horizontal application puts on private agents, concluding that the obligations of state and nonstate actors may differ in intensity. Take for example *Daniels v. Scribante and Another*, a case of the South African Constitutional Court.[120] Living in conditions of utter disrepair, Yolanda Daniels began to improve the dwelling she rented on Chardonne Farm at her own expense. The property manager, Theo Scribante, argued that the relevant statutory law and constitutional provisions granted her no right to

---

[118] Robert Alexy, *Theory of Constitutional Rights*. See also Georg Sommeregger, "The Horizontalization of Equality"; Ulrich Preuss, "The German *Drittwirkung* Doctrine and Its Socio-political Background."

[119] For cases with facts and outcomes similar to *Lüth*, see also the South African Constitutional Court case *Khumalo v. Holomisa* (CCT53/01) [2002] ZACC 12, and the US Supreme Court case *New York Times v. Sullivan* 376 U.S. 254 (1964).

[120] *Daniels v. Scribante and Another* (CCT50/16) [2017] ZACC 13.

change the property without his or the owner's consent. Moreover, they argued that they had no positive duty to pay for any modifications she made to improve her living conditions. Tending to the social and historical context surrounding the case, the South African Constitutional Court ultimately decided that Daniels did, in fact, have a right to live in conditions that were up to standard and, more specifically, that this was required by her right to human dignity. Moreover, Scribante and the property owners were not necessarily exempt from covering these costs. Still, the Court acknowledged certain limits to the duties that Daniels's right demanded of Scribante. In the majority opinion, the Court observed that private persons can only rely on "their own pockets" or private funds as opposed to public sources of revenue. Justice Madlanga explains, "It would be unreasonable, therefore, to require private persons to bear the exact same obligations under the Bill of Rights as does the State."[121] Because the capacities, resources, and status of private and public institutions are not identical, their constitutional duties are not equal.

Nevertheless, the capacity of, or burden on, private entities is neither the only nor the most important consideration in determining whether rights should be applied horizontally. In *Daniels*, the Constitutional Court developed criteria introduced in earlier cases,[122] explaining the considerations upon which the horizontal application of rights depends:

> Whether private persons will be bound depends on a number of factors. What is paramount includes: what is the nature of the right; what is the history behind the right; what does the right seek to achieve; how best can that be achieved; what is the "potential of invasion of that right by persons other than the State or organs of state"; and, would letting private persons off the net not negate the essential content of the right?[123]

This explanation of the South African Constitutional Court's decision suggests that much more enters the calculation than the burden that horizontal application may create for private entities. Rather, the court puts much weight on the importance or status of a given right, such as how constitutive a right is of a larger constitutional project, as well as

---

[121] Ibid., para. 40.

[122] See *Khumalo v. Holomisa*, in which the South African Constitutional Court decided that the horizontal application of Section 8(2) of the South African Constitution depends in part on the potential of private entities to impinge on rights, but also, importantly, on the "intensity of the constitutional right in question" (para. 33).

[123] *Daniels v. Scribante and Another*, para. 39.

what the right's realization will require. One can see this in the Constitutional Court's consideration of "the nature of the right" and "the history behind the right." In such criteria, the Court considers the status of particular rights weighed against standards of justice, as well as the meanings that arise out of particular historical and cultural contexts. Some rights are so important, universally and locally,[124] the argument goes, they demand parity across the polity, governing even actions in what one might otherwise understand to be a private space.

Duty in Horizontal Application

In addition to parity, the horizontal application of rights also engenders certain duties akin to republican understandings of civic duty. Specifically, in obligating private entities to promote the constitutional commitments of a polity, horizontal application holds individuals accountable for others' rights, generating constitutional duties as they take up the mantle of their fellow citizens' equal status. Of course, liberal political thought also depends on a belief in human equality. But again, one who subscribes to the liberal conception of freedom as noninterference may dispute the way horizontality seeks equality through enlisting private entities for public projects. On the other hand, the idea that one has duties with respect to one's fellow citizens is part and parcel of the republican community to which Pettit refers.[125] That one would have obligations to one's fellow citizens as an extension of pursuing the good of the polity is beyond dispute in almost any version of the republican tradition. Therefore, while not necessarily incompatible with liberal thought, this understanding of duty is a natural result of the republican conception of freedom as nondomination.

This connection between horizontality and citizens' duty is apparent in various scenarios, such as when courts apply rights horizontally to achieve an outcome that might have been attainable through the conventional vertical model as well. For example, in *Mohini Jain v. State of Karnataka*, the Indian Supreme Court decided that it was unconstitutional for private universities to charge certain capitation fees, insofar as such fees would obstruct the Indian Constitution's guarantee of equality (in Article 14) and right to education (implied by

---

[124] Ibid., para. 51.
[125] Pettit, *Republicanism*, 125–126.

Article 21).[126] However, these rights plausibly could have been secured through alternative means, perhaps through government subsidies to offset the cost of applying to private universities, or through making public universities more accessible.[127] When a court applies horizontally a right that government might have secured through state action, it seems to assume the distinct goal of compelling private entities to respect and guarantee the rights of others. Horizontal application thus becomes just as much about the duties of those private entities charged with protecting rights as about protecting the rights-bearer.

A similar impulse underlies those instances in which a court imposes a penalty on private actors in addition to whatever steps are necessary to ensure that the rights-bearers' rights are secured. Consider the case of *M. C. Mehta v. State of Tamil Nadu*, in which the Indian Supreme Court held that employing children younger than fourteen in match and firework factories violated Article 24 of the Constitution. The offending employers were required to pay a fine to the "Child Labour Rehabilitation-cum-Welfare Fund" in order to provide for children who might otherwise be compelled to seek employment.[128] While this penalizing impulse hoped to deter future violations of rights, it also spurred private actors to participate in the promotion of particular rights and the values underlying them.

In *Daniels v. Scribante and Another*, this preference for horizontality, and a category of constitutional duties for individuals, was described more broadly.[129] In deciding that landlords must permit tenants to live in accommodations with requisite standards of dignity, the South African Constitutional Court did more than simply hold private entities to account for public values. Rather, the Court decided that economic and social rights could directly create obligations of private individuals and nonstate actors.[130] This entails the much broader conclusion that

---

[126] *Mohini Jain v. State of Karnataka* (1992) 3 SCC 666. See Stephen Gardbaum, "Horizontality in the Indian Constitution," in *The Oxford Handbook of the Indian Constitution*, ed. Sujit Choudhry, Madhav Khosla, and Pratap Bhanu Mehta (Oxford: Oxford University Press, 2016), 600–613, at 608.

[127] For similar reasoning with respect to horizontality, see Mark Tushnet, "The Issue of State Action/Horizontal Effect in Comparative Constitutional Law," *International Journal of Constitutional Law* 1 (2003), 79–98.

[128] *M.C. Mehta v. State of Tamil Nadu* (1996) 6 SCC 756; Gardbaum, "Horizontality in the Indian Constitution," 605.

[129] CCT50/16 [2017] ZACC 13.

[130] See also Aoife Nolan, "*Daniels v. Scribante*: South Africa Pushes the Boundaries of Horizontality and Social Rights," I-CONnect, December 20, 2017, www.iconnectblog

constitutional commitments may create *positive* obligations for private individuals and nonstate actors. In other words, individuals against whom a right is applied horizontally may not simply have to refrain from acting in a particular way, but may have to take positive action in pursuit of the commitments of the polity.[131] In this understanding, horizontal application has the reach and power to achieve an equality akin to Pettit's status equality.[132] Insofar as it holds private individuals to not only acknowledge but also actively secure the rights of others, horizontality makes possible an equality that exceeds the typical negative and positive rights, since it encompasses the mutual cooperation and recognition that might enable one to look others in the eye, according to Pettit's republican "eyeball test."

One might object that while the constitutional duties that result from horizontal application ultimately aim toward solidarity among citizens, this would come about by judicial decree in contrast to the more typical republican emphasis on a robust civic culture and contestation.[133] The objection might continue that, in spite of the moderation that courts sometimes practice, the very act of assigning duties to private actors, such as landlords and private universities, only serves to underscore and even crystalize how rights-bearers continue to depend on such entities. In contrast, a remedy more faithful to republican principles would work to free people from dependence on judicial oversight, insofar as freedom as nondomination is possible only in independence from external, likely arbitrary, forces. In response to this objection, that horizontality achieves merely a pretense of republican objectives due to its reliance on government authority rather than civic culture, and top-down implementation, one could argue that the courts (and other institutions) involved in applying rights horizontally offer citizens an education in republican

---

.com/2017/06/daniels-v-scribante-south-africa-pushes-the-boundaries-of-horizontality-and-social-rights.

[131] See also Gardbaum, "Horizontality in the Indian Constitution"; Colm O'Cinnede, "Irish Constitutional Law and Direct Horizontal Effect: A Successful Experiment?" in *Human Rights in the Private Sphere*, ed. Dawn Oliver and Jorg Fedtke (Abingdon: Routledge-Cavendish, 2007), 213–251.

[132] Pettit, *People's Terms*, 37.

[133] Jacobsohn addresses this very point in the Indian context: "The very explicitness of the constitutional recognition (especially in Article 25) that meaningful social reform required attention to the critical role of religion in Indian life might suggest the futility of judicial intervention. Problems of such complicated scope and intricacy would very likely defy Court-mandated solution." See Gary Jacobsohn, *The Wheel of Law* (Princeton: Princeton University Press, 2009), 92.

virtues.[134] While the institutional character and limitations of courts mean that the effects of horizontality will likewise be limited, this practice could potentially serve an instructive role,[135] as well as a kind of stopgap in salient cases.[136]

The next section discusses how the tension – some have called it a difficulty[137] – inhering in judicial review between top-down authority and self-government bears on the question of horizontal application. It begins with the observation that certain scholars who have written on horizontal application were also prominent contributors to the Republican Revival in legal scholarship. Nevertheless, these scholars do not seem to connect horizontality and republicanism in their writings. A potential reason for this may be the simple fact that horizontality is so closely associated with courts, often viewed as less democratic (or, for the purposes of this book, less republican) institutions. The next section thus wrestles with critiques and defenses of judicial decision-making and their applications to horizontality. However, while courts are key actors in questions of horizontality, they may relate to this phenomenon differently depending on the particulars of a given context. For example, constitutional framers, rather than courts, may introduce horizontal application into the constitutional text itself. Thus, the section concludes that republicanesque objections to the role of courts in horizontal application are contingent. Indeed, the histories detailed in subsequent chapters illustrate the varying roles of courts and how different actors relate to the horizontal application of rights in different ways. Moreover, notwithstanding the courts' essential role in this practice, reinvigorating the role that, say, legislative institutions also play in deciding these questions

---

[134] Eoin Daly has directly alluded to the potential of horizontality to advance republican ends, although he has not developed the connection in great depth. See Eoin Daly, "Freedom as Nondomination in the Jurisprudence of Constitutional Rights," *Canadian Journal of Law and Jurisprudence* 28:2 (2015), 289–316, at 306; and Daly and Hickey, *Political Theory*, 77–78.

[135] In the words of Eugene Rostow, "The Supreme Court is, among other things, an educational body, and the Justices are inevitably teachers in a vital national seminar." Rostow goes on to cite the situation of African Americans in the 1950s United States and argues for the good that the Court accomplished in advancing equality in both public and private venues ("The Democratic Character of Judicial Review," *Harvard Law Review* 66:2 [1952], 193–224, at 208).

[136] See Jud Mathews's account of how courts employ horizontality when they find "normative gaps" in existing law (*Extending Rights' Reach* [Oxford: Oxford University Press, 2018], 13).

[137] Alexander Bickel, *The Least Dangerous Branch* (New Haven: Yale University Press, 1986).

would begin to address concerns that horizontal application disproportionately empowers courts. As it happens, such steps may be described as making horizontality more republican in the sense that it refocuses some attention on representative institutions. With such adjustments, the extension of public values to establish parity among, and duties for, private actors may also more closely approximate the republican value of self-governance essential to republican freedom.

Horizontality and the Republican Credentials of Courts

Despite the features of horizontal application that can be understood in republican terms, the expansive role for courts that horizontality potentially entails may give some republican scholars pause.[138] As Bellamy explains, "Courts lack the fundamental democratic quality of allowing an equal input from all affected citizens – their 'right' to author their rights."[139] Such a tension emerges in one strand of republican thought not yet discussed, namely the Republican Revival in legal scholarship. Interestingly, some Republican Revivalists, such as Frank Michelman and Mark Tushnet, have also written on horizontality.[140] However, these scholars never make the connection that horizontality has a republican logic, perhaps because of the nature of their endorsement of republicanism. Tushnet, for example, emphasizes such republican principles as self-government, dialogue, and deliberation,[141] principles that may not easily coexist in an increasingly court-centric world. Indeed, Tushnet has argued that we must "take the Constitution away from the courts."[142]

Frank Michelman finds a role for courts in his republicanism, although his argument is premised on the very fact that there is a deep tension between what he frames as "rule of the people" and "rule of law."

---

[138] Daly and Hickey, *Political Theory*.
[139] Richard Bellamy, "Democracy as Public Law: The Case of Constitutional Rights," *German Law Journal* 14:8 (2013), 1017–1038, at 1030.
[140] Frank Michelman, "Constitutions and the Public/Private Divide," in *The Oxford Handbook of Comparative Constitutional Law*, ed. Michel Rosenfeld and András Sajó (Oxford: Oxford University Press, 2012), 298–317; and Frank Michelman, "The Interplay of Constitutional and Ordinary Jurisdiction," in *Comparative Constitutional Law*, ed. Tom Ginsburg and Rosalind Dixon (Cheltenham: Edward Elgar, 2011), 278–297; Tushnet, *Weak Courts*.
[141] Mark Tushnet, *Red, White, and Blue: A Critical Analysis of Constitutional Law* (Lawrence: Kansas University Press, 2015).
[142] Mark Tushnet, *Taking the Constitution Away from the Courts* (Princeton: Princeton University Press, 2000).

In *Law's Republic*, Michelman states, "Republican thought thus demands some way of understanding how laws and rights can be both the recreations of citizens and, at the same time, the normative givens that constitute and underwrite a political process capable of creating constitutive law."[143] In other words, it is not immediately clear how citizens can be both self-governing and governed by law. As a solution, Michelman argues that courts are distinctly situated to assist the marginalized of society to join the governing body of citizens. For if a polity, taken as a whole, is to be truly self-governing, then all its citizens must possess the requisite agency to govern. According to Michelman, courts can help widen the boundaries to encompass more people as citizens and thus facilitate more perfect self-government. Nevertheless, a tension remains in Michelman's thought, since he elsewhere concedes that the role of the courts ought to remain fairly modest.[144]

Richard Bellamy tries to strike a similar balance in his own scholarship.[145] Drawing on a distinction first employed by Pettit,[146] Bellamy concedes the usefulness of courts for their "editorial" capacity – that is, their ability to force legislatures to reconsider laws that may not have accounted for the interests of every group in the polity.[147] However, he worries that with judicial finality, courts instead begin to exercise an "authorial" role. This is the function of *making* law, which, in a republican understanding of freedom as nondomination, ought to be retained by institutions accountable to and, therefore, controlled by the people, rather than exercised by unelected judges. Bellamy explains that if a court is allowed "to strike down legislation or to read into it its own reading of its fit with constitutional norms, then it is in effect usurping the authorial function of electoral democracy."[148] And indeed, insofar as people disagree so vastly in their views of the "sources and substance" and the

---

[143] Michelman, "Law's Republic," 798.
[144] See the analyses of Michelman's thought in Jeff King, "Social Rights in Comparative Constitutional Theory," in *Comparative Constitutional Theory*, ed. Gary Jacobsohn and Miguel Schor (Cheltenham: Edward Elgar, 2018), 144–166; and William Forbath, "Not So Simple Justice: Frank Michelman on Social Rights, 1969–Present," *Tulsa Law Review* 39 (2004), 631–636.
[145] Bellamy, "Democracy as Public Law."
[146] Philip Pettit, "Democracy, Electoral and Contestatory," in *Designing Democratic Institutions*, ed. Ian Shapiro and Stephen Macedo (New York: New York University Press, 2000), 105–146.
[147] Bellamy, "Democracy as Public Law," 1030.
[148] Ibid., 1036.

"subjects and scope"[149] of rights, one has little reason to entrust judges with answering these inherently political questions about rights, much less with their horizontal application. Bellamy states, "At the level of principle, these disputes have not proved any more resolvable in seminar rooms of philosophy departments than they have among policy makers and citizens."[150] Since reasonable disagreement is inevitable, the republican who is committed to freedom as nondomination may not view courts as proper venues to convene what Eugene Rostow referred to as a "national seminar."[151] Rather, on Bellamy's telling, the authorial implications of rights questions make their resolution a matter for "real democracy."[152]

Tom Hickey also addresses these concerns.[153] Like Bellamy, Hickey is a political constitutionalist in that he views the source, substance, and scope of rights as political questions, rather than as questions with set legal answers to be revealed by judges and lawyers.[154] In this spirit, Hickey joins Bellamy in arguing that judicial review cannot be justified in terms of judges' "epistemic"[155] capacities (i.e., their abilities to reach correct answers), if one is operating in a republican conception of freedom as nondomination. However, Hickey departs from Bellamy in the extent to which he thinks judicial review can be justified in terms of judges' "legitimating"[156] capacity without necessarily usurping the authorial function. This is because courts may actually support those processes by which the people retain control over governing institutions and so bolster their republican liberty. In particular, Hickey cites the ability of judicial review to "smoke out"[157] dubious motives of legislators, draw attention to missed opportunities to accommodate minorities, and allow individuals whose rights may have been violated to raise their grievances.[158] Insofar as these features and capacities work toward

---

[149] Ibid., 1021.
[150] Ibid.
[151] Rostow, "The Democratic Character of Judicial Review," *Harvard Law Review* 66 (1952), 193–224, at 208.
[152] Bellamy, "Democracy as Public Law," 1030.
[153] Tom Hickey, "The Republican Core of the Case for Judicial Review," *International Journal of Constitutional Law* 17 (2019), 288–316.
[154] Ibid., 292.
[155] Ibid., 290–293.
[156] Ibid., 293–297.
[157] Ibid., 305.
[158] Ibid., 300–310. See also John Hart Ely, *Democracy and Distrust* (Cambridge, MA: Harvard University Press, 1980).

legitimating law-making processes rather than seeking correct answers, they become not only compatible with but also potentially instrumental toward a republican understanding of freedom as nondomination. In this way, Hickey argues, even strong judicial review may remain editorial without infringing on the authorial function more properly located in those electoral institutions over which people have more control.

To some extent, the questions underlying Hickey's and Bellamy's arguments about judicial review cannot be avoided in considering horizontal application, given the core role of the courts in this practice. Nevertheless, the role of courts still varies among countries employing horizontal application. For example, a constitutional assembly, rather than a court, may be the body to adopt this practice, mitigating concerns about countermajoritarianism and democratic deficits. This is true of the South African Constitution, which provides for the potential horizontal application of all rights in Section 8, and is arguably true of the Indian Constitution, which includes more targeted horizontality provisions such as Article 15 concerning antidiscrimination. In cases such as these, the finding that courts are less republican than other governmental institutions is only a concern when it comes to the implementation of horizontal application, as opposed to the more fundamental decision to adopt this practice in the first place.

Moreover, other institutions may still serve an important function in determinations of horizontality, even as the courts retain their own role. Constitutional amendments may spur legislators to apply rights horizontally as they look to implement new constitutional commitments. Moreover, legislators may respond to or even anticipate court decisions, essentially creating upstream effects as they legislate with horizontality in mind.[159] Arguably we see such exchanges between institutions in all of the chapters that follow. We see such contests in the United States following the adoption of the Fourteenth Amendment and later the Civil Rights Act of 1964. Moreover, in Germany we see different courts staking different positions on the question of horizontality, which was made more complicated when the European Union introduced its antidiscrimination directives for the Member States.

Court decisions cannot be avoided in conversations on horizontal application and, indeed, comprise a substantial portion of the subsequent

---

[159] I am grateful to Jud Mathews for this insight.

pages.¹⁶⁰ Thus, in some sense, one cannot avoid the question of whether courts employ horizontal application in primarily an editorial or authorial mode. In other words, the question still stands whether horizontal application generally contributes to courts' ability to legitimate those processes that engender republican freedom, or instead raises wholly new political questions that ought to be left to more democratic institutions. Still, while courts play a prominent role in questions of horizontality, they need not have a monopoly on the practice. Rather, courts are one among several governmental institutions that may attempt to shape the private sphere according to constitutional norms.¹⁶¹ A complete telling must thus account for the clusters of relations among institutions that this practice creates and the ways such institutions relate differently to horizontality.¹⁶² Consideration of the range of institutions involved only becomes more important when thinking in republican terms.

Conclusion

Horizontal application constitutes a republican vein within the tradition of liberal constitutionalism. As such, horizontal application still depends on the continued use of the liberal language of rights.¹⁶³ In understanding this innovation in constitutionalism through the lens of republican theory, this chapter does not intend to cast republicanism

---

[160] Indeed, the judiciary often serves as "the vehicle through which questions of 'foundational collective identity' are addressed" (Jacobsohn, *Constitutional Identity*, 14; see also Ran Hirschl, *Toward Juristocracy*, chap. 6).

[161] The "new commonwealth model of constitutionalism" that Stephen Gardbaum finds emerging in various countries may offer yet another alternative ("The Case for the New Commonwealth Model of Constitutionalism," *German Law Journal* 14:12 [2013], 2229–2248). As Gardbaum explains, "The new model blends legal and political constitutionalism across the board in its three sequenced stages of pre-enactment political rights review, judicial rights review, and post-judicial political rights review" (ibid., 2230). In short, this model acknowledges the politics involved in rights adjudication and, consequently, carves out roles for both courts and legislatures in answering these questions. In the terms of this book, something like the new commonwealth model might preserve an element of republican politics even as courts maintain a sizable role in deciding how public commitments should bear on private spaces.

[162] Speaking of American constitutional history but with an eye toward other contexts, Jacobsohn describes "a protracted contest involving multiple interventions by political actors distributed across institutions and between levels of government, all responding differently to pressures emanating from a constantly shifting social landscape" (*Constitutional Identity*, 355).

[163] Duncan Ivison, "Republican Human Rights?" *European Journal of Political Theory* 9:1 (2010), 31–47.

and liberalism as clearly dichotomous, or horizontal application as wholly incompatible with liberal constitutionalism. Rather, it draws attention to how particular features of horizontality reflect and find grounding in republican forms within a larger liberal framework. Previous scholarship understands horizontality in liberal contexts,[164] yet concepts within the republican tradition do more to explain the logic of crucial features, including the parity and duty that horizontal application generates.

In light of these republican features, then, what position does horizontal application occupy as a development in the long tradition of constitutionalism? How can we conceive of its situation and function as a republican vein in liberal constitutionalism? The intellectual history that Kalyvas and Katznelson lay out in their book, *Liberal Beginnings: Making a Republic for the Moderns*, proves instructive on this point. They argue that liberalism grew incrementally and organically out of republicanism to make republican politics practicable in modern times. They explain, "Instead of simply thinking of republican and liberal ideas as rival, external each to the other, we demonstrate that what we recognize today as liberalism in fact was constituted as a conceptual hybrid both against and within republican terminology, ideas, and aspirations ... Political liberalism burst from the shell of a republican chrysalis."[165] Thus, while liberalism eventually took on a life of its own, it was originally intended as a corrective within the republican tradition, bringing the rights of the individual to the fore of politics.[166] A correct understanding of the history, they maintain, locates liberalism and its earliest thinkers as a kind of addendum to republican thought.[167]

In a similar spirit to this historical account, horizontal application works as an adjustment but in the reverse direction, reinjecting

---

[164] Scholars have understood horizontality in the context of social democracy (e.g., Mark Tushnet, *Weak Courts, Strong Rights* [Princeton: Princeton University Press, 2009]) and Rawlsian thought (e.g., Sonu Bedi, "The Scope of Formal Equality of Opportunity: The Horizontal Effect of Rights in a Liberal Constitution," *Political Theory* 42 [2014], 716–738). For arguments that depart from liberalism, see Danwood Mzikenge Chirwa's Marxist and feminist take on horizontality in "In Search of Philosophical Justifications and Theoretical Models for the Horizontal Application of Human Rights," *African Human Rights Law Journal* 8 (2008), 294–311, at 294; see also Gautam Bhatia's labor-republican account in *The Transformative Constitution* (Noida: Harper Collins, 2019), 183.
[165] Kalyvas and Katznelson, *Liberal Beginnings*, 4–5.
[166] Ibid., 5.
[167] Ibid., 8–9.

republicanesque elements into liberal orderings. This qualified return to certain qualities from republican thought may function to bolster liberalism where some critics find that it falls short.[168] Indeed, if liberalism was originally a corrective to republicanism, some critics suggest that liberalism has gone too far in its claims to the neutrality of law, its emphasis on rights and private interests, and so on. This may result in a kind of atomism and self-interestedness detrimental to public life and civic duty. Amid such shortfalls, constitutional actors may and arguably do employ horizontal application as a kind of adjustment to this status quo. In Jud Mathews's words, horizontal application fills certain "normative gaps" in private law.[169] In much the same way that Kalyvas and Katznelson describe liberalism as arising out of a need to correct certain aspects of republicanism in concrete circumstances, so too may we think of horizontal application as arising out of historical particulars to address problems that constitutional actors encounter, and perhaps even to realize more fully certain understandings of liberal constitutionalism itself. Indeed, even as this chapter describes how traditional rights claims are reimagined as ends with the introduction of horizontality, it is still liberal values that form the content of these ends and that are arguably expanded by this process of reimagining.

While this book's republican framework is useful to understand specific features of horizontal application, it also draws attention to potential ways in which horizontal application may not be so republican. Indeed, the role of the courts in applying rights horizontally may exist in some tension with republicanism's emphasis on self-government, as discussed earlier. While the presumed purpose of recognizing rights is to entrench certain protections against the will of the majority, rights of any kind, including rights applied horizontally, are not purely legal questions and do not only inhabit the juristic realm. They are also political questions – high constitutional-political questions, but political questions, nonetheless. Objections to horizontality revolving around the courts thus seem to pose less of a challenge when legislators take part in the conversation or when horizontality is introduced by constitution-makers themselves. In such cases, horizontality bears a stronger connection with those actors

---

[168] On Kavlyas and Katznelson's telling, scholars repeatedly characterize liberalism as giving primacy to "the right over the good; neutral legal procedures rather than substantive values; interests, not virtues; negative instead of positive liberty; and individual persons as distinct from collectivities and the public good" (*Liberal Beginnings*, 15).

[169] Jud Mathews, *Extending Rights' Reach* (Oxford: Oxford University Press, 2018).

and institutions traditionally associated with republicanism, potentially hedging worries about horizontality's homogenizing of private to public and its potential to effect a "juridical coup d'etat."[170] Republicanism's demands of citizens to pursue the common good and to fulfill their civic duties are also accompanied by the promise of republican freedom. As this chapter describes how horizontal application makes analogous demands of citizens in contemporary constitutional orders, constitutional actors would do well to acknowledge the political dimensions of horizontal application, in order that this practice may occur "on the people's terms."[171]

---

[170] Alec Stone Sweet, "The Juridical Coup d'État and the Problem of Authority," *German Law Journal* 8 (2007), 915–927.

[171] Pettit, *People's Terms*.

Equality
Does the Constitution Apply Horizontally?

This book now turns to various constitutional orders to examine republican themes in actual debates over the horizontal application of rights. These contexts raise similar questions about horizontality, although under different circumstances and with different forces in play. These chapters do not constitute case studies in the sense that the selection of contexts aims at providing any causal conclusions; rather they are examinations and, ultimately, illustrations of the republican potential of horizontal application in practice. In Kim Lane Scheppele's words, these chapters begin to construct different repertoires for a republican understanding of horizontality.[1] These chapters are by no means exhaustive, but attempt to draw from contexts that, for one reason or another, are paradigmatic for the question of horizontality. In this way, they together sketch a kind of preliminary picture to understand horizontal application through the lens of republican theory.

Chapters 3 and 4 examine political histories and key court cases from the United States and India, respectively. Together, these histories show how republican themes have figured into discourses that aim to justify the introduction of horizontal application in constitutional politics. (The subsequent two chapters on Germany and South Africa differ in that constitutional actors in these contexts largely *presuppose* a doctrine of horizontality, instead raising questions about how far the practice ought to extend.) In the United States the inquiry begins after the adoption of the Fourteenth Amendment, insofar as the text of the amendment does not explicitly proscribe or provide for horizontal application. In contrast, and partly as a result of lessons learned from the United States' record on racial equality, the Indian framers included in their constitutional text provisions that clearly contemplated horizontality. The inquiry in India, therefore, begins in earnest during the ratification debates. While textual

---

[1] Kim Lane Scheppele, "Constitutional Ethnography," *Law and Society Review* 38:3 (2004), 389–406.

provision need not necessarily translate into jurisprudential action pursuant to horizontality, it sets a different constitutional scene in which the debate will unfold. The common question, then, recurring in both the United States and India, is whether the constitution permits horizontality, in general and in particular cases. As ever, different actors and institutions in both countries have offered varied answers. In those instances where constitutional actors have favored some practice of horizontal application, republican themes of a common good and duties of citizens emerge. Likewise, the primacy of rights less connected to public ends emerges in those arguments wedded to a more traditional vertical model.

In both the United States and India, as well as the other contexts this book considers, some of the most instructive interchanges unfold around the issues of equality and antidiscrimination. That this proves to be a kind of flashpoint in horizontality debates is perhaps unsurprising, as constitutional commitments to equality often engender larger projects and, thereby, more extensive duties than do other commitments. Moreover, the application of some version of these duties to private actors is liable to be tendentious to the extent that they involve the limitation of other rights, often liberty rights.[2]

Both the United States and India have histories tainted by social stratification and caste.[3] Even after adopting constitutional commitments to equality and antidiscrimination, the nature and reach of these commitments hung in the balance in both countries. Indeed, the fact that these countries' constitutions include remedial provisions raises questions about the scope and horizontal application of their commitments – whether the rights in their constitutions entail only a limited or formal equality or a more ambitious vision, and whether these rights obligate state actors only or nonstate actors as well.[4] As systems of inequality are frequently rooted in individual practices and beliefs, both countries

---

[2] Georg Sommeregger, "The Horizontalization of Equality: The German Attempt to Promote Non-discrimination in the Private Sphere via Legislation," in *The Constitution in Private Relations*, ed. András Sajó and Renáta Uitz (Utrecht: Eleven, 2005), 33–53; Laurie Ackermann, *Human Dignity: Lodestar for Equality in South Africa* (Cape Town: Juta, 2012), 326–327.

[3] See Bruce Ackerman, *Revolutionary Constitutions: Charismatic Leadership and the Rule of Law* (Cambridge, MA: Harvard University Press, 2019); Martha Nussbaum, "Ambedkar's Constitution: Promoting Inclusion, Opposing Majority Tyranny," in *Assessing Constitutional Performance*, ed. Tom Ginsburg and Aziz Huq (Cambridge: Cambridge University Press, 2016), 295–336.

[4] Andrew Clapham, *Human Rights Obligations of Non-state Actors* (Oxford: Oxford University Press, 2006); Stephen Gardbaum, "The 'Horizontal Effect' of Constitutional Rights," *Michigan Law Review* 102 (2003), 387–459; Mattias Kumm, "Who Is Afraid"; Mattias Kumm and Victor Ferreres Comella, "What Is So Special about Constitutional

naturally have had to confront whether and how new commitments to equality and nondiscrimination would bear on the private sphere. Early decisions launched different political-constitutional discourses that would evolve amid later opportunities to revisit the meaning of equality – whether as a right in a more formal or limited sense, or a more extensive end toward which to endeavor across spheres.

Chapters 3 and 4 show how constitutional actors in the United States and India debated the role private actors would play in securing constitutional commitments, particularly equality and nondiscrimination. At least some constitutional interpreters in both contexts understood the public–private divide as crucial to respecting rights and determining what actors maintained constitutional duties at all. That is, only public or state actors were deemed responsible for upholding constitutional rights. In contrast, other interpreters emphasized broader ends they found in the constitution, defining constitutional requirements and duty-bearers based on what the constitution ultimately aimed to accomplish. While the public–private divide persists, these latter constitutional arguments admit more space in which to find duties for private actors. Republican-inflected discourses tend to emerge from such constitutional understandings.

While constitutional actors in the United States and India have taken up similar questions regarding horizontal application, the particular challenges naturally differ between countries. One of the major questions that confronted constitutional actors in the United States was whether the Constitution's commitment to equality provided congressional authority to enforce that equality in privately owned places of public accommodation. The Centrist Republicans distinguished between civil and social rights in a way that cabined equality's reach, while Radical Republicans insisted on a more capacious understanding of congressional power to secure this end. Similar questions were resurrected decades later during the Civil Rights Movement when different actors, including the demonstrators, made similar constitutional arguments. In contrast to the US Constitution's Fourteenth Amendment, the Indian Constitution included stronger textual basis on which to argue that equality and, more specifically, antidiscrimination would indeed require cooperation from private actors. The crucial questions were, therefore, concerned with the status of horizontality as a matter of fact and application, rather than with the foundational principles. For example, the Indian Supreme Court confronted questions about what

Rights in Private Litigation?" in *The Constitution in Private Relations*, ed. András Sajó and Renáta Uitz (Utrecht: Eleven, 2005), 241–286.

the rights guarantees of Part III of the Constitution meant for duties of private entities and, controversially, whether the constitutional ends articulated in the Directive Principles of Part IV might translate into any enforceable duties of private actors.

The comparison between the United States and India is not to suggest a false equivalence either in their histories or in their constitutional projects. Indeed, both inequality and equality have taken different forms in each country's experience, and their constitutional states of affairs are the result of many historical accidents. From the Reconstruction Era through the years of Jim Crow, blatant racism pervaded much of America, including many of its governing institutions. Moreover, the laissez-faire understandings of politics that prevailed at the time the Fourteenth Amendment was adopted sustained early formulations of the state action doctrine, favoring a vertical model of rights. On the other hand, not even eighty years after American Reconstruction, India's constitutional moment emerged into a different time and world. While both the caste system and religious conflict continually plagued the country, the fact that the Indian Constituent Assembly coincided with the adoption of the Universal Declaration of Human Rights attests to the fact that this was a new era for understandings of equality and rights in general. Given such historical contingencies, it is unsurprising that the pursuit of equality in these countries would raise somewhat different issues and take different forms.

Viewing the arguments of constitutional actors through a republican lens reveals theoretic potential in the discourses. More often than not, these actors did not intend to draw from republican theory, yet these chapters show how their arguments do track a republican logic. Moreover, these chapters identify a category – a republican category, as it were – of discursive-political resources constitutional actors can employ, and have employed, when contemplating whether to introduce a practice of horizontality. On this basis, it is instructive to draw from such different constitutional orders – one, a product of the eighteenth century and committed primarily to classical political rights; the other, one of the most ambitious constitutions of the Global South and assuming a wider array of rights obligations. The theoretical nature of this project calls for examining the crucial questions across time and place in this way. As the following two chapters illustrate, many of the answers offered show a common republican parlance across time and place, characterized by arguments pointing toward a common good and new duties of citizens.

3

The United States

Equality Along the Public–Private Divide

Scholars frequently treat the United States' constitutional experience as a kind of ideal type when it comes to private actors' duties. In particular, the US Supreme Court has repeatedly affirmed, even against competing interpretations and efforts of Congress, that the Fourteenth Amendment's guarantee of equal protection creates constitutional duties only for state actors. Of course, the Thirteenth Amendment abolished slavery in all sectors of the polity; beyond this provision, however, the Civil War Amendments did not admit of additional guarantees against private action. Nor did they, in the Supreme Court's understanding, permit Congress to pass legislation pursuant to these new constitutional commitments that might generate something like duties of private actors.

This is the official story that was passed down through case law and that, eighty years later, would prompt the Indian constitutional framers to adopt alternate language in their 1950 Constitution, as Chapter 4 will discuss. Key figures involved in drafting India's Constitution understood its ends as largely different from the American counterpart insofar as they aimed to give broad effect to equality and nondiscrimination rights across spheres of life. Through the twentieth and twenty-first centuries, constitutional discourse in the United States would continue to assume some version of the Court's "state action doctrine," the idea that only government action triggers rights protections or, put differently, that only the state maintains constitutional duties. Such arguments insist on maintaining the divide between public and private, and often may be read as embracing an understanding of liberty resembling freedom as noninterference. To this extent, such accounts seem to resist a republican interpretation. It would be problematic, however, to understand such discourses in simply liberal terms. Indeed, initially they were clearly employed to defend or preserve racist and other illiberal strains of American politics and thought. Moreover, while perhaps rights-centric in prioritizing certain rights, such as to property, such arguments did not necessarily emerge from balancing other rights (let alone ends), at least not in any meaningful sense. Rather, they often depended on diminishing the rights-bearing status of black persons, in addition to rejecting an understanding of equality as a shared public project.

If the dominant discourse emerging from US constitutional history is so strongly wedded to the state action doctrine, what role does this chapter serve in a book on republican interpretations of horizontality? First, in certain cases, these arguments from American constitutional history serve as a useful foil to such republican concepts as a common good, shared ends, duties of citizens, and the like. Consistent with the typical scholarly consensus of American constitutionalism on these matters, this chapter finds occasion to examine discourses attached to traditional conceptions of constitutionalism that largely persisted even as the political culture shifted over time in favor of, for example, a further-reaching conception of equality. Indeed, the extent to which American constitutional discourse remains linked to traditional accounts of constitutionalism comes into sharper relief as Chapter 4 will turn to the Indian constitutional experience.

On the other hand, this book's interpretive project and general focus on discourses rather than, say, a certain country's dominant schools of thought offer occasion to consider other threads of constitutional argumentation in the American context, some of which may be understood in a republican light. For example, a strong basis for a republican interpretation and even explicit invocation of republican principles exists in dissenting and concurring opinions, such as Justice Harlan's famous dissent in the *Civil Rights Cases* (1883).[1] Moreover, important landmarks outside of case law, such as the sit-in protests and subsequent Civil Rights Act of 1964, show republican resonances in the ends at which they aim, even as they simultaneously show some attachment to vertical conceptions of rights inherited from official precedent. Even while the state action doctrine largely continued to dominate strict legal accounts, these episodes of constitutional politics in the twentieth century occurred against a backdrop of shifting understandings of equality and of the attendant duties of private actors. In the United States, arguments related to understandings of freedom, traditional accounts of constitutionalism, racism, and a combination of these tend to countervail against horizontality, and particularly the horizontal application of equality, in the discourse. On the other hand, some arguments reveal the potential for

---

[1] *Civil Rights Cases*, 109 U.S. 3 (1883).

republican readings even in the United States, foregrounding a more extensive project of equality for the polity that engenders not merely rights but duties of citizens as well.

Expanding the scope of study beyond the framework of the state action doctrine, this chapter concludes by examining those episodes in which constitutional commitments were in fact applied to private relationships. In *New York Times v. Sullivan* (1964), for example, the Court applied freedom of speech principles to overturn traditional formulations of the common law of defamation.[2] Moreover, in turning to the states, this chapter draws attention to the important reality of American federalism, and the fact that positive law at the subnational level includes no explicit state action requirement. A version of indirect horizontal application has thus expanded and contracted in various states at various times, with arguments about the duties of private actors under state constitutions sometimes taking on a republican character. While much in the prior sections (those focusing on the state action doctrine) turns specifically on rights related to equality, these latter sections (depicting some practices of indirect horizontal application at the subnational level) engage a broader range of issue areas. Moreover, while the particular issues applied horizontally vary between states, they often evince a turn from rights-centric arguments, couched in terms of noninterference, to greater openness to particular ends of the community articulated in the state constitutions.

In some ways, beginning the contextually based chapters of this book with the United States sets a kind of baseline for traditional understandings of constitutionalism from which horizontal application departs. However, it also illustrates the complexity inherent in constitutional discourse, a theme that recurs in various forms throughout the rest of the book. This chapter draws out complexity in the versions of horizontality and corresponding republican themes that do emerge in the American discourse, despite strong doctrinal ties to a state action requirement. In subsequent chapters, in contrast, complexity emerges more often in the arguments that seem to countervail against horizontality once it has been established. Differently situated institutions and actors continually wrestle with the reach and limits of horizontal application. In the constitutional history that follows, and in putting this American experience loosely into conversation with that of India in Chapter 4, constitutional actors may be read as debating the extent to

---

[2] *New York Times v. Sullivan*, 376 U.S. 254 (1964).

which certain constitutional rights are understood as a kind of shared public project, or a common good with the potential to implicate even private actors. Different repertoires[3] of constitutional experience thereby emerge with each of the following chapters as arguments related to constitutional ends, rights, and duties unfold across different circumstances. At the same time, specific themes recur, such that the concepts introduced in Chapter 2 carry over in helpful and revealing ways.

Defining a New Commitment to Equality

In the first session of the Thirty-Ninth Congress, Senator Jacob Howard explained that the purpose of the proposed Fourteenth Amendment to the Constitution was to "[abolish] all class legislation in the States and [do] away with the injustice of subjecting one caste of persons to a code not applicable to another."[4] In this way the Republicans of the post-Civil War era hoped the forthcoming changes to the Constitution would set the stage for effecting the equality of all people throughout the states. Hence the Thirteenth, Fourteenth, and Fifteenth Amendments were ratified between the years 1865 and 1870. The text of each of these was clear enough. The Thirteenth Amendment abolished slavery. The Fourteenth Amendment extended citizenship to "all persons born or naturalized in the United States," and guaranteed the equal protection of the laws and due process of law to people in every state. The Fifteenth Amendment guaranteed that the right to vote would not be contingent on one's race. Congress quickly moved to exercise the power the amendments granted to enforce the new constitutional commitment to equality. To this extent, Congress, as opposed to the courts, had some preliminary say in determining what the new commitment to equality would require in practice. In the ensuing years, Congress enacted several laws in pursuance of these amendments, including the Civil Rights Act of 1875, which guaranteed, among other things, "'full and equal' enjoyment of inns, public conveyances, and places of public amusement, regardless of race." As justification for this legislation, Congress cited its power to enforce both the Thirteenth Amendment's ban on slavery and the Fourteenth Amendment's guarantee of equal protection.

---

[3] Kim Lane Scheppele, "Constitutional Ethnography," *Law and Society Review* 38:3 (2004), 389–406.

[4] Congressional Globe, 39th Cong., 1st Sess. 2766 (1866). See also Cass Sunstein, "The Anticaste Principle," *Michigan Law Review* 92:8 (1994), 2436.

Even at the time the Civil Rights Act of 1875 was passed, Congress was fairly divided on whether legislating on public accommodations exceeded its constitutional powers, to say nothing of what policies might be prudent in a turbulent time.[5] A strong contingent from the southern states sought to limit the progress of Reconstruction as much as possible, and the Republican Party was itself divided on how to understand and interpret the new commitment to equality. While the Radical Republicans were eager to read the new amendments as much more comprehensive in their reach, the Centrist Republicans were content to extend freed persons an equality limited to political and legal spheres more strictly understood.[6] This range of positions with respect to the new amendments were on full display when the Civil Rights and Enforcement Acts were eventually challenged in court. In a series of cases, known collectively as the *Civil Rights Cases* of 1883, the Supreme Court was tasked with offering its own interpretation of the Civil War Amendments and the extent to which Congress did or did not act within its proper limits in its subsequent legislation. In these cases, black plaintiffs sued for being excluded from theaters and transportation facilities, in violation of the Civil Rights Act of 1875. The white owners of those businesses argued that Congress had no authority to regulate their establishments under the Thirteenth and Fourteenth Amendments. In an eight-to-one decision, the Court ruled in favor of the business owners.

In the opinion of the Court, Justice Joseph Bradley addressed the extent of congressional authority in the context of each amendment. The Thirteenth Amendment, he conceded, had no state action requirement. That is, the amendment prohibited slavery with respect to the actions both of the state and of private or nonstate actors. However, the Court did not accept the plaintiffs' argument that their exclusion from such public places as theaters and transit facilities amounted to "badges of slavery."[7] To accept this interpretation, Justice Bradley maintained, would be to "[run] the slavery argument into the ground."[8] On Bradley's telling, black persons had already been granted their "essential freedoms" in their civil and political rights, and calling any act of private

---

[5] Pamela Brandwein, *Rethinking the Judicial Settlement of Reconstruction* (Cambridge: Cambridge University Press, 2011), 342.
[6] Ibid.
[7] *Civil Rights Cases*, para. 21.
[8] Jack Balkin and Sanford Levinson, "The Dangerous Thirteenth Amendment," *Columbia Law Review* 112:7 (2012), 1472.

discrimination a badge or incident of slavery would render the actual protection meaningless. In private correspondences, Bradley further worried that capacious interpretations of the Thirteenth Amendment would impose "another kind of slavery" on white proprietors.[9] Moreover, he took issue with Congress's legislative efforts as he did not see (or refused to see) how private gatherings might be distinguished from privately owned businesses in a principled manner. Bradley wrote: "Surely a white lady cannot be enforced by Congressional enactment to admit colored persons to her ball or assembly or dinner party."[10]

In this way, Bradley redrew the lines that Congress had initially drawn as to what equality would mean and require under the US Constitution. Freedom extended only so far as to grant civil and political rights. So long as black persons had such freedoms, the Thirteenth Amendment could not (and, Bradley's argument implies, should not) do more for them. Moreover, although Bradley conceded that the Thirteenth Amendment did not include a requirement for state action, underlying his reasoning on this constitutional provision was a palpable urgency that the Court nonetheless maintain a strict line between public and private, and maintain that line in a particular place. Specifically, the Thirteenth Amendment only required individuals in private spheres not to have slaves. But it did not require anything more of individuals, especially not in private arenas. Anything more, in his words, would make black people the "special favorite of the laws."[11]

Bradley's reasoning with respect to the plaintiff's Fourteenth Amendment arguments reflected a similar urgency to maintain a line between public and private. The difference was that the text of the Fourteenth Amendment does include language that raises the question of state action. The text of the amendment reads:

> *No State* shall make or enforce any law which shall abridge the privileges or immunities of citizens of the United States; *nor shall any State* deprive any person of life, liberty, or property, without due process

---

[9] Ibid., 1472. Levinson and Balkin suggest that, even in 1883, a plausible argument could have been made for reading the Thirteenth Amendment more expansively. Justice Harlan's dissenting opinion exemplifies such a reading. However, the majority of the Court was not keen on adopting such an interpretation given the fact that the Thirteenth Amendment did not have a state action requirement.

[10] Balkin and Levinson, "The Dangerous Thirteenth Amendment," 1472.

[11] *Civil Rights Cases*, para. 25. See also Pamela Brandwein, "A Lost Jurisprudence of the Reconstruction Amendments," *Journal of Supreme Court History* 41 (2016), 330.

of law; nor deny to any person within its jurisdiction the equal protection of the laws.[12]

To the extent that the text of the Fourteenth Amendment has a state action requirement, its application depends on some prior understanding of what constitutes state action (or state neglect, as it were[13]) as opposed to purely private action. Looking to draw such a line between public and private, Justice Bradley considered the requirements and content of the right to equality. In making this determination, he relied on the distinction between civil rights and social rights that he had begun to develop in his 1874 Circuit opinion for *United States v. Cruikshank*.[14] Pamela Brandwein explains that, during the framing of the Fourteenth Amendment, "Centrist and Radical Republicans agreed on a core body of *civil rights*: contract, property, suing, testifying, and equal redress for injuries. For centrists, access to public accommodations, schools, intermarriage were typically social rights."[15] Brandwein explains that while the Radical Republicans would have both civil and social rights protected by the Fourteenth Amendment, Centrist Republicans drew this distinction for the very purpose of omitting social rights from the guarantee of equal protection.[16] Bradley pursued this line of argument in the *Civil Rights Cases*, setting the initial limits for the reach of equality in the polity.

Justice Harlan's lone dissent in the *Civil Rights Cases* undertakes a task different from Bradley's line-drawing project and comes to an alternate interpretation of the new amendments. In his dissent, Harlan argued against Bradley's narrow account, explaining that the Thirteenth Amendment protects against more than slavery per se. Indeed, on his telling, the Thirteenth Amendment calls for a more capacious interpretation that includes the abolition of certain corollary "badges and incidents" of slavery. Thus, contrary to Bradley's reading, the Thirteenth Amendment equipped Congress to contend with the many "burdens and disabilities" that freed persons confronted as a direct result of centuries of

---

[12] US Constitution, Amendment 14, Section 1, emphasis added.
[13] One of Brandwein's primary objects in *Rethinking the Judicial Settlement of Reconstruction* is to reveal how original formulations of state action, even by more centrist actors, were capacious enough to include instances of state neglect (Brandwein, *Rethinking*; see also Brandwein, "Lost Jurisprudence," 334–335).
[14] Brandwein, *Rethinking*, 16.
[15] Brandwein, "Lost Jurisprudence," 341.
[16] Brandwein, *Rethinking*, 60–86.

enslavement.[17] Full abolition of slavery, full freedom in any meaningful sense, required protection of "those fundamental rights which were the essence of civil freedom" and protection from "all discrimination against [freed persons], because of their race."[18] According to Harlan, "the essence of civil freedom" thus extended further than Bradley conceded to include the very venues that the Civil Rights Act proposed to regulate, namely, "inns, public conveyances, and places of public amusement."

Harlan understood the ability to use inns and public conveyances as part and parcel of a rudimentary conception of freedom and, as such, comprising the freedom the Thirteenth Amendment intended to guarantee. Indeed, services such as these institutions offer are "so far fundamental as to be deemed the essence of civil freedom," no less than those rights the majority of the Court did concede.[19] That the agents of these institutions are technically nonstate actors does not detract from the fact that they maintain public significance and power over the enjoyment of the rights in question. Harlan explains, "[N]o matter who is the agent, or what is the agency, the function performed is *that of the State.*"[20] In this account, these agents were executing public functions in offering these services and therefore may be subject to Congress's efforts to give effect to the guarantees of the Thirteenth Amendment. In the Court's decision to rule otherwise, he explained, freed persons are "robbed of some of the most essential means of existence, and all this solely because they belonged to a particular race which the nation has liberated."[21]

Apart from this argument that the regulations of the Civil Rights Act follow from the Thirteenth Amendment's guarantee of freedom, Harlan also explains that access of all-comers to inns and public conveyances is a principle rooted in common law. In this light, the Court's rejection of the Civil Rights Act becomes even more significant as not simply a rejection of one possible interpretation of a constitutional amendment, but a rejection of longstanding common law intended to regulate such private interchange. On this point, Harlan quotes Justice Joseph Story:

> An innkeeper is bound to take in all travelers and wayfaring persons, and to entertain them, if he can accommodate them, for a reasonable compensation, and he must guard their goods with proper diligence .... If an

---

[17] *Civil Rights Cases*, para. 34.
[18] Ibid., para. 35.
[19] Ibid., paras. 35, 39.
[20] Ibid., para. 38, original emphasis.
[21] Ibid., para. 40.

innkeeper improperly refuses to receive or provide for a guest, he is liable to be indicted therefor .... They (carriers of passengers) are no more at liberty to refuse a passenger, if they have sufficient room and accommodations, than an innkeeper is to refuse suitable room and accommodations to a guest.[22]

On this basis, Harlan highlights the public nature of such institutions as inns and public conveyances. With this "*quasi*-public employment," he explains, comes "certain duties and responsibilities to the public," to serve all guests without distinction as to race or color.[23]

Harlan's opinion goes on to consider the Civil Rights Act's attempt to regulate "places of public amusement." While such places as theaters do not necessarily qualify as "the most essential means of existence," they may still be understood as public in the sense that proprietors devote their property "to a use in which the public has an interest." To this extent, Harlan explains, these institutions operate only under the license of law, and so, the authority to establish and maintain them is public in nature. Harlan concludes on this basis that such institutions must "submit to be controlled by the public *for the common good.*"[24]

This line of thinking, that privately owned institutions operating under the law must align with *the common good*, makes explicit a republican significance inhering throughout Harlan's opinion. In the Thirteenth Amendment and Civil War Amendments more generally, Congress rearticulated the polity's *res publica* to include a conception of freedom now comprising racial equality. This project involved not only the abolition of slavery but also the abolition of those badges and incidents that contradicted this new articulation of the common good. Thus, Congress affirmed in the Civil Rights Act that "since the nation has established universal freedom in this country for all time, there shall be no discrimination, based merely upon race or color, in respect of the accommodations and advantages of public conveyances, inns, and places of public amusement." In other words, Congress established universal freedom as an end for the broader political community, including sectors of the private sphere, and sought to realize this object in both law and fact.

As Harlan understood the Thirteenth Amendment to be as much about discrimination on a broad scale as about the institution of chattel slavery in particular, so too did he understand the Fourteenth

---

[22] Ibid.
[23] Ibid., para. 41.
[24] Ibid., para. 42, emphasis added.

Amendment as transcending a strict understanding of legal or formal equality to include all the "privileges or immunities fundamental in republican citizenship."[25] His more expansive interpretation of equality and citizenship comes through when he explains that the Fourteenth Amendment and, specifically, the citizenship clause of Section 1 guarantee "[e]xemption from race discrimination in respect of the civil rights which are fundamental in *citizenship* in a republican government."[26] He goes on to read Congress's Section 5 enforcement power in light of this comprehensive understanding of citizenship. Given his broad reading, the new amendments seem to *require* Congress to take positive action to give these new constitutional commitments full effect, as it so attempted in the Civil Rights Act. Harlan explains the rationale undergirding the Fourteenth Amendment accordingly: "To meet this new peril to the black race, that the purposes of the nation might not be doubted or defeated, and by way of further enlargement of the power of Congress, the Fourteenth Amendment was proposed for adoption."[27]

In this way, Harlan relies on the citizenship clause to justify Congress's authority to legislate pursuant to the Fourteenth Amendment. He argues that the Amendment's language is "distinctly affirmative in character,"[28] not simply prohibiting the states from violating the new commitment to equality, but empowering Congress to give effect to the Civil War Amendments. Ought not Congress to have the constitutional authority, he questions, to "do for human liberty and the fundamental rights of American citizenship what it did ... for the protection of slavery and the rights of the masters of fugitive slaves"?[29] Harlan would thus have Congress pursue a notion of citizenship encompassing much more than a simple checklist of traditional legal criteria.[30] Rather, the Civil War Amendments aimed at more than legal equality in citizenship, on Harlan's telling, to bring equality even into certain private spheres, encompassing even citizens and private actors into this constitutional project. He states:

---

[25] Ibid., para. 47. See also Christopher R. Green, "The Original Sense of the (Equal) Protection Clause: Subsequent Interpretation and Application," *George Mason University Civil Rights Law Journal* 19 (2009), 260–264.
[26] *Civil Rights Cases*, para. 56.
[27] Ibid., paras. 43–44.
[28] Ibid., para. 46.
[29] Ibid., para. 53.
[30] I am grateful to Gary Jacobsohn for this insight.

> It was perfectly well known that the great danger to the equal enjoyment by citizens of their rights as citizens was to be apprehended not altogether from unfriendly State legislation, but from the hostile action of corporation and individuals in the States. And it is to be presumed that it was intended by that section to clothe Congress with power and authority to meet that danger.[31]

In this way, Harlan's account of the amended constitution might be described as embracing a project or, one might say, ends, much more than did Bradley's. Indeed, his opinion reveals how the Civil War Amendments might have marked, in the words of Jacobsohn and Roznai, the beginning of a kind of step-by-step revolution toward more complete racial equality.[32]

From the debate between Radical and Centrist Republicans to the exchange between Justices Bradley and Harlan, a range of interpretations of equality and the Fourteenth Amendment entered the constitutional discourse. Specifically, what the Fourteenth Amendment's guarantee of equal protection meant for public accommodations, and in particular whether access to public accommodations was properly considered a civil right, seemed an open question. According to Charles Calhoun, "For most Republicans ... the good society entailed [civil and] political equality but not social equality."[33] In spite of its more marginal status in early debates, however, the Radical Republican argument illustrated the range of possibilities for the Fourteenth Amendment, including a more republican interpretation of equality that included a social dimension and implicated a wider range of actors. Indeed, other iterations of this general position would recur in the constitutional politics of the twentieth century as the state action doctrine continued to be debated.

Ultimately, the Centrist Republican conception of what equality required triumphed in the *Civil Rights Cases*, along with a particular understanding of a strict line between public and private spheres, with public accommodations located decidedly on the private side. In so prioritizing the rights of proprietors, these interpretations likewise pointed toward a priority of freedom as noninterference. At the same time, while this interpretation in some ways tracks traditional liberal

---

[31] *Civil Rights Cases*, para. 5.
[32] Gary Jacobsohn and Yaniv Roznai, *Constitutional Revolution* (New Haven: Yale University Press, 2020), 166.
[33] Charles Calhoun, *Conceiving a New Republic* (Lawrence: Kansas University Press, 2006), 13.

understandings of constitutionalism and the public–private divide, the continually ascriptive character[34] of the era's politics and political discourse defies calling these arguments simply liberal.[35] As the idea that only state action triggered constitutional rights endured in American jurisprudence, some later arguments were attached to liberal commitments of a certain stripe and not (always) adulterated with the same racist overtones. This is arguably true, for example, of such arguments as Herbert Wechsler's famous call for neutral principles, discussed below.

Alternate discourses would also reappear in the ensuing decades, some of which may be read as making equal protection into a larger constitutional project, even a common good, and effectuating duties for at least some citizens in turn. These arguments often approximated or even embraced versions of horizontality, echoing Harlan's dissent and themes this book conceives in terms of republicanism. Specifically, these discourses begin to consider the possibility that private actors may have duties qua private actors to the extent that their actions bear on certain public projects. In other cases, these arguments seem intent on more closely tracking the Court's initial settlement in the *Civil Rights Cases*, perhaps reaching conclusions that are similar to Harlan's, but justifying new duties of citizens more on the basis that certain private actors resembled public institutions and less on the way they bear on public or constitutional ends, such as equality, even as private actors. While both styles of argument might result in duties of private actors, the former depends more on the public–private divide that grounds the state action doctrine. Thus, while both formulations arguably are heirs to Harlan's judgment, instances of the latter may be read in a more republican light.

---

[34] Rogers Smith, *Civic Ideals* (New Haven: Yale University Press, 1999).

[35] In *Rethinking the Judicial Settlement of Reconstruction*, Pamela Brandwein shows that the *Civil Rights Cases* did not necessarily entail "the rejection of black property, contract, safety, and voting rights." However, these actions would all be justified in the name of the *Civil Rights Cases* in the years of Jim Crow (Brandwein, *Rethinking*, 3; Brandwein, "Lost Jurisprudence," 345). See also Brandwein's recounting of Stephen Breyer's dissent in *United States v. Morrison*, 529 U.S. 598 (2000): "Justice Breyer suggested that the canonical 1883 decision, the *Civil Rights Cases*, never considered the kind of claim advanced by the federal government in the *Morrison* case, namely, that Congress was authorized under the Fourteenth Amendment to remedy the failure of state actors to punish gender-motivated violence" (*Rethinking*, xi). While only so much can actually be attributed to the *Civil Rights Cases* itself on Brandwein's and, indeed, Breyer's accounts, much of the subsequent development of the state action doctrine has still been argued in the name of this early decision.

Harlan's dissent offered plausible alternative interpretations of the Civil War Amendments that translated the commitment to equality into a more far-reaching project potentially applying to members of civil society. As the sections that follow suggest, however, constitutional actors and legal scholars continually questioned the status of such arguments vis-à-vis American doctrinal history and even liberal constitutionalism in general. The Court's judgments remained largely fixed on keeping intact a version of the state action doctrine, rather than on explicitly implicating private actors in a constitutional project of racial equality. Therefore, with a few notable exceptions, the arguments that tended to prevail in subsequent years remained premised on the public–private divide, even as many constitutional actors and members of the public grew more sympathetic to a broader conception of equality.

Revisiting Equality's Requirements in the Twentieth Century

After decades of an equality defined by "civil not social" and "separate but equal," the Court and American populace in certain ways became receptive to a more capacious understanding of the content and requirements of equality. That the Court might in fact pursue a line of constitutional argument that allowed equality rights to reach private spaces seemed plausible when the Court briefly embraced a broader understanding of state action. In the 1948 case *Shelley v. Kraemer*, homeowners in St. Louis adopted a restrictive racial covenant that prevented African Americans and other minorities from purchasing properties in their neighborhood. The covenant stated that no property shall be "occupied by any person not of the Caucasian race, it being intended hereby to restrict the use of said property ... against the occupancy as owners or tenants of any portion of said property for resident or other purpose by people of the Negro or Mongolian Race."[36] When one of the homeowners party to this covenant sold his house to an African American family by the name of Shelley, others in the neighborhood asked the courts to uphold the restrictive racial covenant as a private contract to which they had all voluntarily agreed. The Supreme Court of Missouri decided to enforce the covenant on the basis that it was a purely private contract and did not bear on the state's obligation to uphold the Fourteenth Amendment's commitment to equal protection. This was a

---

[36] *Shelley v. Kraemer*, 334 U.S. 1 (1948), para. 5.

matter of private action, rather than state action. However, on appeal, the US Supreme Court found that the very act of enforcing the covenant did constitute state action. In the Opinion of the Court, Justice Vinson explained that "the full panoply of state power"[37] was ultimately responsible for preventing the Shelley family from occupying the home they had purchased. To this extent, one could not honestly say that the state had "merely abstained from action, leaving private individuals free to impose such discriminations as they see fit."[38] While the Court could not prevent the drafting of such covenants, neither could it enforce them without directly participating in discriminatory actions, thereby violating the Fourteenth Amendment.

In this way, the Court seemed to locate one path forward from the strictures of Bradley's initial reasoning and subsequent developments that continually left Congress bereft of any power to implement a broader equality. Indeed, in the years leading up to the sit-in protests, some spectators hoped that *Shelley*'s move to recognize the Court's enforcement of private contracts as constituting state action might next lead to the Court's reinterpretation of the Fourteenth Amendment to require equal access to public accommodations.[39] However, others were less optimistic about the impact of this case, whether for reasons of strategy or reasons of principle. Today, legal scholars understand *Shelley* as "a singular case" and as the Court's attempt to "[put] aside doctrinal complexities in order to attack an immoral and socially destructive practice."[40] Indeed, this decision does constitute a kind of high-water mark in the Court's willingness to stretch the bounds of the state action doctrine so as to hold private actors accountable for constitutional principles. No major case after *Shelley* follows similar reasoning. While the Court would in some ways find workarounds to the state action doctrine, it quickly reverted back to a more limited understanding of state action, particularly in those cases that did not raise the issue of racial equality.

That retrospective analyses find *Shelley* to be anomalous in US constitutionalism is not altogether surprising when viewed in the light of early accounts of the case. Some legal scholars, including many who were

---

[37] Ibid., para. 19.
[38] Ibid.
[39] Christopher Schmidt, "The Sit-Ins and the State Action Doctrine," *William and Mary Bill of Rights Journal* 18 (2010), 785.
[40] Ibid., 784.

sympathetic to a broader equality, faulted the Court for its reasoning and even the outcome it reached in *Shelley*. Herbert Wechsler, for example, famously criticized the Court for departing from "neutral principles" of the law, explaining:

> That the action of the state court is action of the state ... is, of course, entirely obvious ... What is not obvious, and is the crucial step, is that the state may properly be charged with the discrimination when it does no more than give effect to an agreement that the individual involved is, by hypothesis, entirely free to make.[41]

In other words, according to Wechsler, while state action was present in the general sequence of events surrounding the *Shelley* case, one could not honestly say that state action was responsible for the particular discrimination at issue, namely the restrictive covenant. The state may have had a hand in the covenant's enforcement, but it was not the source of the discriminatory act. Any decision to the contrary, Wechsler argued, was merely a result of the Court's wanting to reach a more favorable outcome rather than adhere to neutral principles of the law. The fact that such dissents came from parties that were likely to welcome the outcome in *Shelley* as a practical matter speaks volumes of the dominance of the state action doctrine at the time. While the Court in *Shelley* had technically granted the premise that only state action was accountable to constitutional obligations, it departed from the thrust of the *Civil Rights Cases* in that constitutional standards ultimately governed the behavior of private actors.

That many scholars and jurists objected to the Court's decision at the time is not to say that the issue of state action was settled in constitutional argumentation, however. Indeed, *Shelley* and other cases such as *Marsh v. Alabama* (1946)[42] led some to question the state action doctrine as traditionally understood.[43] Louis Henkin, for example, suggested in a 1962 article that the Court should have decided *Shelley v. Kraemer* by weighing the Shelley family's right to equality against the other homeowners' liberty to enter a contract.[44] He explains, "Under today's

---

[41] Herbert Wechsler, "Toward Neutral Principles of Constitutional Law," *Harvard Law Review* 73:1 (1959), 29.
[42] In this case, the Supreme Court decided that a privately owned company town was required to respect the right to freedom of speech under the First Amendment insofar as the town had certain public features and functions.
[43] Schmidt, "The Sit-Ins," 784.
[44] Louis Henkin, "*Shelley v. Kraemer*: Notes for a Revised Opinion," *University of Pennsylvania Law Review* 110:4 (1962), 473–505.

concepts of due process, we have suggested, the state may not forbid a person to be whimsical or capricious in his social relations or as to whom he will admit to his home."[45] In other words, a certain arbitrariness in private action must be permitted if liberty in a meaningful sense is to endure. But this arbitrariness or whimsy that characterizes social relations (and that amounts to a conception of freedom as noninterference in these spaces) does not extend to all spheres, Henkin argues. His treatment of rights begins to resemble horizontal effect, explaining how the Court should have engaged in a process of balancing to determine which right ought to triumph in this particular instance. More often than not, he thinks, equal protection will triumph, given the commitments of the Constitution. But again, in his telling the Constitution does permit and even protects a certain ability of individuals to act arbitrarily with respect to the company they choose to keep. And so, the Court cannot but account for such freedoms of association as well. To balance these freedoms, Henkin explains, Shelley should have asked that the "state not prefer the old contract over his new one, that it not lend support to organized zoning for an improper purpose, to a discrimination which has no basis but race and serves no purpose but prejudice."[46] Hence, while different rights may have been at stake here, the facts of the case and the commitments of the Constitution favored the Shelleys.

Henkin's heterodox take on state action never gained traction.[47] Indeed, something closer to Wechsler's understanding seemed to stick in American legal discourse and in the Court's own arguments. Just a couple of years after *Shelley*, the Supreme Court actually denied certiorari of a case in which the New York Court of Appeals had "found no state action in a racial discrimination claim against a private housing developer."[48] The Supreme Court opted to deny cert in spite of the fact that "the developer had received extensive state support in the form of land condemnation, street closings, and a twenty-five year tax exemption for a New York case just a couple of years later."[49] In the end, the argument in

---

[45] Ibid., 498.

[46] Ibid., 496–497.

[47] At least Henkin's approach did not gain traction in the United States. Other countries do practice something very close to what Henkin proposes in their doctrines of horizontal effect. See, for example, Laurie Ackermann's take on South African constitutionalism (*Human Dignity: Lodestar for Equality in South Africa* [Cape Town: Juta, 2012], 271–273).

[48] *Dorsey v. Stuyvesant Town Corp*, 299 N.Y. 512 (1949).

[49] Schmidt, "The Sit-Ins," 783.

Shelley was the exception that proved the rule, a fact that became even clearer as the Supreme Court began to confront the cases resulting from the sit-in protests. Even as the Court largely ruled in favor of protestors, finding ways to help them evade trespass laws during the sit-ins of the early 1960s, it abided by the discursive status quo of the state action doctrine.[50]

The Civil Rights Act Redux

Around the time that Congress was debating the Civil Rights Act of 1964, the Supreme Court was deciding *Bell v. Maryland*.[51] In this case, twelve African American students were refused service in a Baltimore restaurant and convicted of criminal trespassing. As Christopher Schmidt explains it, "[T]he question came down to which party was the primary lawbreaker, the discriminating proprietor or the sit-in demonstrator."[52] Given its favorable rulings in the sit-in cases of the previous terms, the Court might have taken this opportunity finally to overturn or at least revisit the conclusion of the *Civil Rights Cases*. And indeed, Justices Douglas and Goldberg were in favor of doing just this throughout the deliberations. Even in the earlier case of *Garner v. Louisiana* (1961), Douglas wrote in his dissent: "Restaurants, whether in a drugstore, department store, or bus terminal, are a part of the public life of most of our communities. Though they are private enterprises, they are public facilities in which the State may not enforce a policy of racial segregation." Three years later, and with the Civil Rights Act of 1964 on the cusp of passing in the legislature, court observers speculated whether the time was ripe to reconsider the constitutional question – were private business owners obligated by the equal protection clause?

Even while a majority of the Court was sympathetic to the protesters, other considerations were in play that, scholars argue, led the Court to vacate and remand the decision back to the Maryland Court of Appeals. Schmidt makes much of the fact that Justice Black was disquieted by the methods of the protestors, for example. Eager to maintain law and order and not to stamp civil disobedience with the Court's

---

[50] McKenzie Webster, "The Warren Court's Struggle with the Sit-In Cases and the Constitutionality of Segregation in Places of Public Accommodations," *Journal of Law and Politics* 17 (2001), 373–408.
[51] *Bell v. Maryland*, 378 U.S. 226 (1964).
[52] Schmidt, "The Sit-Ins," 784.

endorsement,[53] Justice Black, along with Justices Harlan (II) and White, decided in favor of the restaurant owner. The remaining six justices wavered between considering the constitutional question and taking the intermediate step of vacating and remanding, since Maryland had recently passed laws against discrimination in public accommodations. Led by Justice Brennan, the justices seeking the more moderate line put much weight on the fact that the Civil Rights Act was about to pass Congress. If they could prevent any disruption of this progress by avoiding a (doctrinally) controversial decision, then so much the better.

Members of the public sympathetic to the Civil Rights Movement were largely unconcerned and even unaware of such jurisprudential hurdles, however. In fact, a major impetus behind the sit-in protests was the widespread conviction that the principle of equality advanced in *Brown v. Board of Education* ought to apply to public accommodations as well. Moral and constitutional consistency, they argued, required nothing less. Martin Luther King, Jr. described the demand for equality in access to public accommodations as "the logical extension of the school segregation struggle."[54] This popular understanding, that the constitutional commitment to equality directly bore on private spaces, received the imprimatur of other public figures as well, including Dwight Eisenhower[55] and John F. Kennedy.[56] Almost as if to draw from Justice Harlan I's conception of citizenship in the *Civil Rights Cases*, President Kennedy stated that the "right to be served in facilities which are open to the public" was an "elementary" right and one of "the privileges of being American."[57] In his 1963 message to the American people on civil rights, he said:

---

[53] Ibid., 798–801.

[54] Ibid., 788.

[55] Martin Luther King, Jr., "A Creative Protest" (February 16, 1960), in *The Papers of Martin Luther King, Jr., Volume V*, ed. Clayborne Carson, Tenisha Hart Armstrong, Adrienne Clay, and Susan Carson (Berkeley: University of California Press, 2006), 368; Dwight D. Eisenhower, "The President's News Conference" (March 16, 1960), in *Public Papers of the Presidents of the United States: Dwight D. Eisenhower, 1960–1961* (Washington, DC: US Government Printing Office, 1961), 293–302. See also Schmidt, "The Sit-Ins," 788.

[56] John F. Kennedy, "Radio and Television Report to the American People on Civil Rights" (June 11, 1963), in *Public Papers of the Presidents of the United States: John F. Kennedy, 1963* (Washington, DC: US Government Printing Office, 1964), 468–470. See also Schmidt, "The Sit-Ins," 790.

[57] Kennedy, "Radio and Television Report," 468–470; see also Schmidt, "The Sit-Ins," 790.

> If an American, because his skin is dark, cannot eat lunch in a restaurant open to the public, if he cannot send his children to the best public school available, if he cannot vote for the public officials who represent him, if, in short, he cannot enjoy the full and free life which all of us want, then who among us would be content to have the color of his skin changed and stand in his place?[58]

In this light, at least some constitutional actors and members of the general public viewed equality at lunch counters, restaurants, and the like as no less constitutive of the equality the polity had committed to in the Fourteenth Amendment and clarified in *Brown*. Such arguments seem unconcerned with maintaining a line between public and private, inasmuch as they understood equality as a project that implicated a broad range of actors across the American polity.

Even those who were more aware of the doctrinal complexities of state action and equal protection did not necessarily view these precedents as insurmountable. In a 1960 article, for example, the *Washington Post* described the state action doctrine as "an evolving thing."[59] It stated:

> An assertion that would have been laughed out of court 20 years ago may be an established right today after a long step-by-step process of fashioning a new rule. The courts may not rule today that Negroes have a right to eat beside white persons in private stores. They might so rule three or five or 10 years from now after taking it a piece at a time.[60]

The observation that "a long step-by-step process" might be underway suggests that alternate interpretations of the state action doctrine and equality were, in fact, in play in discourses during those decades, despite the various reiterations of Bradley's early take on the Fourteenth Amendment. The Court might have decided, for example, that African Americans had "a right to eat beside white persons," thereby reinterpreting the state action doctrine to conform to the emerging public understanding and, as it happens, to be closer to Justice Harlan's conception of citizenship in the *Civil Rights Cases*. Even the Chief Justice himself thought it possible that the jurisprudence might unfold in this way. In speaking of the Court's practice of avoiding the merits and instead deciding the sit-in cases on more procedural issues, Earl Warren explained that he had hoped that the Court "could take these cases *step*

---

[58] Kennedy, "Radio and Television Report," 468–469; see also Schmidt, "The Sit-Ins," 790.
[59] Richard L. Lyons, "Lunch 'Sitdown' a Legal Puzzler," *Washington Post*, March 27, 1960, E5; see also Schmidt, "The Sit-Ins," 785.
[60] Ibid.

by step, not reaching the final question until much experience had been had."[61] As Warren thus admitted the possibility and even some desire to develop the state action doctrine, in retrospect it was telling that these reflections came within a more general explanation of why the Court had not yet taken such steps.

Various oral and written statements suggest that many of the justices initially considered decoupling Section 1 of the Fourteenth Amendment, establishing the legal principle of equal protection, from Section 5, establishing Congress's enforcement power.[62] This would allow the Court to "*follow* Congress in redefining the meaning of the Equal Protection Clause – that is, the congressional interpretation of equal protection would then be adopted by the Court as a self-enforcing constitutional right."[63] Even Justice Harlan, who ultimately dissented from Brennan's majority opinion in *Bell v. Maryland,* indicated some willingness prior to the decision to consider this rationale, since it would have allowed the Court to tread lightly with respect to the jurisprudential precedent.[64] Members of Congress floated this possibility, too, during deliberations for the Civil Rights Act of 1964. Nevertheless, this decoupling strategy would not control the decision in *Bell v. Maryland,* nor would it serve as the primary authorization for Congress's Act, as discussed below.

Despite the potential doctrinal workaround of decoupling Sections 1 and 5, to say nothing of the favorable state of public opinion, the majority opinion in *Bell* ultimately avoided the constitutional question altogether. Scholars suggest a variety of factors contributing to the Court's anemic judgment, from Justice Black's fears of endorsing civil disobedience, to the strategic calculation of how their decision might

---

[61] Del Dickson, ed., *The Supreme Court in Conference (1940–1985): The Private Discussions behind Nearly 300 Supreme Court Decisions* (Oxford: Oxford University Press, 2001), 718, emphasis added; see also Schmidt, "The Sit-Ins," 791.

[62] Leon Friedman, ed., *Argument: The Complete Oral Argument before the Supreme Court in Brown v. Board of Education of Topeka, 1952–1955* (New York: Chelsea House, 1969), 94–103; Robert H. Jackson, Memorandum 11 (March 15, 1954) (on file with Library of Congress, Manuscript Division, Papers of Robert H. Jackson, Box 184); see also Schmidt, "The Sit-Ins," 805.

[63] Schmidt, "The Sit-Ins," 805.

[64] Dickson, *The Supreme Court in Conference,* 720, n211; Transcript of Oral Argument, *Heart of Atlanta,* 379 U.S. 241 (no. 515), reprinted in Philip B. Kurland and Gehard Casper, eds., *Landmark Briefs and Arguments of the Supreme Court of the United States: Constitutional Law, Volume 60* (Arlington: University Publications of America, 1975), 573; see also Schmidt, "The Sit-Ins," 806–807, 818–819.

affect the contemporaneous efforts of Congress.[65] Moreover, some cost is generally attached to the process of revisiting and revising precedent – perhaps particularly as the precedent was itself understood as protecting rights. In dissent, Justice Black seemed to echo Justice Bradley's argument in the *Civil Rights Cases*: "[The Fourteenth Amendment] does not destroy what has until very recently been universally recognized in this country as the unchallenged right of a man who owns a business to run the business in his own way so long as some valid regulatory statute does not tell him to do otherwise."[66] The underlying argument here was that the Fourteenth Amendment maintained a particular distinction between public and private, and the regulation of public accommodations fell decidedly on the side of private, nonstate action. So while the states were free to root any antidiscrimination law in their own commitments to equality, the US Supreme Court at least had to abide by the line-drawing project defined decades earlier in the *Civil Rights Cases*, as well as respect the particular place at which Bradley had located this line, which prevented the application of equality in public accommodations.

Even the majority opinion shows concern on the part of Justice Brennan and those justices joining him not to depart too quickly or drastically from what they took to be the requirements of doctrine. Perhaps their concerns were primarily strategic or prudential; however, even this suggests that these distinctions between public and private and state action and nonstate action were rooted in legal discourse to such a degree that caution was warranted. That the general public's understanding of equality's requirements had shifted enormously by this period only throws the point into sharper relief. In the end, even the activist Warren Court was not up to the task of redefining equality as a constitutional matter, to uproot the conceptions of public and private that had developed around equality in the form of the state action doctrine.

Contemporaneous with the Court's deliberations in *Bell v. Maryland*, Congress held debates similar in both subject matter and intensity. In working to pass the Civil Rights Act of 1964, members of Congress

---

[65] Schmidt, "The Sit-Ins," 791–792.
[66] *Bell v. Maryland*, 378 U.S. 226 (1964). It is interesting that Black joined the majority in both *Marsh v. Alabama* and *Shelley v. Kraemer*. These cases blurred the lines between public and private but also granted the premises of state action and so maintained some semblance of this distinction. Nevertheless, this does not by itself explain why Black did not join Brennan's conciliatory opinion. Christopher Schmidt offers a compelling explanation in that Black was deeply concerned about the impact the sit-in protests would have on the rule of law more generally. See Schmidt, "The Sit-Ins," 798–802.

considered whether they might rely on their enforcement powers under Section 5 of the Fourteenth Amendment. This basis was clearly more germane to the questions at issue than, say, the alternative basis of Congress's power to regulate commerce. Moreover, a few of the Court's recent decisions (some concerning the sit-ins and others state action) served to suggest that at least some of the justices might welcome the shift in constitutional understanding this would inevitably entail. On the other hand, relying on the power to regulate commerce likely provided a safer basis on which to ensure this new Civil Rights Act withstood lawsuits. Indeed, even if less clearly connected to issues of discrimination and equality, the Commerce Clause would not pose the same challenge to the regnant precedent and might consequently be more successful at achieving the legislators' intended ends.

Even despite the high stakes of the issue of civil rights, Congress did not seem to accept its position "as a coequal branch on matters of constitutional interpretation" and deferred instead to the Court's 1883 precedent.[67] Schmidt's account points to a painful irony in Congress's deferential attitude. In his telling, the Court was actually looking to Congress to act on the constitutional issue. As described above, the Court had in its deliberations considered decoupling the first and fifth sections of the Fourteenth Amendment, which would have allowed Congress to advance its own understanding of equality rights in law under its enforcement power.[68] Nevertheless, the Court's "evolving position on this question was largely hidden from view," leaving members of Congress ignorant of these developments among the judges.[69] Ultimately Congress cited its power to regulate commerce as the primary constitutional basis on which it passed the Civil Rights Act. While it also cited its enforcement power under the Fourteenth Amendment, this provision was clearly auxiliary.

Not long after the Civil Rights Act became law in 1964, proprietors began to challenge Title II's requirement that people not be denied access to public accommodations on the basis of race. In such cases as

---

[67] Schmidt, "The Sit-Ins," 773.

[68] Speaking of the justices, Schmidt explains, "Among themselves at least – for only hints of this would reach published Court opinions – they recognized that a congressional definition of state action (under Section 5) might go beyond a judicial definition (under Section 1)" ("The Sit-Ins," 804). Douglas resisted this possibility in hopes that the Court would take a stronger line on equality and so truly confront the precedent of the *Civil Rights Cases* (Schmidt, "The Sit-Ins," 808).

[69] Schmidt, "The Sit-Ins," 808–809.

Katzenbach v. McClung[70] and *Heart of Atlanta Motel v. United States*,[71] the Court confronted the question of whether Congress acted within its constitutional powers in its recent legislation. Moreover, the Court considered what part of the Constitution gave Congress this authority. Although Congress had relied primarily on the Commerce Clause, that the law mentioned the Fourteenth Amendment at all kept Section 5 in play as a possibility. Even at this stage, however, when the Court was in such a position that it could defer to Congress, it upheld Title II on the basis of the Commerce Clause alone, "refusing to evaluate the alternative Fourteenth Amendment rationale to which most of the Justices felt Congress had not committed itself."[72] The justices considered the possibility in conference, but in the end only Douglas and Goldberg wanted to address Congress's Section 5 enforcement powers.[73] And so, what broad sectors of the country had come to understand as a requirement of constitutional morality – an end for the polity to pursue – remained cordoned off from the perspective of constitutional law, to be regulated simply as a matter of commerce and not implicating competing constitutional rights. Neither Congress nor the Court disrupted or modified what they took to be the original settlement of this constitutional question from the nineteenth century.

By prioritizing a vertical logic, the arguments predominating in American constitutional discourse may be read as rejecting, at least as a theoretical matter, a particular understanding of racial equality as a shared project and as creating duties beyond a fairly narrowly defined public space. One might cite such developments as the Civil Rights Act as a counterpoint. And indeed, many horizontal initiatives often do occur in the form of statutory law. The Civil Rights Act has itself become quasi-constitutional in nature,[74] and many states have done much to combat

---

[70] *Katzenbach v. McClung*, 379 U.S. 294 (1964). This case concerned a restaurant – within close proximity of state and interstate highways – that refused access to African American customers. Against the arguments of the restaurant proprietors, the Court upheld the 1964 Civil Rights Act that drew upon Congress's power over interstate commerce to outlaw discrimination in public accommodations.

[71] *Heart of Atlanta Motel v. United States*, 379 U.S. 241 (1964). Similar to *Katzenbach v. McClung* and decided on the same day, this case involved a motel that refused access to African American customers. Again, the Court upheld the 1964 Civil Rights Act outlawing discrimination in this context.

[72] Schmidt, "The Sit-Ins," 772.

[73] Ibid., 819–820.

[74] See William N. Eskridge and John Ferejohn, *A Republic of Statutes: The New American Constitution* (New Haven: Yale University Press, 2010).

discrimination in their own antidiscrimination laws even prior to 1964.[75] However, from a theoretic perspective, that the Civil Rights Act continues to be grounded in Congress's commerce power, rather than the principle of equality, seems to demote its status in the constitutional landscape from the start. Even as the law requires private actors not to discriminate on the basis of race, it would not seem to be for the sake of any duty to fellow citizens nor any constitutional goal or project.[76] Whether this lower constitutional status carries consequences with respect to actual outcomes or impact is beyond the scope of the present book.[77] What this book aims to do is reveal and clarify the republican concepts undergirding the theoretical situation of this constitutional discourse.

Law Along the Public–Private Divide

The sit-in protests may have posed the question of whether to rethink concepts of public and private with respect to the particular issue of racial equality. Yet, constitutional discourse, particularly from the Court, illustrates how the precedent in the *Civil Rights Cases* persisted in constitutional thinking concerning the public–private divide. Key actors continued to adhere to the state action doctrine in some form, rejecting the chance to recast the line between public and private spaces, or even to approximate a republican logic that conceived a role in the broader constitutional project for private actors as such, not unlike Justice Harlan's dissent. Although certain circumstances seemed to favor such a decision, the state action framework still rose above these alternative understandings as a matter of constitutional law – probably owing to precedent, institutional interests, and doubtless other political and attitudinal factors, as scholars have variously suggested.

---

[75] Some scholars lament the dearth of antidiscrimination legislation in India as a conspicuous gap in legal efforts to achieve greater equality. See Tarunabh Khaitan, "Reading *Swaraj* into Article 15: A New Deal for All Minorities," *NUJS Law Review* 2:3 (2009), 420–432.

[76] See Helen Hershkoff on the expressive value underlying these questions ("'Just Words': Common Law and the Enforcement of State Constitutional Social and Economic Rights," *Stanford Law Review* 62 [2010], 1527). See also Corey Brettschneider, *When the State Speaks, What Should It Say?* (Princeton: Princeton University Press, 2012).

[77] On the other hand, recent cases show the fragility of statutes for the very reason that they do not enjoy the same entrenched status as constitutional law. One need not look further than *NFIB v. Sebelius* 567 U.S. 519 (2012) to see that the Court has periodically reined in Congress's commerce power, or *Shelby County v. Holder* 570 U.S. 529 (2013) to see that even such a milestone as the Voting Rights Act is not beyond incursion.

While legal scholars have long recognized the state action doctrine as a "conceptual disaster area,"[78] the Court has continued to work within and around this framework. Particularly in the realm of civil rights, the Court has decided that privately owned institutions that are somehow "entangled" with the state or that serve what are traditionally thought of as "public functions" can, in fact, be regulated as state actors. Though these workarounds may bring the Court to the outcomes it desires, they reach such conclusions only by expanding the definition of the state, arguably preserving the core of Justice Bradley's legacy, rather than obligating private actors to constitutional commitments to equality. Perhaps it is not surprising that the Court has employed these doctrines of "entanglement" and "public function" in the area of civil rights more than any other.[79] Indeed, this is a realm in which the country has patently shifted its thinking as evinced in the sit-ins and the public's constitutional understanding of these and later protests, as described earlier. In other words, these workarounds to the state action doctrine have occurred precisely where the polity has changed its position on a clear set of issues in fairly decisive fashion.

While, historically, the state action doctrine was often employed to nefarious ends, scholars and constitutional actors acknowledge the value of preserving some private sphere beyond the reach of public values and in distinguishing between state and nonstate action.[80] Sometimes the Court has preserved this doctrine even when reaching outcomes that are unpalatable or worse. The staying power of this framework is on full display in the infamous *DeShaney v. Winnebago County* case,[81] when the majority of the Court persisted in a strict conviction that constitutional rights obligated only state actors, arguably in spite of alternative interpretations that might have mitigated tragic circumstances.

A small child by the name of Joshua DeShaney suffered serious abuse at the hands of his father. Wisconsin Social Services reported to the

---

[78] Charles L. Black, Jr., "The Supreme Court, 1966 Term – Foreword: 'State Action,' Equal Protection, and California's Proposition 14," *Harvard Law Review* 81 (1967), 95.

[79] See, for example, *Reitman v. Mulkey* 387 U.S. 369 (1967) and *Moose Lodge v. Irvis* 407 U.S. 163 (1972). See also Jud Mathews, *Extending Rights' Reach* (Oxford: Oxford University Press, 2018), 9.

[80] See Louis Seidman and Mark Tushnet, "The State Action Paradox," in *Remnants of Belief: Contemporary Constitutional Issues* (Oxford: Oxford University Press, 1996), 49–71. Indeed, even those arguing in favor of horizontality hardly prescribe abandoning these concepts altogether.

[81] *DeShaney v. Winnebago County*, 489 U.S. 189 (1989).

residence several times on suspicions of abuse but did nothing to remove the child permanently from his father's custody. The abuse continued until the boy suffered irreversible brain damage with which he would live for the rest of his life. Learning what had happened only after it was too late, the boy's mother argued that the state was culpable insofar as it knew about the situation but did nothing to protect her son's positive right to liberty under the Fourteenth Amendment. In a 1989 opinion by Chief Justice Rehnquist, however, the Supreme Court ruled that the Fourteenth Amendment did not establish an affirmative duty of the state to protect against *private* abuse. Because Joshua's injuries were inflicted by a private party, the harm at issue could not properly be described as state action. Moreover, neither did any negligence on the part of the social worker constitute a harm insofar as this was an instance of state *in*action as opposed to state action. Thus, the Constitution did not offer any rights protections to Joshua. His only remedy was found in the fact that the father had been convicted of child abuse.

The state action doctrine thus persists, and persists in rigid form, even in the face of tragedy. Perhaps the idea that "state neglect" be counted as state action might have led to a different outcome in *DeShaney*.[82] While this understanding of state neglect was widely accepted in equality-based claims in the nineteenth century, Brandwein explains how it fell away from the jurisprudence after a few decades.[83] Even without the concept of state neglect, however, the Court might have reached a different outcome, according to Justice Brennan's dissent. He argues that the state *had* acted from the very moment that it established the Department of Social Services, taking upon itself a duty to protect vulnerable citizens even in their private homes.

Gary Jacobsohn offers a framework to evaluate this alternative outcome in *DeShaney* against the decision the Court actually reached. Specifically, he analogizes constitutional interpretation with the classic dramatic genres of comedy and tragedy. In much the same way that comedies conclude with happy endings, typically only after some manipulation and absurd turns of events, so too can we imagine "judges exercising creativity in the pursuit of acceptable outcomes."[84] On the

---

[82] Brandwein, *Rethinking*, 242–243.
[83] Ibid.
[84] Gary Jacobsohn, "Dramatic Jurisprudence," in *Constitutional Stupidities, Constitutional Tragedies*, ed. William Eskridge and Sanford Levinson (New York: New York University Press, 1998), 115.

other hand, in contrast to comedic figures, the tragic hero inevitably is "unable to escape the necessary consequences of his actions," try as he may.[85] Likewise, constitutional interpretation can have a tragic character, as when judges insist on "rigorous judicial adherence to norms of objectivity derived from neutral principles,"[86] even when alternative plausible interpretations might have been available. In *DeShaney*, one might say that Brennan's and Blackmun's opinions tend toward the comedic while Rehnquist's errs on the side of the tragic.[87]

Both approaches have their problems, however. Of the comedic approach, Jacobsohn explains that some "will find in these efforts an unfortunate subversion of the liberal constitutionalism of the Founding Fathers."[88] Even if a person were convinced that a particular outcome was morally superior, it may not follow that the Constitution could support that outcome without unacceptable levels of twisting or manipulation. Meanwhile, practitioners of the tragic approach are vulnerable to the different tendency of subscribing to an "exaggerated sense of law's determinacy."[89] Jacobsohn ultimately comes to the sober conclusion that constitutional interpretation is best understood in *tragicomic* terms, in which judges "strive for an accommodation between necessity and manipulation, between the obligation to find the law and the temptation to make it."[90] While this conclusion resists easy categorization and certainly calls upon judges to exercise their discerning capacities, it seems that neither tragedy nor comedy can by itself encompass a full account of the constitutional project.

Jacobsohn concludes that *DeShaney* seems to "represent a failure of judicial imagination,"[91] suggesting that the Court might have reached a more favorable outcome, perhaps along the lines of Brennan's opinion, without doing damage to constitutional structures. In support of this diagnosis, that the judges did have more latitude to reach a different conclusion than Rehnquist maintained, Jacobsohn points to the "degree of interpretive freedom manifest in the ambiguities surrounding the state

---

[85] Ibid.
[86] Ibid., 116.
[87] One might also say that Herbert Wechsler's account of *Shelley v. Kraemer* was more tragic in the conclusions it reached.
[88] Jacobsohn, "Dramatic Jurisprudence," 115.
[89] Ibid., 116.
[90] Ibid.
[91] Ibid., 117.

action doctrine."⁹² Notwithstanding this possible interpretive freedom, much argumentation in the history of state action jurisprudence seems to be characterized by similarly tragic interpretations when the Court and other actors might have understood the Constitution otherwise – perhaps acknowledging, in more instances, the way certain private spaces hold public significance and, therefore, bear on constitutional projects, permitting Congress to act on this basis.⁹³ This stops short of a republican logic that would understand new constitutional commitments as generating ends for the polity and therefore duties of citizens. In admitting such plausible alternative interpretations, however, the Court might have also permitted the kind of step-by-step transformation of which Earl Warren later spoke, all while preserving more traditional understandings of the public–private divide and constitutionalism. Interestingly, other sectors of American constitutional discourse have shown greater openness to pursuing such lines of argumentation, and even departing from traditional understandings in favor of something like horizontal application.

Beyond the Public–Private Divide: Speech and the States

As this history of discrimination-related moments in constitutional politics has shown, the state action doctrine and accompanying interpretations of individual rights have long been a feature of American constitutional politics. Even actors arguably sympathetic to republican-esque broad ends regarding equality or antidiscrimination measures show attachment to discourses characterized by a kind of rights-centrism and the public–private divide. These cases do not constitute the only format in which constitutional duties of private actors have been considered (and, perhaps, dismissed), however. Indeed, certain exceptional cases follow a logic that could easily be understood as a version of indirect horizontal application,⁹⁴ such as reforming the common law according to constitutional standards. Most notable among these is the

---

⁹² Ibid.
⁹³ The possible exception that proves this rule is *Shelley v. Kramer*. However, some critics, such as Herbert Wechsler, might dispute whether an alternative ruling would have stretched the Constitution too far to its detriment, as Jacobsohn says is possible with the comedic approach.
⁹⁴ *Shelley v. Kraemer* certainly matches this description of approximating indirect horizontality, as well. However, the rationale of the decision in this case does also depend on a conception of state action.

1964 case *New York Times Co. v. Sullivan*.⁹⁵ This famous decision involved the police commissioner for the city of Montgomery, Alabama, suing for defamation after the *New York Times* published a full-page advertisement criticizing the sheriff and Alabama police for their mistreatment of civil rights demonstrators. While the broader criticism itself was not in question, the advertisement did include some inaccuracies about the specific circumstances and actions taken against the protestors, forming the basis for the defamation suit.

In a unanimous decision, the Court argued that the common law rule of defamation governing private actors had to show sufficient parity with the rights commitments of the US Constitution. However, the application of the law of defamation in the lower courts did not give due weight to the commitment to freedom of speech under the First Amendment. On this basis, the Court introduced its "actual malice" standard, arguing that criticisms of public officials, such as the police commissioner, enjoyed broader First Amendment protections than, say, potentially defamatory speech against private individuals. Insofar as criticism of government and public officials was an essential justification for protecting the freedoms of speech and of the press at all, the defamed had to demonstrate that the defendant made the defamatory statement with actual malice, rather than simply demonstrate that the statement was false. In short, constitutional values (in this instance, free speech) required a higher standard than that traditionally set by the common law on matters of defamation.

New York Times v. Sullivan thus constitutes a clear, albeit rare, instance of horizontal application in the United States.⁹⁶ Unsurprisingly, the Court did not acknowledge it in these terms in the same way as have apex courts of other countries. However, simply considering the logic of the decision, this US case may even create stronger horizontal protections for speech than do analogous cases in such countries as Germany⁹⁷ and South Africa.⁹⁸ Specifically, *Sullivan* concludes with more than a simple call for lower courts to consider the influence of constitutional commitments on private law, or for the Supreme Court to do so in future cases. Instead, under the aegis of the

---

[95] *New York Times Co. v. Sullivan*, 376 U.S. 254 (1964).
[96] Stephen Gardbaum, "The 'Horizontal Effect' of Constitutional Rights," *Michigan Law Review* 102 (2003), 387–459.
[97] See the discussions of the *Lüth* case in Chapters 2 and 5.
[98] See the discussion of *Du Plessis v. De Klerk* and *Khumalo v. Holomisa* in Chapter 6.

freedom of speech, the Supreme Court actually strikes down the state common law at issue. The strength of First Amendment commitments in the United States, therefore, translates to comparatively strong duties of individuals, even if indirectly.[99]

In an important article, Stephen Gardbaum argues that *Sullivan* sheds light on a larger potential logic latent in the US Constitution, and particularly in the Supremacy Clause of Article 6, paragraph 2.[100] He argues that this clause establishing the supremacy over the states of all federal law, including the Constitution, effectively calls for a broader practice of indirect horizontal application.[101] While the arguments it employs have appeared only rarely in case law of the US Supreme Court, *New York Times v. Sullivan* nonetheless maps out a potential avenue for additional constitutional duties of private actors in the American context. Put differently, the state action doctrine turns out not to be the only doctrinal pathway for understanding private actors' duties – both their history and their future. Indeed, in a post-*Sullivan* constitutional landscape, rights commitments may be said to have a broader reach, so that the freedom of speech is more than a right one may claim against government, but a source of constraint and obligation in private law and relationships as well. In sum, the requirements of freedom of speech come to impact private actors and thereby narrow, somewhat, the public–private divide.

A complete picture of virtually any question of constitutional politics in the United States warrants some consideration of American

---

[99] In this case and others across contexts concerning the right to free expression, the duty often involves yielding to another's right and perhaps suffering some harm that might result from another exercising that right. In human rights scholarship, this might be considered as a duty to respect, as opposed to protect or fulfill, a right.

[100] Gardbaum, "'Horizontal Effect' of Constitutional Rights."

[101] On the other hand, Mark Tushnet describes how the jurisprudential particularities arising from the United States' federal structure limit the Supreme Court's ability to develop something like a doctrine of indirect horizontality in certain ways. Insofar as the states have "final authority for developing the nonconstitutional law applicable within their jurisdictions," the Supreme Court cannot readily force them to abandon such laws that may run counter to the national constitution. Tushnet describes a hypothetical scenario in which an employer, operating in a state with an employment-at-will rule, fires an employee for being a member of a disfavored political party. The fact that the national constitution protects a right to free speech or association does not impel any change to the employment-at-will doctrine or this application of it (Tushnet, "The Issue of State Action/Horizontal Effect in Comparative Constitutional Law," *International Journal of Constitutional Law* 1 [2003], 79–98, at 87).

federalism.¹⁰² And indeed, when it comes to the relationship between public and private spheres and the question of horizontal application, the experience of several states complicates the picture scholars have typically painted in focusing exclusively on the national constitution. Scholars such as Helen Hershkoff, John Dinan, and Emily Zackin have documented well the way in which state constitutions enrich our understanding of the American rights tradition.¹⁰³ Specifically, they challenge the conventional wisdom that American constitutionalism is preoccupied with negative rights, and with what government may not do. Instead, these scholars illustrate how state constitutions provide for positive rights, and even how state governments are charged with securing certain ends. Dinan goes so far as to suggest that positive rights provisions in state constitutions "can give expression to the fundamental goals and values of a polity."¹⁰⁴

In this same spirit, consideration of the constitutional traditions and case law of the states demonstrates that the state action doctrine does not by itself govern the question of constitutional duties of private actors in the United States. While *New York Times v. Sullivan* may be an exceptional case at the national level of constitutional politics, this manner of applying constitutional commitments to common law norms has happened with greater frequency, and less doctrinal restraint, across the several states.¹⁰⁵ Indeed, this book's republican framework offers a helpful lens to analyze the issues that emerge at this subnational level of constitutionalism. While much of this chapter has recounted arguments about how private actors within the states ought to relate to the national constitution's commitment to equality, the chapter now concludes by considering how the states themselves have understood how private actors relate to the states' constitutional ends. In the terms of this book, one might say that rights in the states have sometimes been interpreted as more than mere rights for which to hold government accountable, but as

---

¹⁰² See Robinson Woodward-Burns, *Hidden Laws: How State Constitutions Stabilize American Politics* (New Haven: Yale University Press, 2021); Emily Zackin, *Looking for Rights in All the Wrong Places* (Princeton: Princeton University Press, 2013); John Dinan, *The American State Constitutional Tradition* (Lawrence: University of Kansas Press, 2006).

¹⁰³ See Helen Hershkoff, "The New Jersey Constitution: Positive Rights, Common Law Entitlements, and State Action," *Albany Law Review* 69 (2006), 553–559; Hershkoff, "Just Words"; Dinan, *State Constitutional Tradition*; Zackin, *Looking for Rights*.

¹⁰⁴ Dinan, *State Constitutional Tradition*, 221.

¹⁰⁵ Hershkoff, "Just Words," 1524–1525.

larger ends, perhaps a kind of *res publica* at a subnational level, sometimes implicating private actors as well. In these instances, the strict division between public and private has proven less entrenched, such that courts apply state constitutional values to common law rules, giving further "expression to the fundamental goals and values of a polity."[106]

In the important case of *Pruneyard Shopping Center v. Robins* (1980),[107] the Supreme Court suggested that the state constitutions may be interpreted to protect rights against private actors. The case involved high school students soliciting signatures at a local shopping center. The center's security guards asked the students to leave, as they had not attained a permit from the owners. The students sued the center for violating both their right to freedom of speech under the US Constitution and their right to petition the government under the California State Constitution. When the US Supreme Court ruled in favor of the students, several state governments and, more specifically, state courts began to evaluate a state action requirement for constitutional rights in their subnational contexts. State constitutions do not explicitly prescribe developing common law in line with constitutional commitments in the same way as, say, the South African Constitution does.[108] However, *Pruneyard* seemed to constitute an invitation to apply state constitutional rights on a broader scale than the state action doctrine permitted for rights in the national constitution.[109] In the wake of *Pruneyard,* several state courts expanded (and, in some cases, later contracted) the application of constitutional norms to such entities as "shopping centers, universities, insurance companies, banks, utilities, private clubs, and possessory lienors."[110] Hershkoff explains how interpretive practices of state courts can resemble "those of jurisdictions abroad, such as India and South Africa, in which courts achieve the horizontal application of constitutional norms in disputes involving nongovernmental actors using the pathways of private law doctrine."[111]

---

[106] Dinan, *State Constitutional Tradition*, 221.
[107] *Pruneyard Shopping Center v. Robins*, 447 U.S. 74 (1980).
[108] Hershkoff, "Just Words," 1525.
[109] John Devlin, "Constructing an Alternative to 'State Action' as a Limit on State Constitutional Rights Guarantees: A Survey, Critique, and Proposal," *Rutgers Law Journal* 21 (1990), 819–902.
[110] Ibid., 823–824.
[111] Helen Hershkoff, "State Common Law and the Dual Enforcement of Constitutional Norms," in *New Frontiers of State Constitutional Law: Dual Enforcement of Norms*, ed. James A. Gardner and Jim Rossi (Oxford: Oxford University Press, 2011), 154.

While *Pruneyard* remains controversial and different states continue to decide these questions in varied ways,[112] the fundamental point is that state constitutions maintain greater interpretive space, less concretized precedent, and perhaps lower stakes in terms of scope and ability to revise – in short, fewer obstacles from pursuing a version of indirect horizontality.[113] Likewise, constitutional politics within the states may be interpreted through this book's republican lens. With greater latitude as to structuring the duties of – or at least relations between – private actors, constitutional discourses within the states might more easily transcend the kind of rights-centrism on display in many accounts of the national constitution, and may be more likely to articulate ends that involve the cooperation of private actors.

In an article examining the relationship between socioeconomic rights and indirect horizontality in the states, Hershkoff argues:

> [S]tate constitutional socio-economic rights fit comfortably within this conception of rights as constitutive of a shared polity. They aim not only to secure the material improvement of a single claimant, but also to protect a particular kind of political culture that values a shared interest in specified public goods such as free public schooling or safe workplaces.[114]

Her description of a conception of "a shared polity" and of a "political culture that values a shared interest" typifies the kind of republican tone this book locates in discourses surrounding horizontal application. It is this language of shared public ends that many public figures and protestors employed in the Civil Rights Movement. While this manner of argumentation did not gain much traction as a doctrinal matter at the national level, scholarship suggests that constitutional actors may more easily speak, and have spoken, in these terms at the state level.[115] Indeed, Hershkoff elsewhere explains how the New Jersey Supreme Court has enforced "social and economic rights as a matter of state constitutional law" and likewise has "refused to enforce common law entitlements when they interfere with activities that are vital to democratic life – speech, association, privacy, and the stability of adequate

---

[112] Devlin, "Constructing an Alternative," 823.
[113] Helen Hershkoff, "The Private Life of Public Rights: State Constitutions and the Common Law," *New York University Law Review Online* 88:1 (2013), 1–23.
[114] Hershkoff, "Just Words," 1553–1554.
[115] Dinan, *State Constitutional Tradition*; Zackin, *Looking for Rights*; Hershkoff, "New Jersey Constitution."

housing."[116] In this way, the possibility of prioritizing what is constitutional in both public and private spaces, a kind of public morality or common good in the terms of this book, emerges clearly in the states.

Of course, the US federal structure has permitted some of the great evils of American history. However, it has also permitted broader rights protections tailored to the particular needs, interests, and commitments of actors and citizens in a given state. Zackin argues this to great effect, opening her book with an example of grassroots efforts advocating for coal miners' rights that resulted in detailed protections in the 1870 Illinois Constitution.[117] Indeed, a range of examples of horizontal application, and more liberal understandings of state action at the subnational level, illustrate how states may pursue different priorities or ends, as they choose to apply some rights expansively and not others. John Devlin describes how New York courts have maintained a state action requirement for speech rights,[118] but have understood due process rights to apply more broadly.[119] Hershkoff also offers several examples, including cases about enforcing equality norms in places of work in Washington,[120] modifying "at will" employment policies in Michigan,[121] and balancing property and speech rights in Oregon[122] – each of which resulted from invoking state constitutional rights commitments, admittedly to varying degrees, in private interactions.

In *McCulloch v. Maryland*, Justice John Marshall argued that the ability of the national government to speak directly to American citizens, as opposed to speaking to them only through the state governments, was an essential characteristic of sovereignty.[123] In a somewhat similar vein, the ability to speak to citizens on matters both public and private seems

---

[116] Hershkoff, "New Jersey Constitution," 558.
[117] Zackin, *Looking for Rights*, 1–2.
[118] Devlin, "Constructing an Alternative," 823fn11, 824fn22.
[119] See *Sharrock v. Dell Buick-Cadillac, Inc.* (45 N.Y. 2d 152, 379 N.E.2d 1169, 408 N.Y.S.2d 39 [1978]) involving a state lien law that permitted private garages to auction property without the opportunity to be heard in advance. The New York Court of Appeals decided that the state lien law was unconstitutional, in contrast with the national precedent in a similar case decided in the same year, *Flagg Bros. v. Brooks* (Devlin, "Constructing an Alternative," 854–857).
[120] *Roberts v. Dudley*, 993 P.2d 901, 911 (Wash. 2000). See Hershkoff, "State Common Law and the Dual Enforcement," 157–158.
[121] *Toussaint v. Blue Cross & Blue Shield of Michigan*, 292 N.W.2d 880, 885 (Mich. 1980). See Hershkoff, "State Common Law and Dual Enforcement," 159–160.
[122] *Lloyd Corp. v. Whiffen*, 773 P.2d 1294 (Or. 1989). See Hershkoff, "State Common Law and Dual Enforcement," 162.
[123] *McCulloch v. Maryland*, 17 U.S. 316 (1819), 404–405.

to be yet another important aspect of sovereignty. Hershkoff explains, "State common law, as an aspect of state sovereignty, helps to publicize issues, transcend boundaries, and test the constitutional waters by offering case-by-case elaborations of constitutional norms in discrete situations."[124] That the states in some ways retain greater ability than the national government to apply constitutional commitments in private spaces is important. It harkens back to early debates between the Federalists and Antifederalists about the nature and locus of American political community, and even anticipates future debates in such quasi-federalist arrangements as the European Union. Indeed, as Chapter 7 will show, the question of horizontality in the European Union is theoretically tied to larger questions of political community and integration, as individual Member States reckon with potentially conflicting commitments coming from the top, that is, from EU institutions. Echoing debates over federalism in the United States, some political actors and observers worry about what horizontal application at a supranational level could mean for the sovereignty of Member States.[125] On the other hand, some are ready to have the European Court of Justice exercise horizontality in a more robust form, as it would serve to confront more directly the question of what kind of a moral community the European Union will be.[126]

In this understanding, the question of horizontality relates to the question of where moral or political community exists and the particular commitments comprising that community. In republican terms, the discourses surrounding these issues in such places as the United States and the European Union may be read as articulating a kind of common good with the potential to shape even private relationships. Indeed, in addition to what material outcomes these questions and decisions might engender, they also have an important expressive element, that is, the "effect of the constitutional norm might be ... [to signal] approval or disapproval of particular forms of private behavior."[127] The question, then, becomes whether these discussions ought to take place among the subunits or in more centralized fora. The answer to this question varies

---

[124] Hershkoff, "State Common Law and Dual Enforcement," 165.
[125] Johan van der Walt, *The Horizontal Effect Revolution and the Question of Sovereignty* (Berlin: De Gruyter, 2014).
[126] Eleni Frantziou, "The Horizontal Effect of the Charter of Fundamental Rights of the EU: Rediscovering the Reasons for Horizontality," *European Law Journal* 21:5 (2015), 675.
[127] Hershkoff, "Just Words," 1527; see also Brettschneider, *When the State Speaks*.

both within the United States and across other federal systems.[128] While the US federal structure proves important to a wide range of constitutional questions, including the possibility of horizontal application, it is less important as a consideration in, say, India, where an understanding of state citizenship does not exist to the same degree that it does in the United States, and a transformative constitutional project arguably permits less deference to state governments than that found in American federalism.[129]

Relative to the US national government, and even the state governments of many other countries, the American states have fewer barriers to debating questions of constitutional ends and citizens' duties. This is not to deny the good reasons that may exist for maintaining a state action doctrine, say, in some desire to preserve a sphere of autonomy in private life.[130] Hershkoff acknowledges how this desire "goes to the heart of the liberal project and to the importance of constitutional values" and that it "raises fundamental questions about private life and its relation to collective goals."[131] Perhaps the tendency of state constitutions to consider material concerns more than federal constitutions warrants greater emphasis on "collective goals," an emphasis that necessarily "constrains our private sense of possibility" more than is generally true at the national level.[132] Such normative considerations are beyond the scope of the present book. However, this book's republican framework offers a richer lexicon and an analytic lens through which to understand more fully the implications of these constitutional questions, even across levels of government.

Conclusion

Various factors – political, legal, historical – have undoubtedly contributed to the constitutional history of state action and horizontal

---

[128] For a similar discussion, see Christina Bambrick, "'Neither Precisely National Nor Precisely Federal': Governmental and Administrative Authority in Tocqueville's Democracy in America," *Publius: The Journal of Federalism* 48:4 (2018), 586–606.

[129] Granville Austin, *Working a Democratic Constitution* (Oxford: Oxford University Press, 1999); Nicholas Robinson, "Expanding Judiciaries: India and the Rise of the Good Governance Court," *Washington University Global Studies Law Review* 8:1 (2009), 1–69; *S. R. Bommai v. Union of India* 1994 AIR 1918 (1998).

[130] Hershkoff, "The Private Life of Public Rights," 20–22.

[131] Ibid., 22.

[132] Ibid.

application in the United States. The purpose of this chapter is not to provide a causal explanation of the outcomes. Rather, this chapter offers one setting, with others to follow, in which to examine discourses surrounding the question of horizontality according to the analytic concepts developed in Chapter 2. For those familiar with American constitutionalism, the emphasis on individual rights and the public–private divide will be unsurprising. However, this book's interpretive lens facilitates the specific work of analyzing the language and arguments surrounding these developments. Ultimately, this interpretive lens helps to illuminate threads with republican undertones, even in American constitutional discourses. We see these republican threads in concurrences, dissents, other constitutional dynamics not strictly part of court-driven doctrinal development, and in state courts and constitutions. Republican themes fit comfortably, and sometimes are explicitly invoked, in such statements as Harlan's famous dissent in the *Civil Rights Cases*,[133] and in his successors' concurrences and dissents in the sit-in cases. To think of the United States strictly as a kind of ideal type for doctrines of state action, as is common, thus misses much that is potentially important from a political theoretic standpoint.

That the United States would have had some version of a state action doctrine seems inevitable given the text of the Fourteenth Amendment and the conventional liberal understandings of constitutionalism. Indeed, even Harlan I's dissent appreciates some distinction between public and private spaces. At the same time, Harlan and successors such as Douglas were ready to acknowledge the significance certain private spaces carried for citizenship and racial equality, as the Radical Republicans had envisioned when they championed the Civil Rights Act of 1875. While a kind of rights-centrism prevails in the predominant doctrinal story, even the archetypal case of state action that is the United States reveals discourses pointing toward certain ends of the community – ends that some constitutional actors came to understand as too constitutive to justify preserving a wholly insulated private sphere. These debates gradually grew out of the transformative constitutional moment embodied in the Civil War Amendments; in contrast, Chapter 4, which is on India, will show how an entire constitutional project, at least on many accounts, was oriented toward transforming both public and private spheres from the beginning. In many ways, the question of horizontal application still

---

[133] *Civil Rights Cases*, 109 U.S. 3 (1883).

has had to be worked out; indeed, it is still being worked out. In another sense, however, it is a question inhering in the Indian Constitution itself. Some of the most influential Indian framers defined their goals in explicit contrast with the rights-centrism that American constitutionalism has come to represent, favoring instead a dynamic constitution centered on equality and nondiscrimination as collective ends.

4

India

Citizens' Duties in Aspiring to Equality

Despite a range of interpretations of what the Fourteenth Amendment requires and permits, doctrinal practice in the United States remains wedded to a dividing line between public and private, between state and nonstate action. Some provisions of the Indian Constitution likewise stipulate that certain rights control only state action, and some constitutional interpreters have indeed foregrounded such provisions. However, more capacious interpretations of rights, indeed of rights as ends, have contributed to the official constitutional story from its earliest days. From arguments of key framers to later Supreme Court judgments, Indian constitutional discourse often understands rights as requiring more for their protection and fulfillment in comparison with American rights. Amid yet another history tainted by inequality and caste, such crucial political figures as Dr. B. R. Ambedkar, who himself was a Dalit, aimed to fashion a constitution that would break down divisions and ameliorate discrimination. Hence, several constitutional provisions admitted space for the possibility that rights be grounded in larger constitutional ends from which private actors were not necessarily insulated. Examining Indian constitutional arguments through this book's republican framework reveals a theoretic potential in the discourse. Indeed, various episodes since the Constitution's adoption in 1950 have been marked by arguments echoing concepts like a common good and duties of citizens. All this has occurred in a context where, like the United States, the reach and nature of equality itself hung in the balance.

In the same way that the US debate cannot be summed up solely in terms of state action or verticality, neither does the Indian debate show an uninterrupted trajectory toward horizontality. Not all of the Indian framers, much less the array of constitutional actors since the Constitution's adoption, subscribed to the same vision of equality, nondiscrimination, and social justice for India. In the years leading up to the Constitution's framing, Jawaharlal Nehru, the independence activist and first prime minister, acknowledged that the Indian constitutional moment might be born of merely a "semi-revolutionary situation."[1] Nehru thus showed some confidence that India was approaching the moment in which it would reconstitute itself, as well as a kind of realism that the impetus for such a revolution likely would not pervade the country as a whole. He was right; many did remain tied to structures of oppression that ran contrary to the eventual constitutional vision.[2] Picking up on this idea of a "semi-revolutionary situation," Jacobsohn and Roznai further suggest that the Indian polity at the time of independence might have been comprised of only "a semi-revolutionary people."[3] Even by the time the framers adopted and drafted the Constitution, they point out, divergent strands of thought and conflicting positions contributed to the final document – some supported the project of secularism and equality, while others were inclined to constitute the country on the basis of Hindu nationalism. Even into the twenty-first century, scholars find both transformative and more nationalist conservative interpretations of the Indian Constitution among political actors and institutions.[4]

In addition to this different interpretation vis-à-vis the place of equality and nondiscrimination in the Constitution, Granville Austin describes competing understandings of the very content and requirements of these rights. This comes in his account of three "strands" underlying the Indian Constitution's philosophy: "protecting and enhancing national unity and integrity; establishing the institutions and spirit of democracy; and fostering a social revolution to better the lot of the mass of Indians."[5] While many observers and constitutional actors understood these three to be "mutually dependent and inextricably intertwined,"[6] these strands also would come to exist in some tension.[7] Most relevant to this book, the traditional rights that one might associate with the second strand's "institutions and spirit of democracy" did not always sit comfortably with the third strand's more ambitious goal of "social revolution." While

---

[1] Presidential Address to the Indian National Congress, Lucknow, April 12, 1936.
[2] Gary Jacobsohn and Yaniv Roznai, *Constitutional Revolution* (New Haven: Yale University Press, 2020), 153–154.
[3] Ibid., 153.
[4] Tarunabh Khaitan, "Killing a Constitution with a Thousand Cuts: Executive Aggrandizement and Party-State Fusion in India," *Law and Ethics of Human Rights* 14:1 (2020), 49–95; Gautam Bhatia, *The Transformative Constitution* (Uttar Pradesh: HarperCollins, 2019), xx–xxvii.
[5] Granville Austin, *Working a Democratic Constitution* (Oxford: Oxford University Press, 1999), 6.
[6] Ibid.
[7] Ibid., 38.

the former was manifested in the Constitution primarily in Part III's guarantees, such as equality, the latter appeared in Part IV's Directive Principles, including the call to institute affirmative action programs (known as reservations) to benefit those populations who were subjected to discrimination.[8] Although the Directive Principles of Part IV were technically nonjusticiable, they were essential to understanding the constitutional vision as a transformative one, charging the state to transcend traditional formulations of rights in favor of more substantive ends across Indian society.[9]

Austin's account, therefore, anticipates both a static element and a dynamic element in the new constitution. Whereas the static provision for, say, the right to equality in Part III, Article 14 would by itself support a more conservative tendency, a more aspirational substantive equality, what Marc Galanter calls the Constitution's "compensatory theme,"[10] arguably comprises a more comprehensive and dynamic vision. Figures like Ambedkar and Nehru, who sought transformation, urged that the Indian project could only be realized fully in recognizing the dynamic element, thus contending "step by step" with a still-unreceptive political culture.[11] These two elements are likewise present in ensuing jurisprudence of the Indian Supreme Court, which displays both conservative and transformative bents in the handful of decisions in which it has confronted the horizontal application of rights to private actors.[12]

In the interest of taking stock and thinking comparatively, in the United States we saw a kind of crescendo of disharmony in constitutional discourses over time, as the limited equality that prevailed in the *Civil Rights Cases* (*pace* the Radical Republicans) did not rest easily with the

---

[8] These Directive Principles largely reflect what Ambedkar would refer to as "economic democracy" (*Constituent Assembly Debates, Vol. 7* [New Delhi: Lok Sabha Secretariat, 1986], 494). And indeed, many provisions among these Directive Principles were included as an effort to keep members of the socialist party at the negotiating table during the Constituent Assembly debates.

[9] In many ways, this division between Parts III and IV of the Indian Constitution tracks what might have been in the US context had constitutional actors pushed for a decoupling of Sections 1 and 5 of the Fourteenth Amendment. Specifically, the US Supreme Court might have been charged with upholding a more formal understanding of equality under Section 1, whereas Congress might have assumed the role of realizing something more, perhaps a kind of substantive equality, under its Section 5 enforcement powers.

[10] Marc Galanter, *Competing Equalities: Law and the Backward Classes in India* (Berkeley: University of California Press, 1984), 381, 364. See also Jacobsohn and Roznai, *Constitutional Revolution*, 173.

[11] Jacobsohn and Roznai, *Constitutional Revolution*, 145.

[12] Bhatia, *The Transformative Constitution*, xx–xxvii.

way understandings of equality shifted during the Civil Rights Movement of the 1960s. In contrast, we see disharmony at the very start in India, in the juxtaposition of Ambedkar's and Nehru's aspirations with the broader political situation that promised to hamper their vision. Whereas disharmony between public discourses and the official constitutional line proved to be a kind of terminus in America when the US Supreme Court would not revisit the reach of equality during the sit-in protests, it is better characterized as a discursive starting point in Indian constitutionalism since, for many, nondiscrimination and fraternity were ends toward which the country needed to strive but that required more than what some sectors of the polity would permit.[13]

It is in a similar spirit that Jacobsohn and Roznai identify a kind of "step by step revolution" in India, involving both "steps backwards and forwards,"[14] that incrementally furthered more ambitious understandings of the constitutional project at least in certain moments.[15] This same understanding led the Indian framers to provide for horizontal application in several constitutional provisions. Moreover, much about the early constitutional debates possessed a republican valence,[16] sometimes explicitly so. Both during the framing and in later episodes of constitutional politics, such republican proclivities can be seen in arguments about transcending more limited understandings of equality and extending duties beyond state actors to involve private actors as well. Likewise,

---

[13] Contrast this with Jaffa's early account of the American Framers whose Lockean foundations took equality to be a kind of status quo that could be taken for granted. On Jaffa's telling, it was only with Lincoln's subsequent interpretation that equality came to mean more – indeed, it became an end toward which the polity continually needed to work (Harry Jaffa, *Crisis of the House Divided* [Chicago: University of Chicago, 2009], chap. 14).

[14] Jacobsohn and Roznai, *Constitutional Revolution*, 149.

[15] Two decades into the twenty-first century and with a regnant BJP, many political observers and scholars are more cynical of whether Indian politics will fulfill its more expansive constitutional promises into the future.

[16] In contrast with the many accounts that portray India as departing from traditional liberal understandings, Rochana Bajpai ("Liberalisms in India: A Sketch," in *Liberalism as Ideology: Essays in Honour of Michael Freeden*, ed. Ben Jackson and Marc Stears [Oxford: Oxford University Press, 2012]) and C. A. Bayly (*Recovering Liberties* [Cambridge: Cambridge University Press, 2012]) do find liberal elements in Indian political history. Specifically, Bajpai identifies colonial, nationalist, and radical liberal strands running through different eras of the polity's constitutional thought. However, her account encompasses liberalisms of the welfarist variety that are more democratically inclined and often critical of laissez-faire postures. Put differently, the variants of liberalism that Bajpai finds are those that are more likely to find common ground with much in republican theory.

the handful of cases in which the Court has considered horizontal application have often cast the issues at stake in terms that may be conceived of as republican, often deployed in service to transformative understandings of the constitutional project. Indeed, the foundations for such ends-oriented arguments that support horizontal application were established with the 1950 Constitution.

At the same time, arguments less amenable to transformative interpretations, including those respecting horizontal application, persist in constitutional discourse. In certain ways, a continued diversity in the discourse is more conspicuous in Indian constitutional history than in other contexts this book considers insofar as the Indian Supreme Court decides cases in panels, called benches, selected by the chief justice, rather than *en banc*. In other words, only a few justices at a time, rather than the whole thirty-four member court,[17] will typically be charged with deciding a case. Outcomes are thus largely contingent on the composition of those benches and make more tenuous any claims about the court's doctrinal trajectory. Nevertheless, for the purposes of this book, the practice of deciding cases in benches may put more constitutional understandings on the table for examination. Doctrinal trends may be more difficult to locate, but discursive threads across eras and court cases are quite discernible.

This context engenders arguments similar, in both range and substance, to those that Chapter 3 examined in the United States. Indeed, what follows shows a continual choice in Indian constitutionalism between more transformative and conservative constitutional discourses, with the former generally correlating with the horizontal application of rights. Nevertheless, this chapter also reveals new discursive possibilities when the horizontal application of a range of equality and nondiscrimination rights is more explicitly provided for in the constitutional text and framers' visions. Of course, a court's choice to pursue a more transformative or restrained line cannot but be influenced by such contingencies as institutional strength (or limitations, as the case may be) and political will.[18] However, pursuant to this book's project to take constitutional

---

[17] This reflects the number of judges on the court, including the chief justice, as of the 2019 Supreme Court Amendment Act. At the time of the Constitution's adoption, the Court comprised eight judges, including the chief justice, and did sit *en banc*.

[18] The Indian Supreme Court is often counted among the strongest in the world. See, for example, Michaela Hailbronner, "Transformative Constitutionalism: Not Only in the Global South," *American Journal of Comparative Law* 65:3 (2017), 547–548; and Stephen Gardbaum, "What Makes for More or Less Powerful Constitutional Courts?"

discourses as the focus, the primary concern here is to foreground more theoretic lessons, highlighting the potential republican lines of thinking as Indian constitutional actors, operating amid pervasive inequality, contemplate how the horizontal application of rights might grow out of the constitutional project. From cases ranging from labor to education emerge an interpretation of the Constitution as a far-reaching and public project, where public values are not constrained to particular rights formulations, issues, or spheres but potentially implicate all corners of life and a vast cross-section of the Indian populace.

Freedom and Fraternity: Drafting a New Constitution

The Indian independence movement's leaders and constitutional framers sought unity and equality in the country's founding.[19] A decade after independence, Nehru articulated the new constitutional project as "to promote fraternity, assuring the dignity of the individual and the unity of the nation."[20] "Fraternity" was thus considered a major factor in securing individual dignity and rights, to say nothing of the very unity of the newly constituted polity.

This same idea, that relations between citizens are crucial to the success of a democratic India, runs through the deliberations preceding ratification.[21] Members of the Subcommittee on Fundamental Rights believed that citizens' duties should not be neglected amid so much discussion of rights. K. T. Shah cautioned that "the constitution would be incomplete, and even futile, if equal stress were not laid on obligations

---

Duke Journal of Comparative & International Law 29:1 (2018), 31–36. Nevertheless, some scholars dispute whether this account holds in such historical moments when having a strong court would count the most – for example, when the government has taken authoritarian turns during the Emergency Era and during the BJP's present dominance. Even the 1978 Maneka Gandhi case, frequently cited as a great turning point for the Indian Supreme Court, has certain limitations in that the petitioner did not have her passport returned to her after the government had seized it arbitrarily (remote interview with Gautam Bhatia, March 24, 2021). Regardless of how one comes down on the actions of the Indian court, as with any court, it cannot but be influenced by the larger constitutional politics of any given moment.

[19] Manjeet Ramgotra, "India's Republican Moment," in *The Indian Constituent Assembly: Deliberations on Democracy*, ed. Udit Bhatia (New York: Routledge, 2018), 219.

[20] Ibid., 213.

[21] See, for example, Shiva Rao, *The Framing of India's Constitution: Selected Documents*, Vol. II (Bombay: N. M. Tripathi, 1966), 38–48.

corresponding to rights,"²² and that "every one of these rights [in the draft Statement of Fundamental Rights] would be impossible to realise, unless, side by side, toleration is cultivated and enforced."²³ Shah goes on to develop this idea in a way that makes it immediately relevant to the subject of horizontal application, speaking of "the seeming conflict in certain rights due, so to say, to the right of one person or of one group becoming the obligation of another."²⁴ This explanation of a "conflict between rights" and of rights becoming "the obligation of another" gets to the heart of horizontality's republican character, as it generates new duties in a liberal context.

Throughout these deliberations, the framers seemed to be more concerned with cultivating a culture of mutual obligation among fellow citizens than a more specific doctrinal understanding of horizontality as it might develop in constitutional law. That many of the framers sought a culture of fraternity and understood private actors as having obligations to one another is a far cry from the state action requirement through which equality came to be understood in the American context. And indeed, the United States' experience with equality (and inequality) had a direct influence on this stage of drafting of Indian constitutional rights to equality.²⁵ In his draft articles and notes, the Father of the Indian Constitution himself voiced concern to avoid the discrimination that had lingered in the United States as a result of constitutional actors' formulations of divides between private and public, state and nonstate action. B. R. Ambedkar's draft articles explicitly dealt with access to public accommodations, eligibility for various offices, and the like.²⁶ In his notes on these particular draft articles, Ambedkar states that he borrowed language for some of the provisions from the Civil Rights Acts

---

[22] Ibid., 38. This general emphasis on duties would manifest further when the Forty-Second Amendment to the Constitution would incorporate certain fundamental duties of citizens (see Article 51A of the Indian Constitution). Though not justiciable by themselves, the Supreme Court has rendered these fundamental duties justiciable through ordinary law or when attached to a fundamental right (Mahendra Singh, "India: Protection of Human Rights against State and Non-state Action," in *Human Rights in the Private Sphere*, ed. Dawn Oliver and Jorg Fedtke [Abingdon: Routledge-Cavendish, 2007], 181–182).
[23] Rao, *The Framing of India's Constitution, Vol. II*, 39.
[24] Ibid., 40. See also 38–48.
[25] P. K. Tripathi, "Perspectives on the American Constitutional Influence on the Constitution of India," in *Constitutionalism in Asia: Asian Views of the American Influence*, ed. Lawrence Beer (Baltimore: University of Maryland School of Law, 1988), 78.
[26] Ibid.; Rao, *The Framing of India's Constitution, Vol. II*, 86.

of 1866 and 1875, "passed by the Congress of the United States of America to protect the Negroes against unequal treatment."[27]

Whereas in the American context Justice Bradley worried that these laws would force whites to endure "another kind of slavery"[28] and Justice Black later worried that reading the Fourteenth Amendment to guarantee equal access to public accommodations would limit liberty too much, Ambedkar and others in the Subcommittee on Fundamental Rights were intent not to understand equality simply in terms of private and public. In Ambedkar's own words, "Discrimination is another menace which must be guarded against if the fundamental rights are to be real rights. In a country like India where it is possible for discrimination to be practiced on a vast scale and in a relentless manner fundamental rights can have no meaning."[29] In this way, deliberations during the constitutional drafting and subsequent debates often understood equality as necessitating at least some cooperation from private actors.

The Subcommittee on Fundamental Rights did not ultimately adopt Ambedkar's draft articles, but did bring articles before the Constituent Assembly that aimed at securing the right to equality, including the prohibition of discrimination in public accommodations (Article 15), untouchability[30] (Article 17), *begar*[31] and forced labor (Article 23), and child labor (Article 24). Insofar as the problem of inequality did not distinguish between spheres of life, so too did these provisions presume to bring the new public commitments to equality and nondiscrimination into private spaces.[32] Many framers' preoccupation with encompassing private entities in the constitutional plan, and particularly the

---

[27] Rao, *The Framing of India's Constitution*, Vol. II, 96; Tripathi, "Perspectives on the American Constitutional Influence," 78–79.

[28] Jack Balkin and Sanford Levinson, "The Dangerous Thirteenth Amendment," *Columbia Law Review* 112:7 (2012), 1472.

[29] Rao, *The Framing of India's Constitution*, Vol. II, 96; Tripathi, "Perspectives on the American Constitutional Influence," 78–79.

[30] The Civil Rights Act of 1955 implemented Article 17 by making untouchability an offense and creating a mechanism for prosecution (Sudhir Krishnaswamy, "Horizontal Application of Fundamental Rights and State Action in India," in *Human Rights, Justice, & Constitutional Empowerment*, ed. C. Raj Kumar and K. Chockalingam [Oxford: Oxford University Press, 2007], 52).

[31] *Begar* is a system of forced labor historically practiced in India.

[32] Citing Article 15(2) and Article 21 (guaranteeing the right to life), Krishnaswamy explains that "the majority of rights are expressed in broad and general terms and ambivalent about who they are addressed to." He continues to explain that Articles 17, 18, and 23 expressly impose constitutional obligations on nonstate actors (Krishnaswamy, "Horizontal Application of Fundamental Rights," 52).

commitment to nondiscrimination, is evident in Article 15. This Article prohibits discrimination in two separate clauses: one aimed at the state, and the other aimed at private individuals or nonstate actors. Both clauses employ the same language and specify the same protected categories: "religion, race, caste, sex, place of birth or any of them."[33] Though these clauses possess almost identical content, the framers nevertheless thought it necessary to include both in the final Constitution, with Sardar Vallabhbhai Patel going so far as to say both were "absolutely essential."[34]

In some ways, however, the inclusion of two separate clauses – one obligating state entities, and another private nonstate entities – complicates the story. On the one hand, the fact that the framers thought it was necessary to specify that a right obligated the state suggests a departure from the traditional model in which one could assume that rights only *ever* obligated the state.[35] On the other hand, implicit in the fact of these separate clauses is the idea that private and public entities are distinct, and perhaps that their obligations are different. Indeed, Patel describes prohibitions of private discrimination in arenas like restaurants and hotels as "a completely different idea" from the state's obligation not to discriminate.[36] Moreover, in detailing additional private establishments, such as "wells, tanks, bathing ghats, roads and places of public resort," Article 15(2b) prohibits discrimination only in situations in which these establishments are "maintained wholly or partly out of State funds or dedicated to the use of the general public."[37] Similarly, Article 14 guaranteeing equality before the law has a state action requirement.

---

[33] See Article 15, clauses 1 and 2, of the Indian Constitution; *Constituent Assembly Debates, Vol. 3* (New Delhi: Lok Sabha Secretariat, 1986), 426; Stephen Gardbaum, "Horizontality in the Indian Constitution," in *The Oxford Handbook of the Indian Constitution*, ed. Sujit Choudhry, Madhav Khosla, and Pratap Bhanu Mehta (Oxford: Oxford University Press, 2016), 603; see also the discussion on gender and "social equality" in Rao, *The Framing of India's Constitution, Vol. V*, 185.

[34] *Constituent Assembly Debates, Vol. 3* (New Delhi: Lok Sabha Secretariat, 1986), 426; Gardbaum, "Horizontality in the Indian Constitution," 603.

[35] Singh, "India: Protection of Human Rights," 188–189.

[36] Ibid..

[37] T. K. Raj offers a compelling interpretation of this antidiscrimination provision as prohibiting discrimination in the context of "public services," that is, "those services vital to modern social life such that their deprivation would seriously disadvantage a dignified life" ("Private Discrimination, Public Service and the Constitution," *Indian Law Review* 6:1 [2022], 34).

The text reads: "The State shall not deny to any person equality before the law or the equal protection of the laws within the territory of India." Though the framers maintained ambitious ideas of the duties of citizens, they still distinguished between state and nonstate actors in matters of law and politics.

The framers were unlikely to collapse the categories of public and private completely given how this distinction largely defines liberalism and given the generally different capacities of state and nonstate actors.[38] Indeed, as in other jurisdictions, the importance of the distinction decreases as the means and power of private entities increase.[39] Nevertheless, the Indian framers' recognition of some distinction between public and private actors created ground on which a young Supreme Court would argue against horizontal application, at least in particular instances if not writ large. At the same time, much in these early constitutional debates reflects a kind of republican vision of the polity's problems that the Constitution was designed to address with its attendant duties of citizens. Likewise, the debates and ultimate text do not contain anything quite like the Centrist Republicans' understanding in postbellum America that drove a wedge between social and civil rights. Rather, the debates reveal comparatively broad consensus during the framing of the Indian Constitution that a right to nondiscrimination required both.[40] Discrimination from any corner of society had to be fought if fundamental rights were to be "real rights" and "have meaning."[41] In this way, Ambedkar and other Indian framers articulated a conception of the Constitution as transformative and, as such, necessarily dynamic. And while traditional understandings about the requirements of equality and nondiscrimination remained present in the discourse, a larger role for private actors in realizing such rights of fellow citizens gained new momentum in constitutional understandings.

---

[38] Legal theorists have argued in various ways that the state's heightened constitutional duties do not necessarily entail that private actors are immune to constitutional commitments. See, for example, Nicholas Bamforth, "The Public Law–Private Law Distinction: A Comparative and Philosophical Approach," in *Administrative Law Facing the Future: Old Constraints and New Horizons,* ed. Peter Leyland and Terry Woods (Oxford: Blackstone Press, 1997), 136–159; and Tarunabh Khaitan, "The Duty Bearers," in *A Theory of Discrimination Law* (Oxford: Oxford University Press, 2015), 195–213.

[39] Singh, "India: Protection of Human Rights," 191.

[40] Rao, *The Framing of India's Constitution, Vol. V,* 185.

[41] Ibid., 96; Tripathi, "Perspectives on the American Constitutional Influence," 78–79.

The Conservativism of the Early Supreme Court

That the Constitution distinguishes between private and public spaces, and between state and nonstate actors, figured into some of the Supreme Court's earliest decisions. These followed other countries' practices, and the conventions of constitutionalism more generally, to confine the application of rights to the state.[42] Early decisions conforming to this conventional understanding include *PD Shamdasani v. Central Bank of India* (1952)[43] and *Vidya Verma v. Dr Shiv Narain Verma* (1956).[44] Nevertheless, these are also ambiguous cases, insofar as the constitutional language alone offers interpretive space in which the Court might have applied the rights in question to private actors had they been so inclined. In these early cases, however, the Court employed a kind of canned understanding of constitutionalism, with only perfunctory consideration of how the Indian Constitution might call for something more or something different. Quoting an earlier case, Justice Bose writes in *Vidya Verma*, "[A]s a rule constitutional safeguards are directed against the state and its organs and that protection against violations of rights by individuals must be sought in the ordinary law." Sudhir Krishnaswamy describes this approach as "stipulative and unreasoning" for its inattention to how the constitutional text and its theoretical basis could lead to a different understanding of the scope of fundamental rights.[45] Indeed, it takes as granted conventional accounts of constitutionalism, conceiving of rights as creating a relationship between individuals and the state, and

---

[42] Singh, "India: Protection of Human Rights," 189.
[43] *PD Shamdasani v. Central Bank of India*, AIR 1952 SC 59. "The petitioner was aggrieved by the bank's sale of his shares to recover a debt owed by him." He petitioned the court by a writ action to enforce his fundamental right under the former Articles 19(1)(f) and 31 (1). Chief Justice Patanjali Shastri dismissed the petition on the basis that the language and placement of these constitutional provisions in Part III suggest they apply only to state action. As a side note, Articles 19(1)(f) and 31 were both amended out of the Constitution and replaced with Article 300-A (Krishnaswamy, "Horizontal Application of Fundamental Rights," 55–56).
[44] *Vidya Verma v. Dr Shiv Narain Verma*, AIR 1956 SC 108. The husband of the petitioner presented the Supreme Court with a habeas corpus petition to "release his wife from the custody of her father, alleging a violation of her fundamental right to life and liberty protected under Article 21." Justice Vivian Bose followed the Court's decision in *Shamdasani* to conclude that Article 21 was not intended to protect life and liberty against private individuals (Krishnaswamy, "Horizontal Application of Fundamental Rights," 56–57).
[45] *AK Gopalan v. State of Madras* (1950) SCR 88, 204; see also Krishnaswamy, "Horizontal Application of Fundamental Rights," 57.

not considering that they might embody certain ends for the polity as a whole. Nevertheless, these two cases did not foreclose the possibility of such an understanding and the future development of horizontality insofar as they limited their analysis to the individual rights provisions in question "instead of deciding the issue wholesale."[46] In fact, later cases do show a Court understanding the polity's issues in more republican terms and embracing a dynamic constitutional project[47] aimed at more ambitious understandings.

In addition to resisting any move toward horizontal application at this early stage, the Court also resisted government efforts to make good on the new constitution's "compensatory themes," articulated in the Directive Principles that charged the government with working toward a more substantive equality. In *State of Madras v. Champakam Dorairajan*, the Supreme Court struck down a state initiative that reserved specific spaces in government jobs and universities for members of lower castes.[48] Whereas the State of Madras had relied on Article 46 of the Directive Principles[49] in pursuing this policy, the Supreme Court operated on a more narrow understanding of the ends of equality and nondiscrimination grounded in a prioritization of Article 16(2),[50] prohibiting discrimination, over other provisions in that same Article 16 that permitted greater complexity.[51] Similar to the early cases directly concerning horizontal application, the Court here chose to emphasize some aspects of the Constitution over others, maintaining that quotas in government jobs violated equality under the law. Further, whatever preference the Court already had toward a more conservative interpretation was reinforced all the more by the fact that the Directive Principles

---

[46] Krishnaswamy, "Horizontal Application of Fundamental Rights," 56.
[47] Jacobsohn and Roznai, *Constitutional Revolution*.
[48] *State of Madras v. Champakam Dorairajan*, AIR 1951 SC 226; see also Jacobsohn and Roznai, *Constitutional Revolution*, 173.
[49] This Article reads: "The State shall promote with special care the educational and economic interests of the weaker sections of the people, and in particular, of the Scheduled Castes and the Scheduled Tribes, and shall protect them from social injustice and all forms of exploitation."
[50] "No citizen shall, on grounds only of religion, race, caste, sex, descent, place of birth, residence or any of them, be ineligible for, or discriminated against in respect of, any employment or office under the State."
[51] See, for example, Article 16(4): Nothing in this article shall prevent the State from making any provision for the reservation of appointments or posts in favour of any backward class of citizens which, in the opinion of the State, is not adequately represented in the services under the State.

were nonjusticiable, in contrast with the equal protection of the laws and other such rights in Part III of the Constitution, the protection of which was clearly within the courts' purview.[52]

In response to such judgments "impeding the fulfillment of government's perceived responsibilities" under the Directive Principles,[53] parliament passed the Constitution Act of 1951. In this First Amendment to the Constitution, a parliament, largely composed of the same members that had drafted the Constitution,[54] pushed back against the Supreme Court's restrictive decision in *State of Madras v. Champakam Dorairajan*. The Amendment aimed to clarify a series of rights under Part III of the Constitution, including the rights to property and to equality, in order to preempt further claims that they somehow stood in the way of state-initiated reservation programs. In this way, such affirmative actions to assist historically deprived populations could not be challenged on the basis of discrimination.[55] Jacobsohn and Roznai explain this as "a step forward in the dialogical advancement of a dominant, if not indisputable, view about achieving distributive justice in the polity."[56] However, the Court did not take even a constitutional amendment as the final word on the question, waging an ongoing battle for power with parliament in the ensuing years.

A couple of decades, as well as several significant decisions and constitutional amendments, later, the Court had a considerable opportunity to push back against parliament in *Kesavananda Bharati v. State of Kerala*.[57] In this decision, the Court established what has become a crucial concept of Indian constitutionalism, known as the Basic Structure Doctrine, the idea that "specific features of the Constitution are deemed sufficiently fundamental to the integrity of the constitutional project to warrant immunity from drastic alteration."[58] The initial cause

---

[52] Jacobsohn and Roznai, *Constitutional Revolution*, 162–163.
[53] Austin, *Working a Democratic Constitution*, 97.
[54] Jacobsohn and Roznai, *Constitutional Revolution*, 173fn99.
[55] For a discussion on similar issues in the context of the United States, see Reva B. Siegel, "Equality Talk: Antisubordination and Anticlassification Values in Constitutional Struggles over Brown," *Harvard Law Review* 117 (2004), 1470–1547.
[56] Jacobsohn and Roznai, *Constitutional Revolution*, 174. It is worth noting that the First Amendment has a complicated history and has been employed to a range of ends. In fact, many Indian scholars and commentators view it as limiting certain rights, such as freedom of expression. I am grateful to Tarunabh Khaitan for calling my attention to this blended history.
[57] *Kesavananda Bharati v. State of Kerala* (1973) 4 SCC 225.
[58] Jacobsohn and Roznai, *Constitutional Revolution*, 161.

(and effect) of this decision was to declare that the Court in fact had power to determine if an amendment passed by parliament (specifically, the Twenty-Fourth and Twenty-Fifth Amendments) went so far as to destroy, rather than simply modify, the Constitution's basic structure. In particular, a narrow majority of the Court argued that while amendments could enact some limitations to individual rights, the Constitution permitted such limitations only to a point. The initial impetus for this judgment was, admittedly, to stem parliament's power against the judiciary. However, this same Basic Structure Doctrine would gain additional legitimacy when parliament did pass dubious constitutional amendments. Indeed, the doctrine has been often enlisted to the cause of a more capacious understanding of the Indian constitutional project, including the support of the Directive Principles and even the expansion of horizontal application.[59]

The Supreme Court thus assumed a fairly conservative posture in the years immediately following the Constitution's adoption. It conceived of individual rights in such a way as to deter parliament's efforts to enact transformative legislation and, moreover, insisted on a vertical model of rights that limited the influence of constitutional values in private spaces. Constitutional debates and particular provisions distinguishing between state and nonstate action rendered such early decisions against horizontal application viable.[60] Nevertheless, these readings did not accrue in Indian constitutional politics the same entrenched status we see in the more limited interpretations of equality that followed the United States' Fourteenth Amendment. Indeed, even if the state were the primary guarantor of rights, a larger project, grounded in the debates and constitutional text, aimed at the polity's more thorough transformation.[61] Citing such constitutional understandings, the Indian Supreme Court would ultimately give indirect horizontal application to Article 14's guarantee of "equality before the law" and "equal protection of the laws" *in spite of* its state action requirement and would not just support reservations but support them in private spaces, too. Nevertheless, it took years of political conflict and institutional consolidation before the

---

[59] Nick Robinson, "Expanding Judiciaries: India and the Rise of the Good Governance Court," *Washington University Global Studies Law Review* 8:1 (2009), 28–30.

[60] Such as *AK Gopalan v. State of Madras* (AIR 1950 SC 27), *PD Shamdasani v. Central Bank of India* (1952 AIR 59, 1952 SCR 391), and *Vidya Verma v. Dr Shiv Narain Verma* (1956 AIR 108, 1955 SCR (2) 983).

[61] Bhatia, *The Transformative Constitution*, 2019; Hailbronner, "Transformative Constitutionalism."

Court began to make such arguments. Nehru might have explained this as part of the step-by-step revolution[62] that depended as much on political will as on the theoretic potential of the foundations established by the framers.

From Rights to Ends: Toward a Broader Constitutional Understanding

Eventually, the Supreme Court acknowledged a constitutional project more comprehensive than its early decisions suggested, specifically in reassessing the reach of rights in Part III of the Constitution.[63] As early as the 1963 case *State of West Bengal v. Union of India*,[64] the Court began to understand rights as also engendering a broad constitutional program. In this understanding, a right was "an obligation imposed not merely upon the 'State,' but upon all persons to respect the rights so declared, and the rights are enforceable unless the context indicates otherwise against every person or agency seeking to infringe them."[65] In this, we see an operative logic different from the aforementioned cases, in that certain rights might, in fact, create duties "for all persons" according to the commitments of the Constitution. In this way, at least some constitutional actors put greater weight on the requirements of particular articles of the Constitution and, not unlike many US cases, expanding the definition of "the State," per Article 12, to admit further application of rights even under a state action requirement.

In the wake of the Emergency Era of 1975–1977, the Court, chastened by its broad capitulation to executive power, was eager to reassert itself as a defender of all rights and not a mere instrument of the privileged.[66] Emboldened in this way, the Court acted to widen the application of fundamental rights, including through the horizontal application of certain constitutional rights. In *People's Union for Democratic Rights*

---

[62] Jacobsohn and Roznai, *Constitutional Revolution*, 166.
[63] As Krishnaswamy explains, the fact that early cases assessed the reach of *specific* rights rather than deciding the issue of horizontality wholesale gave the court flexibility to decide differently in later cases ("Horizontal Application of Fundamental Rights," 56).
[64] *State of West Bengal v. Union of India*, AIR 1963 SC 1241, 1264.
[65] Ibid.
[66] Singh, "India: Protection of Human Rights," 197. See also Anuj Bhuwania, *Courting the People* (Cambridge: Cambridge University Press, 2017). Bhuwania argues that the Supreme Court has leveraged power to become a majoritarian institution and, in fact, has a poor record when it comes to defending rights.

v. *Union of India* (1982),[67] the petitioners sought to enforce existing labor laws against contractors who were paying less than minimum wage in a construction project. The petitioners argued that the state had failed to enforce these labor laws, but also that the private contractors had violated laborers' right to equality (Article 14), right to life (Article 21), and rights against exploitation (Articles 23 and 24). With respect to the right against "*begar* and other similar forms of forced labor" (Article 23), Justice Bhagwati explained that certain constitutional rights were "enforceable against the whole world."[68] Moreover, he described the right against child labor (Article 24) as "plainly and indubitably enforceable against everyone."[69] Insofar as Article 14 includes a state action requirement, Bhagwati dealt with it somewhat differently. Rather than giving Article 14's right to equality direct horizontal application, as with Articles 23 and 24 where horizontality is basically required by the text, he gave this provision *indirect* horizontal application, expanding the state's duties to ensure that private entities met minimum wage requirements.

Though limited in some ways, *People's Union* is notable for the arguments the Court made in developing horizontal application in Indian constitutional law, particularly on provisions that bear on equality. In spite of some language of state action in the Constitution, *People's Union* illustrates how "differently phrased rights may apply horizontally to a different extent and in a different manner,"[70] and particularly those rights that bear directly upon India's larger project toward equality and nondiscrimination. The concern in this case is clearly not to negotiate equality along a boundary of what is public and what is private, which is arguably how much of the state action discourse in the United States has unfolded. Rather, the Indian Court's interpretation raises the more positively constructed question of how the right to equality may charge private individuals and nonstate actors to act in certain ways. This approach, Krishnaswamy suggests, serves as a kind of model, "as it pays attention to the constitutional text, the nature of the right, and the context in which the right is claimed."[71] In this way, the Court avoids making all disputes automatically subjects of public law while carving out

---

[67] *People's Union for Democratic Rights v. Union of India*, 3 SCC 235 AIR 1982 SC 1473.
[68] *People's Union for Democratic Rights v. Union of India*, AIR 1982 SC 1473 (n. 35) 252-253; see also Krishnaswamy, "Horizontal Application of Fundamental Rights," 58.
[69] *People's Union for Democratic Rights v. Union of India*, AIR 1982 SC 1473 (n. 35) 250; see also Krishnaswamy, "Horizontal Application of Fundamental Rights," 59.
[70] Krishnaswamy, "Horizontal Application of Fundamental Rights," 62-63.
[71] Ibid.

a space to understand equality as creating constitutional obligations for private citizens.[72]

The specific rationale in *People's Union* reveals what is arguably a republican understanding of the issues at hand. As Gautam Bhatia notes, beyond the fact that the workers received an amount less than the minimum wage at the time, the Court focused on the reality of exploitation and force underlying the entire situation. This was not merely a freedom to go about one's life without interference but a freedom from the power of "market forces" from which employers benefited and which they reproduced in turn.[73] Thus, Bhatia identifies a labor-republican understanding of freedom in *People's Union*, one that appreciates the arbitrary power that human-made structures and systems may impose to the benefit of some and at the expense of others.[74] This conception of freedom finds grounding in the Constitution itself, as such figures as Ambedkar took on more than a rights regime, but also confronted the belief that existing orderings were somehow neutral.[75] Instead, the Constitution embraced a "social vision" that called into question existing economic arrangements and relationships that stood to hamper the project of fraternity. In light of such a goal, attempts to dissect the meaning of the word "freedom" were less helpful than considering "what my moral obligations to you are."[76] Indeed, in this understanding, individuals and other private actors inevitably garner some obligations to one another.

The judgment in *People's Union* thus articulates both the problem of forced labor and its solution in republican terms. In contrast to the logic of state action, which does not offer conceptual space to consider the possibility of citizens' duties as such, the Court found basis for a republican logic in the constitutional history and text, not least in such aforementioned provisions as Articles 23 and 24 that imply the possibility of horizontality. The Court might have expanded the concept of state action so as to encompass nonstate actors (such as public accommodations) as a practical matter, an approach employed in both the US and Indian contexts at times. However, no concept of individual

---

[72] Ibid.; see also Bamforth, "The Public Law–Private Law Distinction," and Khaitan, "The Duty Bearers."
[73] Bhatia, *The Transformative Constitution*, 171.
[74] Ibid., 187.
[75] Ibid., 189.
[76] Ibid.

constitutional duty follows from this reasoning. Instead, in *People's Union*, the Court drew from a preexisting lexicon to formulate an understanding of constitutional duty. Admittedly, this case serves as a kind of "signpost to a road not yet taken,"[77] as horizontal application remains nascent in Indian constitutionalism. Nevertheless, the sort of space that *People's Union* makes for private obligation finds its origins in the priorities of the framers, as well as the constitutional text itself. "Appealing to the framers' understandings," Justice Bhagwati explains that Article 23

> is clearly designed to protect the individual not only against the State but *also against other private citizens*. Article 23 is *not limited in its application against the State* but it prohibits "traffic in human beings and begar and other similar forms of forced labour" wherever they are found.[78]

That the framers laid the groundwork for the concept of horizontal application could thereby spare the Indian Supreme Court some of the concerns the Warren Court faced in the 1960s when it too was inclined to conceive of cases in more republican terms.[79]

The Indian Constitution's stronger foundation for horizontality in its constitutional vision comes into sharp relief in a couple of cases that have analogs in the canon of American constitutional law. Although legal scholars dispute the status of these cases from a technical standpoint as instances of horizontal application, they do reveal an underlying core that can be cast in terms of republicanism, particularly when contrasted with the analogous US cases. First, *Vishaka v. State of Rajasthan* (1997)[80] speaks to the issue of the state's duty to protect in ways not unlike the American case *DeShaney v. Winnebago County* (1989).[81] Apart from the usefulness of this case for its parallels with *DeShaney*, *Vishaka* is often considered an important case in its own right for horizontal application in India. *Vishaka* involved a social worker, employed by the State of Rajasthan, who was brutally gang-raped on the premises of her workplace after she attempted to stop a child marriage. A trial court's acquittal

---

[77] Ibid., 207.
[78] Singh, "India: Protection of Human Rights," 202, original emphasis.
[79] It is worth noting that the Indian Supreme Court has not, in fact, shown consistent willingness to continue in this vein. See, for example, Bhatia on *Lingegowd Detective and Security Chamber (P) Ltd. v. Mysore Kirloskar Ltd.* and *State of Karnataka v. Uma Devi* (*The Transformative Constitution*, 207–210).
[80] *Vishaka v. State of Rajasthan*, AIR 1997 SC 3011.
[81] *DeShaney v. Winnebago County*, 489 U.S. 189.

of her attackers served as the impetus for others to file a class suit to establish laws against sexual harassment. Before *Vishaka* was decided in 1997, the only relevant provisions against such abuses were those couple of provisions of the penal code under which the social worker had sued. The petitioners argued that these did not adequately address the hazards to women in the workplace and that the issue should take on a weightier constitutional status.[82] The petitioners stated:

> The failure of the state to establish a legal framework to tackle sexual harassment in the workplace resulted in the violation of a woman's right to equality and against discrimination under Articles 14 and 15, her right to life under Article 21, and her right to "practice any profession" ... protected by Article 19(1)(g).[83]

Thus, petitioners sought to highlight the state's failure to protect rights by way of legislation and, by extension, how this failure directly resulted in the violation of women's rights by private actors.

In his careful reading of the case, Stephen Gardbaum points out that it is not entirely clear who the Court thought responsible for the harm in *Vishaka*. Indeed, given the facts of the case, the primary harm was arguably that which the assailants inflicted against the social worker.[84] But even clearer in the judgment is the interpretation that the state inflicted a harm in failing in its duty to protect citizens from such crimes and from sexual harassment in general. Though this understanding falls short of direct horizontal application, since the perpetrators are not themselves responsible for upholding rights, this latter reading is a clear instance of indirect horizontal application. Indeed, private actors were still held to the rubric of constitutional principles in the positive action the state took to regulate behavior. What previously would have been a matter of mere tort, contract, and criminal law became "a constitutional wrong" in *Vishaka*,[85] as the law was made to accord better with constitutional ends.

Recall Justice Rehnquist's general argument in the American case *DeShaney v. Winnebago County*, that the Constitution's purpose "was to protect the people from the State, not to ensure that the State protected them from each other. The Framers were content to leave the extent of governmental obligation in the latter area to the democratic political

---

[82] Robinson, "Expanding Judiciaries," 9.
[83] Krishnaswamy, "Horizontal Application of Fundamental Rights," 53.
[84] Gardbaum, "Horizontality in the Indian Constitution," 604–605.
[85] Krishnaswamy, "Horizontal Application of Fundamental Rights," 53–54.

processes."⁸⁶ This reasoning and its accompanying interpretation of the founding are a far cry from either of the two suggested readings of *Vishaka*. However one reads it, *Vishaka* does entail the state's positive duty to protect individuals. Moreover, while in India and the United States the framers did look to the democratic political processes to execute such protections, it does not follow that in *Vishaka* such protections were discretionary. Indeed, the Court formulated guidelines instructing that the state should undertake such action as a *constitutional* matter. In *DeShaney*, the US Supreme Court insisted on the presence of state action to trigger constitutional rights protections, and that an inaction that led to a private harm was not adequate. In *Vishaka*, on the other hand, Chief Justice Verma does identify such a positive obligation of the state, thus "widening the scope of application of rights as the court enforces a positive obligation on the state to intervene and decisively alter the relationship between private parties."⁸⁷ Beyond the particular issues of gender equality with which this case was concerned, this reflects the more general divergence between understandings of the US and Indian constitutional projects, the latter being much more concerned with positive steps the state ought to take to remediate such abuses – historical, proximate, and the proximate rooted in the historical.

Also present in *Vishaka*, and absent from *DeShaney*, is the understanding that citizens might have duties to one another under the Constitution. While the remedy in *Vishaka* did not necessarily come by way of the constitutional duties enumerated in Article 51A, insofar as they are not justiciable,⁸⁸ the very fact that Chief Justice Verma cites them shows some continuity with the convictions aired in the Constituent Assembly debates. Krishnaswamy understands these constitutional duties as an "interpretive aid" to the Court.⁸⁹ Therefore, even if not controlling the case as a doctrinal matter, Verma's citing these duties suggests that, at

---

⁸⁶ *DeShaney v. Winnebago County*, 489 U.S. 189.
⁸⁷ Krishnaswamy, "Horizontal Application of Fundamental Rights," 53–54.
⁸⁸ *Surya Narain v. Union of India* (AIR 1982 Raj 1, 1981 WLN 198); see also ibid., 54.
⁸⁹ Another "interpretive aid" that Chief Justice Verma employed in *Vishaka* was the 1979 international treaty known as the Convention on the Elimination of All Forms of Discrimination against Women (CEDAW) (Krishnaswamy, "Horizontal Application of Fundamental Rights," 55). The invocation of this agreement raises interesting questions about the role and limits of supranational and international institutions in developing horizontal rights obligations. This is a particularly salient question in light of the republican framework underlying this book and will be considered more fully in Chapter 7.

some level, "all citizens are under the constitutional obligation not to engage in sexually discriminatory behavior in the workplace."[90] Contrast this outlook with Mary Ann Glendon's account of the United States, wherein she describes the "deafening" silence of anything like citizens' duties in national constitutional law and, in many ways, civic culture.[91]

Another US case that serves as a useful comparison to this moment in Indian constitutionalism is *United States v. Morrison* (2000). Indeed, both *Morrison* and *Vishaka* concern the introduction of legislation to deter and penalize gender-based violence and harassment. However, in passing the 1994 Violence Against Women Act (VAWA), the US Congress was not acting to fulfill any constitutional duty to protect. Indeed, in Rehnquist's opinion in *Morrison*, the Supreme Court decided that the Commerce Clause and Equal Protection Clause did *not* empower Congress to enact certain sections of the law. Respecting the Commerce Clause, the Court argued that punishing gender-based crimes, as VAWA proposed to do, was beyond the purview of the national government and ought to be left to the states. Moreover, the Court argued that the legislature could not rely on the Equal Protection Clause in regulating private relationships. Citing the *Civil Rights Cases* as precedent, the Court maintained that the state action doctrine did not permit bringing constitutional commitments to bear on private actors. Neither did the state action doctrine empower the national government to hold accountable state actors, such as the state legislatures, for their *inaction* to legislate against gender-based crimes.

The decision in *Morrison* illustrates plainly the contention that the US Congress did not have the same constitutional duty to protect, and indeed could not assume such a duty, as did the Indian Parliament. One could argue that the role of federalism in American constitutionalism makes sense of the outcome in *Morrison*. Even though India is also a federal country, the arc of its constitutional jurisprudence places much less emphasis on the unique governing power of its states, perhaps symptomatic of differences in its larger constitutional vision.[92] Nick

---

[90] Krishnaswamy, "Horizontal Application of Fundamental Rights," 54.
[91] Mary Ann Glendon, *Rights Talk: The Impoverishment of Political Discourse* (New York: Free Press, 1991), 77.
[92] Granville Austin explains that, from the adoption of the Constitution, India did not have a robust understanding of citizenship at the state level (*Working a Democratic Constitution*). On the other hand, Vinay Sitapati explains that different states have different understandings of "other backward classes" ("Reservations," in *The Oxford Handbook of the Indian Constitution*, 722).

Robinson explains, "In contrast to the American Constitution, which largely solidified the economic and social status quo even while bringing momentous political changes, India's Constitution was born with an eye towards multiple transformations."[93] Moreover, as the 1994 *Bommai* decision discussed later reveals, such a transformative project on the national scale does not easily allow for significant deference to subnational units. However, separately from the federalism question, the general absence of anything like a duty to protect in the United States is worth noting. The American states could regulate gender-based violence as they wished, but they also could do nothing and face no repercussions, even as state actors. Thus, while the variable of federalism certainly influences constitutional argumentation and the larger story in the United States, the difference between *Morrison* and *Vishaka* also points toward a more basic difference that finds expression in Glendon's insight about the dearth of "duties talk" in the United States. Whereas the Indian Supreme Court in *Vishaka* mandated government action as a constitutional matter, the US Supreme Court rejected Congress's initiative as a constitutional matter.

Another case, which has an American analog in the decision of *Shelley v. Kramer*, may seem to undercut this chapter's argument at first blush. In 2005, the Indian Supreme Court decided *Zoroastrian Cooperative Housing Society v. District Registrar*.[94] This case involved a society that restricted membership only to Parsis. Since housing could only be transferred to members, the practical effect of the agreement was that only Parsis were permitted to buy houses in the cooperative society. Both cases thus involved housing restrictions on the basis of classifications that had particular political salience in their respective contexts – race in *Shelley*, and religion in *Zoroastrian Cooperative*. To this extent, comparing these cases offers a glimpse into how each polity has addressed fundamental questions of equality among citizens in the common area of housing.

Recall that the US Supreme Court decided *Shelley* based on the fact that the Court was an arm of the state and would have been implicated in discrimination contra the Fourteenth Amendment if it were to uphold the restrictive housing covenant. While the decision in *Shelley* technically toes the state action line and distinguishes between public and private spheres, the result clearly approaches and, according to some typologies, even represents a form of horizontal application. Indeed, the case is

---

[93] Robinson, "Expanding Judiciaries," 2–3.
[94] *Zoroastrian Cooperative Housing Society v. District Registrar* (2005) 5 SCC 632.

rightly understood as an anomaly in the long history of state action in the United States. And yet, the Court's conforming to the doctrine of state action still serves to turn attention away from the actual issue of the case, which was a private harm.

Perhaps surprisingly, the decision in *Zoroastrian Cooperative* more closely conforms to a strict state action line, at least in the particular outcome the Indian Supreme Court reaches. Rather than relying on the fact that the Court would in effect be upholding the restrictive housing covenant in deciding in favor of the cooperative society, the Court seems to engage the validity of the cooperative society's agreement itself. While the cooperative society argued its case on the basis of its right to association (Article 19(1)(c)) and minorities' right to cultural preservation (Article 29 (1)), the respondents argued that the restrictive covenant violated public policy, specifically Article 15 of the Constitution that prohibits discrimination in both public and private spaces. Thus, the arguments from both sides invited the kind of substantive analysis the US Supreme Court had avoided in *Shelley*. Although the Court ruled in favor of the cooperative society, however, it is unclear whether they based their decision on the constitutional rights to association and cultural preservation.

Legal scholars have acknowledged that the reasoning in *Zoroastrian Cooperative* is "obtuse,"[95] making it difficult to contend with and nearly impossible to come to any definitive conclusion about the controlling rationale.[96] For these reasons, as well as the potentially important fact that this case was decided only by a two-judge panel,[97] the present

---

[95] Gautam Bhatia, "Exclusionary Covenants and the Constitution – II: The Zoroastrian Co-op Case," *Indian Constitutional Law and Philosophy*, January 12, 2014, accessed January 25, 2019, https://indconlawphil.wordpress.com/2014/01/12/exclusionary-covenants-and-the-constitution-ii-the-zoroastrian-co-op-case, 2.

[96] Assessing the extent to which this particular case will serve as precedent in future similar cases requires acknowledging other contextual factors as well. For example, the Parsis are a minority religion in India and one that the public tends to view favorably. Moreover, the case of the housing cooperative was argued by a prominent Parsi lawyer who became the attorney general of India. (I am indebted to Tarunabh Khaitan for these insights.) Given these forces working in favor of the cooperative, it is not necessarily clear that the outcome of this case would be replicated under different circumstances. On the other hand, this fact is not so important to the present project as this book is concerned more with theoretic potential in constitutional arguments than with constitutional development per se.

[97] Article 145(3) of the Constitution of India suggests that cases decided by five or more judges are more authoritative than those decided by panels of only two or three. See also Andrew Green and Albert H. Yoon, "Triaging the Law: Developing the Common Law on the Supreme Court of India," *Journal of Empirical Legal Studies* 14:4 (2017), 706–710;

account of the case is necessarily tentative. There seem to be two lines of reasoning in *Zoroastrian Cooperative*. On the one hand, although the cooperative society's bylaw preventing the sale of land to non-Parsis had to conform with "public policy," the Court argued that conformity with relevant statutory law, namely the Gujarat Cooperative Societies Act,[98] rather than directly with the Constitution was sufficient. It states:

> So long as there is no legislative intervention of that nature [to eliminate a qualification for membership in the cooperative society based on sex or religion], it is not open to the court to coin a theory that a particular by-law is not desirable and would be opposed to public policy as indicated by the Constitution.[99]

Thus, the Court's argument amounts to a fairly robust state action requirement, insofar as it maintains some separation between parliament's ability to legislate private interchange and the Constitution. On this reading, parliament has wide discretion in setting the parameters of such societies without running the risk of implicating the state in any discrimination in which the society chooses to participate.[100] Indeed, it may legislate so as to permit such restrictive covenants among religious groups such as the Parsis in spite of the constitutional project to render such categories "legally irrelevant."[101] Put differently, private agreements such as the one among the Parsis of this housing cooperative were subject

---

Tarunabh Khaitan, "Equality: Legislative Review under Article 14," in *The Oxford Handbook of the Indian Constitution*; Gardbaum, "Horizontality in the Indian Constitution," 613.

[98] Bhatia, "Exclusionary Covenants and the Constitution – II: The Zoroastrian Co-op Case," 2.

[99] *Zoroastrian Cooperative Housing Society*, (2005) 5 SCC 632; see also Gardbaum, "Horizontality in the Indian Constitution," 611.

[100] Bhatia shows that this may have been inconsistent with prior judgments, however. He quotes the Court in *Delhi Transport Corporation v. DTC Mazdoor Congress*: "[I]n the absence of specific head of public policy which covers a case, then the court must in consonance with public conscience and in keeping with public good and public interest ... declare such practice or rules that are derogatory to the constitution to be opposed to public policy" (Bhatia, "Exclusionary Covenants and the Constitution – II: The Zoroastrian Co-op Case," 2). On this general point, Gardbaum suggests the greater discretion of the court may hinge on whether the legislation in question concerns a mandatory law, "in that the State is prescribing the compulsory terms of private legal relationships," or permissive law, in which "individuals set the terms of their private legal relationships and the State enforces them whatever they are" ("Horizontality in the Indian Constitution," 612).

[101] Bhatia, *The Transformative Constitution*, 122.

only to such regulatory legislation, and not necessarily the Constitution itself.[102]

Zoroastrian Cooperative thus seems to involve a similar reasoning as in *Shelley*, only reaching the opposite outcome, and even going further in that the state ultimately did uphold the covenant in question. Despite constitutional ends, such as rooting out discrimination and fostering equality, that might hold up public principles as a standard even for private projects, this episode (or at least this first reading of it) signals a kind of retreat to conventional understandings of rights contra the Constitution's transformative streak. The Court sidesteps both those constitutional provisions that would assign private actors some role in upholding constitutional commitments and those that call upon the legislature to make law in accord with the Constitution. Instead, the Court seems to carve out anew a space in which private actors may enter into contracts unencumbered by constitutional ends.[103]

An alternative reading of *Zoroastrian Cooperative* that is plausible, albeit underdeveloped in the Court's judgment, is that the Court did engage in constitutional balancing here, and that "its narrow conception of public policy was the *conclusion* and not the premise of its analysis."[104] In other words, the Court did question and ascertain that the cooperative society's particular bylaw conformed to the Constitution, and therefore proceeded on this basis to balance the rights to freedom of association and cultural preservation against the right to be free from discrimination. Indeed, there is some evidence for this in the judgment. The Court states:

> [I]t is open to that community to try to preserve its culture and way of life and in that process, to work for the advancement of members of that community by enabling them to acquire membership in a society and allotments of lands or buildings in one's capacity as a member of that society, to preserve its object of advancement of the community.[105]

---

[102] As Bhatia points out, the court does not seem to account for the fact that the Indian Contract Act does permit the invalidation of contracts and even exception to the enforcement of statutes that run up against public policy (*The Transformative Constitution*, 123).

[103] The stakes of this question come into sharper relief when we consider the perennial issue of housing discrimination in India. Indeed, discrimination on the basis of religion continues to be a problem in the rental and housing markets of many Indian metropolises (remote interview with Gautam Bhatia, March 24, 2021).

[104] Gardbaum, "Horizontality in the Indian Constitution," 612.

[105] *Zoroastrian Cooperative Housing Society*, (2005) 5 SCC 632, para. 33; see also Bhatia, "Exclusionary Covenants and the Constitution – II: The Zoroastrian Co-op Case," 4.

This discussion about preserving one's "culture and way of life" suggests that rights such as those found in Articles 19 and 29 did factor into the Court's judgment, and that the decision in *Zoroastrian Cooperative* did not hinge simply on the right of private actors to enter any manner of contract under statutory law. Rather than base its decision primarily on a state action requirement, the Court did apply these rights horizontally, in this reading. It simply came down in favor of the rights to association and cultural preservation, in this instance, rather than antidiscrimination. Apart from the fact that the Court seems to refer to these competing constitutional rights, this reading is further corroborated by the fact that contractual rights are, historically, not so prioritized as rights of association in Indian constitutionalism.[106] Moreover, which reading is "correct" may matter more for developmental stories than it does for the current theoretical project. That the latter reading of *Zoroastrian Cooperative* is even plausible demonstrates the theoretical potential for a republican interpretation of horizontality in Indian constitutional discourses.

If there is any merit to this second reading, then this case does involve horizontal application to a greater degree than does *Shelley*. Indeed, in this latter reading, *Zoroastrian Cooperative* actually takes up the constitutional substance of the question at stake rather than rely on the fact of judicial enforcement of contracts. One might question, then, how this decision that seemingly favors discrimination comports with the larger purpose of the Indian Constitution. Is not the Indian project founded on the goal of equality and fraternity among all constituent religions, ethnicities, and cultures? The key here may be the fact that the Parsis are a minority population in India. In a similar way, the American case *Wisconsin v. Yoder* allowed Amish communities to make alternative educational choices for their children, thus acknowledging a need to accommodate differences of particular populations, even as they may sit in some tension with other constitutional commitments. Indeed, such efforts toward accommodation are rooted in other constitutional commitments such as cultural preservation. This is not to say that rights of

---

[106] Bhatia, "Exclusionary Covenants and the Constitution – III: Zoroastrian Cooperative and Political Liberalism," *Indian Constitutional Law and Philosophy*, January 13, 2014, accessed January 25, 2019, https://indconlawphil.wordpress.com/2014/01/13/exclusionary-covenants-and-the-constitution-iii-zoroastrian-cooperative-and-political-liberalism. Bhatia points out that this has been the case since the debates of the Constituent Assembly.

association and cultural preservation would always trump rights of non-discrimination. It is unlikely, for example, that such majority populations as adherents to the Hindu faith would have succeeded with the same arguments, since Article 29 of the Constitution refers specifically to minorities' rights to cultural preservation. As Bhatia argues, the Indian Constitution actually "contains the tools to go one step beyond the solutions advanced in other jurisdictions" when it comes to horizontal discrimination, including restrictive covenants. Indeed, with such provisions as Article 15(2), it may bring the principles of equality and non-discrimination to bear directly on private actors engaging in a wide range of transactions, whenever constitutional actors are inclined to do so.[107]

Although one cannot easily sum up the *Zoroastrian Cooperative* case, one also cannot ignore it when considering the question of horizontal application in India, particularly given the case's implications for the larger constitutional objects of equality and nondiscrimination. There are good reasons to adopt different readings of the case and to believe that the case's outcome is circumscribed to the unique set of facts before the Court.[108] While one might be justified to draw conclusions about this case only hesitantly, the later case *Indian Medical Association v. Union of India (IMA)* sheds additional light on the arguments in *Zoroastrian Cooperative*. Whereas *Shelley* is a high-water mark for horizontality in the United States, *Zoroastrian Cooperative* seems to be only one episode in what could be an ongoing thread, pending Court members' understanding of the Constitution's ends and, consequently, their receptivity to the republican elements of horizontality. And indeed, in the *IMA* case that followed a few years later, we see a convergence of discourses concerning the different commitments of Indian

---

[107] Bhatia, *The Transformative Constitution*, 128–131, grounds this argument in the court's capacious reading of Article 15(2)'s term "shops" in *Indian Medical Association v. Union of India* (2011) 7 SCC 179, paras. 112–113. In turn, the court's interpretation grows directly out of the constitutional debates.

[108] Bhatia, "Exclusionary Covenants and the Constitution – IV: Article 15(2), *IMA v. UoI*, and the Constitutional Case against Racially/Religiously Restrictive Covenants," *Indian Constitutional Law and Philosophy*, January 14, 2014, accessed January 25, 2019, https://indconlawphil.wordpress.com/2014/01/14/exclusionary-covenants-and-the-constitution-iv-article-152-ima-v-uoi-and-the-constitutional-case-against-raciallyreligiously-restrictive-covenants, 1. Bhatia explains that "the correctness of Zoroastrian Cooperative rests upon Article 19(1)(c) [freedom of association] read with Article 29 [rights of groups to preserve their culture], and is therefore grounded in its own set of specific facts. It does not serve as precedent for the legality and enforceability of restrictive covenants qua contracts, more generally."

constitutionalism – specifically, to the rights enumerated in Part III and the more compensatory scheme of social justice in Part IV. In this later case, the deciding members of the Supreme Court showed themselves willing to engage all parts of the constitutional project. Moreover, in this case the Court employed horizontal application and did so through a republican manner of argument.

Emerging Duties under the Transformative Constitution

A few antecedent battles in Indian constitutional history laid crucial groundwork for the *IMA* case and expansion of horizontal application. In its early years, the Indian Supreme Court's judgments showed a kind of "static" interpretation of the Constitution.[109] This manifested in its drawn-out battle with parliament, including such episodes as the passing of the First Amendment and the *Kesavananda* case. Moreover, this static interpretation manifested in the Court's early horizontal application decisions, which adhered to a state action requirement with respect to Part III of the Constitution. As Jacobsohn and Roznai explain, "[T]he Court became the perfect embodiment of the disharmonies within the Constitution, as it found itself over time on both sides of the tension inherent in the dual commitment to socio-economic transformation and liberal democratic rights."[110] Such cases as *People's Union* after the Emergency Era and, later on, *Vishaka* show some shift in the discourse on the reach of Part III rights. While *Zoroastrian Cooperative* displays adherence to a strict state action rationale, the obscure nature of this decision could be interpreted as additional evidence of a break from prior understandings, at least among some constitutional actors. In contrast with what some readings of *Zoroastrian Cooperative* might by themselves suggest, later cases reveal some willingness to develop horizontal application further. In particular, the Court has incorporated Part IV of the Constitution, containing the Directive Principles, into its own constitutional purview, a development which certainly bears on the way actors discuss the horizontal application of rights to private actors.

In 1994, the Court decided *S. R. Bommai v. Union of India*, what has been described as the "linchpin in Nehru's step-by-step progression."[111] The case arose amid ongoing violence between Hindus and Muslims

---

[109] Jacobsohn and Roznai, *Constitutional Revolution*, 145.
[110] Ibid., 157.
[111] Ibid., 166.

following the destruction of a mosque in Ayodhya in the State of Uttar Pradesh. The party in power in the state, the Hindu nationalist BJP, was clearly complicit in its negligence to quell the violence. And so, pursuant to Article 356 of the Constitution, the president of India assumed rule over the state. When the state challenged this action, the Supreme Court explained that, in its failure to take steps to put down the violence, the BJP-led government demonstrated that it "could not be trusted to follow the objective of secularism which was part of the basic structure of the Constitution and also the soul of the Constitution."[112] Furthermore, since the Constitution "does not provide for its own demise,"[113] the president's actions were justified as necessary to save the basic structure of the Constitution, including such fundamental principles as secularism as an instrument of equality and the larger catalog of Directive Principles in Part IV.

In *Bommai*, the Court extended the Basic Structure Doctrine of *Kesavananda* beyond constitutional amendments to bear on the actions political actors pursue in the course of ordinary politics. Put differently, apart from the electoral repercussions politicians risk in ignoring the Directive Principles, the decision in *Bommai* established that "a Government will also have to answer for ignoring the Directive Principles of State Policy in a court of law."[114] In this way, the Court embraced within its purview the same Directive Principles previously considered unenforceable, realizing a conviction that motivated many in the Constituent Assembly, namely, that the soul of the Constitution included both Part III and Part IV.[115] *Bommai* thus marks an important moment in the larger constitutional revolution of which Nehru spoke, and a significant point of distinction from the US *DeShaney* case. Specifically, it rendered state *in*action respecting the Directive Principles constitutionally liable and subject to the judgment of the Supreme Court. Moreover, *Bommai* set the stage for applications of horizontality that also incorporated the Directive Principles, as became evident in the *IMA* case.

In *IMA*,[116] the Supreme Court applied *Bommai* to the effect of embracing a transformative constitutional understanding, specifically

---

[112] S. R. Bommai v. Union of India, at 143.
[113] Ibid., at 237.
[114] Jacobsohn and Roznai, *Constitutional Revolution*, 170–171.
[115] Ibid., 158; see also *Minerva Mills v. Union of India*; Shruti Rajagopalan, "Constitutional Change: A Public Choice Analysis," in *The Oxford Handbook of the Indian Constitution*, 138.
[116] *Indian Medical Assn. v. Union of India*, (2011) 7 SCC 179; see also Raj, "Private Discrimination," 26–30.

understanding duties of private actors as emerging not only from some of the rights enumerated in Part III but also potentially from the Directive Principles of Part IV. In short, the Court in *IMA* brought the Basic Structure Doctrine to bear on parliament's efforts to effectuate the Directive Principles by way of constitutional amendment. In addition to the usual issues surrounding the enforceability of social policy and the practice of reservations in particular, however, the Court faced the additional question of how such initiatives applied horizontally. Specifically, it considered the validity of the Ninety-Third Amendment to the Constitution, adopted in 2005, that laid groundwork for legislatures to extend to private actors the charge to maintain reservations in education – essentially guaranteeing a requisite level of representation across spheres of life for members of castes and other groups that had faced systematic disadvantage in Indian society. The Amendment added a fifth section to Article 15 of the Constitution that read:

> Nothing in this article or in sub-clause (g) of clause (1) of article 19 shall prevent the State from making any special provision, by law, for the advancement of any socially and educationally backward classes of citizens or for the Scheduled Castes or the Scheduled Tribes in so far as such special provisions relate to their admission to educational institutions *including private educational institutions, whether aided or unaided by the State*, other than the minority educational institutions referred to in clause (1) of article 30.[117]

Similar to the First Amendment discussed above, this Ninety-Third Amendment aimed to ensure that Article 15's guarantee of formal equality would not be deployed against efforts to realize a more substantive equality. However, that this Amendment applied to *both* public and private educational institutions made it importantly different from prior constitutional developments. Indeed, this Amendment directed the momentum of more capacious understandings of the constitutional project toward private spaces, specifically private educational institutions. Whereas the division between Part III and Part IV of the Constitution (as well as other divisions, as between Article 15(1) and Article 15(2)) had provided grounds on which to circumscribe an already limited conception of horizontal application, the Ninety-Third Amendment began to break down some of these divisions, acknowledging that some constitutional ends would implicate private actors.

---

[117] Constitution of India, Article 15, Section 5, emphasis added. Again see Siegel, "Equality Talk," for a discussion on similar issues in the United States.

Pursuant to this new amendment, the Delhi Act of 2007 prohibited certain educational fees and mandated that a number of seats in all educational institutions be reserved for "Scheduled Castes, Scheduled Tribes and other socially and economically backward classes."[118] In the very next year, a private, unaided professional school in Delhi, called the Army College of Medical Sciences, was founded, admitting to their student body only "wards, or children of current and former army personnel and widows of army personnel, who, the school's defenders claimed, had experienced educational disadvantages relative to the civilian population."[119] The school ranked applicants according to their test scores, but made no distinction on the basis of social, economic, or cultural background, other than meeting the army personnel requirement. Therefore, while the population the school aimed to serve might have faced disadvantages of their own, the school's admission policy did not necessarily benefit those populations belonging to the castes and backward groups the Delhi Act and, by extension, the Ninety-Third Amendment aimed to protect. The appellant argued that the law and amendment were both contrary to the basic structure of the Constitution insofar as they constituted "unreasonable restrictions" under Article 19 (detailing the "Right to Freedom") and were likely to destroy the freedom to maintain such unaided nonminority educational institutions.[120]

In prior years, the Court might have invoked the Basic Structure Doctrine of *Kesavananda* to uphold a more limited or "static" equality that favored the Army College of Medical Sciences' case. Instead, however, the Court followed *Bommai* in that it acknowledged parliament's efforts to implement the Directive Principles and thereby secure a more substantive equality as part and parcel of the larger constitutional project. In this understanding, the Ninety-Third Amendment did not betray the Basic Structure Doctrine, but rather moved the country forward in a protracted constitutional revolution. Moreover, the particular fact that the Amendment and subsequent law included such private institutions as the Army College of Medical Sciences in its efforts to achieve greater

---

[118] Jacobsohn and Roznai, *Constitutional Revolution*, 176fn107.
[119] Ibid., 184.
[120] *Indian Medical Assn. v. Union of India*, (2011) 7 SCC 179, para. 70. While proponents of horizontality should welcome the expansion of horizontality that *Indian Medical Association* constitutes, the facts of this case are such that they might incline even proponents to seek out bounds around this constitutional practice. Specifically, the case's outcome precludes private actors from prioritizing disadvantaged groups that are not among those explicitly delineated by the constitutional project.

equality did not detract from the constitutional vision. Rather, this effort to reach into private spaces was in line with the vision many in the Constituent Assembly articulated – to bring private actors into the fold of the constitutional project and inculcate a conception of fraternity among citizens. Insofar as abuse occurred and inequality existed without distinction between public and private spaces, so too must the Constitution ultimately reach these spaces. The Court seems to adopt this position for itself in the *IMA* case, directly speaking to the relationship between constitutional ends and duties of citizens. It states, "[T]he same concerns of national purpose, goal and objectives that inform the constitutional identity [do not] miraculously disappear in the context of the private sector."[121]

Furthermore, the Amendment in question not only was consistent with the Constitution, in the Court's telling, but actually augmented the fundamental constitutional project that had long aimed at transforming the private sphere to effect equality and even fraternity among citizens. Even apart from the new Clause 5 the Ninety-Third Amendment added to Article 15, the Court briefly acknowledged how the preexistent Clause 2 in Article 15 also serves to ground the Delhi Act of 2007.[122] While, prima facie, this provision simply provides recourse for discrimination in "access to shops, public restaurants, hotels and places of public entertainment," the Court finds in Article 15(2) nothing less than the Constitution's "conception of social justice," a conception meant to apply more extensively than standard definitions of "shops" might suggest.[123] Indeed, the Court maintained, one must read this provision in the context of the polity's "national aspirations of establishing a society in which Equality of status and opportunity, and Justice, social, economic and political." Understood through this lens, private establishments must "not contribute to the perpetuation of unwarranted social disadvantages associated with the functioning of the social, cultural and economic order."[124] The Army College of Medical Sciences was perpetuating such disadvantages by not considering the disparate impact their admission standards had on different populations, thereby hampering the Constitution's end of substantive equality.[125]

---

[121] *Indian Medical Assn. v. Union of India,* (2011) 7 SCC 179, para. 108.
[122] Ibid., paras. 112–114.
[123] Ibid., para. 112; see also Bhatia, *The Transformative Constitution,* 131–139.
[124] *Indian Medical Assn. v. Union of India,* (2011) 7 SCC 179, para. 113.
[125] Ibid., para. 114.

This effort to bring equality into private spaces took many forms over the years, involving different rights from Part III and, as in *IMA*, different Directive Principles from Part IV. Moreover, that the question of horizontal application occurred in the specific area of education was not particularly surprising. Insofar as many Indian schools are privately run, bringing education into line with constitutional ends could not but raise the question of horizontal application. Education was a natural sector in which to give effect to constitutional commitments, as education influences so much of the life and future of a polity, as well as how citizens relate to one another and relate to the Constitution. The upshot of such regulation was that schools, including private schools, faced a real call to action when the Delhi Act required the implementation of reservations. This application of horizontality was never going to be instantaneous or effortless. Indeed, these regulations entailed a fundamental shift in the mission of the Army College of Medical Sciences as initially conceived. But then, the Indian Constitution was never going to be an instantaneous or effortless project. As Jacobsohn and Roznai explain, "Since the greatest potential societal effect of group-based admissions policies implicates the private domain, it is only appropriate that a case confronting that issue directly became the occasion for instructive reflection on India's constitutional revolution."[126] Thus, more than any of the preceding decisions that implicated the question of horizontal application, the *IMA* case shows a clear shift from rights-centric understandings to republicanesque discourses concerning constitutional ends and how those ends involve the cooperation of private actors.

The Future of Horizontal Application?

Observers of Indian constitutional politics may find a worksite for the continued development of horizontal rights in questions of religion – an ongoing issue that strikes at the heart of India's constitutional project. Scholars have described religion in India as "thick" insofar as it occupies a central role in public life in comparison to many other countries today.[127] Many religious practices also stand at odds with constitutional commitments to equality, propagating systems of caste and gender discrimination, for example. Thus, insofar as it adopts a transformative

---

[126] Jacobsohn and Roznai, *Constitutional Revolution*, 175.
[127] Bhatia, *The Transformative Constitution*; Gary Jacobsohn, *The Wheel of Law* (Princeton: Princeton University Press, 2009).

vision, the Indian Constitution could not avoid confrontation with religion.[128] The practical complexity of such reform is clear, as religion is deeply constitutive of many diverse people's lives and even daily habits.[129] Additionally, a kind of theoretical complexity accompanies these issues. In any context, religion serves to introduce an alternate and independent set of standards – one might even say an alternate set of laws – to the conversation.[130] Thus, whereas questions of horizontality always involve balancing, the particular issue of religion raises unique challenges as religious communities within a polity maintain potentially different understandings of, say, the common good. One necessarily confronts the question of whether and how religious groups should be treated like other nonstate actors such as businesses or private employers. While all countries confront such questions in some form, they become more salient in contexts like India, where religion plays a thick role in daily life and constitutional understandings assume ameliorative or transformative ends.[131]

The question of the relationship between religion and politics is as old as both religion and politics. However, to adapt the question to the terms of this book, we might ask how horizontality's function to apply public norms across the polity comprehends the existing norms of religion. To the extent one understands liberalism as requiring a kind of sequestration of religion to a separate private sphere, both for its own sake and for the sake of civil peace, this issue might serve to reveal the reach and usefulness of this book's republican framework. In short, while a constitution inspired by conventional liberal accounts would likely preserve wider latitude for religious practices, a constitution assuming the republican elements that this book identifies with horizontality may be more inclined to take on the moral question of balancing religious and civil

---

[128] Jacobsohn, *The Wheel of Law*.
[129] See Gary Jacobsohn's analysis of the Directive Principles and the Uniform Civil Code in "India: The Ameliorative Aspiration," in *The Wheel of Law*, 91–124.
[130] See Ran Hirschl's discussion of these issues in *Comparative Matters* (Oxford: Oxford University Press, 2014).
[131] This is in contrast with such countries as the United States where religion is generally "thinner." On Jacobsohn's telling, "[T]he greatest assurance that the protection of diversity for all *religious* beliefs will be taken seriously – including those beliefs that violate the spirit of the "self-evident' principles underlying the constitutional agreement – lies in the achievement of *political* assimilation" (*The Wheel of Law*, 58–59).

norms against one another. More specific to the Indian context, the Constitution guarantees both freedom of conscience (Article 25) and group rights that allow a religious denomination to "manage its own affairs in matters of religion" (Article 26).[132] At the same time, both Articles 25 and 26 include limitation clauses that admit of some state regulation of religious practices. Unsurprisingly, these dual commitments have come into conflict time and again. The question, for Indian constitutional actors, is how to adjudicate these sometimes-diverging commitments.

These musings necessarily raise the question of horizontal application and, more specifically, the obligations of religious denominations vis-à-vis constitutional commitments to equality and antidiscrimination. The question comes into sharp relief in the 2018 case *Indian Young Lawyers' Association v. State of Kerala*, often called the *Sabarimala* case, considering whether overseers of the Sabarimala Temple should be made to admit women in spite of the long practice of barring women between the ages of ten and fifty. Indeed, the controversy goes back decades and has continued to be disputed even after the 2018 judgment.[133] The Supreme Court's current habit in such cases is to weigh whether the practice in question constitutes an "essential religious practice."[134] If the Court deems something "essential," then that practice remains protected from regulation under Articles 25 and 26. If not, then that religious denomination incurs duties to adjust their practices to align better with, say, the constitutional principle of equality. And indeed, the Court decided in the *Sabarimala* case that restrictions to temple entry were not essential to Hinduism and, on this basis, regulable.

In some ways, the essential religious practices test seems deferential toward religion, permitting those practices that run up against

---

[132] Interestingly, the Indian ambassador to South Africa advised parties in the South African constitutional negotiations in 1993 to include a commission on considering the protection of minority groups in their constitution insofar as South Africa was contending with similar diversity. Ultimately, after extensive debates, the Constitutional Assembly opted only to include individual rights rather than group rights in the Final Constitution. However, Chapter 9, Section 185 of the Final Constitution does establish the Commission for the Promotion and Protection of the Rights of Cultural, Religious, and Linguistic Communities (remote interview with Sheila Camerer, March 3, 2021; remote interview with Nicholas Haysom, October 26, 2020).
[133] "Congress Proposes Law to Bar Entry of All Women to Sabarimala Shrine," *The Federal*, February 7, 2021, accessed April 25, 2021, https://thefederal.com/states/south/kerala/congress-proposes-law-to-bar-entry-of-all-women-to-sabarimala-shrine.
[134] Bhatia, *The Transformative Constitution*, 146–155.

constitutional commitments if they are *essential*.[135] As with any issue raising the question of horizontality, however, religious authorities may still be called to support such public projects as promoting equality, as we saw in the *Sabarimala* case. The essential religious practices test poses unique challenges, moreover, in that it entangles the Court in "knotty questions of religious and theological doctrine."[136] Indeed, some criticize the merits of this doctrinal test on the very basis that it charges the state with evaluating and defining the content of religion.[137] Gautam Bhatia, for example, proposes an antiexclusion principle to decide such cases, calling on the Court instead to determine how religious practices bear on secular ends, rather than try to discern the essential practices that should be a matter internal to a given religion.

In addition to being grounded in text and history, an antiexclusion principle avoids the difficulty of a court attempting to discern a religion's essential practices. Instead, this principle operates on a basis that the Constitution itself adopts and cognizes. Arguably, in this understanding a republican logic is more pronounced, as nonstate actors are held to account for the constitutional project regardless of how it might bear on their religion. Put differently, the antiexclusion principle explicitly operates from the perspective of the state, whereas the essential practices test at least presumes to operate from the perspective of the religion in question, in spite of the aforementioned difficulties of this approach. While the antiexclusion principle is more upfront in its prioritization of constitutional principles, this posture may well be constitutive of any project understood as transformational. In a similar vein, Bhatia explains:

> [T]he constitutional text itself exhibits reformist intentions; and scholars of Indian secularism have repeatedly differentiated it from its liberal

---

[135] Along similar lines, Chiara Cordelli argues that a "right to democracy" ought to be enforced even within "large and hierarchical churches," and that "this right is not overruled by claims to freedom of religious association and church autonomy." Interestingly, Cordelli's account hinges on an ability to distinguish between essential and nonessential beliefs or practices, imposing democratic norms only on the nonessential in order to preserve some autonomy of religious organizations. In other words, she wants to "democratize organized religion, but stops short of imposing substantive egalitarian norms on churches" (Cordelli, "Democratizing Organized Religion," *Journal of Politics* 79:2 (2017), 587).

[136] Bhatia, *The Transformative Constitution*, 167.

[137] In some ways this may invite comparison with a kind of Rousseauian account of civil religion (*The Social Contract, Book IV*, chap. 8).

Western counterpart, noting its "ameliorative" or "contextual" nature, which specifically envisages State intervention into religion in order to achieve certain substantive values.[138]

While a transformative project is likely to call for a prioritization of public values in most any context, this seems especially true in a country like India where the project itself has been defined in terms of reshaping deeply rooted religious practices. Put differently, such a transformative project as found in India, by definition, prioritizes the ultimate realization of constitutional ends over certain religious practices.

Cecile Laborde argues in favor of treating religion differently from how "separationist" models, such as the essential religious practices test, propose. Specifically, she argues for a "minimal secularism," maintaining that religion ought not to be singled out for special treatment when it clashes with public projects, particularly "liberal democratic ideals."[139] Rather, in her telling, religion should be subject to regulation in much the same way as any other area of life. Evidence of such alternative approaches seems to be present in both India's constitutional text and history. In fact, a couple of justices have hit upon a similar approach in their judgments – specifically, Chief Justice Sinha in his dissent from the 1962 case *Saifuddin v. State of Bombay*, and Justice Chandrachud in his concurrence to the *Sabarimala* judgment. Both judges focus on the impact of each respective case on the public project of antiexclusion, as Bhatia and Laborde advocate, rather than have their argument hinge on any elaboration of religious doctrine.[140]

Another emergent issue that potentially triggers horizontal application is the rights of same-sex couples. In 2009, the Delhi High Court decided *Naz Foundation v. Union of India*, overturning a colonial-era provision in the penal code that criminalized homosexual activity on the basis of Article 14 (Equality Before Law), Article 15 (Prohibition of Discrimination), and Article 21 (Protection of Life and Personal Liberty).[141] Soon after the case was decided, Tarunabh Khaitan described

---

[138] Bhatia, *The Transformative Constitution*, 154.
[139] Cécile Laborde, "Minimal Secularism: Lessons for, and from, India," *American Political Science Review* 115:1 (2021), 3.
[140] Bhatia, *The Transformative Constitution*, 166–168.
[141] In its decision, the Delhi High Court goes out of its way to treat discrimination on the basis of sexual orientation in private spaces. See para. 104: "Article 15(2) incorporates the notion of horizontal application of rights. In other words, it even prohibits discrimination of one citizen by another in matters of access to public spaces. In our view, discrimination on the ground of sexual orientation is impermissible even on the

the judgment as a natural conclusion given the principles of the Indian Constitution. He states, "Given the liberal, secular and egalitarian Constitution of India, it is the opposite result that would have surprised constitutional lawyers."[142] And yet, that is exactly what the Supreme Court did four years later. In *Koushal v. Naz Foundation,* the Supreme Court overturned the Delhi High Court's 2009 decision and, with it, what Khaitan had described as a "new deal for all minorities."[143] The Court cited in its reasoning the "principle of presumption of constitutionality" of legislation and the need to ground important decisions in the principles of the Indian polity rather than of foreign jurisdictions (as the Delhi Court had).[144] Finally, in the back-and-forth fashion that, Jacobsohn and Roznai argue, defines the arc of India's constitutional history, the Supreme Court revisited the issue in 2018, this time ruling in favor of decriminalization. The Court stated:

> [T]he Indian Constitution is first and foremost a social document. The majority of its provisions are either directly aimed at furthering the goals of the social revolution or attempt to foster this revolution by establishing the conditions necessary for its achievement ... The Constitution of India recognises, protects and celebrates diversity. To stigmatise or to criminalise homosexuals only on account of their sexual orientation would be against the constitutional morality.[145]

In this way, the Court ultimately argued in its unanimous decision that "the constitutional morality" required this new application of the equality principle in India.[146]

Insofar as the decriminalization of homosexual activity involved questions about the penal code, this particular sequence of cases implicated

---

horizontal application of the right enshrined under Article 15." See also Tarunabh Khaitan, "Reading *Swaraj* into Article 15: A New Deal for All Minorities," *NUJS Law Review* 2:3 (2009), 427–429.

[142] Khaitan, "Reading *Swaraj* into Article 15," 420.
[143] Ibid., *Suresh Kumar Koushal & Anr v. Naz Foundation & Ors*, AIR 2014 SC 563.
[144] Jacobsohn and Roznai, *Constitutional Revolution*, 262.
[145] *Navtej Singh Johar and Others v. Union of India*, AIR 2018 SC 4321, para. 80; see also ibid., 266.
[146] Some maintain that strategic motives also underlie this judgment. Specifically, outgoing Chief Justice Deepak Misra desired to leave his post on a high note after facing criticism for being progovernment. This case proved to be an easy win insofar as activists had already done much to change public perception with respect to gay rights, and the government at this point did not seek to defend the penal code. Indeed, the court would have been unlikely to decide the case differently (remote interview with Gautam Bhatia, March 24, 2021).

only the state and state action. Nonetheless, the Court seized upon the opportunity in its 2018 decision to lay groundwork to extend rights obligations further. It stated:

> It is not only the duty of the State and the Judiciary to protect this basic right to dignity, but *the collective at large also owes a responsibility to respect one another's dignity*, for showing respect for the dignity of another is a constitutional duty. It is an expression of the component of *constitutional fraternity*.[147]

From the beginning, the Indian constitutional vision was one of "fraternity." In this light, it is somewhat unsurprising that the Court would gesture toward implications for private actors even as the case itself created obligations only for the state. As a practical matter, this digression in the Court's argument may foreshadow future moves to hold public accommodations accountable for this extension of the Constitution to gay rights, contingent, of course, on individual justices' inclination to develop horizontal application further and to do so in the particular arena of gay rights.[148]

Apart from laying judicial groundwork for horizontality in such dicta described above, a symbolic element pervades this and other decisions,[149] in a way similar to how the Constitution itself includes both material and expressive elements. In discussing the significance of the Directive

---

[147] *Nautej Singh Johar and Others v. Union of India*, AIR 2018 SC 4321, para. 134, emphasis added.

[148] As explained earlier, the proclivities of individual justices, arguably, are an even more important consideration in the Indian context than other jurisdictions insofar as cases of the Indian Supreme Court are assigned and decided in panels. (For a related discussion, see Green and Yoon, "Triaging the Law.") This means that the future development of horizontality depends on cases that raise the issue at all being assigned to justices inclined to develop the practice further. The fact that Justice Dhananjaya Chandrachud assumed the role of chief justice in November 2022 bodes somewhat well for horizontality in India as he wrote the concurring judgment that would apply Article 17 horizontally in *Indian Young Lawyers' Association v. State of Kerala*, also known as the *Sabarimala* case. Of course, other important variables remain in play, including party and institutional relations and even the pipeline of cases (remote interview with Gautam Bhatia, March 24, 2021).

[149] The Court speaks similarly in a couple of other passages in the 2018 judgment. See para. 52: "In a constitutional democracy committed to the protection of individual dignity and autonomy, the state and every individual has a duty to act in a manner that advances and promotes the constitutional order of values"; and para. 250: "To change the societal bias and root out the weed, it is the foremost duty of each one of us to — stand up and speak up against the slightest form of discrimination against transgenders that we come across."

Principles, Marc Galanter explains, "The compensatory discrimination policy is not to be judged only for its instrumental qualities. It is also expressive: through it Indians tell themselves what kind of people they are and what kind of nation."[150] In a similar vein, in the most influential understandings of the Indian constitutional project, the public and the private were never essentially distinct; rather, both spheres speak equally and speak together to what "kind of people" and "what kind of nation" India aims to be.

Conclusion

While it would be an overstatement to say that Indian constitutionalism includes a developed practice of horizontality, this chapter shows certain republican theoretic themes in the discourse that have the potential to support more extensive horizontality, particularly with respect to equality rights. In various episodes, constitutional actors have connected the success of the constitutional project with what transpires in private spaces. From the arguments of such crucial figures as B. R. Ambedkar to the 2011 *IMA* case, understandings of private actors as having constitutional duties emerge. Indeed, some constitutional actors have understood such duties to emerge not only from those rights enumerated in Part III but also potentially from the Directive Principles of Part IV. Contrast this with the early adoption of a strict vertical model in the United States. That there exists a separate private sphere not subject to constitutional standards steers much of the discourse in that context. This is true even in spite of arguments of the Civil Rights Movement premised on more ambitious understandings of equality and of citizens' duties. In both contexts we find some republican potential in early formulations and ensuing debates concerning equality's horizontal application. As courts and constitutional actors continually question whether horizontality emerges from the constitution, however, the discourses in these two constitutional orders tend to exhibit different presuppositions – namely, presupposing vertical relations in the United States, and admitting, or creating, space for some understanding of horizontal relations in India.

---

[150] Galanter, *Competing Equalities*, 562; see also Brettschneider, *When the State Speaks*. The theme of expressive value that some perceive in applying rights horizontally will recur throughout these chapters.

CONCLUSION

The aforementioned cases notwithstanding, the Indian Supreme Court has not frequently enforced constitutional commitments to equality and antidiscrimination in its case law. Likewise, these commitments have often proven not to take root in civil society as a practical matter, as evinced in ongoing social boycotts and the lack of national antidiscrimination law.[151] However, these established constitutional commitments continually inform debates to presuppose that public ends bear on private spaces and that private entities may have constitutional duties. Recurring in Indian constitutional discourse, including in official accounts, is an understanding of equality as seeking more substance, and as aiming toward fraternity among citizens. In this way, Indian constitutionalism points toward a horizontal project, and one that constitutional actors frequently articulate in republican terms.

---

[151] The Anti-Discrimination and Equality Bill was introduced by Shashi Tharoor, MP, in 2017 but lapsed with the dissolution of the Lok Sabha (Tarunabh Khaitan, "Anti-Discrimination Bill Project," accessed September 13, 2022, https://sites.google.com/site/tarunabh/Home/discrimination-law).

Transformation
How Far Does the Constitution Apply Horizontally?

Chapters 3 and 4 have examined debates in the United States and India over the simple question of whether constitutional rights can be applied horizontally. Both nations have faced the decision of whether equality rights may be enforced in privately owned spaces such as public accommodations and housing. In the *Civil Rights Cases*, the US Supreme Court roundly rejected Congress's efforts to give horizontal application to equality. Against Justice Harlan's admonitions that such protections were requisite to republican citizenship, Justice Bradley and the rest of the Court argued that relegating the reach of this right to state actors only was necessary if the country was to avoid "another kind of slavery." Meanwhile, state constitutions have generally had more latitude to apply rights horizontally, even if they have not always done so. Moreover, horizontal interpretations of constitutional rights have emerged in popular understandings and discourses in such moments as the Civil Rights Movement. Expressly concerned with cultivating fraternity among citizens, on the other hand, the Indian framers, provided for the application of equality rights against private actors in Article 15 of the Constitution. While this right to equality has taken time to be activated in private spaces as a practical matter, observers of Indian constitutional politics perceive further development of horizontal application in line with these early foundations. Nevertheless, this is far from an established practice in Indian constitutional law and politics, and so the question of how horizontal application grows out of the Constitution remains a live one.

Chapters 5 and 6 center on the slightly different question of the *extent* to which the constitution applies horizontally in new contexts, again examining how republican-inflected discourses emerge in debates. In both Germany and South Africa, the question of whether the constitution applied horizontally was answered early on and can be taken as granted. Therefore, rather than ask whether horizontality had any role in the constitutional plan, debates in these contexts have been more concerned with the *extent* and *limits* of horizontal application – to what rights, to what actors, and under what circumstances.

The debates these chapters recount also tend to treat horizontal application as a mechanism to transform private spaces, as the Constitutions of both Germany and South Africa were drafted in pursuit of immense societal transformation.[1] Confronting histories of systemic injustice and genocide, constitutional actors in both countries enshrined values such as human dignity with power to govern across public and private spheres and even to establish duties for both public and private actors. From drafters to judges, constitutional actors pointed toward a need for parity in the way these values governed across spheres, establishing a common standard or, in republican terms, a kind of common good for a wider scope of the polity. The practice of horizontality was treated as not merely another tool to protect rights, but one that could facilitate transformative ends. What specifically this would mean for private actors' duties, however, remained a question.

Early on, each country departed from the conventional liberal logic that rights only created obligations for the state. The German Federal Constitutional Court introduced indirect horizontal effect, or *Drittwirkung,* soon after its institution in the *Lüth* case. Moreover, South African constitutional framers explicitly provided for horizontal application in the Final Constitution. The constitutional discourses that unfolded after each country's founding moment reveal aspirations among some to create a new kind of society. German scholar Georg Sommeregger describes horizontality in terms of promoting a kind of constitutional morality or introducing "society's common moral yardstick" into private spaces.[2] Moreover, he characterizes the later expansion of horizontal application to equality rights as part of a process of "enlarging the circle of members of the polis."[3] Similarly, Nick Friedman argues how South Africa's doctrine of horizontal application was part and parcel of the Constitution's transformative project.[4]

In both contexts, however, horizontal application was also contested from the beginning. Academics and jurists alike debated the virtues and

---

[1] Jacobsohn and Roznai, *Constitutional Revolution,* 111–112.
[2] Georg Sommeregger, "The Horizontalization of Equality: The German Attempt to Promote Non-discrimination in the Private Sphere via Legislation," in *The Constitution in Private Relations,* ed. András Sajó and Renáta Uitz (Utrecht: Eleven, 2005), 53.
[3] Ibid., 49.
[4] Nick Friedman, "The South African Common Law and the Constitution: Revisiting Horizontality," *South African Journal on Human Rights* 30:1 (2014), 67.

vices of this new legal-constitutional mechanism. Would accepting the Basic Law as a standard for Germany's entire legal system threaten its time-honored civil law and specialized courts? Would horizontal application usurp the function of the South African legislature to decide political questions and such matters as appropriations? What would become of individual autonomy if private actors were now also responsible for protecting and promoting constitutional rights? As Frank Michelman puts it, the "ghosts" of the conventional liberal wisdom persisted in constitutional discourse in different ways,[5] even as both constitutions committed to real and thoroughgoing transformation. Most obviously, courts in both Germany and South Africa have predominantly practiced indirect, rather than direct, horizontal application, ostensibly creating a buffer in the way public values come to bear on private actors. Perhaps the German courts had particular incentive to tread lightly as no national high court had previously claimed the ability to apply constitutional rights horizontally in the 1950s.[6]

Actors argued for further limits to horizontal application based on their interpretations of the constitutional projects. For example, certain corners of the German legal world have long valued autonomy (*Privatautonomie*). While this value has certainly undergone transformation in legal discourse since the reframing of the Civil Code in the nineteenth century, constitutional drafters recommitted to such individual rights in the wake of the Second World War. Likewise, elements of a conventional liberal wisdom have lived on in constitutional discourses, including in ways that touch on horizontal application. This translates to the way constitutional actors have treated claims of equality and nondiscrimination differently from other rights. For example, equality and nondiscrimination were long adjudicated according to the lower standard of reasonableness review, while most enumerated freedoms in the German Basic Law enjoyed more robust proportionality review.[7]

---

[5] Frank Michelman, "Constitutions and the Public/Private Divide," in *Oxford Handbook of Comparative Constitutional Law*, ed. Michel Rosenfeld and András Sajó (Oxford: Oxford University Press, 2012), 304.

[6] Alec Stone Sweet and Kathleen Stranz, "Rights Adjudication and Constitutional Pluralism in Germany and Europe," *Journal of European Public Policy* 19:1 (2012), 92–108. Some exceptions are the treatment of speech in the Weimar Constitution and in new state constitutions before the adoption of the Basic Law. See Peter Quint, "Free Speech and Private Law in German Constitutional Theory," *Maryland Law Review* 48:2 (1989), 258.

[7] Stone Sweet and Stranz, "Rights Adjudication," 100. This early treatment of equality is often attributed to the law professor and justice of the Constitutional Court Gerhard

Moreover, the few times that rights related to equality were applied in private spaces occurred through the Federal Labor Court rather than the Constitutional Court, or directives of the European Council requiring heightened antidiscrimination policies in Member States. Only recently has the Constitutional Court itself taken up this question, most notably in the 2018 *Stadium Ban* case.[8] While horizontality itself has long been accepted in Germany, its application to equality rights continues to be a subject of debate, frequently treated as running up against private autonomy.[9] Indeed, unlike the state, private individuals are "free to decide who they favor or disadvantage, with whom to conclude contracts and to whom to grant access to their property, their pub or their hotel."[10]

On the other hand, equality has featured more prominently in South African constitutional experience and discourse, enjoying pride of place alongside dignity and freedom. According to former Justice of the Constitutional Court Laurie Ackermann, these three values are impossible to separate from one another and even define one another in the South African constitutional project.[11] The South African Court has still argued for limits to horizontal application, for example, applying rights to private actors indirectly by way of common law and statutory law. However, the Court has not set apart any one area of rights as a limit on horizontal application, as has been true of equality in Germany. Indeed, the end of realizing equality across spheres has characterized much of South African constitutional discourse, such that even definitions of autonomy are suffused with a concern for equality.[12] Although South Africa's Constitution is comparatively young, there has been much discussion of horizontal application as the practice has developed, from *Du Plessis v. De Klerk* in 1996 (which showed some signs of Michelman's liberal ghosts) to later cases such as *Daniels v. Scribante* in 2017 (which

---

Leibholz. His formulations of equality amounted to a different standard of review until around the 1980s and 1990s, as well as a narrower focus on political and gender equality (interview with Christoph Möllers, Berlin, 9 December 2019).

[8] 1 BvR, 2080/09, April 11, 2018.
[9] Interview with Christoph Möllers, Berlin, December 9, 2019.
[10] Fabian Michl, "Wer darf wen 'diskriminieren'? Zum Nichtannahmebeschluss in Sachen Hotelverbot (1 BvR 879/12)," *VerfBlog*, October 12, 2019, https://verfassungsblog.de/wer-darf-wen-diskriminieren.
[11] See generally Ackermann, *Human Dignity*.
[12] Some scholars have understood the relationship between autonomy and equality in similar ways in the Indian context. See, for example, Tarunabh Khaitan, "Reading *Swaraj* into Article 15: A New Deal for All Minorities," *NUJS Law Review* 2:3 (2009), 420–432.

suggests that private actors potentially have duties with respect to their fellow citizens' socioeconomic rights). Even as many have argued for limiting horizontal application in South Africa, constitutional actors largely embrace this practice as a constitutional requirement, including the parity and duties that horizontal application activates across a range of values.

Perhaps unsurprising given these countries' transformative aspirations, scholars often identify German and South African constitutionalism as archetypes for horizontal application. In fact, Germany's experience with horizontal application influenced members of the South African Constitutional Assembly, and both countries have explicitly debated horizontality in academic as well as juristic fora. Considering these constitutional discourses alongside each other offers promising ground to carry out this book's project of examining debates through the lens of republican concepts.

5

Germany

New Tensions Amid Radiating Values

Just a few years after it was established in 1951, the Federal Constitutional Court decided that the principles of Germany's new Basic Law needed to be considered in adjudicating public and private action alike. In many ways, the Court's judgment in the landmark *Lüth* case simply mirrored the constitutional drafters' urgency to protect the constitutional order against the future rise of authoritarianism and rights abuses. Such a project arguably required some ability to reach a wider expanse of society in the way horizontal application (*Drittwirkung*) permitted. Following *Lüth*'s paradigmatic account of the need for a kind of parity across spheres, much of the content of subsequent court decisions and the language of other constitutional actors may be read as tracking a republican mode of discourse. The protection of individual rights remained essential in a postwar world. However, rights were often discussed in terms of broader ends, ends which a range of actors within the community were called upon to uphold.

This reorientation to secure an "objective order of values," to use the words of the Court deciding *Lüth*, might be viewed as compatible with other aspects of German political tradition as well. The statist and welfarist orientation of German public law, for example, may also be described as establishing the larger political community's role in securing certain positive ends. In addition, while social welfare is often pursued through means different from horizontal application, a state already charged with such positive objectives might easily regulate private behavior in parallel fashion to horizontality. Winfried Brugger offers a communitarian account of German constitutionalism that makes clear how there is space for such objectives. Ultimately, he describes the German constitutional order in terms of "liberal communitarianism,"[1] attempting to balance individual rights and collective goals. In Brugger's

---

[1] Winfried Brugger, "Communitarianism as the Social and Legal Theory behind the German Constitution," *International Journal of Constitutional Law* 2:3 (2004), 431–460.

telling, the communitarianism of German constitutionalism does not require foregoing individual rights, as some might conclude from the term "communitarianism," but does comprehend certain collective goals of the community to which individual rights may give way, despite the typical priorities of liberal constitutionalism.

This dual liberal-communitarian portrait that Brugger paints portends a place for both horizontal application and certain countervailing factors in German constitutional debates. Horizontal application was adopted early on, but only after serious debates and institutional tensions. Indeed, although German governance is often understood to have statist proclivities, other aspects of German politics have roots in liberalism and, at least in the nineteenth century, a kind of libertarian liberalism at that.[2] Taking a cue from Louis Hartz,[3] legal scholar Peter Quint explains that the German Basic Law reflects a similar concern with classical liberal rights to what we find in American constitutional-political history.[4] An insistence on maintaining the integrity of private law as separate pervades the civil law tradition and, in certain ways, the Basic Law's own codification of autonomy and other classical liberal rights.[5] However, while regard for a robust private sphere maintains some hold in German legal history, the new constitutional order enshrined a set of values that such actors as the Constitutional Court would understand as governing increasingly more sectors of German society.

In the terms of this book, the practice of horizontal application, rooted in the language of an objective order of values, tended to a republican interpretation, presupposing a common constitutional morality for which even private actors were understood to be on the hook. While quickly incorporated into legal practice, however, horizontality was also

---

He contrasts this category of "liberal communitarianism" with "a substantive, conservative communitarianism," and a more "egalitarian-universalistic" vision (459–460).

[2] Peter Quint, "Free Speech and Private Law in German Constitutional Theory," *Maryland Law Review* 48:2 (1989), 249.

[3] Louis Hartz, *The Liberal Tradition in America* (New York: Harvest, 1991).

[4] Quint, "Free Speech and Private Law," 249. It is important to note that German liberalism is different from what is sometimes called Manchester liberalism. Specifically, Germany's liberal values were consistently embedded in a larger context of societal values, giving rise to a social welfare streak at certain times even when such liberal values as *Privatautonomie* were ascendant. This is in contrast with other forms of liberalism that place greater emphasis on laissez-faire capitalism in conjunction with classical liberal values (interview with Christoph Möllers, Berlin, December 9, 2019).

[5] Gary Jacobsohn, *Constitutional Identity* (Cambridge, MA: Harvard University Press, 2010), 15.

limited in the German Constitutional Court's jurisprudence in that it was not generally applied in such areas as antidiscrimination and equality. In arguments for autonomy, republican interpretations encountered obstacles around these issues into the twenty-first century. In contrast with discourses about a larger constitutional moral order articulating certain ends and the possibility of duties for private actors, cases concerning antidiscrimination and equality engendered discourses much more centered on individual rights, and particularly rights that might run up against broad commitments to equality. Thus, in developing horizontal application, constitutional actors would allocate duties in such a way that insulated private actors from duties related to equality. Instead, the Court primarily applied classical political and civil rights horizontally, couched in language that conceptualized them as common ends, requiring parity across spheres and triggering duties of citizens.

In this way, the discourses employed on the topic of horizontality have gradually made constitutional commitments over into a kind of common good, obliging more actors and spaces in what has traditionally been understood as the private sphere. Jacobsohn and Roznai explain how the adoption of the Basic Law "signals the moment when the foundation for achieving a new identity in that country was established."[6] Horizontal application has served as an instrument to ensure this new identity is realized in toto.[7] The reorientation toward an objective order of values and, by extension, certain common ends precipitated by the Basic Law thus offers ground for a republican interpretation of horizontal application in this context.

This chapter begins by describing the pedigree and commitments underlying Germany's civil law tradition and how interpretations of this tradition interact with interpretations of new commitments assumed under the Basic Law. The chapter proceeds with a discussion of horizontal application, centering on its treatment in German legal scholarship and practice. In particular, theoretical and institutional understandings related to Germany's civil law tradition sometimes run up against newer constitutional aspirations, in general and when applied horizontally. For several decades, discourses pointing toward the pursuit of parity and recognition of private actors' duties in horizontal application only extended to more traditional constitutional commitments, as described above. This came to a head and began to shift in 2005 and 2006, when the

---

[6] Gary Jacobsohn and Yaniv Roznai, *Constitutional Revolution* (New Haven: Yale University Press, 2020), 111.
[7] Kumm, "Who Is Afraid."

German Parliament attempted to pass antidiscrimination legislation to fulfill directives from the EU. The controversy surrounding this antidiscrimination legislation, particularly from certain corners of industry and religious groups, evinced an enduring liberal ethos in the discourse, still occasionally in tension with the incremental efforts toward greater societal cohesion that underlie the practice of horizontality. More recently, in the *Stadium Ban* case,[8] among other cases, the Constitutional Court took up the question of the horizontal application of equality and began to speak about this constitutional value in language that may be interpreted in republican terms.

The Public–Private Divide in Germany's Legal Tradition

Certain corners of German law long maintained presuppositions of individualism and autonomy, both in the structure of the legal system and in the content of the law itself. As was the case in many European countries in the nineteenth century, the German system comprised two distinct categories of law and, corresponding to those categories, independent systems of courts.[9] The Civil Code constituted the private law, "the body of rules that seeks to do justice between private individuals and which does not ordinarily concern the state as a party,"[10] while the public law pertains to "obligations or regulations of the political organs of the state."[11] These systems of law originally operated independently of one another and, in general, did not intersect.

German jurists located the Civil Code in the ancient tradition of Roman law, thus endowing private law and its practitioners with great prestige. On the other hand, the public law was relatively new and primarily concerned with the administration of social insurance and welfare programs following Bismarck's 1890 reforms.[12] Public law thus lacked the same storied history and reputation for rigor that came to be associated with the Civil Code. Nevertheless, jurists understood the distinction as indispensable. Indeed, by separating the rules governing the state from those governing private relations, the law both delineated a

---

[8] *Stadium Ban*, 1 BvR, 2080/09, April 11, 2018.
[9] John Henry Merryman, *The Civil Law Tradition*, 3rd ed. (Stanford: Stanford University Press, 2007); Alan Watson, *The Making of the Civil Law* (Cambridge, MA: Harvard University Press, 1981), 144–157.
[10] Quint, "Free Speech and Private Law," 255.
[11] Ibid., 256.
[12] Ibid.

separate sphere of private life and outlined ostensibly neutral rules of engagement for private interchange.[13] Quint explains:

> The apparatus of the state was excluded from private law, except to the extent necessary for the judiciary to allocate the private rights recognized by the Civil Code, and these rights generally implied a maximum of individual autonomy and a minimum of intervention to redress individual or group inequalities already existing in society.[14]

Thus, the Civil Code reflected what Philip Pettit calls freedom as non-interference.[15] Though both public and private law were necessary to governance, it was the Civil Code, the private law, that jurists credited with preserving freedom for Germany. In contrast, even when the Weimar Constitution later adopted a long list of rights, these rights were deemed judicially unenforceable[16] and still failed to occupy the same position as did the Civil Code in the German imagination.

Apart from the systemic structure that allowed for the referee of private relationships separately from the constraints of public law, the substantive content of law and belief in the Civil Code's neutrality shows liberal predilections of a certain kind in the contemporaneous legal world. In particular, the rules of private law "were thought to enhance a more general freedom of individuals not to be interfered with by the state – particularly in commercial relationships but also in other areas of everyday life."[17] Thus the Civil Code promised order and protection in such areas of private interchange as contracts, torts, inheritance, and family relationships. Indeed, some continue to point to the Civil Code as an essential source of freedom for the German people, even after the

---

[13] This calls up such arguments as Herbert Wechsler's call for neutral principles ("Toward Neutral Principles of Constitutional Law," *Harvard Law Review* 73:1 [1959], 1–35), on the one hand, against the likes of Robert L. Hale ("Coercion and Distribution in a Supposedly Non-coercive State," *Political Science Quarterly* 38 [1923], 470–494) and Tushnet (*Weak Courts, Strong Rights: Judicial Review and Social Welfare Rights in Comparative Constitutional Law* [Princeton: Princeton University Press, 2008]); see also Kumm, "Who Is Afraid," 341–342, 365–366.

[14] Quint, "Free Speech and Private Law," 255.

[15] Philip Pettit, *On the People's Terms* (Cambridge: Cambridge University Press, 2012), chap. 1.

[16] Kumm, "Who Is Afraid," 342, goes on to explain that this decision not to make rights justiciable was, at least in part, a result of observation of the United States' experience with a Supreme Court.

[17] Quint, "Free Speech and Private Law," 256.

adoption of the Basic Law.[18] Moreover, such guarantees as those of private autonomy (*Privatautonomie*) were "highly cherished" for their role in securing a new middle class seeking economic freedom in the nineteenth century.[19] Thus, notwithstanding a few exceptions,[20] the bourgeois idea "that contracting parties are formally free and equal"[21] and that private transactions ought not to be hindered defined much of the substance of German law until the early twentieth century, when certain elements of such precepts were called into question.

From Neutral Rights to Constitutional Ends

The perception of neutrality of the Civil Code was disputed in the early twentieth century as scholars and political actors observed that political choices undergirded decisions pertaining to both the code's legislation and interpretation. Severe economic crisis also generated a new urgency to modify the private law to meet the escalating needs of the country.[22] Later, in the wake of the Second World War, the realization that the Weimar Constitution could be so easily leveraged to serve odious political ends further exposed the problems of striving for value neutrality in the law.[23] As political and constitutional reformers moved to amend Germany's Civil Code and adopt a new Basic Law, the country's constitutive principles underwent a kind of transformation. To be sure, the Weimar Constitution was a significant influence on the new constitution, and the Civil Code was initially imported into the new regime unamended. Nevertheless, new commitments and historical memory

---

[18] See ibid., 263, including fn. 60 paraphrasing Günther Dürig, "Grundrechte und Zivilrechtsprechung," in *Festschrift Zum 75. Geburtstag von Hans Nawiasky*, ed. Theodor Maunz (Munich: Isar Verlag, 1956), 157–190.
[19] Jorg Fedtke, "Drittwirkung in Germany," in *Human Rights and the Private Sphere*, ed. Dawn Oliver and Jorg Fedtke (Oxford: Rutledge-Cavendish, 2007), 129.
[20] Most notably the general clause of the BGB, Section 138. This provision in the Civil Code was intended to allow legislators to regulate private behavior according to social norms (Quint, "Free Speech and Private Law," fn. 18; Georg Sommeregger, "The Horizontalization of Equality: The German Attempt to Promote Non-discrimination in the Private Sphere via Legislation," in *The Constitution in Private Relations*, ed. András Sajó and Renáta Uitz [Utrecht: Eleven, 2005], 33–53).
[21] K. Zwiegert and H. Kotz, *An Introduction to Comparative Law*, trans. Tony Weir (Oxford: Oxford University Press, 1987), quoted by Quint, "Free Speech and Private Law," fn. 25; see also Morton J. Horowitz, "The History of the Public/Private Distinction," *University of Pennsylvania Law Review* 130 (1982), 1423–1428.
[22] Kumm, "Who Is Afraid," 341–342.
[23] Quint, "Free Speech and Private Law," 262.

imbued the law with new meanings. Most notably, dignity figured prominently in the new constitution. The very first provision of the Basic Law states, "Human dignity shall be inviolable. To respect and protect it shall be the duty of all state authority."[24] Such an emphasis on dignity is consistent with liberalism's concern for the individual and even expands on Kantian strands some scholars identify in earlier instantiations of German law.[25] In his book *Human Dignity*, Aharon Barak states that there is "no other constitution in which human dignity has such a central role."[26] Indeed, that dignity is enshrined as Germany's supreme constitutional value, never to be amended, reflects its uncompromising rejection of the abuses of human dignity inflicted by the Third Reich.

While this new commitment to dignity certainly comports with the more liberal threads of Germany's legal tradition, it depends less on a conception of separate public and private spheres, even as it continues to operate in a civil law system. Indeed, with this and other additions to the Basic Law, the content and very purpose of fundamental law expands.[27] Barak explains that most approaches to understanding the role of dignity in German constitutionalism employ the context of "the framework of society. Human dignity is not the human dignity of a person on a desert island."[28] In this way, we see a shift from the individualism and aspiration to value neutrality of the nineteenth century to something of a moral proposition for how the individual ought to be treated in German society and, by extension, what society itself ought to look like. Returning to the provision of the Basic Law, the second clause reads: "To *respect* and *protect* [dignity] shall be the duty of all state authority."[29] Barak explains that this provision has the potential to make both negative and positive

---

[24] Basic Law Article 1 Section 1.

[25] See Quint, "Free Speech and Private Law," 255, and accompanying citations: Hans Hattenhauer, *Die Geistesgeschichtlichen Grundlagen Des Deutschen Rechts*, 3rd ed. (Heidelberg: Müller, 1983); Karl Larenz, *Methodenlehre Der Rechtswissenschaft* (Berlin: Springer Verlag, 1975).

[26] Aharon Barak, "Human Dignity in German Constitutional Law," in *Human Dignity: The Constitutional Value and the Constitutional Right* (Cambridge: Cambridge University Press, 2015), 231.

[27] As David Robertson explains, constitution-makers no longer restrict the constitutional text to the structure and limits of government, but rather articulate aspirations and even an identity for the polity, as well ("Thick Constitutional Readings: When Classical Distinctions Are Irrelevant," *Georgia Journal of International and Comparative Law* 35 [2007], 277–331); see also Jacobsohn, *Constitutional Identity*.

[28] Barak, "Human Dignity in German Constitutional Law," 236.

[29] Basic Law Article 1, Section 1, emphasis added.

demands of government.³⁰ The duty to respect requires that the state not do anything to offend human dignity, a principle that seems to grow fairly naturally out of the liberal threads of the German legal tradition. The duty to protect, on the other hand, seems to require that the state take some positive action in pursuance of human dignity, though the text itself does not specify what this ought to entail. Almost a decade after the adoption of the Basic Law, the Federal Constitutional Court offered additional meaning and clarity on this duty to protect, interpreting it to require the defense of human dignity against violations by private actors.³¹

In this way, human dignity emerges as both a value, or an end, of the German constitution and a right. As a value, it constitutes the basis of the German polity and, to this extent, engenders a kind of "common good." The important distinction between subjective and objective rights, explained in Chapter 2, further illuminates this development. To reiterate, subjective rights align with the typical conception of rights as justiciable and as giving rise to claims against particular parties, usually the state. In contrast, objective rights comprise the broader values or ends of a given constitutional order.³² Objective rights are not immediately justiciable, though sometimes judges may decide cases in ways that derive duties from them. Discussing this shift to extract some understanding of values, of a common good, out of what formerly would have been mere rights claims, Habermas discusses the now-recurring commitment to human dignity in national constitutions today. He states:

> "Human dignity" performs the function of a seismograph that registers what is constitutive for a democratic legal order, namely, just those rights that citizens of a political community must grant themselves if they are to be able to *respect* one another as members of a voluntary association of free and equal persons. *The guarantee of these human rights gives rise to the status of citizens who, as subjects of equal rights, have a claim to be respected in their human dignity.*³³

---

[30] Barak, "Human Dignity in German Constitutional Law," 237–238.
[31] BVerfGE 7, 198 (1958); BVerfGI 39, 1 – Abortion I (1975); see also Jud Mathews, *Extending Rights' Reach* (Oxford: Oxford University Press, 2018), 68–72.
[32] Robert Alexy, *A Theory of Constitutional Rights* (Oxford: Oxford University Press, 2010); see also Quint, "Free Speech and Private Law," 261–262.
[33] Jurgen Habermas, "The Concept of Human Dignity and the Realistic Utopia of Human Rights," *Metaphilosophy* 41:4 (2010), 469, emphasis in the original.

If a constitution proposes an encompassing principle to guide a polity, a "seismograph" as Habermas puts it, then it is no longer a stretch to argue that citizens, too, will have some duties in conformity with this standard. Put differently, human dignity begins to clear the normative jungle formerly occupied by the nineteenth-century commitments to neutrality and individualism, thereby preparing German constitutional ground for the kind of parity across spheres and duties of private actors that horizontal application would ultimately actuate.[34]

This concept of objective rights thus serves as an intellectual bridge in constitutionalism, expanding the meaning of rights to encompass a kind of public morality. In the terms of this book, this move to conceive of dignity as the moral basis for the constitutional order gestures toward a new paradigm of parity, governing and creating duties for actors across spheres according to a common standard. While the Basic Law does not explicitly take this step, dominant accounts of its vision as well as its specific content have laid groundwork for such an interpretation. We get one such glimpse into the expanse of the German constitutional project from Jorg Fedtke's explanation of the years during the Third Reich, of the "climate of fear, terror and oppression, which went far beyond the many single instances of human rights infringements by the regime."[35] He states:

> Nazi ideology permeated society as a whole – the working environment, the arts, journalism, the scientific community, architecture, the church, schools and universities, social relationships, local communities where people went about their daily lives, and even the allegedly safe nucleus of the family home.[36]

As the pathologies and abuses had transcended spheres of life, the reconstituted German law had to be adequately equipped to effect change across spheres as well. Specific provisions in the original text of the Basic Law suggest as much. In addition to the commitment to human dignity, Article 1 Section 3's statement that rights bind the judiciary "as directly applicable law" begins to challenge the understanding of the role of courts in the civil law tradition, that the judiciary's role was simply to administer the Civil Code amid private transactions.[37] Indeed, the idea

---

[34] See also the *Elfes* case, BVerfGE 32, 6 (1957).
[35] Fedtke, "*Drittwirkung* in Germany," 128.
[36] Ibid., 128–129; see also Laurie Ackermann, *Human Dignity: Lodestar for Equality in South Africa* (Cape Town: Juta, 2012), 322.
[37] Fedtke, "*Drittwirkung* in Germany," 127.

that rights bind the judiciary could be interpreted as a charge that judges continued to remain accountable to constitutional rights and values in the very process of applying the Civil Code.

On such questions, Article 9 Section 3 guarantees the "right to form associations to safeguard and improve working and economic conditions" against all actors, regardless of occupation or profession.[38] Thus, the constitutional drafters left little guesswork about the extent of this provision's application. Though this and the aforementioned provisions in the Basic Law in some sense signaled a certain capaciousness of the constitutional project, their presence also seemed to cut in the opposite direction. Specifically, the act of stating when private actors were implicated by the commitments of the Basic Law was construed as implying that the remainder of the text obligated only state actors. And indeed, it was not long after the Basic Law was adopted that jurists and legal scholars began wrestling with these questions.

Debating Horizontality in the New Constitutional Order

Although the apex courts of the German legal system had already been charged with ensuring consistency *within* each branch of civil law,[39] the prospect of horizontal application suggested for the first time the possibility of consistency, or parity, across areas of law. While some of the content of the Basic Law set the stage to break from the old paradigm and to adopt some version of horizontal application, it did not necessarily entail horizontal application by itself.[40] Indeed, the reconstituted law provoked more questions than it answered with respect to the relationship between private law and public law and the obligations of private actors with respect to public law. And it certainly did not settle the question of German constitutional identity, particularly respecting the weight the civil law's values would maintain in light of the evidently transformative additions to German fundamental law. Much was unsettled regarding horizontal application in the ensuing years as the twentieth century progressed.

---

[38] Ibid., 126.
[39] Quint, "Free Speech and Private Law," 256.
[40] Fedtke explains that "the existence of an objective duty of the state to protect individual private interests need not necessarily translate into a subjective right of individuals to invoke this protection in court" ("*Drittwirkung* in Germany," 150).

Given Germany's plural court system, these questions were as much about constitutional identity as they were about institutional power. Indeed, jurists from every area of law weighed in. Many legal scholars and jurists initially reacted by falling back on the orthodoxy of civil law systems, namely, that public law, now the Basic Law, had no influence on private disputes.[41] Some argued that the council responsible for the Basic Law simply was not authorized to adopt a constitution that affected private relationships, even if it had wanted to. Public law was, by definition, meant to give protection against government institutions insofar as they possessed more power, in contrast with private law that was framed to govern relationships among equals.[42] Still others argued against horizontal application in terms drawn from the Basic Law itself. As explained earlier, a few specific provisions suggest that the state has a duty to protect against private abuses (Article 1, Sections 1, 3) or that certain private relationships are, in fact, held to a constitutional standard (Article 9, Section 3). The presence of such provisions could imply that other parts of the Basic Law were not intended to bear on private relationships.

Other scholars challenged the conventional wisdom that the civil law system required a strict separation between public and private law. Quint explains the argument made by some that earlier conceptions of basic rights did not in fact distinguish between public and private offenders.[43] Presumably, too, recent events had demonstrated the ways in which private entities could inflict great harm, whether in consort with state authorities or independently. Hans Carl Nipperdey, chief judge of the Federal Labor Court from 1954 to 1963, believed as much and led the Labor Court in arguing for a conception not merely of horizontal application but of *direct* horizontal application, meaning the Constitution itself could create duties of private individuals rather than simply influence private interchanges through private law.[44] In a series of cases,

---

[41] Quint cites many German scholars who rehearse these classic arguments (255–257); see, for example, I. K. Zweigert and H. Kotz, *An Introduction to Comparative Law*, trans. Tony Weir (Oxford: Oxford University Press, 1987); Larenz, *Methodenlehre Der Rechtswissenschaft*, 48; Gustav Radbruch, *Einführung in die Rechtswissenschaft*, ed. Konrad Zweigert (Stuttgart: Koehler, 1980), 103–105; Franz Wieacker, *Privatrechtsgeschichte der Neuzeit*, 2nd ed. (Göttinggen: Vandenhoeck & Ruprecht, 1967), 479–483.

[42] Quint, "Free Speech and Private Law," 257.

[43] Ibid.

[44] Ibid., 259.

before and even after the Constitutional Court decided *Lüth*, the Labor Court adopted this position that basic rights, and particularly those rights that are most constitutive to the German project, could be deployed directly against private individuals. Indeed, these rights were so important as to constitute "general rules for the governance of all of society."[45] Nipperdey and other advocates of direct horizontal application cited elements of the Basic Law itself in support of their position. For example, Article 20 Section 1's description of the polity as "a democratic and social federal state" suggests that some intervention of the state in private affairs was permitted "to ameliorate various forms of societal, rather than governmental, oppression."[46]

The Labor Court certainly had strategic incentives to argue in favor of direct horizontal application, insofar as this move allowed the Labor Court to touch what was previously beyond its reach – the Basic Law. Indeed, this approach would effectively place the Labor Court alongside the Constitutional Court as "an alternative source of constitutional adjudication."[47] Other jurists and scholars of private law came to opposite conclusions, however, fearing that the ultimate result of horizontal application would be not to expand the domain of the private law courts, such as the Labor Court, but to expand the role of the Constitutional Court as overseer of private law. Arguably, such jurists and scholars had reason to resist horizontal application also, to ensure their status as experts and final arbiters in their respective areas of law.[48]

Within these strategic considerations one may interpret a real intellectual disagreement, a clash of visions, about the identity of the new German constitution and how seemingly competing values would relate in the future. Some scholars understood the system of law to be essentially the same as before. Human dignity and other values that gained expression in the Basic Law certainly changed the landscape of constitutional law but, such arguments maintained, bore neither on the essential civil law framework nor on the governance of private relations. Others, most notably Nipperdey, took the new content of German fundamental law to be more transformative, to include a new charge to

---

[45] Ibid., 260; Mathews, *Extending Rights' Reach*, 28.
[46] Quint, "Free Speech and Private Law," 260; see also Article 28, Section 1 of the Basic Law.
[47] Mathews, *Extending Rights' Reach*, 44.
[48] Fedtke, "*Drittwirkung* in Germany," 139. A similar set of concerns motivated institutional tensions between the South African Supreme Court of Appeal and the Constitutional Court after the latter was established under the new constitutional dispensation.

order civil society according to the principles of the Basic Law.[49] Many parties had a stake in these questions and found support for their preferred answers in the particular factors they chose to emphasize out of the seeming disharmony[50] – whether they found an institutional separation built into the civil law, which was thought also to support individual autonomy, or perceived an expanded social character the Basic Law introduced to the constitutional-legal schema. Such interpretations appear in particular decisions of the civil courts leading up to the Constitutional Court's decision in *Lüth*.

In 1954, the Federal Court of Justice first held that personality rights (i.e., the right to freely develop one's personality under Article 2) could be applied horizontally in the *Schacht* case.[51] Just six months later, the Labor Court would argue for direct horizontal application, declaring that certain rights were so constitutive to the Basic Law that they ought to apply to public and private actors alike.[52] The case involved an employee who was fired for distributing pamphlets in support of the Communist Party at his workplace, thus implicating Article 3 Section 3 (prohibiting discrimination on the basis of political views) and Article 5 Section 1 (guaranteeing the freedom of expression).[53] Though the Court decided in this particular case that the employer had dismissed the employee for reasons not related to political censorship, they took the opportunity to declare that the Basic Law did create rights obligations for employers and other private actors. Quint translates part of the opinion, that certain fundamental values "entered into [the basic legal] framework, and neither the organization of a workplace nor agreements nor acts of legal peers should be allowed to contradict those values ... Thus these basic rights affect not only the relationship of the individual citizen to the state, but also the interrelationship of the citizens as legal equals."[54]

---

[49] Fedtke, "*Drittwirkung* in Germany," 140.
[50] Jacobsohn, *Constitutional Identity*, 15.
[51] BGHZ 13, 334, https://law.utexas.edu/transnational/foreign-law-translations/german/case.php?id=740. Nuno Ferreira explains that this case determined that "private letters can only be published with the consent of their authors and under the terms defined by them" as a function of the right to free development of personality (*Fundamental Rights and Private Law in Europe: The Case of Tort Law and Children* [New York: Routledge, 2011], 34).
[52] 1 BAGE 185, 191 (1954); Ferreira, *Fundamental Rights*, 34.
[53] Fedtke, "*Drittwirkung* in Germany," 139–140.
[54] Quint, "Free Speech and Private Law," 260, fn. 47; 1 BAGE 185, 193 (1954).

The Labor Court thus staked its territory in the debate over the nature of the Basic Law and its ability to reach private relationships. The Basic Law, the Court argued, furnished guidelines (or an *ordre public*) for organizing the larger German society. While the catalog of individual rights in the Basic Law[55] certainly featured in these decisions and continued to form the content of German law, the Court also drew from the idea of social justice (*Sozialstaatsprinzip*) present in Articles 20 and 28 to justify their broader view of what the Basic Law aimed to accomplish.[56] Moreover, although the Labor Court's reasoning was grounded in a conception of freedom, it was a more expansive conception that sought to account for the realities of power relationships and discrepancies in bargaining positions.[57] One might say, in the terms of this book's republican framework, that it transcended freedom as noninterference in favor of something akin to freedom as nondomination.

The Labor Court would continue in this vein a few years later in the *Zölibat*[58] decision. In this case, a woman was dismissed from her job at a hospital when she got married, as she had violated a term of employment requiring that workers remain single. The Court considered deciding the case on the basis of certain potentially relevant provisions of the Civil Code.[59] However, it instead opted to continue developing the concept of direct horizontal effect of constitutional rights, deciding the case on the basis of Article 6 Section 1 (protecting marriage and the family) as well as Article 2 Section 1 (guaranteeing free development of personality).[60] The Court doubled down on the claim of its previous decisions that private relationships and transactions ought not to contradict the *ordre public* established by the Basic Law. Nipperdey argued:

> A number of constitutional rights do not merely guarantee individual freedom against the power of the state, but rather are ordering principles for society, which have immediate significance even for the private legal dealings of citizens amongst one another. The Senate [of the Court] has also previously indicated, that private law agreements, legal transactions and undertakings may not be set in opposition to that which one may call

---

[55] Fedtke "*Drittwirkung* in Germany," 137.
[56] Ibid., 139–140; 1 BAGE 185, 193 (1954).
[57] Fedtke, "*Drittwirkung* in Germany," 139–140; 1 BAGE 185, 193 (1954).
[58] 4 BAGE, 274 (1957).
[59] For example, the public policy or "good morals" general clauses, which I will discuss later on.
[60] Mathews, *Extending Rights' Reach*, 45.

the ordering structure, the *ordre public* of the actual political and legal regime.[61]

The immediate result of this line of argument was to expand the protections offered by constitutional rights by recognizing employers and other private actors as themselves having constitutional duties. Nevertheless, Nipperdey's reasoning reveals an additional innovation that constitutional rights mandate a particular social order. What in one sense was an expansion of rights protections was in another sense a directive that private actors "uphold the public order and the common good."[62] In this way, the Labor Court argued for a constitution that weighted parity in applying the Basic Law greater than the prior distinctions of the civil law system, and that weighted constitutional ends and their corresponding duties greater than certain exercises of rights.

In arguing specifically for direct horizontal application, moreover, the Labor Court showed some readiness to dismantle the distinction between public and private, previously thought essential in guaranteeing individual freedom.[63] Jud Mathews suggests that the constitutional theory underlying such decisions in the Labor Court had an "anti-individualistic and antiliberal" bent.[64] In fact, some German scholars find enough in these decisions to argue that "this orientation toward the priority of collective interests over individual interests reflects a holdover from the labor law doctrines of the Third Reich."[65] Nipperdey's interpretations track the pre-Basic Law version of private law, which was "a very value-laden, not liberal, national socialist private law."[66] The "national socialist, anti-liberal . . . way of doing politics" informed the private law so that it almost always privileged the objective order over the subjectivity we find

---

[61] 4 BAGE, 274 (1957); Mathews, *Extending Rights' Reach*, 45.

[62] Mathews, *Extending Rights' Reach*, 45.

[63] Even still the Labor Court showed some hesitance, setting a high bar for direct horizontal application in insisting that the rights violation be of the gravest nature (Quint, "Free Speech and Private Law," 259–260, 265).

[64] Mathews, *Extending Rights' Reach*, 45. He later states, with less qualification, that the Labor Court's decision to apply direct horizontal effect reflected its "statist orientation to the project of constitutionalism" (46).

[65] Mathews, *Extending Rights' Reach*, 45, and accompanying citation: Thomas Henne, "Die neue Wertordnung in Zivilrecht – speziell Familien-und Arbeitsrecht," in *Das Bonner Grundgesetz: Altes Recht und neue Verfassung in den ernsten Jahrzehnten der Bundesrepublik Deutschland (1949–1969)*, ed. Michael Stolleis (Berlin: Berliner Wissenschafts-Verlag, 2006), 21.

[66] Interview with Christoph Möllers, Berlin, December 9, 2019.

in liberalism.⁶⁷ Put differently, Nipperdey "domesticizes, civilizes, constitutionalizes that idea [of prioritizing the objective] into German labor law."⁶⁸ The Labor Court's judgments put much weight on the capacity of rights to dictate social goods and thereby expressed much confidence in restructuring institutions that were previously thought necessary to protect freedom in the German constitutional order. Put differently, the discourses coming out of the Labor Court at this time suggest a readiness, indeed an eagerness, to adopt a conception of the common good in labor law, governing even private sectors according to objective public values.

Despite the Labor Court's argument that the Basic Law established a new *ordre public*, the question of horizontal application was by no means settled. In its decisions, the Labor Court had identified one possible equilibrium amid the disharmony in German law as it had been reconstituted, choosing to emphasize the principles of the Basic Law as obligating a wider expanse of German society and even obligating private actors directly. This was in contrast with the legal orthodoxy that still persisted even after 1949 when the Basic Law was adopted, that separation between public and private spheres and systems of law was essential and served such values as *Privatautonomie*. The Federal Constitutional Court would refer to these positions as two "extreme" views,⁶⁹ suggesting that there could be another, intermediate interpretation of the German constitutional order and, moreover, that such an alternative may be preferable. And indeed, just a few months after the Labor Court decided the *Zölibat* case, the Constitutional Court offered its own take on the question of horizontal effect as the supreme authority responsible for interpreting the Basic Law.

The *Lüth* Case: Challenging and Preserving Civil Law

In 1958, the Constitutional Court handed down the *Lüth* decision,⁷⁰ a case that continually features in scholarship as foundational for the practice of horizontal application. The facts of the case appear in Chapter 2, but I present them again here for the sake of a thorough

---

[67] Ibid. Möllers follows Alexy in the way he employs the terms "objective" and "subjective."
[68] Interview with Christoph Möllers, Berlin, December 9, 2019. According to Möllers, that such developments would come from the Labor Courts was unsurprising given that labor laws are "the least liberal private law" to the extent that they comprise the most regulation.
[69] *Lüth*, BverfGE 7, 198 (1958); Quint, "Free Speech and Private Law," 258.
[70] BVerfGE 7, 198 (1958).

analysis. After being acquitted of war crimes for producing an anti-Semitic film during the war, former Nazi propagandist Veit Harlan directed a new film in 1950, the title of which translates to *Immortal Beloved*. In response, journalist Erich Lüth called for a boycott of the film. Harlan, in turn, called for an injunction against Lüth on the grounds that he intended to harm Harlan's economic prospects. The district court in Hamburg granted the injunction, only for it to be overturned in 1958 when the Federal Constitutional Court finally weighed in. As explained in Chapter 2, the Constitutional Court took issue with the fact that the lower court had not properly accounted for the Basic Law's "order of objective moral and legal principles" – that is, the fact that the Basic Law establishes not only subjective rights (that create rights obligations between particular parties) but also principles to guide the life of the broader polity. These principles had a "radiating effect" on all sectors of German law for which all courts had to account. The lower court had consequently erred when it held that the Civil Code alone governed the case's outcome without considering how the values of the Basic Law might intervene in the calculus. The Constitutional Court was careful to stipulate that this was still ultimately a dispute between private persons and, as such, ultimately governed by the Civil Code. Nevertheless, Lüth's right to the freedom of expression (guaranteed under Article 5 Section 1) was also relevant to the question at hand as a commitment of the Basic Law. Moreover, though all provisions of the Basic Law were potentially relevant to such calculations, the right to freedom of expression was of particular import insofar as it was "absolutely constitutive" (*schlechthin konstituierend*) in a liberal constitutional order.[71] The fact that this was a dispute between private actors did not exempt the courts from considering how the relevant provisions of the Civil Code comported with the commitments of the Basic Law and particularly such foremost guarantees as the freedom of expression.

That the Constitutional Court's decision in *Lüth* employed a doctrine of horizontal effect would seem to follow from the Labor Court's preceding decisions. Indeed, both Courts conceive of rights as objective values aiming toward a common good of society. Moreover, both grounded their decisions in a concession that such values could be abused in the context of private relationships and interactions with the state alike. Crucial, however, was the difference in mechanisms employed by each

---

[71] Quint, "Free Speech and Private Law," 283.

court. In *Lüth* the Constitutional Court struck a kind of middle ground in deciding that the values of the Basic Law applied to private actors only indirectly, that is, by way of their influence on private law. Thus, government actors across branches were charged with ensuring the compatibility of law with constitutional values, from the initial processes of legislation to the interpretation of law in courts. In so reasoning, the Constitutional Court charted a middle path between two "extremes," departing from a strict understanding of the separation between public and private law as well as from the Labor Court's argument that the Basic Law itself creates duties of private actors. First proposed by eminent law professor Günter Dürig, this intermediate position of indirect horizontal effect was quickly accepted, even praised, by scholars and jurists alike.[72]

The decision in *Lüth* and the particular way in which the Constitutional Court developed horizontal effect for the German polity marked a sort of moment of truth with respect to both the larger architecture of law and courts, as well as the actual content of law. With respect to the architecture of law and courts, some legal scholars have questioned whether the indirect effect that *Lüth* introduces actually produces outcomes different from those that would be produced under direct horizontal effect. Both ultimately entail the balancing of rights, the argument goes, even if the indirect method involves the intermediate translation into private law.[73] While this is an important point and perhaps true in some cases, it does not fully appreciate the theoretic difference between these methods of horizontal application given the particularities of the German system, or the practical fact that constitutional actors themselves view them as meaningfully different. In its formulation, the Constitutional Court arguably found a balance between competing narratives associated with the old civil law system and the primacy of new constitutional values. More than a mere symbolic difference, moreover, the adoption of indirect horizontal effect has the practical result of keeping the civil law, and all its attendant discourses, relevant in such balancing considerations. The Constitutional Court did not decide that the Basic Law controlled all outcomes, just that it had to be *considered* against the existing rules of the civil law.[74] In this way, the

---

[72] Ibid., 265, fn. 66; Ackermann, *Human Dignity*, 321.
[73] Kumm, "Who Is Afraid"; Mathews, *Extending Rights' Reach*.
[74] As Chapter 6 will recount, certain judgments in South African constitutional law have, in a similar way, attempted to carve out space for areas such as contract law and common law more generally.

Court preserved the potential of the Civil Code, and its attendant discourses, to factor into cases as a separate source of content and values.

In navigating old and new legal traditions in this way, moreover, the compromise in *Lüth* had the practical effect of preserving largely intact and distinct systems of law and courts. As Michelman explains, horizontal application in Germany is limited by the very fact that it operates in a dualist system of civil law and constitutional law.[75] Following *Lüth*, the Constitutional Court did expand its power to hold civil law questions up to a constitutional standard.[76] Nevertheless, even after *Lüth*, the Court spoke of "honoring this restriction of its competence"[77] and of not using this new power to encroach on the interpretive role of its counterpart apex courts. It insisted that courts at every level and even the legislature show due consideration for the principles of the Basic Law, but did not insist on any particular interpretation of these principles, so long as the ordinary courts' balancing was not egregiously off.[78] Furthermore, the private law courts remained the final interpreters in their respective areas of law wherein the Constitutional Court largely refrained from interfering. Indeed, beginning in *Lüth* and continuing in subsequent horizontality cases, the Basic Law's influence reaches only to a couple of specific provisions in the Civil Code known as the "general clauses." One of the most important of these, Section 826 of the Civil Code, states: "Whoever intentionally causes injury to another person in a manner contrary to good morals has the duty of compensating for that injury."[79] The Civil Code's reference to "good morals" seems to admit some external

---

[75] Frank Michelman, "The Interplay of Constitutional and Ordinary Jurisdiction," in *Comparative Constitutional Law*, ed. Tom Ginsburg and Rosalind Dixon (Cheltenham: Edward Elgar, 2011), 289–290.

[76] In arguing that the Basic Law influences the duties of private actors not directly but in the way constitutional values influence the civil law, the Constitutional Court was reasserting its role as the supreme interpreter of the Basic Law. Whereas direct horizontal effect served to give the Labor Court a significant say in interpreting constitutional principles and their effect on private actors, by insisting that the question in *Lüth* was at base one of civil law, the Constitutional Court also reinserted itself into the equation. On such an approach, the civil courts would once again engage directly with the civil law and, in theory, rely more on the Constitutional Court's interpretations of the constitutional law (Mathews, *Extending Rights' Reach*). Though this argument makes sense in the abstract, it is not necessarily borne out by subsequent cases, such as *Mephisto* (see Quint, "Free Speech and Private Law").

[77] Michelman, "Interplay," 289.

[78] Interview with Justice Dieter Grimm, Berlin, December 4, 2019.

[79] Quint, "Free Speech and Private Law," 349; for discussions of *Lüth*, see "Free Speech and Private Law," 284–285, and Sommeregger, "Horizontalization of Equality," 43.

standard of evaluation,[80] and the Constitutional Court exploited this opening to bring the principles of the Basic Law to bear on private law. In so doing, however, it effectively limited its own interpretive authority to these particular provisions so as not to fashion itself as a "super ordinary court"[81] that can reinterpret any provision of the Code as it wishes. In those instances when the Constitutional Court cannot reach a "constitutionally satisfactory solution" without breaching jurisdictional divides, it actually looks to the legislature to revise the law.[82] Thus, "simultaneous, colliding commitments"[83] persist in Germany's practice of indirect horizontal effect, as separate systems of law and courts persist alongside the idea that the Basic Law sets the standard across spheres.

In addition to preserving a separation of public and private systems and structures, *Lüth* may be described as sustaining a kind of liberal, rights-centric discourse with respect to the content of the law. Of course, the Court endorsed the need to propagate a *society* committed to certain common norms – the freedom of expression was prioritized in *Lüth* in part for its public value and not solely for Lüth's private interests and rights as an individual.[84] At the same time, the particular right of freedom of expression, even while enforced as a societal norm, is familiar and valued as an individual right in the liberal tradition. In the terms of this book, then, should *Lüth* be understood to signify a primacy of liberal, and not republican, discourses? Recall Chapter 2's account of horizontal application as a republican vein in liberal constitutionalism. The republican interpretation advanced here does not claim that liberal values are no longer present, but that horizontality engenders new modes of discussing and disseminating these (and other) values, such that they may

---

[80] Indeed, the presence of these general clauses in the Civil Code suggests that legislators in the nineteenth century had already accepted the idea that social values might bear on the private legal order. However, the norms underlying these clauses were generally weak (interview with Christoph Möllers, Berlin, December 9, 2019). With *Lüth*, we see a formalization and even expansion of this mechanism in the Civil Code, as the Basic Law came to form the content of "good morals." Previously legislators maintained the primary role in defining what "good morals" meant, thus keeping the discussion within the realm of private law. After *Lüth*, however, the content of "good morals" would come from a standard external to private law, namely, the Basic Law itself. From this point on, the Constitutional Court necessarily involved itself and the Basic Law in private matters, thus bringing public values explicitly to bear on private orderings.

[81] Michelman, "Interplay," 289.
[82] Ibid., 290.
[83] Ibid.
[84] Quint, "Free Speech and Private Law," 284; Sommeregger, "Horizontalization of Equality," 43.

be interpreted no longer merely as rights but often come to be discussed as ends. Freedom of expression is described in *Lüth* not only as a right but also as part of the content of an "objective moral order," a kind of common good for which a wider range of actors becomes responsible. Also worth noting is the role dignity plays in *Lüth*'s defense of freedom of expression, as discussed earlier. Discourses of human dignity characterize much postwar constitutionalism and, in its common associations with social welfare, generally ask more of society than do older accounts of liberalism.

The Basic Law and *Lüth*'s interpretation of it thus marked a change in German law, turning the putative neutrality of Weimar toward a system of objective values. Nevertheless, the Constitutional Court preserved certain traditional understandings present in interpretations of the Civil Code and contrary to the Labor Court's endorsement of direct horizontal application. Indeed, in one telling, the Constitutional Court adopted indirect horizontal effect in lieu of direct effect in an effort to preserve a particular conception of liberty and prevent it from turning into a duty, per se.[85] In sum, while new language about the obligations of private individuals emerged with this new societal morality, older discourses emphasizing individual rights and such values as autonomy persisted. Perhaps illustrative of this, on the very same day the Court decided the *Lüth* case, it handed down another decision in which the right to freedom of expression itself gave way to "certain traditional property interests."[86] Various episodes in the years following *Lüth* evince persistent disharmony in constitutional discourses, efforts both to preserve old structures and understandings and to foster a common obligation to constitutional norms in society.

As the Court in *Lüth* preserved some domain for private law in settling on indirect horizontal application, some perceive the "reassertion of private law" in such subsequent decisions as the *Mephisto* case.[87] This 1971 decision involved a novel, entitled *Mephisto*, whose main character was modeled on the life of German actor Gustaf Gründgens. Klauss Mann, the author, had formerly been friends with Gründgens. While Mann admitted that certain details of the character were based on the actor's life, he insisted that he did not intend the novel to be a portrait of any particular person. Nevertheless, Gründgens's heir filed an action

---

[85] Interview with Justice Dieter Grimm, Berlin, December 4, 2019.
[86] 7 BVerfGE 230, 1958; Quint, "Free Speech and Private Law," 286–287.
[87] 30 BVerfGE 173 (1971); see also Quint, "Free Speech and Private Law," 291.

against Mann under the Civil Code's general clause 823(l), providing a civil remedy against infringement on "the life, body, health, freedom, property" of Gründgens.[88] In its judgment, the Constitutional Court interpreted the *constitutional* rights of human dignity and free development of personality (Articles 1 and 2, respectively) to encompass – that is, elevate to constitutional status – these rights formulated in the Civil Code.[89] In other words, the Civil Code actually gave content to the Basic Law, insofar as the Court incorporated these traditional formulations into its understanding of human dignity and personality. In this way, these rights could be balanced against and even take precedence over such rights as to artistic endeavor (Article 5 Section 3) that occur in the Basic Law explicitly.[90] One might speculate how *Mephisto* and other cases might have differed had the Labor Court's approach of direct horizontal application gained traction. Specifically, constitutional rights obligations would have applied to private actors directly. Thus, private law would not serve as a necessary intermediary or enjoy the same opportunity to bear on decisions as a unique source of values.

While *Mephisto* goes further than many cases in the extent to which the Civil Code informs constitutional interpretations, it is not unique in putting into dialogue private law and the Basic Law and, more to the point, holding up the private law as a source of values in its own right. The earlier *Blinkfüer* case also translated the Civil Code into constitutional terms, finding that the freedom of the press (Article 5 Section 1) supported claims under the aforementioned clause 823(1) of the Civil Code. In this case, the leftist magazine *Blinkfüer* won against the freedom of expression of a conservative publisher calling for a political boycott of the magazine.[91] Moreover, in the 1973 *Soraya* case, the Constitutional Court leveraged the constitutional right to personality in order to compel a remedy corresponding to the Civil Code's protection of personality

---

[88] 30 BVerfGE 173 (1971); see also Quint, "Free Speech and Private Law," 291, fn. 147.
[89] Mathews, *Extending Rights' Reach*, 60.
[90] Quint, "Free Speech and Private Law," 297.
[91] Although both *Lüth* and *Blinkfüer* concerned the freedom of speech, the Constitutional Court distinguished their facts and, consequently, the balancing of rights in each respective case. Specifically, the Court argued that the calls for a boycott in *Blinkfüer* extended beyond the realm of speech to involve the leveraging of one big publisher's economic power against a smaller newspaper. This, the Court determined, allowed the latter's freedom of the press to prevail against what, at first blush, might have seemed to be simply the freedom of speech of the former (interview with Justice Dieter Grimm, Berlin, December 4, 2019).

rights. On the one hand, some argue this step constitutes a rewriting of the Civil Code to align it with the Basic Law, insofar as the Code expressly states that "intangible and nonpecuniary harms" could *not* be rewarded for damages.[92] However, with the introduction of horizontal application, even its indirect form, we would expect that constitutional values bear on private law in such ways. What is unique in the German jurisprudence, and what we see in such cases as *Blinkfüer*, is the way the Civil Code maintains a certain stature in argumentation and is put into dialogue with the Basic Law, in spite of the primacy and "radiating effect" of the latter.[93] That this maintenance of traditional structures is not universal will come into sharper relief in Chapter 6's discussion of the common law of South Africa, which, after some institutional and doctrinal struggles, is more completely beholden to the South African Constitution and which, importantly, falls entirely within the jurisdiction of the South African Constitutional Court to uphold or modify.

Initial Limits and Persisting Tensions in Horizontality

The tensions that accompanied the move toward horizontality continued not only in institutional and legal divisions between the private law and public law but also arguably in understandings of the Basic Law itself. As the previous section explained, the Basic Law's commitment to such values as human dignity revised more traditional understandings of rights, the public–private distinction, and other liberal values. Still, Jorg Fedtke interprets the catalog of rights in the Basic Law as having continuity with prior understandings and as basically "classical-liberal in character."[94] Following human dignity as the foundational value come "an extensive range of individual freedoms," including,

> the right to life and physical integrity, religious freedom, free speech and freedom of the press and the media, protection of marriage and the family, freedom of assembly and association, privacy of correspondence and telecommunications, freedom of movement within the federal territory, the protection of economic activity, inviolability of the home, and the protection of property.[95]

---

[92] Mathews, *Extending Rights' Reach*, 64.
[93] Ibid., 140.
[94] Fedtke, "*Drittwirkung* in Germany," 137.
[95] Ibid.

INITIAL LIMITS AND PERSISTING TENSIONS   171

In addition to these enumerated rights, the right to "free development of personality" has since been interpreted by the Constitutional Court as a kind of "catch-all right," protecting a vast range of liberty interests so as to make the Bill of Rights essentially comprehensive.[96] After a couple of decades, the priority of these rights seems to have settled into the popular imagination. Jud Mathews explains that 1959–1974 constituted "the high phase of liberalization in Germany."[97] Mathews cites as evidence a series of public opinion polls conducted in Germany between 1949 and 1963 that asked respondents to rank different rights in order of importance. In 1949, 35 percent of respondents identified freedom from want as most important, in contrast with 26 percent who selected freedom of expression. By 1963, in contrast, only 15 percent of respondents selected freedom from want, while 56 percent identified freedom of expression as most important. Moreover, in a 1964 poll, German voters ranked freedom as a more important value than either order or prosperity.[98]

This apparent surge in liberal values also tracks the sorts of rights that tended to be applied horizontally, in this particular era and in general. The aforementioned cases illustrate the prevalence of such rights as freedom of expression, freedom of the press, and free development of personality in Germany's earliest and most foundational horizontality cases.[99] It was in this rights context and larger milieu that horizontality developed and came to be accepted in German legal practice. The "objective system of values," propagated with horizontality, engendered discourses among constitutional actors concerning the need for parity across spheres of life. As the above cases illustrate, however, such arguments for parity remained tied to a particular catalog of rights and liberties and yielded to separate systems of law and courts. And so, it was in this context that the civil courts also adopted the practice of horizontality, particularly after a few cycles of judges had the chance to complete clerkships at the Constitutional Court and return home to their primary court appointments in the ensuing years.[100] Moreover, with the

---

[96] Barak, "Human Dignity in German Constitutional Law," 231.
[97] Mathews, *Extending Rights' Reach*, 53.
[98] Ibid., 53, fn. 10. Perhaps these trends in understandings of rights and freedom also bear connection to developments related to the Cold War.
[99] For a more comprehensive list that further illustrates this point, see Gert Bruggemeier, Aurelia Colombi Ciacchi, and Giovanni Comandé (eds), *Fundamental Rights and Private Law in the European Union: Volume 1* (Cambridge, UK: Cambridge University Press, 2010), 277–279; see also Ackermann, *Human Dignity*, 328.
[100] Interview with Justice Dieter Grimm, Berlin, December 4, 2019.

adoption of the additional feature of the individual constitutional complaint, by which individual citizens could directly raise claims of constitutional violations, horizontal application became part of the "daily job" of the Federal Constitutional Court.[101]

Even still, the civil courts dispute how the Constitutional Court applies constitutional values to private law in certain instances, sometimes questioning the definitions of such terms as "property," "takings," and "freedom of contract" as employed in constitutional law.[102] Admittedly, any objections now come in the context of discrete cases rather than as wholesale challenges to horizontal application as a practice.[103] That horizontal application has largely been accepted, though, is not to minimize the changes it brought to German civil law. For the first time, private lawyers had public lawyers telling them they interpreted the law incorrectly, and these private lawyers initially feared that the public lawyers would remake private orderings in the image of public law.[104] In this book's terms, their worries reflect how the Basic Law and, more specifically, the mechanism of horizontal application would bring a new parity across German systems of law and spheres of life. Meanwhile, the traditional, largely liberal ethos historically associated with private law lived on in such people as Werner Flume, a towering figure in German private law who emphasized freedom of contract throughout his decades-long career. Flume and others like him went so far as to argue that German constitutional law had become nothing less than an instrument by which "to objectify the private liberal free coordination of subjects through contract."[105]

While Flume's perspective was continually present, it remained a mere strand of German legal thought, as horizontal application was increasingly embedded in legal practice. Of course, the nature of the rights applied horizontally in early cases did not typically call for a deep change in German society or in the behavior of individual private actors. A kind of rights-centricity could coexist alongside the language of this new

---

[101] Ibid. Although a vast majority of the thousands of cases heard by the Constitutional Court each year are the result of individual complaints, Justice Grimm estimated that violations are found only in 2 percent of cases. This small number corroborates the contention that the whole system of courts has come to apply horizontality, and in a way the Constitutional Court generally deems acceptable.
[102] Interview with Christoph Möllers, Berlin, December 4, 2019.
[103] Interview with Justice Dieter Grimm, Berlin, December 4, 2019.
[104] Ibid.
[105] Interview with Christoph Möllers, Berlin, December 9, 2019.

constitutional morality in discourses surrounding horizontal application. One might describe those duties with which private actors were charged as growing out of accepted orthodoxy and already part of the societal status quo. In contrast, when the conversation eventually turned to the horizontal application of equality rights and antidiscrimination, the tenor of the discourse shifted. Old anxieties seemed to be resurrected and new anxieties born as certain constitutional and private actors expressed concern over the impact of new applications of horizontality on individual liberty and autonomy. In the arguments and events of ensuing years, sectors of both the juristic and general populations seemed to treat these developments as a turn to ensconce certain constitutional rights as ends in themselves and to do so at greater expense to other rights than had previously characterized horizontality.

Equality in the Private Sphere

While the early questions surrounding horizontality largely subsided, constitutional actors rarely applied Article 3's right to equality horizontally until recently. It seems to have taken the outside force of the EU to initiate such an expansion, when the European Council directed Member States to implement antidiscrimination measures in 2000.[106] Only after these developments did the German Constitutional Court depart from its conservative approach to Article 3's equality provisions to consider the possibility of their horizontal application.[107] Scholars explain how the Court previously considered equality cases under the lower standard of "arbitrariness review as opposed to a more intensive proportionality review."[108] Laurie Ackermann, former justice of the South African Constitutional Court, tells a similar story of German constitutionalism:

---

[106] The exception to this delay is the way in which parliament largely rewrote Book 4 of the Civil Code, governing family law, in the decades following the Basic Law's adoption to conform to Article 3 of the Basic Law, and conform to contemporary views about the equal status of mothers and fathers (Mathews, *Extending Rights' Reach*, 67–68). Such revisions came almost entirely through parliament, however, rather than through the courts. Moreover, this was the only part of the Civil Code that was so overhauled as a result of the adoption of the Basic Law.

[107] *Stadium Ban*, 1 BvR, 2080/09, April 11, 2018.

[108] Mathews, *Extending Rights' Reach*, 80; Stone Sweet and Stranz, "Rights Adjudication and Constitutional Pluralism in Germany and Europe," 100.

As point of departure the Basic Law, by "upgrading" ("*Aufwertung*") the freedom "flowing from human worth" and by making a primary choice in favour of personal freedom, places it beyond doubt that thereby freedom is also sanctioned as between equals, as against demands of equality.[109]

Günter Dürig offers a coinciding account, seeing freedom under the Basic Law as "the primary manifestation" of human dignity[110] and, moreover, that "a preference for freedom as against equality has been established."[111]

The few times that equality was applied horizontally before the EU introduced its directives occurred in the Labor Court, consistent with that court's approach to horizontal effect since the 1950s.[112] The Labor Court has been quicker to rely on the constitutional commitment to equality in adjudicating fair relations between employer and employee.[113] Insofar as the labor courts' jurisdiction is circumscribed to labor law, the German legal community generally acknowledges that their area warrants more searching consideration of social power and even the continued application of *direct* horizontal effect.[114] In light of this tendency of the labor courts to give more weight to equality, it is not surprising that they largely allied with the European Court of Justice (ECJ) after the issuance of the 2000 antidiscrimination directives. The High Labor Court even asked the ECJ for preliminary references about the requirements of

---

[109] Ackermann, *Human Dignity*, 326. Interestingly, Ackermann thinks that South Africa ought to heed Germany's example in limiting the extent to which the Basic Law's right to equality applies to private law (327). Stephen Ellmann calls for similar limits in his article "A Constitutional Confluence: American 'State Action' Law and the Application of South Africa's Socioeconomic Rights Guarantees to Private Actors," *New York Law School Law Review* 45 (2001), 21–75. As the next chapter demonstrates, however, the South African Constitution lays groundwork for a more progressive practice of horizontality, which often, albeit not always, is manifested in the Constitutional Court's judgments.

[110] Ackermann, *Human Dignity*, 326.

[111] Ibid., 327.

[112] Ibid., 328.

[113] Stone Sweet and Stranz explain that the Labor Court has even employed its own invented "General Clause on Equality" to this end ("Rights Adjudication and Constitutional Pluralism in Germany and Europe," *Journal of European Public Policy* 19:1 [2012], 98).

[114] The Labor Court continued to employ direct horizontal effect through the 1980s without much resistance. Indeed, some even reason that "the one-sided relations of social power" that tend to characterize employment cases justify a higher accountability to constitutional standards than is necessary for other private relationships (Quint, "Free Speech and Private Law," 265, fn. 66).

these new policies, while the Constitutional Court instead followed along only to the extent that was required.

Although equality was certainly present in the Basic Law, it did not feature prominently in the context of private relations, a fact arguably consistent with the emphasis on *Privatautonomie* in certain sectors of German law discussed earlier. While German politics long possessed a strong welfarist streak, the value of equality did not extend further, for example, to include principles of antidiscrimination vis-à-vis gender, race, national identity, and the like. It may be the case that provisions for social welfare were understood as the functional equivalent of these protections, rendering the latter superfluous. Indeed, people from various sectors of civil society argued that such protections against discrimination would amount only to costly "red tape" and higher burdens of proof for private actors.[115] Ultimately, the external force of the EU shifted this status quo and pushed for the stronger horizontal presence of equality principles in the form of antidiscrimination legislation. The two directives that the European Council required in national law included Council Directive 2000/43/EC (the Racial Equality Directive) and Council Directive 2000/78/EC (the Employment Equality Framework Directive). The former aimed to bring all public and private law into line with EU equality norms, specifically concerning racial and ethnic discrimination. The latter directive, in contrast, aimed only to influence employment law, but required equal treatment across a range of classifications, including "sex, racial or ethnic origin, religion or belief, disability, age or sexual orientation."[116] The German Parliament first attempted to implement these directives in the Anti-Discrimination Act (ADG) of 2001.[117] The Act generated much controversy from all sectors

---

[115] Interview with Alexander Tischbirek, Berlin, December 9, 2019. Tischbirek explained that police unions were particularly concerned about the higher burden of proof they would have to satisfy.

[116] Sommeregger, "Horizontalization of Equality," 36; Mathews, *Extending Rights' Reach*, 79.

[117] Georg Sommeregger summarizes the changes the Act proposed:

> It would have regulated the conclusion, termination, content, and execution of contracts whose objects are goods and services offered in a market situation, (i.e., publicly), and in particular, contracts of purchase or sale, rent, credit, and insurance. Both direct and indirect discrimination would have been prohibited, and, new for German law, so would harassment. A striking feature of the rules of evidence was the intended reversal of the burden of proof in favor of the plaintiff. The defendant would, in other words, be called to adequately and convincingly prove his/her lack of

of German society, as politicians, jurists, and many others in civil society argued the Act "would go too far in curtailing the principle of private autonomy."[118] Others argued that it was in fact necessary not to exempt "predominant sectors of social life from scrutinization" in order to take nondiscrimination seriously.[119]

In his contemporaneous analysis of the arguments surrounding the ADG, Georg Sommeregger recounts some scholars' worries about the proposed legislation:

> The introduction of equality in the private sphere by doctrines of horizontality is in substance mandated virtue imposed by the state on the individual. As Karl-Heinz Ladeur put it, "In a liberal society there should be a difference between prosecution of public discrimination against citizens and public invasion of privacy in order to impose 'correct' views on citizens." In this criticism the state appears as a missionary that tries to make citizens morally "good."[120]

While preserving a private sphere permits diversity of views, abolishing the public–private divide, as the new legislation was understood to do, would entail "subjecting private action to the same moral yardstick (or values) as are valid for public agents."[121] The argument continues that this would result in "crushing ... the possibility of private choice by 'public virtue.'"[122] The prospect of bringing the value of equality to bear on private spaces thus yielded strong reactions for the very reason that it would require individuals in the private sphere to adhere to a public formulation of a kind of common good. Sommeregger stipulates, however, that this parity (what he calls "value monism") was only required in select areas and with respect to particular categories. The legislation did

---

intent to discriminate. Another new item was the right of associations to take legal action (*Verbandsklagerecht*) on behalf of the victim of the alleged discrimination. Associations could even have proceeded without the consent of the victim.

("Horizontalization of Equality," 39)

[118] Sommeregger, "Horizontalization of Equality," 37–39; Mathews, *Extending Rights' Reach*, 81; Fedtke, "*Drittwirkung* in Germany," 154. Sabine Berghahn also describes the reactions of churches and other religious organizations in Ben Knight, "European Court of Justice Tells German Churches to Respect EU Discrimination Law," *Deutsche Welle*, September 11, 2017, accessed July 9, 2019, https://p.dw.com/p/2nMsu.
[119] Sommeregger, "Horizontalization of Equality," 44.
[120] Ibid.
[121] Ibid.
[122] Ibid.

not entail a blanket requirement that all private choice conform to public standards, but only that some private choices conform. On this basis, he concludes that the legislation "did not introduce a new paradigm but shifted the line between uncensored and censored private behavior (too far for some), with the result that the private sphere is decimated without being liquidated conceptually."[123] The appropriateness of such shifting of the public moral yardstick into private spaces ultimately amounts to a political question, the answer to which likely depends on a given country's particular history, commitments, and public opinion.

In many ways, these fears about the consequences for autonomy echo those same fears articulated in the run-up to the *Lüth* case in the 1950s. Nevertheless, the antidiscrimination legislation stirring up those fears is different from the initial move to horizontality in *Lüth* in a couple of ways. First, the content of the rights in question is qualitatively different from those that had been given horizontal effect in prior decades.[124] Sommeregger explains, "In the horizontalization of other fundamental rights the fundamental tension between liberty and equality is in the background, whereas in the case of the antidiscrimination legislation it comes to the fore because of the fact that equality itself is the object of

---

[123] Ibid., 48.

[124] Rather than depend entirely on a distinction between liberty and equality, Sommeregger goes further to explain this as a difference between two concepts of equality. This distinction is analytically useful and achieves a level of nuance, often lost in similar discussions, insofar as classical liberalism consistently counts equality among its foundational principles. He states:

> In the public sphere, equality equals the principle of non-discrimination-... In the private sphere, equality refers to the equal standing or equal autonomy, of the individuals relative to each other, i.e., the lack of hierarchy, or "natural" equality ... The passing of anti-discrimination legislation means the transferal of the logic of equality in the public field (constitutional law field) to private law/private relationships. The introduction of the logic of equality-non-discrimination into private law, which hitherto functioned on the logic of equality-as-autonomy, means that in the private sphere, the "state" element of the public formula (i.e. the relationship state v. individual) is transferred to the "individual" element of the private formula (relationship individual v. individual). The result of the substitution is that the individual (now in the place of the state) has a duty not to discriminate (on the grounds spelled out by the law), but can no longer oppose its own rights to autonomous choice. The space formerly filled autonomously and arbitrarily by individuals is now filled by the state, and filled with the common standard of the community.
> ("Horizontalization of Equality," 46–47)

horizontalization."[125] This book's argument presumes that horizontal effect *always* entails parity, insofar as it always brings public values to bear in private spaces. Thus, even when more negative, classical rights are at issue in a case, one of the parties will still be required to conform to those attendant values of the Constitution – for example, the freedom to develop human personality in *Mephisto*, or the freedom of the press in *Blinkfüer*. To this extent, the EU directives and subsequent legislation of the German Parliament were not different, but simply added new rights to the catalog of those that would in some way be applied horizontally.

At the same time, the nature of the duties incurred is somewhat different in comparing negative classical rights with equality rights horizontally applied. The difference in duties is even more apparent in the potential positive duties of private actors considered in the context of South Africa in Chapter 6. Presumably, this heightened potential for the constitutional duties of private actors might be felt all the more in some corners given certain regnant elements of German legal history and tradition, such as the system of civil law, recounted earlier. Moreover, the consensus that such values inspired was in certain ways embodied in the liberal surge of the postwar years. In Sommeregger's terms, a kind of "value monism" with respect to these more classical rights did not give rise to controversy. When the prospect of individual duties pertaining to antidiscrimination arose, however, many expressed anxiety that the consequent new duties would touch subjects that comprised a continued "value pluralism" in German society. Put differently, regarding the ADG, some private actors expressed that the content of those rights for which private actors would be held responsible would potentially conflict with their priors.[126]

---

[125] Sommeregger, "Horizontalization of Equality," 45.

[126] Jud Mathews recounts some of the cases that followed the AGG (the legislation that ultimately was successful following the ADG). He states:

> A number of cases concern indirect discrimination on the basis of language: for example, the state labor court in Nuremberg ruled that a job requirement of "very good knowledge of German" in a job posting for a software specialist could be evidence of discrimination. Cases concerning unequal treatment on the basis of religion have been numerous, and their outcomes have often turned on whether equal treatment would infringe the employers' own confessional rights. A Muslim dental trainee had a right to wear a headscarf at work, according to a labor court in Berlin, but a Protestant hospital could legally forbid a Muslim nurse from wearing a headscarf, according to the state labor court in Hamm. The Federal Labor Court ruled that it could violate the AGG for an employer to fire a Muslim

Unlike the early judicial debates that preceded *Lüth*, the shift to apply equality and, more specifically, antidiscrimination horizontally occurred through legislation, first through the European Council and then the German Parliament.[127] Whereas the practice of horizontal effect in courts applies rights obligations to private actors in single, isolated cases, the developments following the EU directives came through legislation and, therefore, amounted to a change in the very "base-line of private law."[128] Claims to autonomy, people feared, would no longer be balanced or weighed on a case-by-case basis, but would necessarily yield to equality. As Sommeregger puts it, "The moral standard (one and only) of the community trumps the individual moral standards (resting on personal choice) of the individuals in the specific fields."[129] While a common objection to horizontal application is that courts are not politically accountable in the same way as legislatures, the more typical objection to the ADG was less about the venue of decision than about "this move of public virtue into the private sphere" at all, regardless of origin.[130]

When it comes to the horizontal application of equality and the debates surrounding the ADG, the republican framework of this book amounts to more than an interpretive lens. Rather it captures and

> warehouse employee for declining on religious grounds to move alcohol, and a labor court in Stuttgart ruled that a Catholic organization could fire a teacher for entering a same-sex civil union.
>
> Courts have also considered gender discrimination claims in a number of contexts, reaching various results. A labor court in Cologne held that an airline's minimum height requirement for pilots could constitute a form of indirect discrimination, while the state labor court in Mainz held that employers may give women preferential access to parking spaces. A series of cases concerns unequal access to discos and nightclubs, on the basis of gender or race. A man won a 300 euro judgment against a dance club in Berlin that turned him and his friends away because, according to the bouncer, "you guys are too many men." A dark-skinned law student in Bremen won his claim that he was turned away from a disco on account of his race because several witnesses confirmed his account and the defendant could not prove its claim that he was in fact turned away because he was dressed unfashionably.
>
> (*Extending Rights' Reach*, 83–84)

[127] Of course, this situation raises questions about the relationship between EU and national processes. I bracket this issue here as it is the focus of Chapter 7. See also Johan van der Walt, *The Horizontal Effect Revolution and the Question of Sovereignty* (Berlin: De Gruyter, 2014).
[128] Sommeregger, "Horizontalization of Equality," 48.
[129] Ibid.
[130] Ibid., 47.

articulates how many political and private actors themselves interpreted these developments. Sommeregger's account, for example, suggests that many recognized the reach of public values into more sectors of society as establishing a kind of common good, likely to entail more extensive duties of private actors and compromise of private interests. Again, this is in contrast with the kinds of rights that had previously been applied horizontally in German constitutional practice, such as freedom of expression and freedom of the press, that did not typically require extensive positive action on the part of private actors. On some level, the Basic Law and *Lüth*'s interpretation of it were always premised on a need to build a polity on certain common values after the Second World War; however, this commonality had only extended so far into the private sphere prior to the EU's antidiscrimination directives. On this basis, perhaps it is unsurprising that the impetus to extend horizontal application further came from EU institutions, that is, sources external to Germany.

Ultimately the ADG failed under this political opposition to public mores in the private sphere. Moreover, the ensuing controversy led parliament to change the law actually to allow more discrimination, specifically in lessening protections for workers dismissed from their jobs on the basis of age.[131] Nevertheless, EU institutions stood their ground on the issues at stake when, in the 2005 *Mangold* case, the ECJ described antidiscrimination as one of the EU's "general principles" that ran deeper than the recent directives, thereby insisting on German compliance. While the Constitutional Court, in response, might have reasserted "control over equality law in Germany," it followed the ECJ and, indeed, the German Labor Court, so as not to appear an opponent of equality.[132]

In 2006, the German Parliament managed to pass the General Equal Treatment Act (AGG) in fulfillment of the EU directives. Most decisions related to this legislation have since been issued by the civil courts and labor courts rather than the Constitutional Court.[133] Indeed, very few cases invoking the AGG have been litigated at the federal level. Scholars suggest a couple of different factors to explain this, such as the difficulty certain groups (and particularly vagrant populations) have in accessing the German courts, as well as the short, two-month timeline individuals

---

[131] Mathews, *Extending Rights' Reach*, 82.
[132] Ibid.
[133] Ibid., 83.

have to file antidiscrimination suits.¹³⁴ Moreover, certain aspects of the EU directives have long remained unimplemented, specifically those areas such as education that fall under the competencies of the *Länder* (German federal states). Several states have attempted to implement these aspects of the antidiscrimination directives, but have been largely unsuccessful. Indeed, the same concerns surrounding the ADG and AGG have resurfaced in these subnational arguments.¹³⁵ Amid myriad other factors figuring into these debates, some more resistant arguments may be understood in historical terms. Specifically, antidiscrimination had not previously been emphasized in German legal culture as much as civil liberties, "having comparably weak roots in the tradition of fundamental rights (and their adjudication by the FCC) as well as in public perception."¹³⁶ In this light, the hesitance displayed in arguments from various corners of German society is not necessarily surprising.

Equality and the Future of Horizontal Effect

After the events surrounding the EU directives and the AGG, whether and when Article 3's equality provisions might apply horizontally also became the subject of much debate. The arguments surrounding these later debates offer additional insight for interpreting horizontality in a republican light. The Constitutional Court finally took up the question of the horizontal application of Article 3 in 2018 in the *Stadium Ban* case. In this case, a sixteen-year-old fan of a German football club was permanently banned from a stadium for disorderly behavior.¹³⁷ The individual filed a constitutional complaint, arguing that the ban violated his constitutional right to the free development of personality "in light of the paramount significance of football for social life and the importance attached to it by the general public and society."¹³⁸ Although the Constitutional Court agreed that the facts of the case did implicate questions of constitutional rights, they found the issue was not the youth's right of personality but his right to equality under Article 3(1)

---

¹³⁴ Interview with Alexander Tischbirek, Berlin, 9 December 2019.
¹³⁵ Michael Wrase, "Anti-discrimination Law and Legal Culture in Germany," in *Antidiscrimination Law in Civil Law Jurisdictions*, ed. Barbara Havelková and Mathias Möschel (Oxford: Oxford University Press, 2019); interview with Alexander Tischbirek, Berlin, 9 December 2019.
¹³⁶ Wrase, "Anti-discrimination Law," 141.
¹³⁷ *Stadium Ban*, 1 BvR, 2080/09, April 11, 2018.
¹³⁸ Ibid., para. 6.

insofar as he was treated differently from other stadium attendees. Thus, the task of the courts was to balance this protection against unequal treatment under Article 3(1) against the football club's guarantee of private property under Article 14(1).

The Court was careful to stipulate, however, that Article 3(1) "does not give rise to an objective constitutional principle," such that private actors would generally have a duty to uphold equality rights. Rather, the Court reiterated the liberal precept that "all persons have the freedom to choose – according to their own preferences – when, with whom, and under what circumstances they want to enter into contracts, and how they want to make use of their property in this context." The young fan's equality rights under Article 3(1) only applied to the football club, a private actor, in this instance because of the particular nature of the football club and the stadium. Specifically, these were institutions generally open to the public, forming a central part of social life, and maintaining a kind of monopoly over the sport of football. Even while subject to Article 3 requirements in this particular case, however, the Court determined that the football club had not acted arbitrarily in banning the young fan, but that the unequal treatment was justified by his conduct.

In many ways, the *Stadium Ban* case raised more questions than it answered. While on the one hand, it seemed equality rights might now apply horizontally, the extent to which this hinged on the particular facts of the individual case remained unclear. Legal scholars found a kind of ambivalence in the judgment and speculated that the Court may have had trouble reaching a consensus.[139] Indeed, one could simultaneously read it as preparation for more to come or as a careful attempt to cabin the outcome to this single decision. The picture would only become murkier in the following year when the Court decided two additional cases concerning Article 3(1)'s equality guarantee. The first of these was simply a preliminary injunction that the Third Way, a far-right political party, filed against Facebook after the social media platform identified some of its posts as hate speech and temporarily restricted the party's ability to post content.[140] The facts raised questions about Facebook's

---

[139] Interview with Christoph Möllers, Berlin, 9 December 2019.
[140] 1 BvQ 42/19, 22 May 2019. In this case, Facebook acted on the basis that the hate speech violated its own community standards. However, it is worth noting that Germany's 2017 Network Enforcement Act (NetzDG) also creates obligations of communications companies, such as Facebook, to restrict hate speech. The law has faced much criticism

obligations with respect to equal treatment and whether social networks would be subject to Article 3 obligations, as was the football club in the *Stadium Ban* case. However, the Court decided only the question of injunction, granting the Third Way's petition, rather than taking on the constitutional question at stake.[141]

A few months later, the Constitutional Court confronted the possibility of the horizontal application of equality yet again when an official of the extremist right-wing National Democratic Party of Germany made a reservation for a wellness hotel. The hotel owner notified him that he could not stay, explaining that the official's "political opinions were incompatible with the hotel's mission to ensure that each and every guest could enjoy an excellent wellness experience."[142] The Court reiterated the principle it articulated in the *Stadium Ban* case, that private actors were not subject to equality guidelines as a general principle, but only under specific circumstances. Ultimately, the Court decided that those specific circumstances simply were not present here; unlike the football club, the wellness hotel did not form a central part of social life and did not maintain a monopoly. Therefore, the party official could claim no right against which to balance the hotel owner's right to property (Article 14(1)) and freedom to conduct a business (Article 12(1)). Moreover, the Court clarified that the prior *Stadium Ban* case had only treated the General Equality Clause of Article 3(1), rather than the Anti-Discrimination Provision of Article 3(3). While the Court explicitly left open the possibility that this provision might require something of private actors, it did not follow from the ruling that they are prohibited from discriminating on the basis of political opinion. Again, as Fabian Michl explains, private

---

for delegating too much responsibility to private corporations. Maintaining the balance between freedom of expression and protection against hate speech, critics argue, ought to be a function of public actors. Legal scholars predicted early on that the law would come before the Constitutional Court before long (interview with Holger Greve, Berlin, December 9, 2019).

[141] The Constitutional Court has also considered, albeit in *obiter dictum*, the possibility that social media companies may be responsible for upholding other rights commitments as well. In a 2011 case (1 BvR 699/06 [22 February 2011]) the Court determined that an airport was directly bound by fundamental rights obligations as a result of the state's involvement in the airport's operations (akin to the "entanglement" exception to the state action doctrine in the United States). In para. 59 of the opinion, the Court briefly suggests that telecommunications companies may also be directly bound to fundamental rights obligations, such as the freedoms of expression and assembly, when they assume traditionally public functions (akin to the "public function" exception to the US state action doctrine).

[142] 1 BvR 879/12, August 27, 2019.

individuals "are free to decide who they favor or disadvantage, with whom to conclude contracts and to whom to grant access to their property, their pub or their hotel."[143] In this same spirit, the Court decided for the hotel in the name of freedom, once again not even reaching the question of balancing.

Where does this sequence of cases leave the question of equality's horizontal application and, more specifically, a republican interpretation of horizontality? In many ways, the arguments of these judgments hinge on facts unique to the cases at hand – the cultural significance of football in Germany, for example, or historical experience with extreme parties. In Germany, a football stadium is not simply a sports arena but a public forum where citizens go to associate and participate in civic life. Full participation in society may be said to require admission in such a space, while the same cannot be said of the wellness hotel. Setting aside consideration of the factors that might explain the constitutional development itself, the arguments playing into these equality cases show an implicit hesitancy that is arguably relevant to a republican interpretation. Specifically, the judgments point toward a particular way of carving up the private sphere, as the Court understands certain private actors and spaces as contributing to (or detracting from) a kind of common good more than others. Insofar as certain private actors hold greater public import, they are more subject to constitutional values and accrue duties. Contextual particulars are crucial here, as football and a football stadium would not necessarily have the same meaning attached to them elsewhere and, consequently, would not be so relevant to a republican interpretation.

Rights and larger commitments related to equality in Germany thus bring to the fore discursive insights that bear on republican interpretations of horizontality. As explained previously and is true in other contexts, equality is often interpreted as requiring more of private actors than other rights commitments and, to this extent, shows the reach of a republican interpretation amid contextual particulars. Generally, discourses surrounding the horizontal application of equality have been weaker and more hesitant than, say, in the horizontal application of freedom of expression or freedom of the press in Germany. Considering the arguments that arose from the ADG/AGG saga and

---

[143] Fabian Michl, "Wer darf wen 'diskriminieren'? Zum Nichtannahmebeschluss in Sachen Hotelverbot (1 BvR 879/12)," *VerfBlog*, October 12, 2019, https://verfassungsblog.de/wer-darf-wen-diskriminieren.

later debates focused on Article 3, the effect of constitutional values has not radiated so decisively when it comes to equality. However, later judgments have treated some spaces and actors in a way that suggests their heightened public significance or historical meaning and, on this basis, assign constitutional duties related even to equality.

Conclusion

In *Lüth*, the Constitutional Court declared that the Basic Law engendered an objective order of values and, thus, that the constitutional project aspired to influence broader reaches of society than had prior constitutions. In this way, the Court's language signaled a transformative project for a reconstituted Germany. The idea that constitutional values should radiate beyond traditional bounds set a course for a project clearly more ambitious than traditional understandings of constitutionalism. Nevertheless, the fundamental structure of the legal system remained in place with *Lüth*, as the Court acknowledged that private law contributed to "the autonomy of the individual – and to the public good – and therefore should remain in effect ... even when confronted by the countervailing objective and public values of constitutional law."[144] The Constitutional Court thereby reaffirmed the presuppositions of the civil law system so that the Basic Law could influence the private law but not supplant it.[145] In pursuing this moderate course, the Constitutional Court in some sense nestled into the disharmony that had emerged between an enduring civil law tradition and the propagation of public values in private spaces.[146]

While horizontal application in some forms was broadly accepted and assumed into legal practice, a tension reminiscent of that latent in *Lüth* would surface in later debates surrounding the horizontal application of equality. In particular, the EU directives in 2000 aimed to add equality and antidiscrimination to the catalog of those commitments for which private actors would be responsible. As far as certain private actors and

---

[144] Quint, "Free Speech and Private Law," 263.
[145] Quint explains that "the fact that the action remains a private law action may have a significant limiting effect on the scope of the Constitutional Court's review" ("Free Speech and Private Law," 273). Whereas, in the United States, an actor can be held to a constitutional standard if he or she can be shown to be sufficiently entangled or serving a public function, private relationships remain private relationships in Germany and are governed as such even while being influenced by the Basic Law.
[146] Michelman, "Interplay," 289–290.

even some constitutional actors were concerned, this step to subject private spaces to constitutional ends went too far in encroaching on individual rights. While antidiscrimination legislation growing out of the EU directives ultimately passed the German Parliament, related questions about the horizontality of equality rights continue to be adjudicated in the Constitutional Court and other fora.

Describing the German constitutional project as transformative[147] can be helpful to understand what the constitutional drafters were up to in the wake of the Second World War, how the Constitutional Court interpreted that project in the following decade, and perhaps even later efforts to give greater effect to such values as equality. A transformative constitution makes clear space for something like horizontal application, which by definition extends constitutional commitments further into society than traditional understandings of constitutionalism would admit. Indeed, the history recounted in this chapter continually raises the question of what a transformative constitution might require in general and, more specifically, require of private actors. It is at this juncture that a republican interpretation becomes helpful.

This book's republican framework does not necessarily provide normative answers to questions about what a transformative constitution should ask of private actors. Rather, it offers an interpretive lens to understand actors' arguments around these questions. On the one hand, in debates about horizontal application in Germany, we might perceive an embrace of constitutional ends as a kind of common good and, consequently, an embrace of the corresponding duties that follow citizens. On the other hand, arguments in later debates surrounding equality suggest reservation concerning particular ends and the resulting "value monism," to use Sommeregger's phrase. Indeed, an easy embrace of ends and duties is not evident in the later sequence of events or in the arguments pertaining to antidiscrimination. Instead, the discourses emerging from later debates about equality favor more conventional understandings of rights, aligned with a conception of separate spheres, separate systems of law and courts, and so on. Put differently, this book's theoretic lens evinces complexity in the German context, namely, a waning of republican-inflected language about constitutional ends or a common good and renewed emphasis on rights discourses.

---

[147] Michaela Hailbronner, "Transformative Constitutionalism: Not Only in the Global South," *American Journal of Comparative Law* 65:3 (2017), 527–565.

In Chapter 6, similar insights emerge out of the South African context, arguably the paragon of transformative constitutionalism. Debates in both Germany and South Africa largely presuppose that public ends will bear on private spaces to some extent. Yet, how far and in what ways these public ends can reach vary across these constitutional contexts and even across institutions and individual actors within each context. Under the new dispensation in South Africa, debates have centered not so much on whether constitutional commitments may apply horizontally in one space or another but on what such commitments may require specifically of private actors, say, with respect to positive rights. As ever, factors countervailing against horizontal application also influence the debates; political interests rooted in the Apartheid era, as well as a kind of legal formalism, correlate with more traditional articulations of rights. At the same time, much of the constitutional discourse from a range of actors includes some basic admission that the South African constitutional project aims for and requires more of its citizens than other constitutional orders.

6

South Africa

Toward Societal Transformation

Among the numerous national constitutions adopted throughout the twentieth century, that of South Africa stands out for the transformation to which it aspires. Frank Michelman goes so far as to describe it as "postliberal."[1] In the early 1990s, the long-dominant National Party, which had perpetrated Apartheid, and the African National Congress (ANC), founded in response to the racist system, approached the negotiating table to reconstitute the country. Horizontal application fit naturally in this transformative project. As Apartheid had permeated all spheres of life, so too would such values as dignity, equality, and freedom[2] need to suffuse even private life. In this understanding, the constitution could not but call for parity between public and private spaces and hold at least some private actors responsible for these new commitments. A certain egalitarian bent consequently characterized much of the discourse, as distinct from more traditional discourses that emphasize classical political rights over socioeconomic rights, and vertical relationships over horizontal.

Whereas Germany's adoption of horizontal application came through the Federal Constitutional Court's decision in *Lüth*, much of the groundwork for horizontal application in South Africa was laid in the deliberations preceding the adoption of the Constitution. Ultimately, the text of the Final Constitution itself provides for broad application of horizontality. Indeed, Nick Friedman describes horizontality as practically necessary given the nature of the constitutional project. He states:

> Firstly, [horizontal application] commits individuals to the rebuilding of the ethical relations so radically shattered during apartheid, through the undertaking of legal duties to improve their communities. Secondly, given

---

[1] Frank Michelman, "Constitutions and the Public/Private Divide," in *Oxford Handbook of Comparative Constitutional Law*, ed. Michel Rosenfeld and András Sajó (Oxford: Oxford University Press, 2012), 311.

[2] South African Constitution, Chapter 1, Section 1.

the enormous task of reconstruction faced by the new South Africa, the limited resources of the state, and the grossly unequal and enormous wealth which resides in the private sector, horizontality breathes new hope into the possibility of creating a more equal and just society in the medium term. Thirdly, by requiring individuals to uphold their moral duties towards one another and to cooperate in realising a new vision for a shared future, horizontality reaffirms the human dignity of those who bear such duties as much as it does those who benefit from their performance. Insofar as direct horizontality contributes to the realisation of substantive equality and the establishment of the conditions necessary for an autonomous life, it promotes freedom and fosters a culture in which the infinite worth of each person is respected and valued.[3]

Republican principles can easily be read into this account of horizontality and the South African constitutional project – the recognition of duties vis-à-vis community, moral duties of one to the other, a shared future. Also striking is the way Friedman attributes dignity (a concept with a long republican pedigree) to duty-bearers and rights-bearers alike. There is a sense here in which the maintenance and execution of constitutional duties presupposes membership in a common project. In this light, the South African Constitution and the large-scale malaise it aims to ameliorate make clear space for horizontality and a republican interpretation of horizontality at that.

What specific role, then, does this chapter play in the book's project to interpret the practice of horizontal application through the lens of republican political theory? First, that the South African project aimed at thoroughgoing transformation in the way and to the degree it did sets it apart from other constitutional contexts this book considers. Of course, Germany's Basic Law can and has been described as transformative.[4] The German Federal Constitutional Court accordingly adopted horizontal application on the basis that constitutional principles create an "order of objective moral and legal principles" that "radiates" to both public and private spheres of life, as described in Chapter 5.[5] However, the Constitutional Court set limits on horizontality in the realm of equality

---

[3] Nick Friedman, "The South African Common Law and the Constitution: Revisiting Horizontality," *South African Journal on Human Rights* 30:1 (2014), 67; see also Aoife Nolan, "Holding Non-state Actors to Account for Constitutional Economic and Social Rights Violations: Experiences and Lessons from South Africa and Ireland," *International Journal of Constitutional Law* 12:1 (2014), 76.

[4] Michaela Hailbronner, "Transformative Constitutionalism: Not Only in the Global South," *American Journal of Comparative Law* 65:3 (2017), 527–565.

[5] *Lüth*, BVerfGE 7, 198 (1958).

rights, limits which only began to be broached some fifty or sixty years after *Lüth* was decided. In contrast, issues directly connected to equality, such as housing and education, have gained increasing salience in South African constitutional politics. While both the German and South African Constitutions have been dubbed transformative, the South African Constitution's explicit and broad provision for horizontal application arguably points toward a different conception of transformation and thus provides different ground on which to read horizontality as republican. From early initiatives of the ANC to later decisions of the Constitutional Court, South African constitutionalism proves quite receptive to republican interpretations and often echoes republican values.

However, some scholars and political observers take issue with this characterization of the South African Constitution as transformative. Emile Zitzke argues that what are often seen as transformative aspirations in South African private law and human rights do not ultimately address the problems arising from the country's colonial past. Specifically, the new order's Eurocentric roots inhibit full decolonization, a level of transformation that might be possible if African concepts were employed as meaningful reference points instead.[6] Perhaps more critically, Joel Modiri emphasizes how, as a product of negotiation and compromise, the new constitution actually preserves the interests and powers initially secured through racial oppression.[7] The space of this book does not allow for the full discussion these critiques merit. At the same time, the fact that the book's project is primarily analytical and theoretic, rather than normative, allows some liberty to take the South African Constitution at face value – to consider the transformation it does imply, though a different and more transformative project may be conceivable. As this book maintains, horizontality exists within the liberal constitutional milieu even as it marks a kind of digression from certain renderings of that milieu. At the same time, it seems safe to say that, as a descriptive matter, the South African Constitution does mark

---

[6] Emile Zitzke, "A Decolonial Critique of Private Law and Human Rights," *South African Journal on Human Rights* 34:3 (2018), 492–516. In the next section, this chapter discusses one such African concept for which Zitzke advocates, namely *ubuntu*, showing how it bears potential connection to the practice of horizontality. Nevertheless, in discussing horizontality, one can never fully abandon such arguably Eurocentric concepts as "rights." Moreover, as I discuss below, some scholars argue that even ubuntu has been co-opted by the liberal constitutionalist context to which it is sometimes applied.

[7] Joel M. Modiri, "Conquest and Constitutionalism: First Thoughts on an Alternative Jurisprudence," *South African Journal on Human Rights* 34:3 (2018), 300–325.

some real change from the prior order, though that change falls short of certain normative assessments.[8]

Even within the scope of this project, however, fears that the new order is not sufficiently transformative may be borne out in the way constitutional actors reconcile horizontal application with continuities from the prior order. Although key framers were clear, and the constitutional text explicit, in providing for horizontality, certain factors, both persisting from the prior system and emerging in the new, seem to countervail against this practice in particular instances. Indeed, differently situated constitutional actors have related differently to horizontality. As institutions and actors bring their various interests to the constitutional political table, it is to be expected, even in what is arguably an optimal context, that different actors may be more or less disposed to develop horizontal application. This chapter thus follows the same dynamic as previous chapters in finding more compelling republican interpretations in certain moments and spaces than others. While we ascertain their full weight in the light of South African history, law, and politics, these considerations offer important insights into horizontality more generally as well.

This chapter proceeds by uncovering republican interpretations of horizontality in various South African constitutional debates, paying particular attention to founding debates and the early landmark case, *Du Plessis v. De Klerk*, before turning to more recent developments. This chapter also addresses those factors that, in South Africa, have seemed to countervail against horizontal application. They include persistent priorities of the formerly dominant National Party, oppositional institutional interests not unlike the early debates between private and public lawyers in Germany, and a highly formalist legal culture. As in foregoing chapters, attention to these factors is not intended to set up a developmental argument, but to set the full contextual scene on which to analyze constitutional discourses surrounding horizontality and bring the republican lens to bear. Insofar as such factors are inseparable from, and even

---

[8] Some pieces that actually appear alongside the articles by Zitzke and Modiri are more confident in the transformative foundations that the Constitution establishes, attributing persisting pathologies instead to the way democratic politics has evolved (or, rather, has sometimes failed to evolve). See Firoz Cachalia, "Democratic Constitutionalism in the Time of the Postcolony: Beyond Triumph and Betrayal," and especially Dennis M. Davis, "Is the South African Constitution an Obstacle to a Democratic Post-colonial State?" both in *South African Journal on Human Rights* 34:3 (2018), 375–397, 359–374.

constitutive of, constitutional politics, so too will they bear on a republican interpretation of this constitutional practice.

Foundations for a Republican Interpretation: Ubuntu and Democracy

While those involved in the constitutional deliberations would not necessarily have described the constitutional project in terms of civic republicanism, communalistic elements have long figured into South African political culture. Specifically, the concept of *ubuntu* dates back to precolonial times, encompassing a rootedness in community and inescapable connectedness to neighbor. Praeg describes it as "a political economy of obligation"[9] and a "logic of interdependence."[10] Markedly different from political narratives focusing on the individual, ubuntu speaks to an interconnectedness and capacity for friendship among people as human beings. The Constitutional Court has made some use of the concept in its judgments, with Justice Mokgoro describing it as "an idea based on deep respect for the humanity of another"[11] and "part of our rainbow heritage."[12]

Some object that ubuntu is hollowed out by attempts to apply it to the liberal structures of South African constitutionalism.[13] The Constitution simply does not admit space for ubuntu's full-blown communalism, the argument goes, nor can ubuntu be employed to support such typically liberal structures as rights, courts, and the like. The very fact that courts are entrusted with enforcing the Constitution poses an obstacle in that they tend to understand conflicts as clashes of rights in contrast with the community-mindedness that ubuntu espouses.[14] Others have been more optimistic with respect to ubuntu's contributions to South African constitutionalism.[15] We see such optimism in Justice Sachs's judgment in *Port Elizabeth Municipality v. Various Occupiers*,[16] a case in which a

---

[9] Leonhard Praeg, *A Report on Ubuntu* (Pietermaritzburg: University of KwaZulu-Natal Press, 2014), 33.

[10] Ibid., 47.

[11] *Dikoko v. Mokhatla*, 2006 (6) SA 235, 2007 1 B.C.L.R. 1, paras. 68–69 (CC).

[12] *S v. Makwanyane*, 1995 (3) SA 391, para. 308 (CC).

[13] Stacy Douglas, "Ubuntu versus Ubuntu: Finding a Philosophy of Justice through Obligation," *Law Critique* 26 (2015), 305–312; Anthony O. Oyowe, "Strange Bedfellows: Rethinking *Ubuntu* and Human Rights in South Africa," *African Human Rights Law Journal* 13 (2013), 103–124.

[14] Douglas, "Ubuntu versus Ubuntu," 310.

[15] Thaddeus Metz, "Ubuntu as a Moral Theory and Human Rights in South Africa," *African Human Rights Law Journal* 11 (2011), 532.

[16] *Port Elizabeth Municipality v. Various Occupiers*, (CCT 53/03) [2004] ZACC.

white landowner attempted to evict extremely poor black families who had lived on the land for years. Drawing on ubuntu, Justice Sachs required the parties to "engage with each other in a proactive and honest endeavor to find mutually acceptable solutions" before resorting to such adversarial measures as eviction. He explained:

> The spirit of *ubuntu*, part of the deep cultural heritage of the majority of the population, suffuses the whole constitutional order. It combines individual rights with a communitarian philosophy. It is a unifying motif of the Bill of Rights, which is nothing if not a structured, institutionalized and operational declaration in our evolving new society of the need for human interdependence, respect and concern.[17]

The Court would rely on similar reasoning in such later cases as *President of South Africa v. Modderklip*,[18] discussed later, actually shying away from the language of rights in favor of a call for neighborliness.

For some, the concept of ubuntu has thus served as a counternarrative or supplement, aligning South African constitutionalism with the maxim that "[a] person is a person through other persons."[19] Put differently, ubuntu potentially brings something new to the constitutional table in the very act of bringing something quite old, not unlike this book's republican interpretation of horizontality. What Chapter 2 argues to be republican features of horizontal application bring to constitutionalism an understanding of the polity conceived as a whole, as well as an understanding that citizens have duties to one another. In a similar way, ubuntu conjures a conception of constitutionalism that transcends the individual, evinced in Justice Sachs's judgment in *Port Elizabeth Municipality*. He explains that "those seeking eviction should not rely on "concepts of faceless and anonymous squatters automatically to be expelled as obnoxious social nuisances,"[20] and that "those who find themselves compelled by poverty and homelessness to live in shacks on the land of others, should be discouraged from regarding themselves as helpless victims, lacking the possibilities of personal moral agency."[21] Thus, Justice Sachs concludes, "Wherever possible, respectful face-to-face

---

[17] Ibid.; see also Justice Albie Sachs, *The Strange Alchemy of Life and Law* (Oxford: Oxford University Press, 2009), 105–109.
[18] *President of the Republic of South Africa and Another v. Modderklip Boerdery (Pty) Ltd* (CCT20/04) [2005] ZACC 5, para. 54, quoting Albie Sachs's opinion in *Port Elizabeth Municipality v. Various Occupiers*.
[19] Metz, "Ubuntu as a Moral Theory," 536.
[20] *Port Elizabeth Municipality v. Various Occupiers*, para. 41.
[21] Ibid.

engagement or mediation through a third party should replace arms-length combat by intransigent opponents."[22]

Ubuntu arguably offers a philosophic tradition, already existing in South Africa, to buttress a republican interpretation of horizontal application. While not self-consciously or explicitly connected with republicanism, ubuntu tracks certain republican ideals in its calls for mutual respect among citizens.[23] And indeed, the Court invokes ubuntu in crucial horizontality cases, including *City of Johannesburg v. Blue Moonlight Properties*[24] and *AB and Another v. Pridwin Preparatory School*,[25] discussed later. The point of comparing ubuntu and republican ideas is not to create a false equivalence between them, but rather to sketch the full contextual space that could admit a republican reading of horizontal application. Indeed, ubuntu is a primary reason there is more such space for a republican reading of horizontality in South Africa than in nearly any other context in the world. As Chapter 2 explains, horizontal application seems to call for a new theoretical reference point that this book sums up in the concept of the common good – the sheer idea that there is a good of the community of which to speak, one that extends beyond individual rights to encompass some consideration of shared ends. However, what ultimately is contained in, or what substance is meant by, the common good is at least partly contingent on the politics of the place.[26] Likewise, ubuntu emphatically is not about individual rights but rests on the essential nature, even the priority, of community. Therefore, in addition to tracking a similar orientation toward the communal, the concept of ubuntu is noteworthy as it potentially offers some substantive content, even if at a high level of abstraction, to understand what exactly the common good might involve in this context.[27]

In addition to this age-old principle of ubuntu, early proposals of the ANC also point toward something of a communal approach to treating

---

[22] Ibid., para. 39.
[23] See, for example, Chapter 2's discussion of Philip Pettit's "eyeball test."
[24] *City of Johannesburg Metropolitan Municipality v. Blue Moonlight Properties 39 (Pty) Ltd and Another* (CC) [2011] ZACC 33, para. 38.
[25] *AB and Another v. Pridwin Preparatory School and Others* (CCT294/18) [2020] ZACC 12, para. 61.
[26] Of course, one may meaningfully argue that certain understandings of the common good are better (or worse) than others. Variations of the concept have appeared in different schools of thought, even nefarious ones.
[27] It is worth noting, however, that even ubuntu has come to be imbued with different meanings, as the spectrum of political persuasions, from liberals to communists, lay claim to fulfilling this principle.

South Africa's pathologies. Democracy would become the ANC's constant refrain, as the party put its faith in the change it hoped would follow from enfranchising the population's actual majority. Moreover, the cooperation even of private actors within the public project was key. In a certain sense, bringing public and private standards under a more common regulative umbrella could serve to democratize law and politics, rather than exempting one corner of law to follow a different, perhaps less demanding standard.[28] In this democratized understanding, no space of society exists beyond the fundamental law to which "the people" have ascribed their consent, provided that the people are in fact consenting to and creating that law.

Giving voice to these commitments, among others, the ANC Constitutional Committee drafted its 1991 Bill of Rights for a New South Africa even prior to the negotiations and convening of the Constitutional Assembly.[29] While this document would not be adopted wholesale into the Final Constitution, it offers a clear articulation of the solutions key actors envisioned would solve South Africa's problems. Relevant to the present project, Article 14(1) states, "In its activities and functioning, the State shall observe the principles of non-racialism and non-sexism, and encourage the same in all public and private bodies." In a similar vein, Article 14(3) continues, "The State and all public and private bodies shall be under a duty to prevent any form of incitement to racial, religious or linguistic hostility and to dismantle all structures and do away with all practices that compulsorily divide the population on grounds of race, color, language, or creed." And finally, Article 16(3) on Enforcement states, "The terms of the Bill of Rights shall be binding upon the State and organs of government at all levels, and where appropriate, on all social institutions and persons." Such early proposals clearly imply a republicanesque diagnosis of the situation and republican prescription for what a new, democratic South Africa would require. References to how the state should direct both public and private action, as well as to the duties of private bodies to dismantle divisive social structures, contemplate something like horizontal application.

---

[28] I am indebted to Heinz Klug for this insight.
[29] Zola Skwyiya, "A Bill of Rights for a New South Africa: A Working Document by the ANC Constitutional Committee," *African Journal of International and Comparative Law* 3 (1991), 601; ANC Constitutional Committee, "A Bill of Rights for a Democratic South Africa: A Working Draft for Consultation," *African Journal of International and Comparative Law* 3 (1991), 608.

Moreover, such formulations seem to conceive of these duties not as separate from or supplementary to the public project but as constitutive of a vision or good that could only be achieved in common.

The proposed Bill of Rights continues with Article 15 establishing the possibility that legislation might limit the exercise of rights, and beginning to outline the conditions under which such limitations could occur for the sake of maintaining "an open and democratic society."[30] As Chapter 2 suggested, limitation clauses are arguably a precondition for horizontal application, insofar as they acknowledge that individual rights might give way to broader ends, whether to the rights of others or to certain communal goods. Such limitations may not amount to full-blown duties, necessarily, but they do entail some concession of limits to exercising one's own rights. Following the Canadian Charter as an example, the South African drafters, therefore, took the crucial step to preserve limitations analysis in both the 1993 Interim Constitution (Chapter 3(33)) and the Final Constitution (Chapter 2(36)).[31] By the Interim Constitution's adoption, the early articulations of horizontality in the ANC's 1991 Bill of Rights, mentioned above, had been dropped, with no mention of private bodies in Chapter 3(7) on the "Application" of rights. While the ANC's vision offers robust ground for a republican interpretation in early proposals for horizontal application, the omission of horizontal application from the 1993 text likewise reveals the presence of other forces in the constitutional story running up against this republican interpretation.

The Interim Constitution: A First Step "to Make the Best Constitution in the World"

The process by which South Africa adopted its new constitution is well known.[32] The National Party (what historically had been the white Afrikaner ethnic nationalist party) and the ANC (founded for the purpose of ending Apartheid) agreed to pursue a two-stage constitution-making process, beginning with an Interim Constitution negotiated between the parties that would set the terms for a Final Constitution.

---

[30] ANC Constitutional Committee, "A Bill of Rights for a Democratic South Africa," 619.

[31] Dennis M. Davis, "Constitutional Borrowing: The Influence of Legal Culture and Local History in the Reconstitution of Comparative Influence – The South African Experience," *International Journal of Constitutional Law* 1:2 (2003), 187.

[32] Remote interview with Nicholas Haysom, October 26, 2020. Mr. Haysom explained how those involved in the negotiations saw the opportunity as "the only shot we get to make the best constitution in the world."

Ultimately the Constitutional Court would prescribe nine changes to the draft text before certifying the country's new vision in the Final Constitution. The choice to conduct a multistage process was a conscious attempt to navigate an issue ubiquitous in constitution-making but especially salient in the South African context, namely, the challenge of balancing majoritarian rule with the protection of minority rights.[33] In South Africa, this meant facilitating the transition to democracy by abolishing racial elections and granting universal suffrage, a move likely to cast white populations in the role of political minority in the new government. The Interim Constitution was thus an effort to begin the constitution-making process by setting initial terms on which all the major parties could agree.[34]

As the ANC came to the negotiating table with such aspirations as they had articulated in their 1991 Bill of Rights, so too did the National Party come with goals of its own, namely, to secure a space for itself in public and private life as it assumed minority status.[35] On this basis, National Party representatives initially advocated for group rights in the new constitution, specifically for the recognition of the Afrikaner population as a group with such rights as to education in its own language.[36] The concept of group rights was met with great suspicion, however, from both domestic and international voices. With the possibility of group rights roundly rejected, the National Party ultimately changed tack to pursue individual rights instead, especially strong property rights,[37] as well as a high degree of autonomy in private spaces and at local levels. Indeed, local governments were not even discussed at this stage of the deliberations and would remain racialized through the 1990s.[38]

---

[33] Ibid.; Heinz Klug, *Constituting Democracy: Law, Globalism, and South Africa's Political Reconstruction* (Cambridge: Cambridge University Press, 2010).

[34] See Klug, *Constituting Democracy*. The two-stage process attempted, too, to address the concerns of other populations that would also assume minority status, including the Zulus and their particular objection to their king's diminished status under the new constitution. Violent conflict ensued and, ultimately, the Zulu population refused to participate in the deliberations (remote interview with Nicholas Haysom, October 26, 2020).

[35] At this stage of the process, only fringe groups on the far right were interested in preserving the racially exclusivist politics of years prior (remote interview with Hoyt Webb, November 16, 2020).

[36] Remote interview with Nicholas Haysom, October 26, 2020.

[37] Remote interview with Sheila Camerer, March 3, 2021.

[38] Klug, *Constituting Democracy*.

This early stage of constitution-making was an exercise in pragmatism and compromise, arguably to a degree exceeding many other nations' processes. The goal at this interim stage was simply to commence a conversation the parties would be willing to continue into subsequent years. As a practical document, the Interim Constitution rolled back many facets of the ANC's early proposals. The proposed practice of horizontal application, for example, was dropped. Relatedly, the text shows some shift in emphasis toward such rights as to property, departing somewhat from the vision of the 1991 Bill of Rights. In the terms of this book, that which might have supported republican understandings – say, a vision of ends related to elevating the socioeconomic status of black populations – was effectively dropped at this stage to accommodate other rights and interests.[39] Recounting this dynamic in his memoir, Justice Sachs explains how "[t]he dialectic of legal development was such ... that concepts intended to assuage the anxieties of the whites inevitably aroused the concerns of the blacks."[40]

Although direct horizontal application was omitted from the text of the Interim Constitution, the subject did arise in the deliberations. Mindful of Apartheid's deep-seated legacy in the social fabric, this was a natural question for ANC representatives to consider as they aimed beyond formal rights protections at thoroughgoing transformation.[41] Insofar as private actors would maintain great power, framing rights as only the state's responsibility, rather than shared by citizens or other private actors, might have impractically constrained the larger project.[42] Interestingly, however, the prospect of applying rights horizontally was debated both among and within parties involved in the deliberations of the Interim Constitution.[43] Despite some consensus that the new constitution was bound to bring sweeping change, less clear was the role of horizontal application in this project. Members across the parties feared the real possibility that a clumsy formulation of horizontal application would have far-reaching and unintended consequences.

---

[39] Sachs, *Strange Alchemy*, 165–166.

[40] Ibid., 166. Justice Sachs describes how many, including some black law students, feared that a bill of rights stood to benefit whites more than anyone.

[41] Nolan, "Holding Non-state Actors."

[42] Lourens Marthinus Du Plessis and Hugh Corder, *Understanding South Africa's Transitional Bill of Rights* (Kenwyn: Juta, 1994), 113.

[43] Richard Spitz offers a detailed account of the discussions and shifting positions on this question (Richard Spitz with Matthew Chaskalson, *The Politics of Transition: A Hidden History of South Africa's Negotiated Settlement* [Oxford: Hart, 2000], 268–278).

Noting the global trend toward horizontality, the Technical Committee on Fundamental Rights included horizontal application in the original proposal for the Interim Constitution.[44] Unsurprisingly, representatives of the National Party and the libertarian Inkatha Freedom Party were wary of this provision, pushing instead for a vertical model to obligate only state actors and not change so drastically the status quo that privileged whites.[45] Moreover, the Communist Party also expressed hesitation about horizontal application, but their criticism stemmed from fear of its bidirectionality, or the possibility that corporations could claim rights against private individuals, too.[46] In such an understanding, horizontal application could be abused by "economically powerful institutions in areas which do not properly fall within the ambit of an instrument for human rights protection."[47]

Despite early articulations of horizontal application in the ANC's 1991 Bill of Rights and the Technical Committee's proposal, a gap emerged even among those who favored significant change under the new constitutional dispensation. For example, in Spitz's telling, Halton Cheadle and Albie Sachs disagreed on this question, Sachs counting himself among those who thought horizontal application necessary to prevent the privatization of Apartheid.[48] Spitz also attributes this divide to various party members' consultation with such law professors as Laurence Tribe. Apparently, Tribe cautioned the committee on rights against horizontal application, for the common reason that legislatures, rather than courts, are better suited to regulating private relations.[49] Likewise, Chief Justice Michael Corbett commented on a draft expressing the judiciary's opposition for similar reasons, asserting that horizontal application would bring judges into policy debates that ought to happen in politically accountable branches of government. On the other hand, others' worries cut in the other direction, that cementing horizontal

---

[44] Du Plessis and Corder, *Understanding*, 111.
[45] Spitz, *Politics of Transition*, 269.
[46] Section 7(3) also entitled "juristic persons" to rights, reflecting another trend in constitutionalism that found its roots in the German Basic Law. For their part, the South African drafters tried to delimit this provision by making its application contingent on the nature of the right (as opposed to the nature of the juristic person) (Du Plessis and Corder, *Understanding*, 116–117).
[47] Du Plessis and Corder, *Understanding*, 111–112; remote interview with Nicholas Haysom, October 26, 2020.
[48] Spitz, *Politics of Transition*, 271. Ironically, Sachs would decide against horizontal application in the early decision of *Du Plessis v. De Klerk*, discussed later.
[49] Spitz, *Politics of Transition*, 271; see also Du Plessis and Corder, *Understanding*, 112.

application of particular rights in the Interim Constitution would prevent courts from employing broader interpretive powers to apply additional rights horizontally in the future.[50]

Key drafter Halton Cheadle initially worried that horizontal application would empower "judges, particularly those appointed by the Nationalist régime to intervene in areas in which a democratically elected Parliament should be legislating."[51] The fact that the ANC presumably would become the majority party in the new parliament sheds further light on the hesitance of party affiliates to hand over additional power to the courts. As a practitioner of labor law, Cheadle also worried that horizontal application would bring too much within the purview of the Constitutional Court to the detriment of those issues and institutions dedicated more specifically to fair labor practices. Indeed, his concern was not unlike that of some German practitioners of labor law in the years leading up to *Lüth*. Spitz suggests that such worries over horizontal application were symptomatic of the presence and different preoccupations of academics and practitioners in the Assembly.[52] The academics were generally convinced that some provision of horizontal application was essential to realizing constitutional values writ large. In contrast, the practitioners initially were more inclined to preserve traditional distinctions in law, often for the simple reason that they were not clear on how this novel constitutional mechanism would operate in practice, but could see the potential repercussions of a careless execution.

Some of these apprehensions of what horizontal application might amount to seem to conjure up possible interpretations of horizontal application, beyond a republican one. The concerns of Professor Tribe, Chief Justice Corbett, and Halton Cheadle, for example, give voice in different ways to the objection, taken up in Chapter 2, that horizontal application's reliance on courts may be antirepublican. Such institutional questions may be tied to substantive matters, moreover – for example, whether the courts could be trusted to place due weight on such issues as fair labor, or instead would give priority to more traditional rights. A picture begins to emerge of how horizontal application could fit interpretations that are not clearly republican by keeping rights and the

---

[50] Du Plessis and Corder, *Understanding*, 112; Spitz, *Politics of Transition*, 271, 274.
[51] Spitz, *Politics of Transition*, 271.
[52] Ibid., 279.

individual at the center of the inquiry, rather than initiating a kind of reordering to prioritize certain ends and community.[53] Put differently, the fact that private actors may come to have duties to one another may not necessarily entail a common good that has assumed priority, but may in fact be designed to preserve the individual and individual rights above all.

In this way, these debates over the Interim Constitution reveal the question of whether horizontal application would ultimately be employed to further the ANC's early articulations of a new constitutional vision, or simply serve as another means by which private interests were furthered – whether the old interests connected with the Apartheid regime or a new set of private interests altogether. Indeed, this is not unlike the criticisms discussed earlier about the way ubuntu has come to be coopted by a rights-centric narrative. It is worth noting, however, that in these debates, neither the National Party nor corporate interests ever pushed for horizontal application. And indeed, those corners of the ANC and its allies who voiced concerns were presumably thinking through more extreme and marginal scenarios of how this practice could be employed. Ultimately, the ANC and its allies came to support horizontal application, judging that the capacity of this practice to achieve the ends of the ANC's constitutional vision outweighed any potential threats.

Despite the balance ultimately weighing in favor of horizontality, the rights committee led by Cheadle[54] would adopt a vertical model for the Interim Constitution, omitting reference to direct horizontal application while still admitting something like indirect horizontality.[55] Section 7(1) in the chapter on rights, for example, does not list the judiciary among the state organs bound by constitutional rights. Du Plessis and Corder suggest that this provision should, nevertheless, be read as including the judiciary if it is to cohere with other parts of the Constitution.[56] Specifically, they mention Section 4(2)'s statement of the Constitution's supremacy, binding "*all* organs of state at all levels of government."[57] The Interim Constitution did not embrace a robust practice of horizontal

---

[53] On the other hand, Chapter 7 on the European Union illustrates how a kind of common good might be constructed around more economic considerations.
[54] Spitz, *Politics of Transition*, 278.
[55] Du Plessis and Corder, *Understanding*, 112.
[56] Ibid., 112–113.
[57] Ibid., 112.

application, but also did not preclude it altogether. Presumably, as was its stated goal, it aimed at a kind of middle ground in light of the need for consensus both within and between parties. The Interim Constitution remained uncommitted to direct horizontal application, but also took steps to avoid a strict state action doctrine of the American stripe.

Amid the general caution surrounding horizontal application at this early stage, the committee also agreed to what became known as "seepage provisions" in Section 35(3). This section states: "In the interpretation of any law and the application and development of the common law and customary law, a court shall have regard to the spirit, purport and objects of this Chapter."[58] This formulation would not be unusual as justification for the horizontal application of rights in other contexts. Indeed, it resembles the reasoning of the German Federal Constitutional Court in *Lüth*, that the Basic Law's objective order of values necessarily informed the interpretation of all other areas of law. To this extent, the Interim Constitution left an opening for some form of horizontal application and even laid groundwork for constitutional rights to trump customary law.[59] But while it required judges to take constitutional principles into consideration, it did not provide any mechanism that would *require* judges to take the affirmative step of reassessing private law.[60]

More than a mere placeholder, the Interim Constitution came with the promise that the National Party's voice would maintain a significant level of volume even as the ANC grew louder. Following the adoption of the Interim Constitution in November 1993 was the first nonracial election in April 1994, allowing the ANC to assume its status as, in fact, representing the majority of South Africans after some 350 years of disenfranchisement. Even in later stages of the process, however, the Constitutional Assembly offered protection to the National Party, such as through high thresholds for adopting certain provisions into the Final Constitution, including the Bill of Rights, which required a noteworthy 75 percent affirmative vote.[61]

---

[58] Interim Constitution of South Africa, Section 35(3). Danwood Mikenge Chirwa, "The Horizontal Application of Constitutional Rights in Comparative Perspective," *Law, Democracy, and Development* 10:2 (2006), 38.
[59] Du Plessis and Corder, *Understanding*, 114.
[60] Remote interview with Dennis Davis, December 2, 2020; Du Plessis and Corder, *Understanding*, 116; Dikgang Moseneke, "Transformative Constitutionalism: Its Implications for the Law of Contract," *Stellenbosch Law Review* 20:1 (2009), 6.
[61] Remote interview with Nicholas Haysom, October 26, 2020.

The Court at a Crossroads: *Du Plessis v. De Klerk*

In the years the Interim Constitution was effective, from 1993 to 1997, the question of horizontal application remained a live one.[62] Those working on Theme Committee Four on Fundamental Rights in the Constitutional Assembly and others in the ANC parliament began to coalesce around the earlier consensus reflected in the 1991 Bill of Rights regarding the need for something like horizontal application. Indeed, there was a sense of urgency that they had to get this issue right in the Final Constitution. The drafters also viewed the horizontal application of rights against private actors as a way to signal to the larger populace that the Constitution would meet their material needs.[63] National Party members still preferred a vertical model, but chose instead to direct their energies toward protecting property rights, not least because their status had changed from the dominant to opposition party by this later stage.[64] The constitutional drafters thus seemed to reach some settlement on the question of horizontality, reintroducing language that approximated provisions from the 1991 Bill of Rights. The questions that remained about horizontal application were more practical in nature, about specific remedies and finding a formulation sufficiently precise so as not to give courts a carte blanche.

In the meantime, the newly established Constitutional Court contended with the ambiguous language of the Interim Constitution, when it decided *Du Plessis v. De Klerk*. This judgment has received much attention since it was decided in 1996, largely because the majority assumed something like the conventional understandings of public and private spheres, and public and private law, in its interpretation of the Interim Constitution. In short, the Court opted for a more moderated indirect horizontal effect of the German variety rather than the direct horizontal effect for which many had been arguing. Indeed, this case and

---

[62] Delisa Futch, "*Du Plessis v. De Klerk*: South Africa's Bill of Rights and the Issue of Horizontal Application," *North Carolina Journal of International Law and Commercial Regulation* 22:3 (1997), 1011.

[63] Provision for such socioeconomic rights as water, education, and health also served to demonstrate how the new constitution could improve life in concrete ways, garnering legitimacy among the broader population (remote interview with Nicholas Haysom, October 26, 2020).

[64] Remote interview with Dennis Davis, December 2, 2020; First Report of Theme Committee 4 on Block 1 of the Work Programme, *Department of Justice and Constitutional Development*, February 1–14, 1995, accessed October 20, 2020, www.justice.gov.za/legislation/constitution/history/REPORTS/TC4-BLK1S.PDF.

its accompanying judicial rationale made ANC drafters uneasy, contributing to their urgency to follow through with stronger, more explicit provision for horizontal application in the Final Constitution.[65]

In *Du Plessis*, a newspaper reported that South African citizens had been transporting weapons to rebel forces in Angola via covert flights. The newspaper suggested that such private air operators as Gert De Klerk were intentionally fueling the Angolan civil war in order to make a profit. De Klerk sued the newspaper for defamation, arguing that these articles had damaged both his reputation and his business.[66] The decision itself hinged on whether the Interim Constitution could be applied retrospectively insofar as the newspaper (the plaintiffs) sought to rely on Section 15, protecting the freedom of speech and expression, including "freedom of the press and other media." The fact that the Interim Constitution was not adopted until after the articles were published and damages were incurred posed some difficulty to their argument. Implicit in this question of retrospectivity, moreover, was the further question of whether an article of the Constitution could even be brought to bear on a private relationship in the way the newspaper argued. The case made its way to the Supreme Court of Appeal, which decided against the newspaper. Specifically, the Court decided that the Interim Constitution could not apply retrospectively and that the Bill of Rights of the Interim Constitution only had vertical effect.[67] In plain terms, only the state could be said to violate rights such as to freedom of expression; private actors and spaces existed beyond this standard.

The Supreme Court of Appeal was considered to be the final court of appeal in all areas of ordinary law. The question of both retrospectivity and horizontality in the case at hand seemed to implicate constitutional questions, however. Crucial to the outcome of this case was the question of how the common law related to the Constitution: Were such aspects of the common law, such as the rule governing defamation, ultimately subject to the Article 15 commitment to free expression? With such questions straddling the divide between ordinary and constitutional law, the case went to the Constitutional Court. The Constitutional

---

[65] Remote interview with Dennis Davis, December 2, 2020.
[66] Futch, "*Du Plessis*," 1012–1013; Stuart Woolman and Dennis Davis, "The Last Laugh: *Du Plessis v. De Klerk*, Classical Liberalism, Creole Liberalism and the Application of Fundamental Rights under the Interim and the Final Constitutions," *South African Journal on Human Rights* 12 (1996), 363–364.
[67] Futch, "*Du Plessis*," 1012–1013; Woolman and Davis, "The Last Laugh," 363–364.

Court, in turn, agreed with the Supreme Court of Appeal that the Interim Constitution could not apply retrospectively. While this judgment alone would have been sufficient to determine the case's outcome, the Court took the additional step of deciding the question of horizontal application as well.[68] Justice Kentridge cited the Interim Constitution's aforementioned Section 7 to argue that the Constitution included no basis for direct horizontal effect; indeed, Section 7 only obligated the executive and legislature to uphold the Bill of Rights. The Court thus reasoned that the text of the Interim Constitution provided a foundation for a kind of indirect horizontal effect that closely resembled the German practice of *Drittwirkung*. Indeed, Kentridge suggested that horizontal effect in the Interim Constitution resembled the German model more than any other approach to horizontal effect in a national constitution. In this understanding, the Bill of Rights of the Interim Constitution obligated private relationships only insofar as statutes attempted to regulate them.

South Africa was different from Germany, however, in that it maintained a system of common law. This common law, the Court concluded, was not subject to the Constitution in the same way, largely tracking the Canadian take on this question.[69] Of course, Section 35(3) of the Interim Constitution required that a court should have regard for "the spirit, purport and objects" of the Bill of Rights in interpreting any law, and the provision explicitly included the common law in this.[70] Nevertheless, Justice Kentridge suggested that the Constitutional Court was not up to this task, explaining that it simply did not have the capacity to balance matters of common law in the way that would be required in applying horizontal effect. In particular, he worried that in deeming some rule of common law incompatible with the Constitution, the Constitutional Court would have to make law to fill the resulting gap.[71] In addition to actions of parliament in the realm of statutory law, the ordinary courts and particularly the Supreme Court of Appeal were better equipped to apply horizontal application in their "routine common law interpretive work."[72] Kentridge's argument is premised on a specific understanding of law and the work common law does to balance private relationships.

---

[68] Futch, "*Du Plessis*," 1013–1014.
[69] *Dolphin Delivery* [1986] 2 SCR 573.
[70] Interim Constitution of South Africa, Section 35(3); Chirwa, "Horizontal Application," 38.
[71] Futch, "*Du Plessis*," 1019.
[72] David Robertson, "Thick Constitutional Readings: When Classical Distinctions Are Irrelevant," *Georgia Journal of International and Comparative Law* 35 (2007), 303.

In Kentridge's telling, these new constitutional rights were likely to resist balancing in the particular ways that common law decision-making prescribed.[73] In this way, the Constitutional Court's initial formulation of horizontal application was one that preserved traditional boundaries of law, largely intended to isolate private relationships from constitutional obligations directed to the state.[74]

Early critics of the *Du Plessis* decision, Stuart Woolman and Dennis Davis, suggest that the Interim Constitution pointed just as easily, if not more so, to the opposite conclusion. They argue that the Interim Constitution supplies good evidence that the drafters did mean to govern all aspects of law and life, including the common law, as evinced by Section 35(3).[75] The very fact of Justice Albie Sachs's concurring opinion and, especially, Justice Kriegler's dissenting opinion in *Du Plessis* illustrate the plausibility of such alternative reads of the Interim Constitution. We see this tension in Justice Sachs's opinion, in particular. On the one hand, as a core member of the ANC in the decades prior, he recognizes the capaciousness of the South African constitutional project. He states:

> I have no doubt that given the circumstances in which our Constitution came into being, the principles of freedom and equality which it proclaims are intended to be all-pervasive and transformatory in character ... Given the divisions and injustices referred to in the postscript, it would be strange indeed if the massive inequalities in our societies were somehow relegated to the realm of private law, in respect of which government could only intrude if it did not interfere with the vested individual property and privacy rights of the presently privileged classes ... I accept that there is no sector where law dwells, that is not reached by the principles and values of the Constitution.[76]

In this way, Justice Sachs expressed his understanding that the purpose of the South African Constitution differed from the conventional model that prioritized negative rights and sought only to protect against government interference. Indeed, he cites "the circumstances in which [the] Constitution came into being," rooting its normative commitments in a larger understanding of the history of the South African polity. But this understanding was not enough ultimately for Justice Sachs to depart from the majority, as he saw this consideration of constitutional purpose

---

[73] *Du Plessis v. De Klerk*, para. 55; Woolman and Davis, "The Last Laugh," 366–367.
[74] Woolman and Davis, "The Last Laugh," 383.
[75] Ibid., 372; Robertson, "Thick Constitutional Readings," 302.
[76] *Du Plessis v. De Klerk*, para. 177.

as "not the issue" of the case at hand.[77] He explains his more immediate concern that the enforcement of constitutional commitments appropriately depends on the actions of parliament and the Supreme Court of Appeal.[78] Moreover, following Kentridge, he questions whether the Constitutional Court is even equipped to undertake the sort of "social, political, and economic questions" that accompany horizontal application when individuals' rights and duties are weighed against each other.[79] In this way, Sachs straddles the line between the concerns to which Kentridge gives voice in the majority opinion and acknowledgment of certain normative commitments that would seem to accommodate a larger role for the Constitutional Court.

That "the most radical member of the court"[80] could not bring himself to endorse horizontal effect in this instance is revelatory of the sort of crossroad the Court faced in *Du Plessis v. De Klerk*, still operating under the Interim Constitution and well aware of the disconnect between aspiration and the ability to implement those aspirations in local settings. The tension with which Sachs wrestled – of a constitutional vision that clearly implicated the polity as a whole but did not decidedly abandon certain forms of liberal thinking[81] – was not as salient for dissenting Justice Kriegler. After "castigating the majority,"[82] Kriegler states:

> No one familiar with the stark reality of South Africa and the power relationships in its society can believe that protection of the individual only against the State can possibly bring those benefits [of democratic society and justice]. The fine line drawn by the Canadian Supreme Court in the *Dolphin Delivery* case and by the US Supreme Court in *Shelley v. Kraemer* between private relationships involving organs of the State and those which do not, have no place in our constitutional jurisprudence.
>
> ... We do not operate under a constitution in which the avowed purpose of the drafters was to place limitations on governmental control. Our Constitution aims at establishing freedom and equality in a grossly disparate society. And I am grateful to the drafters of our Constitution for having spared us the jurisprudential gymnastics forced on some courts abroad.[83]

---

[77] Ibid.
[78] For a similar discussion in the American context, see Lawrence Sager, *Justice in Plainclothes* (New Haven: Yale University Press, 2006).
[79] Futch, "*Du Plessis*," 1019.
[80] Robertson, "Thick Constitutional Readings," 303.
[81] Michelman, "Constitutions," 304.
[82] Robertson, "Thick Constitutional Readings," 304.
[83] *Du Plessis v. De Klerk*, paras. 145–147.

Kriegler had little patience for the sorts of distinctions that Kentridge and Sachs maintained in their own opinions. Indeed, Section 35(3) and others that Kriegler cites suggest that the "spirit, purport, and objects" of the Constitution govern all law and life in the polity, regardless of the particular institution or court that happens to be acting. Even beyond such specific provisions, however, Kriegler insists on the need to consider the South African constitutional vision as a whole. Due appreciation for the power relationships embedded in South African society and the Constitution's frontal assault on these public and private power structures do not permit the queasiness that Kentridge and others display with respect to the intervention horizontal effect would entail. Kriegler brings his rejection of liberal presuppositions into sharp relief when he accuses the majority of "preying on the fears of privileged whites, cosseted in the past by laissez faire capitalism thriving in an environment where the black underclass had limited opportunity to share in the bounty."[84] Laissez-faire priors may work for other polities, but it is not the basis of the new South African polity, Kriegler argues, and in fact represents much of what the Constitution is combating.

It is not difficult to see how the questions of *Du Plessis* could yield such an array of answers. For example, while the Interim Constitution does not explicitly provide for horizontality, certain provisions like the "seepage provisions" in Section 35(3) could be interpreted as a basis for indirect horizontal application. Kentridge found some grounding for traditional liberal commitments in the Interim Constitution, while Kriegler's more purposive take brought him to a very different conclusion. And indeed, these disparate readings pointed toward a real choice – Robertson describes this as a choice between "thin" and "thick" constitutionalism,[85] while Woolman and Davis understand it as the difference between classical and "creole" liberalism.[86]

An additional, and important, reason for the impasse in *Du Plessis* was the fact that the Interim Constitution maintained separate jurisdictions of the Constitutional Court and the Supreme Court of Appeal. Insofar as the Supreme Court had been the highest court until this time of transition, there was good reason to keep it as supreme in its jurisdiction even after the Constitutional Court was established. Indeed, the continued separation at this stage was indicative of a general distrust of the extent

---

[84] Ibid., para. 120.
[85] Robertson, "Thick Constitutional Readings."
[86] Woolman and Davis, "The Last Laugh."

of the old Supreme Court's loyalty to the new constitution, as well as an initial concession to appease those who worried that the Supreme Court no longer would enjoy primacy in its jurisdiction.[87] This separation of courts preserved in the Interim Constitution provoked the questions we find in *Du Plessis* concerning the relationship between ordinary law, common law, and constitutional law.

This separation of courts is not all that different from that which informed the German Federal Constitutional Court's decision in *Lüth*. Underlying *Lüth* was the similar question of how the Federal Labor Court, as well as other private law courts, related to the Constitutional Court. In *Lüth*, the Constitutional Court asserted itself as the primary and final interpreter of the Constitution; however, it did not prevent other institutions from also engaging in constitutional interpretation. Neither did the Constitutional Court presume to have final interpretive authority with respect to the Civil Code. Indeed, its decision to focus primarily on the general clauses, as explained earlier, shows a kind of self-imposed limit and even deference to other apex courts. Michelman sees all of this as evidence that Germany preserved separate systems of law and courts, even as *Lüth* required that the principles of the Basic Law influence the private law. In the South African context, on the other hand, the separation between the jurisdiction of the Supreme Court of Appeal and that of the Constitutional Court, Michelman thinks, "was always headed for instability."[88] He goes so far as to describe such a system as a "design error" of the Interim Constitution in need of correction,[89] given the vast transformation the ANC and other constitutional actors sought. And indeed, the Final Constitution of 1996 brought significant change, demonstrating that a choice had eventually been made. The Constitutional Court was confirmed as the final arbiter in all areas of law, including matters of common law, and direct horizontal effect of the Bill of Rights became a constitutional requirement. "Under pressure from the idea of a socially transformative, constitutional bill of rights," the Final Constitution united the South African systems of law and courts under a common constitutional standard.[90] With the adoption of the Final Constitution, the institutional structures were more clearly harmonized with the political needs entailed by these new substantive commitments.

---

[87] Michelman, "Interplay," 292.
[88] Ibid.
[89] Ibid.
[90] Ibid.

South Africa as Heir and Foil to German Constitutionalism

Before discussing the specific changes of the Final Constitution and subsequent caselaw on horizontal effect, it is worth fleshing out comparisons between South Africa and Germany, especially as some justices writing in *Du Plessis* explicitly mention the German case.[91] In particular, Justice Laurie Ackermann's opinion in *Du Plessis* compares the South African situation with postwar Germany, finding in these apparent similarities justification to develop an understanding of horizontal application that was also similar. Ackermann maintained that the German Basic Law "was no less powerful a response to totalitarianism, the degradation of human dignity and the denial of freedom and equality than our Constitution."[92] Indeed, he elaborates that a similar stage for the development of horizontal application was set by each country's troubled history. If indirect (in contrast with direct) horizontal effect was good enough for Germany, Ackermann suggests it ought to be good enough for South Africa, too.[93]

Woolman and Davis, however, insist on important differences between Germany and South Africa that, in their view, Ackermann and others paper over. While the German and South African Constitutions were both responses to serious rights abuses and totalitarian regimes, the states of affairs in each postconflict situation were vastly different. After the Second World War, Germany was a "modern, industrialized and relatively egalitarian society. It was into these less than dire circumstances that the [Basic Law] was born."[94] On the other hand, Woolman and Davis wrote:

> Post-Apartheid South Africa could not be more different than post-WWII Germany. It is not united as a nation. It is not linguistically, culturally or politically homogenous. It is not modern, not industrialized, not egalitarian. Thus while vast inequalities in private power may not have been such a problem in post-WWII Germany – and thus made indirect application of the Basic Law palatable – vast inequalities in private power are an inextricable part of the fabric of post-Apartheid South African society –

---

[91] See Futch, "*Du Plessis*," 1016, fn. 54, 1019–1020; Michelman, "Interplay," 291–292; Woolman and Davis, "The Last Laugh," 375.

[92] *Du Plessis v. De Klerk*, para. 92.

[93] Ackermann has been described as one of keenest observers of foreign law, and particularly of German law, among South African justices. See Theunis Roux, "The Dignity of Comparative Constitutional Law," *Acta Juridica* 1 (2008), 185–203, wherein Roux describes Ackermann as "something of a Germanophile" (186).

[94] Woolman and Davis, "The Last Laugh," 375, fn. 45.

and make indirect application of our Constitution an anathema for the majority of our country's citizens.[95]

This explanation gives some historical context for Germany's ability to cling continually to old legal structures, even importing directly many Weimar legal structures. Whereas *Du Plessis v. De Klerk* initially seemed to put South Africa on that same track of preserving some insulation of private relations from constitutional standards, such expressions as Kriegler's condemnation of laissez-faire structures pick up on a progressive shift. And indeed, taking a cue from the ambivalence in *Du Plessis*, the drafters of the Final Constitution made explicit the sheer scope of transformation intended, expanding the Constitutional Court's jurisdiction and clarifying a doctrine of direct horizontal effect. This way, the drafters enabled future judgments to pursue the transformative constitutional project without the need for any "jurisprudential gymnastics." The text and institutions of the Final Constitution were intentionally aligned with transformation and, by extension, with a stronger assertion of direct horizontal application.

The decision of whether and how to apply horizontal application came through different fora in Germany and South Africa – through the Constitutional Court and the Constitutional Assembly, respectively. However, in both cases, the express aim was to respond to histories of violence and to influence the broader social order according to constitutional values. To this extent, Ackermann's comparison in *Du Plessis* is accurate. The parity with which constitutional values applied across public and private spaces manifested differently in each context, however. As explained with respect to Germany, its long tradition of civil law and system of specialized courts, as well as the persistence of the principle of *Privatautonomie*, tracks the way in which horizontal application developed after *Lüth*. Indeed, most cases developed in the context of such classical negative rights as freedom of speech and assembly, with fewer occurring in the realm of equality and antidiscrimination until much later.[96] And when courts and even legislatures did move to bring certain equality rights into private spaces, private interests often resisted. The more traditional rights that make up the content of the German Basic Law as well as certain structural and doctrinal features, therefore,

---

[95] Ibid.
[96] Alec Stone Sweet, "The Juridical Coup d'État and the Problem of Authority," *German Law Journal* 8:10 (2007), 915–927; Laurie Ackermann, *Human Dignity: Lodestar for Equality in South Africa* (Cape Town: Juta, 2012).

map onto a practice of horizontal application that is in some ways more limited. Likewise, while a republican interpretation still emerges in the German turn toward community, this too appears bounded in certain ways, as discussed in Chapter 5.

Comparing German *Drittwirkung* with horizontal application in South Africa bears out Woolman and Davis in their desire to lend nuance to Ackermann's account in *Du Plessis*. In particular, the advance of horizontal application from the Interim Constitution to the settlement of the Final Constitution, to say nothing of the tension internal to *Du Plessis*, points to a real disconnect between the priors of some framers and judges and the ANC's vision articulated in such early documents as the 1991 Bill of Rights and ultimately cemented in the Final Constitution. This was the quandary *Du Plessis* hit upon and which a comparison of Germany and South Africa brings into sharper relief. The formulation of horizontal effect in the Interim Constitution was comparable to that of the German Federal Constitutional Court in *Lüth*, despite the fact that the countries actually faced very different problems.

To be sure, classical liberal rights and freedoms are represented in South African constitutionalism. Indeed, the Constitution founds the polity on "[h]uman dignity, the achievement of equality and the advancement of human rights and freedoms."[97] But these commitments carry unique status and meaning in South Africa. For example, both freedom and equality encompass more than their formal meanings, in that they involve certain material prerequisites as well.[98] Moreover, rather than shy away from certain instances of equality in the context of horizontal effect as in the German case, the South African Constitution actually singles out equality by name as requiring horizontal effect. Chapter 2, Section 9 (4) guaranteeing the right to equality, states:

> No person may unfairly discriminate directly or indirectly against anyone on one or more grounds... [including race, gender, sex, pregnancy, marital status, ethnic or social origin, colour, sexual orientation, age, disability, religion, conscience, belief, culture, language and birth]. National legislation must be enacted to prevent or prohibit unfair discrimination.[99]

Of course, merely providing that the right to equality or right against discrimination has horizontal effect does not entail that a person's right to

---

[97] South African Constitution of 1996, Chapter 1, Section 1(a).
[98] Robertson, "Thick Constitutional Readings"; Ackermann, *Human Dignity*.
[99] South African Constitution of 1996, Chapter 2, Section 9(4).

equality will always prevail against the countervailing right in question. (Section 9(5), for example, suggests that there are instances in which discrimination may be fair.) Nevertheless, the very fact that the South African Constitution so prioritizes equality to specify its provision for horizontal application diverges from the German treatment of the same question.

New Clarity in the Final Constitution

The 1996 Constitution established the Constitutional Court as "the highest court in the republic," with authority to decide constitutional matters as well as any other matter it decides is in its jurisdiction.[100] It was within this new institutional context that the framers entrenched direct horizontal effect as a legal-constitutional practice.[101] In contrast with the ambiguity of the Interim Constitution, the constitutional drafters established horizontal application with uncommon clarity, taking pains to avoid the sort of confusion evident in *Du Plessis v. De Klerk.*

Several provisions across different sections of the final text collectively establish horizontal effect. In contrast to the Interim Constitution that obligated only the actions of the legislature and the executive to the Bill of Rights, Chapter 2, Section 8(1) of the 1996 Constitution provides that the Bill of Rights binds the judiciary as well. In addition, several entirely new provisions concerning horizontal effect were added. Among them were Section 9(4) on the right to equality, described earlier, as well as Section 8(2):

> A provision of the Bill of Rights binds a natural or a juristic person if, and to the extent that, it is applicable, taking into account the nature of the right and the nature of any duty imposed by the right.

In stating that the Bill of Rights binds "a natural or a juristic person," Section 8(2) establishes that rights apply horizontally to obligate both private individuals (natural persons) and other private entities such as firms and corporations (juristic persons). When a panel of experts at the Constitutional Assembly considered this terminology, they found strong reason to bind both natural and juristic persons in view of the goal "not just to root out discrimination by the state but to attack it in its most

---

[100] Ibid., Chapter 8, Section 167.
[101] Spitz, *Politics of Transition,* 279.

pervasive form – discrimination as between citizens."[102] This section goes on to state that the nature of the right and the nature of the duty imposed by the right may influence the outcomes of particular cases when balancing one right against another.[103] Therefore, although horizontal effect establishes parity in applying South African constitutional values across spheres, Section 8(2) creates some space for variation in the way rights obligations apply to private actors as opposed to state actors.[104]

Also in Section 8, the Constitution explains specifically how a court will apply a right horizontally, stating that a court *must* apply or develop the common law in applying horizontal effect. The provision reads:

> When applying a provision of the Bill of Rights to a natural or juristic person in terms of subsection (2), a court
>
> a. in order to give effect to a right in the Bill, must apply, or if necessary develop, the common law to the extent that legislation does not give effect to that right; and
> b. may develop rules of the common law to limit the right, provided that the limitation is in accordance with section 36 (1).

This section seems to take *Du Plessis v. De Klerk* head on, giving all courts, including the Constitutional Court, authority to develop the common law in order to hold private actors accountable for the Bill of Rights. Moreover, as was the case in Section 8 (1), the Constitution acknowledges that some rights will necessarily be limited in the process of balancing. Taken together, these several additions to the Final Constitution mark a clear departure from foregoing renderings of horizontal effect. Indeed, Halton Cheadle had long moved on from any initial concerns to argue the necessity of horizontal effect, drafting Section 8 to provide just the kind of constitutional cause of action the Interim

---

[102] Panel of Constitutional Experts, Technical Committee 4, Draft Memorandum to Chairpersons and Executive Director of the CA, *Department of Justice and Constitutional Development*, March 28, 1996, accessed October 20, 2020, https://justice.gov.za/legislation/constitution/history/LEGAL/CP028036.PDF.

[103] Tom Lowenthal, "*AB v. Pridwin Preparatory School*: Progress and Problems in Horizontal Human Rights Law," *South African Journal on Human Rights* (2020), 271; see also Stephen Gardbaum, "Positive and Horizontal Rights: Proportionality's Next Frontier or a Bridge Too Far?" in *Proportionality: New Frontiers, New Challenges*, ed. Vicki Jackson and Mark Tushnet (Cambridge: Cambridge University Press, 2017).

[104] Ackermann, *Human Dignity*, 267.

Constitution lacked. How consistently jurists would treat this provision as a break from the Interim Constitution was another matter.

In terms of institutional structures, doctrinal specifics, and constitutional content, the South African Final Constitution cemented a clear shift away from the German model. Insofar as both constitutions implemented some version of horizontal application, constitutional standards came to govern public and private spaces alike. In the terms of this book, the turn toward horizontal application can be interpreted as a turn toward certain communal values over sheer individual rights in both places. Nevertheless, from the outset, the particularities of the South African case seemed to invite constitutional actors to extend horizontal application further into private spaces than in the case of Germany. Moreover, subsequent jurisprudence and legislation contributed to a different scope for the parity and duties resulting from the initial communal turn, as constitutional actors in each place incrementally carved up the private sphere in different ways. Thus, while a republican interpretation applies in both experiences, constitutional actors in South Africa now operate in a constitutional context where that interpretation may ultimately ring with more truth at more levels of society.

What remains of this chapter illustrates a republican interpretation of subsequent arguments surrounding horizontal application in South African constitutionalism. Emboldened all the more by the Court's ambivalence in *Du Plessis*, the ANC drafters and those allying with the ANC followed through in their intent to transcend the Interim Constitution by providing an explicit basis for horizontality in the Final Constitution. Nevertheless, much about how horizontal application would develop (or not develop) was left to the discretion of judges and other constitutional actors. As explained earlier, South Africa's experience displays a potential scope for horizontal application, and thus a depth to the republican interpretation, that exceeds that of the German context. Simply put, the commitments of the political community can and have been understood as encompassing more in South Africa and, on this basis, have allowed constitutional actors to make greater inroads into private spaces – including in such areas as housing, education, and even testamentary decisions. At the same time, constitutional actors in South Africa have not always employed this practice in a maximal way. Judges anywhere will always have an interest in drawing lines and developing limiting principles. This seems all the more likely in the case of horizontal application, which marks a departure from conventional understandings and implicates private actors in new ways, intensifying such well-trodden apprehensions in judicial politics as enforcement and funding of courts' directives.[105] Other countervailing factors, such as a pervading formalism in the legal culture, also figure into the practice of horizontal application. Thus, while the constitutional text seems to allow for a robust, republican understanding of the communal, this same text has been employed in more or less expansive ways in the hands of different constitutional actors.

Early Development and Reversion

Albie Sachs and several other justices who joined Kentridge's *Du Plessis* opinion quickly acknowledged the different logics the Final Constitution permitted in *Carmichele v. Minister of Safety and Security*.[106] *Carmichele* established that the courts had an obligation to develop the common law in the light of the Constitution. The case concerned a man, charged with and jailed for assault, who committed another assault after law enforcement had released him on bail. The victim of the subsequent attack argued that police and public prosecutors had "negligently failed to comply with a legal duty" to protect her from a known aggressor.[107] The High Court and Supreme Court of Appeal decided there was no evidence that law enforcement had "acted wrongfully." And so, the applicant appealed to the Constitutional Court. The Constitutional Court, in contrast, rejected tendencies to distinguish between action and inaction on which, for example, the US Supreme Court had relied in *DeShaney v. Winnebago County Department of Social Services*.[108] Rather, a provision similar (though, importantly, not identical) to Section 35(3) of the Interim Constitution provided the basis for the Constitutional Court's decision. Section 39(2) of the Final Constitution states, "When interpreting any legislation, and when developing the common law or customary law, every court, tribunal or forum must promote the spirit, purport and objects of the Bill of Rights."[109] In contrast with the counterpart

---

[105] In *Daniels v. Scribante* (2017) the Court notes how "[p]rivate persons ... fund their conduct from their own pockets," in contrast with the state that relies on public sources of revenue. The Court concludes: "It would be unreasonable, therefore, to require private persons to bear the exact same obligations under the Bill of Rights as does the state" (para. 40).
[106] *Carmichele v. Minister of Safety and Security* (CCT 48/00) [2001] ZACC 22.
[107] Ibid., para. 2.
[108] Ibid., para. 45.
[109] South African Constitution of 1996, Section 39(2).

provision in the Interim Constitution, Section 39(2) explicitly obligates *every* court to attend to constitutional commitments. And so, in a unanimous opinion, the Constitutional Court recognized that it had an obligation to ensure that the common law developed according to such constitutional standards that inhered in the rights as to life, human dignity, freedom, and security.[110] Writing for the Court, Justice Ackermann cites the German Basic Law again, arguing that the South African Constitution also encompassed an "objective, normative value system," and that it was within this value system that the common law needed be developed. Ultimately, the Constitutional Court referred the case back to the initial High Court on the basis that the common law admitted of different possible modifications to accord with constitutional values.[111]

Some question just how radical a break *Carmichele* was from *Du Plessis*. Michelman, for example, argues that the case reveals that the Constitutional Court "internalized some separation," as between systems of law and courts, according to the same traditional paradigm on display in *Du Plessis*. Though all South African law had to conform to the Constitution, he explains, the common law was still developed within its own framework, evinced by the fact that the Constitutional Court sent the case back to the High Court. This, Michelman argues, is not all that different from the system of separate courts and, by extension, the indirect horizontal effect Germany maintains.[112] Indeed, Justice Ackermann's recurring invocation of Germany suggests its continual influence on at least some corners of the Court. Chirwa, on the other hand, points out that the duty to protect that emerges from *Carmichele* is a step removed from a typical liberal framework and particularly from the requirement that state action be present in order to enforce constitutional rights. He highlights how in the South African context the state is "liable for an infringement of a constitutional right by a non-state actor if it fails to take 'reasonable and appropriate measures' to prevent it."[113]

Considering the Constitution's full treatment of rights in private spaces, and particularly Section 8, the South African model clearly goes beyond German *Drittwirkung* as private actors can be charged with rights violations directly, and not simply through the distillation of

---

[110] *Carmichele v. Minister of Safety and Security*, para. 44.
[111] Ibid., para. 56.
[112] Michelman, "Interplay," 292.
[113] Chirwa, "Horizontal Application," 44.

private law.[114] Though such doctrinal differences are important, equally if not more important are how the terms of debate shift and how such differences are, or are not, reflected in understandings of the Constitution's role in the larger society. Does it provide a standard for the larger polity, including duties of private actors, and how does this society ultimately look, given the particular commitments of the Constitution? While a preliminary and cautious step, *Carmichele* does seem to set the doctrinal stage for future expansion of horizontal application. Robertson explains how "a stream of cases" followed *Carmichele* in 2001, all taking as granted that "nothing should stand in the way of the instantiation of constitutional values in the working of the law."[115] Whether this drive for executing the constitutional project would steadily propel the development of horizontal application is a different question.

The year after *Carmichele*, the Court decided *Khumalo v. Holomisa*,[116] representing a concrete step to develop the Constitution's provision for horizontal application in Section 8. Like *Du Plessis* and so many other horizontality cases, *Khumalo* concerned a defamation action. A South African newspaper accused prominent politician Bantu Holomisa of involvement in criminal activities, and he, in turn, sued for damages of defamation. The case came down to the newspaper's right to freedom of expression (Section 16) against Holomisa's right to dignity (Section 10). The newspaper (the applicant) argued that the common law rule of defamation needed to be developed further in order to comply with the constitutional right to freedom of expression. In particular, the newspaper argued that, under a proper understanding of the freedom of expression, plaintiffs ought never to succeed in defamation cases "unless they can establish that a defamatory statement was false."[117]

Writing for the Constitutional Court, Justice O'Regan acknowledged that the freedom of expression had horizontal effect, "given the intensity of the constitutional right in question, coupled with the potential invasion of that right which could be occasioned by persons other than the

---

[114] Ibid., 43; see also Friedman, "The South African Common Law," 66.
[115] Robertson, "Thick Constitutional Readings," 313.
[116] *Khumalo and Others v. Holomisa*, (CCT53/01) [2002] ZACC 12.
[117] Ibid., para. 44. The applicants cite *New York Times v. Sullivan* insofar as the US Supreme Court also required that public figures demonstrate the falsity of a statement. Unlike in *New York Times v. Sullivan*, however, the plaintiffs in *Khumalo* did not argue for an "actual malice" standard. In the judgment of the Court, Justice O'Regan describes this American case as "the high-water mark of foreign jurisprudence protecting freedom of speech" and that many other countries had "declined to follow it" (para. 40).

State or organs of State."[118] Nevertheless, this right had to be balanced against the right to dignity, as it also had horizontal effect. Weighing these two against each other, O'Regan concluded that the common law rules of defamation, in their current state, struck a balance that was, in fact, compliant with both of these constitutional rights commitments. She explained that newspapers and other media would only be charged for defamation when they could not establish that "the statement was true and its publication in the public interest, nor that the publication was reasonable in all the circumstances."[119] However, she also drew attention to the great limitation that shifting the burden of proof to the plaintiff would entail for the right to dignity since it was sometimes impossible to demonstrate the falsity of a claim. Since the newspaper could establish neither the truth nor the reasonableness of the accusations, the Court decided that the common law rules were sound and favored the right to dignity on balance in this particular case.

In Robertson's telling, the earlier *Carmichele* decision had been necessary "to bring the jurisprudence on the development of the common law into line with the much firmer stand taken by the Final Constitution after the weakness of the court's decision in *Du Plessis*."[120] *Khumalo* thus fortified and built on this earlier decision by extending its logic also to apply to relations between private actors. Indeed, with *Khumalo*, constitutional commitments came to comprise the very content of those common law rules governing private relations. Moreover, and perhaps more importantly, under the precedent set by *Khumalo*, the concepts of constitutional rights and duties are not excised as they enter private spaces. Rather, individuals face the prospect that they, too, are accountable for such constitutional rights commitments as freedom of expression or dignity. Justice O'Regan does stipulate the need to consider the intensity and nature of the right before applying it horizontally,[121] and other judges have been at pains to emphasize that the processes of determining the constitutional duties of state and nonstate actors are not equivalent.[122] Even with these caveats, however, the process of balancing and ultimate judgment in *Khumalo* still rest on the recognition

---

[118] *Khumalo and Others v. Holomisa*, para. 33.
[119] Ibid., para. 44.
[120] Robertson, "Thick Constitutional Readings," 313.
[121] *Khumalo and Others v. Holomisa*, paras. 31–33.
[122] Ackermann, *Human Dignity*, 267.

that the Constitution is a source to both rights and duties of private actors.

A degree of caution in a court as new as South Africa's Constitutional Court does not come as a surprise,[123] even in spite of (or perhaps in light of) the promise horizontal application holds for asserting institutional power and jurisdiction.[124] Theunis Roux describes in the early Court a preference for "context-sensitive balancing," or a tendency only to decide the case at hand rather than create broadly applicable rules to apply to future decisions.[125] Stuart Woolman notices and laments a similar tendency a decade after the Final Constitution's adoption, explaining how this practice may cut in either a progressive or regressive direction.[126] To illustrate his concern that the Constitutional Court risked regressing, he cites three cases over a single year in which the Court backpedaled from *Khumalo*'s initial steps to develop horizontality.[127] Such backpedaling is on vivid display in *Masiya v. Director of Public Prosecutions* when the Court omitted any reference to *Khumalo*, instead reverting to *Du Plessis v. De Klerk* as precedent. Woolman describes a hesitance to engage the substance of the Bill of Rights when formulating duties against private actors. In contrast with the documented rationale for which the framers included Section 8 in the Final Constitution, namely, to hold private actors accountable for the *specific* rights, the Court relied on the vague bases of dignity, equality, and freedom[128] and on Section 39(2) concerning constitutional interpretation rather than direct horizontal effect. Of course, such provisions are important, even essential, to South Africa's constitutional project, but they do not perform the function of

---

[123] Theunis Roux, *The Politics of Principle* (Cambridge: Cambridge University Press, 2013).
[124] Johan van der Walt, *The Horizontal Effect Revolution and the Question of Sovereignty* (Berlin: De Gruyter, 2014); Stone Sweet, "Juridical Coup d'État"; Jud Mathews, *Extending Rights' Reach* (Oxford: Oxford University Press, 2018).
[125] Roux, *Politics of Principle*, 305.
[126] Michaela Hailbronner identifies this as a common tendency in courts operating in transformative constitutional orders, as they often employ a more ad hoc methodology to reach just results instead of building a robust body of rules that may constrain future decisions ("Transformative Constitutionalism").
[127] Stuart Woolman, "The Amazing Vanishing Bill of Rights," *South African Law Journal* 127 (2007), 762–794. The specific cases he considers are *Barkhuizen v. Napier* 2007 (7) BCLR 691 (CC); *Masiya v. Director of Public Prosecutions* 2007 (5) SA 30 (CC), 2007 (8) BCLR 827 (CC); and *NM v. Smith* 2007 (5) SA250 (CC), 2007 (7) BCLR 751 (CC).
[128] Woolman, "Amazing Vanishing," 763.

generating specific duties corresponding to enumerated rights as the Section 8 drafters and ANC representatives had earlier envisioned.[129]

The historical record is clear that the ANC intended to effect thoroughgoing transformation in South African law and life, and to do so in part through the mechanism of horizontality. Explained in terms of this book's republican interpretation, the practice of horizontal application has the ability to recast constitutional rights as larger values and thus becomes a means by which to orient more corners of the polity toward the commitments of the new constitution. Why, then, has the Court sometimes avoided applying the Bill of Rights directly to private actors in the way Woolman recounts? Naturally, a confluence of factors will shape judicial decision-making on any issue. One such factor, although by no means the sole or even most crucial one, is how constitutional actors downstream understand the constitutional project. The discourses emerging in and from different cases offer some insight into the range of possible understandings and how those different understandings map onto the more specific question of horizontal application. That some jurists, such as Justice Ackerman, frequently invoked Germany as a point of reference to understand the South African Constitution is telling. Others, such as Justices Sachs, Madlanga, and Moseneke, have been more inclined to define the project on its own terms.[130] Moreover, important debates emerge around the role judges claim for the courts in light of a transformative Final Constitution. Ought judges to employ a jurisprudential minimalism or formalism so that the legislature may spearhead the constitutional project? Or should the Court itself take charge, assuming as much of the project as its institutional capacities permit to ensure the country makes good on its commitments? Considering South Africa's practice of horizontality alongside that of other countries, the Constitutional Court maintains a role in the country's transformative project. Even in its relatively short history, for example, the Court has

---

[129] This hesitancy dovetails in the like and often converging tendency to rely on Section 39(2) in horizontality questions. Much like the provision on which the Court based its decision in *Du Plessis* as well as the German approach, Section 39(2) concerns interpretation rather than actual application, requiring courts to interpret law in a way that "promotes the spirit, purport and objects of the Bill of Rights." Constitution of South Africa, Chapter 2, Section 39(2).

[130] See, for example, Albie Sachs, *The Strange Alchemy of Life and Law* (Oxford: Oxford University Press, 2011); Moseneke, "Transformative Constitutionalism"; Madlanga, "The Human Rights Duties of Companies and Other Private Actors in South Africa," *Stellenbosch Human Law Review* 29:3 (2018), 359–378.

shown itself increasingly willing to apply socioeconomic rights horizontally,[131] not a trivial thing when contrasted with other countries' more bounded practices of horizontality.

On what basis, then, do people like Woolman criticize the Court as unduly minimalist, even regressive? Such critiques typically assess the Court's practice less from a comparative vantage point than from a view internal to South Africa. That is, they weigh the Court's actions against what the Constitution itself seemingly permits, and thus find its development of horizontal application as unnecessarily halting – from the tendency to rely on Section 39(2) rather than Section 8(2), to the invocation of the vaguer constitutional provisions. One might say that the Constitution permits a practice of horizontal application that is all but unfettered, for the very reason that the republican potential of horizontality keeps pace with the reach of the ANC's constitutional vision. But Woolman's account illustrates how this same republican potential may be cause for wariness, as well. Many cases, including the crucial *Grootboom* case discussed later, suggest that the Court was ready to cast the legislature as the primary executor of the ambitious Constitution rather than take on the more positive aspects of the project for itself.[132]

This dynamic confronts the question described at the end of Chapter 2, and elsewhere in this book, regarding courts' status as sufficiently republican bodies to determine whether and when rights apply to private actors.[133] The German Constitutional Court may not confront this tension in the same way as the German Basic Law undertakes a project that is somewhat more modest, at least in certain ways and comparatively speaking.[134] As Mathews explains in his book, the

---

[131] Nolan, "Holding Non-state Actors"; Helen Hershkoff, "Transforming Legal Theory in the Light of Practice: The Judicial Application of Social and Economic Rights to Private Orderings," in *Courting Social Rights*, ed. Varun Gauri and Daniel Brinks (Cambridge: Cambridge University Press, 2008), 268–302.

[132] See also David Bilchitz's criticism; Woolman, "Amazing Vanishing"; Dennis Davis, "Twenty Years of Constitutional Democracy: A Preliminary Reflection," *New York Law School Law Review* 60:1 (2016), 39–54.

[133] One can consider this question either in descriptive or in normative terms. From a more analytic or descriptive perspective, Roux recounts how the early Court went out of its way in the *Bhe* case to treat customary law in a way that appealed to the broader populace (*Politics of Principle*, 248–250).

[134] One might say that the German turn to apply equality horizontally in recent years, detailed at the end of Chapter 5, is an exception that proves the rule or, perhaps more accurately, the beginning of a shift on this matter.

German Constitutional Court was actually eager to assert itself against the other branches and other courts. Michaela Hailbronner notably classifies the Basic Law as transformative;[135] however, the German Constitution is more modest in what it asks, both of state and citizen, compared to the South African Constitution. While Germany's case history suggests a court comfortable with the doctrine (and doctrinal scope) it had a definitive hand in formulating, out of South Africa's case history emerge both discourses that embrace horizontal application and even illustrate its full republican potential, and discourses that attempt to demarcate boundaries to this practice. Early decisions thus show some unevenness in both judicial discourses and ultimate decisions. Later decisions, particularly pertaining to such areas as housing and education that are integral to South Africa's transformation, are a bit more consistent in their embrace of horizontal application and in their display of republican concepts.

The Negative–Positive Divide in Housing and Education

Questions of dignity, free expression, and defamation are by no means novel in horizontality jurisprudence. Nevertheless, in securing the Final Constitution's provision for horizontal application of these rights, *Khumalo* paved the way for other, more distinctive rights of the South African constitutional order also to obligate private actors. These other rights arguably reached deeper into private spaces and, to this extent, could potentially effect transformation all the more. Decisions on housing, education, and even wills and testaments thus emerged, sectors that by themselves signal horizontality extending further into private spaces than in many other contexts. Moreover, the language and arguments in these later decisions reveal the power of a republican interpretation in this context. Language of "neighborliness" and "shared concern" often seems to replace mention of rights altogether, cemented only more in certain invocations of ubuntu. Thus, amid criticisms of some judges' inhibitive formalism and conventional understandings, much in these later decisions may be read through the lens of constitutional ends, rather than mere rights, pertaining to a larger community of private actors maintaining duties vis-à-vis those ends.

---

[135] Hailbronner, "Transformative Constitutionalism."

While finding clear space in more aspirational understandings of South African constitutionalism, many of these new rights commitments threw the courts into somewhat unfamiliar territory. In particular, such socioeconomic rights as health and housing raised new questions about the separation of powers and scarcity of resources, both public and private. In recounting his experience in deciding the important *Grootboom* case, discussed later,[136] Justice Albie Sachs acknowledged the unique difficulties that come with enforcing something such as a right of access to adequate housing, when so much depends on the actions of and resources of legislatures and even private proprietors.[137] Such difficulties first came before the Court in *Soobramoney v. Minister of Health, KwaZulu-Natal* (1997),[138] when a terminally ill man by the name of Soobramoney invoked his right not to be "refused emergency medical treatment" under Section 27(3) and his right to life under Section 11 of the Constitution in order to receive renal dialysis from a state-funded hospital. As Soobramoney was of limited means, seeking care from a public hospital was his only option to sustain his life even a little longer. And yet he remained at the back of the line for the necessary care.

While conceding Soobramoney's right to receive and the state's duty to provide care, the Constitutional Court argued that it was not in a position to compel the state or the hospital to provide care, potentially at the cost of others requiring medical attention. Given that his was an ongoing issue and not a medical emergency, his right was contingent on what resources might be available at any given time, a calculus the Court simply could not make. Soobramoney died shortly after, and criticisms arose about the apparently contingent nature of socioeconomic rights. That medical care was contingent on the availability of resources and even the patient's particular financial means struck many as incongruous with what was supposed to be a transformative constitution, and cast initial doubt on the whole enterprise of socioeconomic rights. In some ways, the Court responded in the *Grootboom* case on housing a few years later, acknowledging its own institutional role in supporting the most

---

[136] *Government of the Republic of South Africa and Others v. Grootboom and Others* (CCT11/00) [2000] ZACC 19.

[137] Albie Sachs, "The Judicial Enforcement of Socio-economic Rights: The *Grootboom* Case," in *The Constitution in Private Relations*, ed. András Sajó and Renáta Uitz (Ultrecht: Eleven, 2005), 79–98; see also Section 25 on property, which both guarantees a right to property and lays out parameters for expropriation.

[138] *Soobramoney v. Minister of Health, KwaZulu-Natal* [1997] ZACC 17.

vulnerable and even its ability to require other institutions to make "reasonable" efforts toward securing such rights.[139]

Housing is a salient and complex issue in South African history. From the outset of European colonialism in the mid seventeenth century through the Apartheid regime of the twentieth century, racially based laws and evictions displaced indigenous peoples leading to widespread impoverishment of black populations.[140] Thus, the South African Constitution provided, "Everyone has the right to have access to adequate housing,"[141] and legislation established various parallel safeguards, from protections for occupiers facing eviction to specialized courts that would see through land reform.[142] The *Grootboom* case concerned a particular settlement, Wallacedene, where only 5 percent of the dwellings had electricity, 25 percent of dwellings had no income at all, and 50 percent of residents were children.[143] Mrs. Grootboom was one among many residing there who had applied for low-cost, state-funded housing, but remained in this increasingly uninhabitable settlement. In the end, the Court decided that Mrs. Grootboom was not entitled to emergency housing, but acknowledged that parliament was charged with taking reasonable action on the issue of housing in general. In the words of Justice Yakoob, "The case brings home the harsh reality that the Constitution's promise of dignity and equality for all remains for many a distant dream."[144] Housing rights are, thus, aspirational in the fullest sense.

---

[139] This is in contrast with the alternative "minimum core" standard, adopted by such bodies as the United Nations, that guarantees a minimum essential level of socio-economic rights provision to which individuals are immediately entitled.

[140] Gaopalelwe Lesley Mathiba, "Evictions and Tenure Security in South Africa," *ESR Review* 19:2 (2018), 13.

[141] Section 26 on housing reads:
"1. Everyone has the right to have access to adequate housing.
2. The state must take reasonable legislative and other measures, within its available resources, to achieve the progressive realisation of this right.
3. No one may be evicted from their home, or have their home demolished, without an order of court made after considering all the relevant circumstances. No legislation may permit arbitrary evictions."

[142] Sandra Liebenberg, "Socio-economic Rights beyond the Public Private Law Divide," in *Socioeconomic Rights in South Africa: Symbols or Substance?* ed. Malcolm Langford, Ben Cousins, Jackie Dugard, and Tshepo Madlingozi (Cambridge: Cambridge University Press, 2013), 77.

[143] Drucilla Cornell, Stu Woolman, Sam Fuller, Jason Brickhill, Michael Bishop, and Diana Dunbar, eds., "Grootboom," in *The Dignity Jurisprudence of the Constitutional Court of South Africa: Cases and Materials* (New York: Fordham University Press, 2013), 415–430.

[144] *Government of the Republic of South Africa and Others v. Grootboom*, para. 2.

Although rooted in the core pathologies of South African history, housing is among the socioeconomic rights that involve such balancing of interests and capacities as to avert full and immediate realization.

While the Constitution specifies that the duty to provide adequate housing falls on the state, the very nature of housing is such that cases frequently involve private relationships. Even in *Grootboom* the Court recognized that a "right of access to adequate housing also suggests that it is not only the State who is responsible for the provision of houses, but that other agents within our society, including individuals themselves, must be enabled by legislative and other measures to provide housing."[145] Those matters considered by the Land Claims Court, such as land restitution and eviction, raise questions of horizontal effect basically by definition.[146] Moreover, several judgments of the Constitutional Court have concerned housing and explicitly address the question of horizontal effect.

In 2005, the Constitutional Court handed down the *Modderklip* decision.[147] The owners of the Modderklip farm permitted some people to settle on the land. However, when thousands occupied the farm, the owners became overwhelmed and offered to sell the land to local authorities to accommodate the new occupants. The authorities refused to purchase and the local police demanded a high deposit to enforce the eviction order Modderklip obtained from a court.[148] In the Supreme Court, Justice Harms acknowledged that housing rights could be enforced horizontally in theory, but decided that it could not in the present case.[149] On appeal, the Constitutional Court did not technically rely on horizontal application, but instead ruled that the state had failed both in protecting the Modderklip company's property rights and in securing the occupants' right to have access to adequate housing.[150] Although the Court chose not to apply horizontal effect explicitly, the Court's remedy still involved balancing rights against each other and, to this extent, necessarily involved cooperation of the parties in securing the rights in question. In particular, the Court argued that eviction was at that point impossible given that, over five years, 40,000 people had come

---

[145] Ibid., para. 35.
[146] I am indebted to Heinz Klug for this insight.
[147] *President of the Republic of South Africa and Another v. Modderklip Boerdery (Pty) Ltd* (CCT20/04) [2005] ZACC 5.
[148] Robertson, "Thick Constitutional Readings," 315.
[149] *Modderklip Boerdery (Pty) Ltd. v. Modder East Squatters & Anor.* 2001 (4) SA 385 (W), para. 31.
[150] Nolan, "Holding Non-state Actors," 82–83.

to settle on the farm and formed their own community.[151] As a remedy, therefore, the Court ordered that the state compensate Modderklip for the use of the land.

Although Modderklip was not responsible for the occupants' right to have access to housing per se, the owners were, ultimately, still responsible for their housing in a practical sense. Moreover, although the occupants were not ultimately understood as trespassing, Modderklip was still entitled to compensation. Of course, the sheer logistics and financial cost of relocating 40,000 people figured into the solution the Court reached. At the same time, the Court's judgment is punctuated with republicanesque ideas. As a discursive matter, the heart of this judgment is nothing less than a call for the private actors involved to participate in larger constitutional ends, to cooperate and even fulfill duties vis-à-vis one another. Quoting Albie Sachs in *Elizabeth Port Municipality*, discussed earlier, Justice Langa recounts the need "to balance competing interests in a principled way and promote the constitutional vision of a caring society based on good neighbourliness and shared concern."[152] In the context of the *Modderklip* case, the difficulty of the immediate circumstances, to say nothing of the longer history that occasioned these circumstances, asks of the parties these same characteristics of neighborliness and shared concern. Put differently, the Court seems to presuppose that the actors involved identify with and share in the values of the constitutional project. Indeed, the very fact that the Court avoided the language of rights in discussing the relationship between the owners and the occupants brings this point into sharper relief. With this choice, "[t]he Court looked to social and economic norms as reflecting a constitutional vision of solidarity that altered the relation of the property owner to the settlers."[153] By avoiding the language of rights in favor of expressions of the collective pursuit of constitutional ends, the case may be read as taking on a more republican cadence.

From an analytical perspective, moreover, attention to the larger constitutional vision articulated in *Modderklip*, rather than the fact that the Court does not understand itself as applying horizontal effect per se, allows the observer to appreciate the extent to which the actors do retain

---

[151] Hershkoff, "Transforming Legal Theory," 296.
[152] *President of the Republic of South Africa and Another v. Modderklip Boerdery*, paras. 53–54, quoting Albie Sachs's opinion in *Port Elizabeth Municipality v. Various Occupiers*.
[153] Hershkoff, "Transforming Legal Theory," 299.

responsibility here and participate in the constitutional project in the ultimate resolution. Indeed, the articulation of the Constitution's commitments in terms of rights is only one possible expression of these commitments, seeing as the South African Constitution itself understands the Republic as founded on the more general values of human dignity, equality, freedom, nonracialism, nonsexism, and so on.[154] Helen Hershkoff finds this approach of avoiding rights language in other contexts, too.[155] This is worth acknowledging for the aforementioned analytical reasons as well as for more substantive reasons to which Hershkoff draws attention. Speaking specifically of *Modderklip*, she explains:

> In the classical conception, common law powers can be used in the holder's discretion to maximize self-utility; the egoistic exercise of power is assumed to conduce toward the general welfare. The presence of social welfare norms in a constitution alters this background assumption. From a constitutive theory of law, the powers assigned to individuals must now be interpreted and applied within the orbit of constitutional commitment and not simply within that of self-regarding concern ... The South Africa Court, thus, made clear that Modderklip's power to control access to the farm could not be extended in a way that would unduly burden the occupants' background right to housing, notwithstanding the fact that the farm owner does not owe a duty of shelter to the settlers. By constraining the exercise of the common law power, the court effectively altered the occupants' legal relation in the sense that they now possessed shelter. But, rather than prescribing rights directly owed from one individual to another, the court instead reshaped a power relationship in a specific context in the light of different facts and circumstances.[156]

While *Modderklip* does not technically employ the language of rights and duties between the private actors, the Court does "reshape a power relationship," as Hershkoff puts it, to balance their conflicting interests against each other. Whereas, in most countries, Modderklip's right to property might have controlled the outcome of the case, here the owners' rights were subject to the broader framework of social welfare norms or, in republican terms, to a particular conception of the common good. This broader normative context does not negate Modderklip's property rights entirely; nevertheless, it does require a general compliance with the constitutional vision. As these norms thus apply across spheres, private

---

[154] South African Constitution of 1996, Chapter 1, Section 1.
[155] Hershkoff, "Transforming Legal Theory," 298.
[156] Ibid., 299.

actors such as Modderklip are brought into the fold of the larger constitutional project.[157]

In the years following *Modderklip*, the Court still contended with the clash between the rights to private property and housing, often invoking the constitutional ethic of neighborliness and ubuntu of *Port Elizabeth Municipality*, discussed earlier.[158] One such case was *Blue Moonlight Properties*,[159] in which a development company sought to evict eighty extremely poor people living on the property the company had recently purchased. The company was aware of the occupiers' presence prior to purchasing, and eviction would all but certainly lead to their homelessness. The City of Johannesburg claimed it had resources to provide emergency housing only for those evicted from publicly owned land. Because these people occupied private property, however, the city could not offer any accommodation.

In *Blue Moonlight Properties* the Court claimed for itself more positive aspects of the constitutional project than it did in *Grootboom*, when it went to great lengths to accommodate the other corners of government. Ultimately, the Court decided that the constitutional guarantees to equality and housing, in fact, required the city to find accommodation

---

[157] In some ways, the facts and judgment in *Modderklip* are comparable to those of the US case *Home Building and Loan Association v. Blaisdell* (1934). In *Blaisdell*, the Court upheld a Minnesota law that issued a moratorium on creditors' remedies at the height of the Great Depression. In particular, Justice Hughes appealed to a broader understanding of the common good to justify what, prima facie, seemed to be a departure from the constitution's contract clause. He writes in the opinion of the Court: "Where, in earlier days, it was thought that only the concerns of individuals or of classes were involved, and that those of the state itself were touched only remotely, it has later been found that the fundamental interests of the state are directly affected; and that the question is no longer merely that of one party to a contract as against another, but of the use of reasonable means to safeguard the economic structure upon which the good of all depends." On Hughes's telling, this apparent deviation from the letter of the Constitution's contract clause actually was necessary to uphold the fundamental aim of the clause itself to "promote conditions of economic stability" (Gary Jacobsohn, *Pragmatism, Statesmanship, and the Supreme Court*, [Ithaca: Cornell University Press, 1977], 188). In much the same way the South African Court was careful not to say that Modderklip was responsible for the occupants' housing rights, the Court in *Blaisdell* similarly argued that it did nothing to damage the principles of contract and property. Rather, it permitted the Minnesota legislation for the very reason that it would further the principle of the contract clause amid economic exigencies. See also Jacobsohn, *Pragmatism*, 183–193.

[158] *Port Elizabeth Municipality v. Various Occupiers*, para. 29.

[159] *City of Johannesburg Metropolitan Municipality v. Blue Moonlight Properties 39 (Pty) Ltd and Another* (CC) [2011] ZACC 33.

for these occupiers although they were on private property. In the meantime, and more relevant to this book, the property owners themselves had a positive obligation[160] pursuant to these same guarantees to equality and housing. Calling for patience, the Court explained that the property owners would have to continue housing these people until city officials could find alternative accommodation.[161] The Court is clear that the company would not have to provide free housing indefinitely, but as long as was required to ensure these people would not be homeless.

Another salient issue for South Africa's constitutional project is education, as significant discrepancies in education were part and parcel of the inequality of Apartheid. And indeed, an important horizontality case decided in the same year as *Blue Moonlight Properties* concerned the right to education. In *Juma Musjid* (2011), the Court considered explicitly whether a socioeconomic right imposed an obligation on a private actor[162] when a private trust took steps to evict a public school that convened on its property. The Constitutional Court decided that the trust had "no primary positive obligation"[163] to provide an education for the students, nor an obligation to make available its property for public use as a school. Nevertheless, the Court found that the trust *did* have "a negative constitutional obligation not to impair the learners' right to a basic education,"[164] pursuant to Section 29 of the Constitution. The Court concluded that the trust had every right to seek an eviction order, but that the courts were not obliged to grant one. Indeed, in evaluating the eviction request, the lower courts were required to consider "the best interest of the learners"[165] and their right to a basic education. Thus, the particular question at issue in *Juma Musjid* was how to balance the right to a basic education and the right to property.[166]

---

[160] Mbuyiseli Madlanga, "The Human Rights Duties of Companies and Other Private Actors in South Africa," *Stellenbosch Human Law Review* 29:3 (2018), 370–372.

[161] *City of Johannesburg Metropolitan Municipality v. Blue Moonlight Properties 39 (Pty) Ltd and Another,* para. 40.

[162] *Blue Moonlight Properties*, decided a few months after *Juma Musjid*, arguably took on this question as well, but did so implicitly. See Madlanga, "Human Rights Duties," 370–372.

[163] *Juma Musjid*, para. 57.

[164] Ibid., para. 60.

[165] Ibid., para. 66; see also Nolan, "Holding Non-state Actors," 83.

[166] *Juma Musjid*, para. 7.

Following the reasoning in *Khumalo*, the Court explained that the horizontal application of rights, including such socioeconomic rights as to education, depended in part on "the intensity of the constitutional right in question."[167] In the context of South African history, the basic right to education did rise to such a level of intensity as to call for a more congruent application to public and private actors alike. The Court explains the particular significance of the right to education in light of the history:

> The inadequacy of schooling facilities, particularly for many blacks was entrenched by the formal institution of apartheid, after 1948, when segregation even in education and schools in South Africa was codified. Today, the lasting effects of the educational segregation of apartheid are discernible in the systemic problems of inadequate facilities and the discrepancy in the level of basic education for the majority of learners.[168]

Thus, much like cases concerning housing, the decision to apply this basic right to education horizontally was grounded in the very purpose of the South African Constitution. The crucial nature of the issue of education, the Court held, warranted summoning private actors also to participate in its remediation or at least to cooperate until an alternative venue for the school could be secured. Both the nature of past abuses and the unique position of many private actors to exercise influence in education were cause to involve such institutions as the Juma Musjid Trust in the constitutional project. As property rights had been formulated to disadvantage the black population during Apartheid,[169] putting other rights, such as to education, on equal footing ensured that claims to private property did not have undue weight and were calibrated to constitutional ends.[170] Moreover, as this decision of the Court to balance these as competing rights departed from the preconstitutional status quo, so too did the decision to cast the issue in terms of the duties of private actors. Aoife Nolan observes how, in *Juma Musjid*, the Court had the option to employ strategies similar to those in *Carmichele* and

---

[167] Ibid., para. 58.
[168] Ibid., para. 42.
[169] The Court states: "Traditionally, because of the clear distinction between public law and private law realms, a private owner could evict any tenant provided that the requirements of *rei vindicatio* were satisfied. Private entities were held to be free to engage in their economic and social interests without state interference. As a result, over emphasis on the differences between the exercise of private and public power often sheltered private power used for public purposes" (*Juma Musjid*, para. 55).
[170] Nolan, "Holding Non-state Actors," 85.

Modderklip that did not invoke constitutional duties of private actors. Instead, however, the Court did speak of duties and found the source of these private obligations in the Constitution itself.[171]

Some fourteen years after the Court first confronted the issue of socioeconomic rights in the *Soobramoney* case, amici in *Juma Musjid* expressed concern that this later judgment might mark a kind of apogee for the Court's jurisprudence in socioeconomic rights. Specifically, they worried the Court would hesitate ever to apply positive rights horizontally since it only applied socioeconomic rights horizontally as a negative matter in *Juma Musjid*.[172] Of course, the Constitution makes no reference to a distinction between positive and negative obligations as a limit on horizontal effect, stating instead that the Court ought to consider "the nature of the right and the nature of the duty imposed by the right."[173] Nevertheless, distinguishing between positive and negative obligations might have offered a more robust limiting principle to those looking for one – whether to shield any vestiges of those laissez-faire priors Kriegler criticized in *Du Plessis*, or to offer cover for a Court that, historically, showed reticence to embrace horizontality's republican logic to extend as far into private spaces as the early ANC vision had aspired.[174] For all intents and purposes, *Blue Moonlight Properties*, decided only a few months after *Juma Musjid*, imposed positive obligations on a private actor, namely, to accommodate people occupying their property while the city arranged for alternative housing. Nevertheless, it did so without using the words "positive obligation," ensuring that this remained a live question in South African constitutional politics until at least the 2017 case *Daniels v. Scribante* and likely beyond as even later cases have shown reticence to speak of positive obligations.[175]

---

[171] Nolan explains: "It is notable that in the Juma Musjid case, the Court was also invited by the applicants to develop the common law of contract and trust in accordance with § 39 (2) of the Constitution and the Court did not do so even though such an approach might have enabled it to avoid addressing § 8(2)" ("Holding Non-state Actors," 88, fn. 145).
[172] Nolan, "Holding Non-state Actors," 83.
[173] Constitution of South Africa, Section 8(2); see also Madlanga, "Human Rights Duties," 373.
[174] Moseneke, "Transformative Constitutionalism."
[175] Meghan Finn speaks of a possible chilling effect resulting from *Juma Musjid*. Specifically, she suggests that litigants will continue to hesitate even to suggest that private actors could have positive obligations, and instead find ways to redescribe obligations in negative terms, since the Court has treated this possibility fairly unpredictably from *Juma Musjid* to *Daniels* and, eventually, *Pridwin*, discussed later (Meghan Finn,

As explained in Chapter 2, the *Daniels* judgment decided that a landlord had a (potentially positive) constitutional obligation to ensure that his tenant lived in conditions consonant with human dignity. Ms. Daniels, the tenant, proposed to improve the property in several basic ways at her own expense: leveling the floor, installing a water supply, adding a ceiling, and so on. Despite the fact that Ms. Daniels's dwelling was basically uninhabitable, the property owner objected on the basis that he might be held responsible for compensating Ms. Daniels for these improvements upon her moving out.[176] If he allowed Ms. Daniels to make these improvements, the owner argued, he assumed a duty that could only be described as positive and, thus, beyond the parameters of horizontal application. This was not simply a negative duty as in *Juma Musjid*, but a positive duty requiring concrete steps on the part of a landlord. The fact that this required more from a private actor than had many past cases was of no moment, however, on the Court's reading of the Constitution – nothing in Section 8(2) foreclosed the possibility that a socioeconomic right could apply horizontally. Thus, the case hinged on balancing the landlord's property rights and the tenant's right to live in dignified conditions, with the Court opting for the latter given Ms. Daniels's dire circumstances.[177] The year after writing the opinion in *Daniels*, Justice Madlanga reflected in a lecture on the decision's significance in unreservedly embracing the Constitution's provision for horizontal application and his hope that the bogeyman of direct horizontal effect as portrayed in *Du Plessis* had "been slain for good."[178]

Describing private obligations in negative or positive terms, as did *Juma Musjid* and *Daniels*, respectively, may be a semantic question in certain instances. Perhaps litigants can basically achieve their desired result regardless of how they frame the issue at hand.[179] As a theoretical matter, however, this constitutes more than word choice. Indeed,

---

"Befriending the Bogeyman: Direct Horizontal Application in *AB v. Pridwin*," *South African Law Journal* 137:4 [2020], 604).

[176] This belief was based on certain provisions of the Extension of Security of Tenure Act (ESTA).

[177] Note that the Court invoked the broad constitutional principle of dignity, rather than a more concrete right, as to housing.

[178] Madlanga, "Human Rights Duties," 374.

[179] This question is considered, for example, by Finn, "Befriending the Bogeyman," 601; Nurina Ally and Daniel Linde, "*Pridwin*: Private School Contracts, the Bill of Rights and a Missed Opportunity," *Constitutional Court Review* 11 (2021), 299, fn. 135; and Leo Boonzaier, "Contractual Fairness at the Crossroads," *Constitutional Court Review* 11 (2021), 229–274.

whether obligations of private actors stop where the language of positive rights begins has implications for the reach of a republican interpretation of horizontal application. On the one hand, extending even negative obligations to private actors encompasses them in the communal project. Indeed, their own rights are limited as they make concessions to (negative) constitutional ends that happen to compete and carry out constitutional duties with respect to their fellow citizens. At the same time, to limit the scope of obligations to the negative reflects some effort not to interfere too drastically in private actors' freedoms – to put limits on the limits, if you will. As explained earlier, limits are entirely predictable as judges stipulate ranges of application for jurisprudential practices. Nevertheless, this particular distinction between negative and positive duties, this potential limit on the content of rights applied horizontality, points to deeper questions (and implicit answers) of how to understand freedom, even if such issues are not actually contemplated by the judges themselves.[180]

As Chapter 2 explained, much scholarship conceptualizes the crucial difference between liberal and republican notions of liberty as consisting in freedom as noninterference and freedom as nondomination, respectively. From a theoretic perspective, the choice not to apply positive obligations horizontally may be read as an understanding of freedom as noninterference and reluctance to restrict individual autonomy in more intrusive ways. By extension, this position tends to deemphasize the ways private actors use autonomy to restrict other rights (such as socioeconomic rights[181]) that could actually be constitutive of alternative understandings of freedom, such as nondomination. As judges thus favor a practice of horizontality limited to negative duties on the one hand, or extending it to positive duties on the other, they effectively chart bounds for how far a republican interpretation might reach in a given case or context. On either understanding, we see a bringing of private actors into the communal space. The question becomes in what ways and how much of the private sphere will be encompassed into the common ends of the

---

[180] Although the very distinction between positive and negative rights has long been questioned (Henry Shue, *Basic Rights: Subsistence, Affluence and US Foreign Policy* [Princeton: Princeton University Press, 1996]), the fact that constitutional actors do make much of it signals the need – from a political theoretic (and even a more general social science) perspective – still to attend to this distinction.

[181] See, for example, Sandra Liebenberg, "The Application of Socio-economic Rights to Private Law," *Journal of South African Law* 3 (2008), 464–480, and *Socio-economic rights: Adjudication under a Transformative Constitution* (Claremont: Juta, 2010).

constitutional project. Scholars such as Sandra Liebenberg argue for the need to take seriously the relationship between socioeconomic rights and equality in the Constitution and thus to resist more traditional understandings that prioritize the negative duties that typically have pride of place in common law.[182] And yet, the foregoing cases show the extent to which the Court's arguments still find different theoretical homes. Later developments show all the more how these theoretic questions are engendered in decisions of the Constitutional Court, as well as the implications of these for a republican interpretation.

A Return to Common Law? Attempting Another Limiting Principle

Just a few months after the Court handed down its judgment in *Daniels v. Scribante*, it decided *Baron v. Claytile Ltd*,[183] which again raised questions of horizontal application in the context of housing and eviction. *Baron* followed *Modderklip* in the sense that the Court was hesitant to assign a private actor duties to guarantee housing rights. In particular, the Court decided that an employer did not have an obligation to continue providing former employees with housing, insofar as the Constitution designated this duty as belonging specifically to the state. To be sure, realizing a right to have access to adequate housing as a matter of fact is a major endeavor. While the primary obligation rested with the state, however, even after *Baron* it is conceivable that private actors be asked to cooperate in much the same way as in *Modderklip* and *Blue Moonlight Properties*. Indeed, courts still retained the ability to decide whether a particular eviction was "just and equitable." Therefore, while the duty to provide adequate housing was technically the state's, a private actor could functionally assume responsibility even for such positive rights as to housing.

The adjacent decisions of *Daniels* and *Baron* in the 2017 term of the Constitutional Court demonstrate how horizontal application is as much a live issue as it is a complicated one. *Baron* in particular shows that the Court maintains some limits on the extent to which private actors have constitutional duties. Nevertheless, even in *Baron*, the Court continued to operate on the basic presumption that private actors could have rights

---

[182] Liebenberg, "Socio-economic Rights beyond the Public–Private Law Divide," 86.
[183] *Barron and Others v. Claytile (Pty) Ltd and Another* [2017] ZACC 24.

obligations. The later *Pridwin Preparatory School* case[184] in some ways illustrates a continued trajectory when the Court took yet a further step in applying rights horizontally to conclude that private schools had a constitutional duty to provide a basic education – specifically that administrators could not dismiss students from the school without giving due weight to the children's right to an education, as through a hearing. The Court argued that this duty existed regardless of any specific terms to which the school and parents contracted. While the Court as a whole seems willing to apply direct horizontality more readily in *Pridwin*, the judgment still leaves many questions related to horizontal application unanswered and perhaps renders them more ambiguous than before.[185] Much of this ambiguity may be traced back to the 2007 case *Barkhuizen v. Napier* and how the judgments in *Pridwin* employ this precedent.[186]

In *Barkhuizen*, the Court declined to apply constitutional principles directly to challenge the terms of a contract, insofar it was a private contract and not a law of general application.[187] Instead, the Court considered whether the terms were reasonable and fair, ultimately giving priority to the principle of "pacta sunt servanda" (that "agreements must be kept") rather than the competing constitutional rights that might have led to some adjustment in the common law. In his majority judgment, Justice Ngcobo explained that this principle of "pacta sunt servanda" itself "gives effect to the central constitutional values of freedom and dignity. Self-autonomy, or the ability to regulate one's own affairs, even to one's own detriment, is the very essence of freedom and a vital part of dignity."[188] These rights, however, are enforced simply through fulfilling the terms of the private contract and preserving existing common law understandings, as opposed to subjecting the contract to other principles arising specifically out of the 1996 Constitution.

---

[184] *AB and Another v. Pridwin Preparatory School and Others* (CCT294/18) [2020] ZACC 12.

[185] Lowenthal, "*AB v. Pridwin Preparatory School*," 266–272; remote interview with Dennis Davis, December 2, 2020.

[186] See the case *Barkhuizen v. Napier* (CCT72/05) [2007] ZACC 5, and Woolman's analysis in his 2007 article. Also Lowenthal, "*AB v. Pridwin Preparatory School*," 5, 11.

[187] In *Barkhuizen,* an insurance contract imposed a ninety-day time limit on the insured's right to initiate legal proceedings after the insurance company rejected a claim. Mr. Barkhuizen, who initiated court proceedings two years after his claim was rejected, argued that the contract terms violated his right to seek redress in a court under Section 34 of the Constitution.

[188] *Barkhuizen v. Napier*, para. 57.

In some ways, *Pridwin* may be read as assuming this position that contracts are insulated from direct constitutional scrutiny. Indeed, some critics, such as Meghan Finn, find that it presumes an even greater degree of insulation than *Barkhuizen* required. While the prior *Barkhuizen* case acknowledged the possibility that constitutional principles could apply indirectly to contracts by reshaping common law understandings, Finn explains, the Court's judgment in *Pridwin* "perpetuates the sense that there are parallel systems of law: one that is shaped by and tested against the Constitution, and another that is autonomous and can be ignored, rather than constitutionally infused."[189] In other words, although the judgment in *Pridwin* ultimately did employ horizontal application, it did so solely on the basis that a constitutional right was invoked and, thus, explicitly in play rather than recognizing that constitutional standards might also bear in some way on the terms of a private contract. In Finn's telling, such a binary framework insulates private contracts to an extent the prior *Barkhuizen* case did not require, undercutting the full transformative potential of a practice of horizontal application.[190]

Such doctrinal questions as these cases raise risk getting technical very quickly. To what, then, does all this amount for the purposes of this book? In many ways, this question of the status of contract law vis-à-vis constitutional values echoes the same concerns of the National Party in the negotiations, of the Supreme Court of Appeal after the establishment of the Constitutional Court, of the majority in *Du Plessis v. DeKlerk*. In later jurisprudential developments such as *Pridwin*, one can likewise read theoretical concerns about what areas of law and life are (or are not) encompassed in the public project. Even under such a transformative constitution as South Africa's, private contracts seem to maintain a specially private status in many judgements of the Court, such that they are not so readily subsumed into the Constitution's transformative project as other areas of law. How horizontality applies to contracts has been contested much more and much longer than the horizontal application of housing rights, for example. In the terms of this book's republican interpretation, one might read in this history and these judgments a reticence to bring the same parity to encompass certain areas of private life into the constitutional domain. Thus, in a similar spirit to the negative–positive duties distinction discussed in the previous section, the arguments underlying these technical doctrinal developments

---

[189] Finn, "Befriending the Bogeyman," 600; see also Ally and Linde, "*Pridwin*," 291.
[190] Finn, "Befriending the Bogeyman," 599–600.

ultimately implicate the discourses to which a republican interpretation may extend.

That there are lingering questions becomes only more apparent when reading *Pridwin*'s judgment alongside *Beadica v. Trustees*,[191] handed down on the very same day and authored by the same justice, Justice Theron, but undoubtedly different. Invoking the principle found in *Barkhuizen* of "pacta sunt servanda" ("agreements must be kept"), in *Beadica*, Justice Theron argues that, in fact, the contract in question ought not to be overturned on the grounds of public policy as the encroachment was not sufficiently severe. Indeed, both the functioning of society and constitutional morality depended on the ability to have one's contracts enforced. So, the question becomes how to square these two cases, *Pridwin* and *Beadica*, seemingly similar in the issues they confront and yet engendering very different discourses. *Pridwin* involved the right of children to an education, a potentially crucial point given the pattern of horizonal application, and the fit of a republican reading of horizontal application, in the context of housing and education.[192] At the same time, Finn and other scholars worry about the way *Pridwin* confines horizontality to just these kinds of clearcut rights issues. While *Beadica* ultimately does not employ direct horizontal application, it also

---

[191] *Beadica 231 CC and Others v. Trustees for the Time Being of the Oregon Trust and Others* (CCT109/19) [2020] ZACC 13. In *Beadica*, a group of black franchisees received funding through an economic empowerment program to acquire franchises from a firm for which they had worked. This consisted of a ten-year franchise agreement and a five-year lease agreement for the business to operate with the option to renew for an additional five years. At the end of five years, the franchisees had not formally asked for the renewal of the lease agreement, seeking renewal only through informal means such as by email or phone. Thus, they faced eviction and, by extension, cancelation of the franchise. If the prior *Modderklip* case parallels the US *Blaisdell* majority opinion, *Beadica* arguably bears similarity with Sutherland's dissent in *Blaisdell*. According to Justice Theron, constitutional values might serve as recourse for those in breach of contract if there were good reasons for the breach. However, in general, courts are charged with upholding contracts pursuant to the principle of legal certainty (interview with Justice Leona Theron, Notre Dame, IN, April 14, 2023).

[192] According to Judge Dennis Davis, the Court has been more sensitive when it comes to cases with closer connection to Apartheid's legacy, such as the dispossession of property. Such cases do not present an abstraction requiring any intellectual leaps. Rather, in cases such as *Daniels v. Scribante*, "There is a visceral, historical thing" that "shouts out from the pages." Effectively, judges are forced to ask, "How can we possibly not come to the aid of a person who is a clear case of a massive cohort of people who are dispossessed of their land throughout the apartheid and colonial period?" (remote interview with Dennis Davis, December 2, 2020).

does not employ the same "parallel systems of law" that Finn fears, but instead seems to signal a return to *Barkhuizen* and the possibility of indirect horizontality in contracts.[193]

If contracts are a useful area to observe different accounts of the reach of South Africa's transformative constitutionalism, then testamentary decisions may offer even more insights. To the extent that wills are among the more personal (or private) of documents one could draw up, testamentary decisions constitute important cases within which to find (or not) the kind of republican discourse with which this book is concerned. The way in which constitutional actors discuss wills and testaments relative to the constitutional project may thus reveal different conceptions of just how far into the private sphere certain actors mean to reach in applying horizontal application. And indeed, while varied in their reasoning, the judgments in the 2021 case *King v. De Jager* prove uncommonly receptive to a republican interpretation.

In *King v. De Jager*, the Court considered a 1902 will stipulating that the testator's farms would be passed down only to male descendants for the subsequent three generations. One of the later beneficiaries bequeathed a portion of the original land to his daughters, however, leading some male descendants to file suit. The Court thus confronted the question of whether the limitation that only male descendants could inherit could be enforced in view of the Constitution's prohibition of discrimination on the basis of gender. In three different judgments, all contrary to the prior decision of the High Court, the Constitutional Court decided that this provision could not be enforced. The first judgment, by Justice Mhlantla, relies on *Barkhuizen*, arguing for the development of common law and the idea that private testamentary provisions could only be enforced as they complied with public policy, including constitutional values.[194] Ultimately, this amounts to a version of indirect horizontality. The majority opinion, penned by Justice Jafta, realized the same outcome that the will ought not to be enforced, but

---

[193] See also Boonzaier, "Contractual Fairness at the Crossroads."

[194] Justice Theron, who joined the Mhlantla opinion, explained the challenge to decide any case "dealing with the will of a person, in both senses." In Justice Theron's understanding, the particular case of *King v. De Jager* turned on the crucial point that the will's stipulation "was not a matter of a particular daughter not inheriting because of a bad relationship. This was a categorical statement that no women could inherit." Such a statement could not be enforced in a constitutional order fundamentally aimed at combating discrimination (interview with Justice Leona Theron, Notre Dame, IN, April 14, 2023).

instead reached this result through consideration of Section 9(3) of the Constitution, against unfair discrimination, as well as the Equality Act of 2000, passed with the express purpose of giving greater effect to such constitutional values. Section 8 of the Equality Act understands unfair discrimination specifically as including "the system of preventing women from inheriting property" and "any practice ... which impairs the dignity of women and undermines equality between women and men."[195] The third judgment by Justice Victor largely agreed with the majority, writing to emphasize the efficacy of the Equality Act as well as the role of *direct* horizontality in ensuring that the existing legislation does indeed protect the right in question.[196]

While largely tracking the reasoning of the majority judgment, Justice Victor's concurrence offers a great deal from which to draw a republican interpretation.[197] She speaks of the need to realize "substantive equality through the lens of transformative constitutionalism."[198] Likewise, she finds that this case is controlled by a capacious interpretation of equality, the Constitution's very raison d'être,[199] in contrast with the impulse to insulate the content of private wills and risk perpetuating Apartheid in private spaces.[200] More than a mere call for balancing competing rights, Victor's concurrence thus articulates the republican conviction that even this exceptionally private sphere of action ought to share in the public project and not detract from constitutional ends. She tellingly concludes by connecting this vision with the principle of ubuntu – in her words,

---

[195] *King v. De Jager*, para. 10.

[196] Ibid., para. 190.

[197] Much of the reasoning in these latter two judgments could be interpreted as running counter to Louis Henkin's arguments, discussed in Chapter 3, that a degree of capriciousness and arbitrariness must be tolerated in more private sectors (Henkin, "*Shelley v. Kraemer*," 498). This was later endorsed by Laurie Ackermann as a possible limiting principle to South Africa's own practice of horizontal application (*Human Dignity*, 268–288).

[198] *King v. De Jager*, para. 224.

[199] Ibid., para. 236.

[200] In ibid., para. 201, Victor states: "It is clear from the scheme and tenor of the Equality Act that it aims to ensure substantive as opposed to merely formal equality. By ensuring that the right to equality can be invoked against private persons, the Constitution acknowledges that colonialism and apartheid were not only facilitated by a repressive state apparatus but also through the complicity of individuals who benefitted directly from an unjust status *quo*. The Equality Act is an acknowledgement that to those on the receiving end of discrimination, the source of the discrimination (be it public or private) matters not."

"the adage that none of us are free until all of us are free."[201] Victor goes on to quote Justice Mokgoro's explanation of the Bill of Rights from a prior case as "an all-inclusive value system, or common values in South Africa" that encompasses, among other values, "group solidarity" and "conformity to basic norms and collective unity."[202] While horizontal application inevitably concerns rights, such accounts as these reveal a different take on the phenomenon – specifically that it may also give rise to certain communal ends and duties to contribute to those ends.

Conclusion

Both the German Constitutional Court and the South African constitutional framers introduced practices of horizontal application with the express intent of breaking from their respective pasts and setting course for a future governed by new constitutional commitments. In their jurisprudential histories, this move to horizontality aspires to a certain parity of governing principles across spheres. Nevertheless, the different content of these respective constitutional projects makes for different articulations and applications of horizontality. The German practice of horizontality finds expression through more classical rights and its civil law tradition. While German *Drittwirkung* still effected parity, initially this parity only extended so far into private spaces before private actors began to resist, as Chapter 5 explained.

On the other hand, the ANC's constitutional vision for South Africa explicitly aimed to upset background assumptions of more traditional accounts of constitutionalism, and upset these assumptions for the purpose of effecting broad change across spheres. Put differently, the broad practice of horizontal application, even in what are traditionally considered more private spaces, aligns with the ANC's constitutional project to transform all sectors of society. A republican logic that public values apply to private spaces exists in other areas of constitutional politics beyond horizontality as well, including statutory developments such as ESTA (the Extension of Security of Tenure Act of 1997) and the complex area of customary law. As to the latter, customary law has been elevated as a recognized source of law in South Africa. Nevertheless, the Constitution still requires parity of tribal law with constitutional

---

[201] *King v. De Jager*, para. 237.
[202] Ibid., para. 239; see also *S. v. Makwayane*, paras. 307–308.

principles.[203] A republican logic thus comes into sharp relief with the reformulation of rules on inheritance[204] and female chiefs[205] according to the Constitution.

From a bird's eye view, horizontal application seems to be expansive in South Africa relative to other countries. Of course, recent cases reveal continued complexity arising from traditional and formalist elements that persist in South African legal culture. However, when the Constitutional Court has chosen to apply horizontality, its language exemplifies a republican conviction that private entities have a role in the larger constitutional project, in contrast with traditional distinctions between public and private and, arguably, in line with the ANC's early vision. In this new constitutional terrain, rights assume more ambitious meanings and continually alter the terms in which relationships among citizens are understood.

---

[203] Sections 15(3), 39(2); see also Liebenberg, "Socio-economic Rights beyond the Public–Private Law Divide," 67, 72–74.

[204] See the foundational case *Bhe v. Magistrate, Khayelitsha; Shibi v. Sithole; SA Human Rights Com v. President of the RSA* 2005 (1) BCLR 1 (CC), deciding that male primogeniture was incompatible with the Constitution.

[205] See *Shilubana and Others v. Nwamitwa* 2009 (2) SA 66 (CC).

7

The European Union

Republicanism in Supranational Context

Prior chapters recounted debates surrounding the horizontal application of constitutional rights to nonstate actors in national contexts. While the particularities of these constitutional orders vary dramatically, comparisons can be made across both time and place. In one way or another, republican themes recur in these discourses, as constitutional actors seek some parity in governing values across spheres and introduce, to a greater or lesser extent, a category of constitutional duty for private actors. As national courts have considered horizontal application, so too has the Court of Justice of the EU considered the extent to which EU law creates obligations for private or nonstate actors.

EU law is typically understood as binding Member States,[1] requiring national institutions to adopt specific legislation or policies. Nevertheless, certain instances of EU law have been interpreted to obligate private actors as well. That EU "regulations" apply to private actors is more or less analogous to national statutes doing the same and, thus, not an issue of serious debate given the legislative function of the European Commission and Council. On the other hand, that such a foundational document as the Charter of Fundamental Rights might have horizontal application has been a source of controversy. Indeed, the constitutional nature of this document raises all of the same objections that jurists and scholars have leveled against horizontal application in national contexts and a host of others stemming from the fact that the EU is a supranational body.

What, then, might this book's republican framework contribute to our understanding of the EU, and particularly horizontality in the EU? What can republican theory illuminate in a context where one cannot so easily take for granted shared commitments and bonds of citizenship? The EU is indeed very different from any other legal order this book considers

---

[1] See, for example, Article 51 of the Charter of Fundamental Rights.

and has been examined by scholars and practitioners in a way that the nation-states this book considers have not. Like the prior chapters, this chapter also recounts countervailing factors working against horizontality, as well as the republican themes that emerge in response. Those factors countervailing against horizontality in the EU's political and scholarly debates are tied up with questions about the very nature and project of the Union. The question of integration and the extent to which the Union itself approximates a republic come into play as political and legal actors debate the place and limits of horizontality in Europe. Indeed, debates in both scholarship and cases of the European Court of Justice (ECJ) track these large questions about the character and aspirations of European unity.

Whereas Chapters 3 and 4 centered on the question of *whether* horizontality can be applied from a constitution, and Chapters 5 and 6 on the question of *how far* the constitution can be applied horizontally, this chapter's inquiry is at a higher level. Specifically, underlying the arguments of scholars and actors in this context is the question of whether and in what ways the ECJ and other actors *may even consider* the question of horizontal application in the first place. Is the EU enough of a political community for its institutions to speak about a discernable private sphere, and therefore potentially to speak to private actors? Or, rather, does its supranational nature somehow serve as a theoretical (and practical) barrier against horizontal application?

These are different sorts of questions than those considered previously, to be sure; however, republican themes emerge from both Eurosceptic and more pro-European perspectives. Republican intuitions certainly underlie those who emphasize the Member States as political communities, but they are also present in those arguments that find potential for something like republican political community and, by extension, horizontality at the Union level. We still see concerns about parity among separate spheres, for example. However, in the European case, the concern is with parity across domestic legal systems with supranational legal commitments. Moreover, whereas prior chapters often recounted constitutional actors resisting horizontality to maintain autonomy in the private sphere, here we see political actors and institutions of Member States trying to maintain domestic autonomy vis-à-vis a broader transnational sphere. Likewise, questions concerning duty arise, but always in the context of larger questions about the nature of European citizenship. Thus, as the republican lens uncovers new theoretical significances in debates over horizontality in the EU, so too do the distinctive features of the EU show additional nuances in a republican conception of horizontality.

In a certain way, horizontality in the EU is actually relatively noncontroversial and is even built into the Union's purpose. Indeed, the Union's original goal of creating a common market necessarily implicates private economic activity and, on this basis, may itself be described as a horizontal project. On the other hand, it is the Member States themselves that are the primary parties to EU treaties. This leads to the distinctive situation in which certain EU legislation, known as directives, do not apply horizontally insofar as they are aimed at the Member States' governments alone. However, the Charter of Fundamental Rights potentially does apply horizontally to private actors, as well as to applications of EU law, but does not necessarily bind the domestic law of individual Member States. Of course, this is in direct contrast with the typical arrangement within many nation-states in which ordinary legislation is the default mode of governing private actors, and higher law applies horizontally only sometimes, if at all. The EU certainly presents an unusual case when it comes to the question of horizontal application. However, it is precisely this unique character that makes the EU experience an important, if singular, bookend to a republican account of horizontality.

With the Charter's introduction and other developments over time, EU law has increasingly transcended its original economic ends to encompass a broader net of political issues and, in turn, has raised questions about the evolving nature of the project. In connecting the horizontal application of the EU Charter with such larger foundational questions about a European *res publica*, the republican framework proves useful. As with prior chapters, it does not attempt to resolve the debates or even to craft one coherent narrative of this dynamic and indeterminate political experiment. Rather, this chapter applies a republican lens in order to appreciate certain theoretical potential in the arguments many European actors and scholars have made in these debates. The first section of this chapter briefly recapitulates some of the theoretical background of prior chapters to lay out more fully the question of republican horizontal application in the context of the EU. The second section turns to scholarship on the EU, examining debates concerning republican politics and citizenship and drawing out the implications of European unity to the more specific subject of horizontal application. This section argues that particular republican resources in the EU, and aspirations of some European actors, bear important theoretical connections with horizontal application. The final section takes a closer look at ECJ decisions and scholarly literature on horizontal application in order to highlight the republican themes that emerge from many of these lines of argument.

The Republican Framework Applied to Europe

This book argues that horizontal application constitutes a republican vein in liberal constitutionalism. This practice applies constitutional rights to create new duties of private actors, thereby achieving greater parity between public values and certain corners of the private sphere. In contrast with traditional understandings in which constitutions create obligations only for the state, judges and other constitutional actors operating on a horizontal understanding derive duties of both state and nonstate actors from the same constitutional source. Much in the same way that constitutional rights insulate certain subjects from the political process, a horizontal understanding shifts the venue for debating questions that arise in the private sphere from the realm of ordinary legislation to more durable, and more fundamental, constitutional law. Horizontal application thus alters traditional premises about the public–private divide to expand the function of a constitution and the scope of constitutional rights.

This republican framework arguably goes further than the conventional liberal logic to help us understand and ground horizontal application in national contexts. But can republicanism bear the same theoretical connection to horizontal application in such supranational contexts as the EU? Much in republican thought presupposes a common sense of polity and citizenship, concepts which many take for granted in national contexts[2] but which people question in the EU. Perhaps scholars and jurists arguing for the horizontal application of the Charter may not as easily appeal to the shared sense of purpose or the sense of common membership that appeared in discourses surrounding horizontality in prior chapters.

---

[2] This is debatable in itself, as Willem Maas explains ("Multilevel Citizenship," in *Oxford Handbook of Citizenship*, ed. Ayelet Shachar, Rainer Bauböck, Irene Bloemraad, and Maarten Vink [Oxford: Oxford University Press, 2017]). Nevertheless, as a practical matter, it is safe to say that the European Union still faces more objections as to legitimacy than do national authorities.

To this extent, it seems possible that scholarly and political commentators might not be able to wield the same republican themes in pursuing horizontality at the continental level. At this high level, horizontality could potentially entail the reshaping of broad swaths of European society, applying the values of the Charter to private actors across Member States. Moreover, this step would admit rights claims of individuals within one Member State against individuals of a separate Member State. But could citizens of two different countries, albeit in the same global region, have duties to one another in the same sense as citizens of the same nation? Such suggestions are not beyond imagination and certainly seem possible today as a technical legal matter. Still, horizontal application in the EU poses a unique set of challenges, prompting additional examination to determine how the republican framework may yet apply in this context.

Republican Aspirations in the EU

Scholars have debated at length whether the EU is compatible with a republican conception of politics and citizenship. This broad, seemingly theoretical question speaks to the more practical issue of building and sustaining the EU as a genuine political community rather than just another international alliance. Moreover, the answer to this question bears on whether a republican account of horizontal application is theoretically possible in this context or if, instead, the case of the EU constitutes a limitation to this argument. Scholars tend to consider the republican credentials of the EU by asking two specific questions. First, to what kind and degree of integration does the European project actually aspire? Second, to what extent does (or can) a European identity permeate the popular imagination? If, per the first question, the ultimate goal is to establish a full-blown political community characterized by common rights and values rather than simply a close-knit international alliance revolving around economics and security,[3] then the ability to foster

---

[3] Aristotle, *Politics*, Book III, part 9 (Stephen Everson, ed., [Cambridge: Cambridge University Press, 1996]). Michel Rosenfeld describes a similar distinction in his discussion of contract as an external relationship, and custom and tradition as pertaining to internal constitution ("The European Treaty: Constitution and Constitutional Identity: A View from America," *International Journal of Constitutional Law* 3 [2005], 320). International relations scholars have considered variations of this question since the start of the Cold War in the concept of "security communities," areas where large-scale violence is unlikely due to shared trust and an emphasis on common interests. Emanuel Adler and Michael

commitment to something like republican politics and citizenship, per the second question, becomes nothing less than an existential concern for the EU. Indeed, the success of the European project comes to hinge on a widespread identification with, as well as some responsibility toward, Europe and one's fellow Europeans.[4] This chapter takes up these two questions in turn, reviewing important relevant debates in the EU in order to lay groundwork for an ensuing discussion of horizontal application.

What is the nature of the European project? Did it originally or does it now include what we might characterize as republican aspirations, as to establishing a distinct *res publica* or a European citizenry? Initially political actors, including judges serving on the ECJ, proceeded as if Europe were primarily an alliance centered around free movement and economics.[5] This mindset is manifested in the phenomenon that EU law sometimes is not effective unless a case involves some crossing of national borders, a fact that can prevent citizens' residing within a country's borders from invoking EU protections, so leading to the phenomenon of reverse discrimination.[6] The ability of law to touch individual citizens seems to be a crucial feature of political community in the full sense of the term.[7] If, then, this sort of crossing of borders is necessary to trigger EU law, Europe is still more of an international community than a federal-supranational one. In this case, the practical reality of the European project cannot but fall short of republican conceptions of the polis and civic feeling, even if Europeans aspire to something more.

Barnett further developed this concept of security communities to include such factors as shared identities and values (*Security Communities* [Cambridge: Cambridge University Press, 1998]).

[4] Jeffrey Checkel's work on the socialization function that institutions serve in Europe addresses this question from an international relations perspective. See, for example, "International Institutions and Socialization in Europe: Introduction and Framework," *International Organization* 59 (2005), 801–826.

[5] Eleni Frantziou, "The Horizontal Effect of the Charter of Fundamental Rights of the EU: Rediscovering the Reasons for Horizontality," *European Law Journal* 21:5 (2015), 657–679; Johan van der Walt also discusses seminal cases, but with a different gloss (*The Horizontal Effect Revolution and the Question of Sovereignty* [Berlin: De Gruyter, 2014]).

[6] Willem Maas, "The Origins, Evolution, and Political Objectives of EU Citizenship," *German Law Journal* 15:5 (2014), 797–819.

[7] For a Tocquevillian account of what governmental authority entails, see Christina Bambrick, "'Neither Precisely National nor Precisely Federal': Governmental and Administrative Authority in Tocqueville's *Democracy in America*," *Publius: The Journal of Federalism* 48:4 (2018), 586–606; see also Madison's *Federalist* 39.

Through a lengthy process punctuated by numerous treaties, actors in favor of the European project now more explicitly aim at securing a shared set of rights and recognition of some sort of constitution.[8] Some more hesitant scholars challenge attempts to apply such domestic concepts to this international context,[9] or label the expansion of the European project "competence creep."[10] Others maintain that this commitment to a common European identity has been the aim of the project from the very beginning.[11] Wherever one falls on these issues, it is difficult to deny the capaciousness and ambition of the European project at least since the Treaty of Lisbon. Therefore, considering the intended degree of integration, at least now it is clear that pro-European actors aspire to something beyond mere economic or security alliance. To this extent, the supranational institution *must* concern itself with questions of political community and citizenship, even if integration remains a stilted process, with such disruptions as Brexit.

While the European project is one of unity and integration, scholars and political actors still interpret differently what this means as a theoretical and practical matter. Some put greater weight on the limits of Lisbon and, previously, Maastricht, arguing that a robust national sovereignty remains a part of the larger plan.[12] Others, in contrast, more readily concede European primacy.[13] However, even those who admit of a larger role for Union governance debate what this means for the Member States. Michel Rosenfeld, for example, understands integration

---

[8] Even if the formal Constitution of Europe failed to garner the necessary support, the content and express purpose of the Treaty of Lisbon is similar enough that one can say that a Constitution of Europe remains the goal.

[9] Nico Krisch argues in favor of a pluralist vision for Europe, as it avoids tensions with diversity that come of applying the concept of constitutionalism beyond the state (*Beyond Constitutionalism* [Oxford: Oxford University Press, 2011]).

[10] In a similar vein, Johan van der Walt follows Dieter Grimm ("Integration by Constitution," *International Journal of Constitutional Law* 3 (2005), 193–208) in distinguishing between de facto and de jure sovereignty assumed by EU institutions (Van der Walt, *The Horizontal Effect Revolution*, 242).

[11] Maas, "Origins, Evolution, and Political Objectives of EU Citizenship."

[12] Leonard F. M. Besselink, "National and Constitutional Identity before and after Lisbon," *Utrecht Law Review* 6:3 (2010), 41.

[13] Frantziou, "The Horizontal Effect of the Charter"; also see Mirjam DeMol's discussion of this question and its implications for horizontal application ("The Novel Approach of the CJEU on the Horizontal Direct Effect of the EU Principle of Non-discrimination: [Unbridled] Expansionism of EU Law?" *Maastricht Journal of European and Comparative Law* 18 [2011], 109–135).

as entailing some prior negation of national identity,[14] while others, such as Willem Maas, emphasize the possibility and practical reality of multi-level citizenship.[15] In some ways, these arguments may constitute a difference in emphasis rather than substance. Nevertheless, these different positions entail real consequences for the status of the EU vis-à-vis Member States, particularly regarding such contested questions as sovereignty and governing authority.

Of course, these debates are not restricted to academic fora. In the *Lisbon Treaty* case the Federal Constitutional Court of Germany sought to protect democratic legitimacy and national-constitutional identity for Germany while remaining open to the EU project of unity.[16] Essentially the Court was willing to cooperate with EU legislation and ECJ decisions, but not at the cost of Germany's sovereignty. Accordingly, the FCC decided that it maintained competence to rule on whether the Treaty of Lisbon was compatible with Germany's larger identity and fundamental commitments. While the Court would concede the "primacy of application of European law," the fundamental principles of the Basic Law could not be annulled. In Rosenfeld's terms, German governing institutions would only participate in the negation of national identity to a point. Nevertheless, this attempt by the German FCC to stake its ground in the ongoing disputes over competence and jurisdiction came only after other decisions that went a long way to assert the primacy of EU law and institutions, including *Van Gend en Loos* and *Costa*, discussed later.[17]

Though there are legal articulations of the European project, as in the treaties mentioned above, what the nature and aspirations of the Union are depends on whom one asks. Is there something akin to a European polis or common good? Are there, in any meaningful sense, European values and European citizens? Or do the Member States remain the primary loci of politics and citizenship? The answers to these questions are largely political and remain to be worked out. Indeed, the answers may exist along a continuum rather than as an either–or formulation.

---

[14] Rosenfeld, "The European Treaty," 325–326.
[15] Maas, "Multilevel Citizenship."
[16] 123 BVerfGE 267 (2009); Gary Jacobsohn and Yaniv Roznai, *Constitutional Revolution* (New Haven: Yale University Press, 2020), 121–136.
[17] *Algemene Transporten Expeditie Onderneming van Gend en Loos v. Nederlandse Administratie der Belastingen*, ECJ 26/62, ECR (1963); *Flaminio Costa v. E.N.E.L.*, ECJ 6/64, ECR (1964).

As Besselink says, this is not a zero-sum game.[18] As long as the European project exists and actors continue to pursue integration, the debates in this context may still be understood through the republican lens. Such integration, though incomplete, may already resemble something like political community as understood in the republican tradition.

Pursuing a Civic Identity for Europe

In light of this republican understanding of debates over the European project, what might the republican lens show us about related questions concerning European citizenship and civic identity? In classical republican thought, one's status as a citizen meant everything; it defined one's rights, duties, and very way of life. It was with one's fellow citizens that a person engaged in political deliberation and so determined the fate of the polity. What, then, does it take to have people identify as fellow citizens of a place? More specifically, can European identity plausibly constitute some degree of individuals' understanding of self and duties? David Miller addresses this issue, explaining the need to have "something that can hold people together despite differences of class, religion, ethnicity, and so forth, and allow them to cooperate politically."[19] He continues to explain that "[t]he mere fact of being subject to the same political system is not sufficient."[20] However, the resources available to classical republics, such as a cultural identity manifested in a common nationality, language, or religion, are not available to European institutions. Moreover, cultural identity cannot be manufactured, as such an imposition of culture would violate the rights of minorities according to our contemporary standards.[21] If European institutions cannot turn to these characteristics to cultivate a sense of peoplehood on the continental level, must they not look elsewhere?

Jürgen Habermas argues that a kind of "constitutional patriotism" may offer sufficient basis on which to found and cultivate a sense of peoplehood. Europeans include individuals of various ethnicities, native languages, and even nationalities, but they may share devotion to a

---

[18] Besselink, "National and Constitutional Identity," 44; also Maas, "Multilevel Citizenship."
[19] David Miller, "Republicanism, National Identity, and Europe," in *Republicanism and Political Theory*, ed. Cécile Laborde and John Maynor (Oxford: Wiley & Blackwell, 2008), 147.
[20] Ibid.
[21] Ibid., 145.

European constitution. Taking this idea to heart, EU institutions and Member States moved to adopt a European Constitution in the Constitution Treaty of 2004.[22] However, this effort failed to garner necessary support for ratification in the national referenda of France and the Netherlands. Those arguing for Habermas's constitutional patriotism post-2004 would have to contend with this mixed history as a result. Perhaps one could cite common values or a shared commitment to such foundational principles as those articulated in the Charter of Fundamental Rights. If European institutions could, in fact, cultivate and sustain a politics centered on such principles, then, Habermas seems to suggest, the prospect of a European civic identity may not be out of reach.

Writing just a few years after the failure of the European Constitution, Miller maintains that these efforts toward constitutional patriotism still come up short. He highlights Habermas's own articulation of the objection that constitutional patriotism is "too weak a bond to hold together complex societies."[23] Miller raises several issues on this point. For one thing, he questions whether the rights articulated in such treaty documents as the Charter are so different from national constitutions that they would, in fact, inspire the requisite devotion to what is distinctly European. After all, do not many countries express commitments as to a right of human dignity[24] and of equality before the law[25]? And how might unity emerge if different actors and institutions among Member States interpret provisions in conflicting ways? In response to such objections, Habermas explains that the focus of loyalty need not be on any definitive account of the treaties but on the "common *horizon* of interpretation" a constitution provides for a people.[26] In other words, it is the very debate about these principles that binds the people,[27] the mere fact of being in dialogue about them, an idea not unlike the contestatory politics that figures prominently in republican thought. Habermas

---

[22] Nico Krisch is skeptical of such efforts and offers an alternative in the form of pluralism in postnational law (*Beyond Constitutionalism*).

[23] Jürgen Habermas, *The Inclusion of the Other: Studies in Political Theory*, ed. Ciaran Cronin and Pablo de Greiff (Cambridge: Polity Press, 1999), 118; see also Krisch, *Beyond Constitutionalism*.

[24] Charter of Fundamental Rights of the European Union, Article 1,

[25] Ibid., Article 20.

[26] Habermas, *The Inclusion of the Other*, 225.

[27] Perhaps, to use Dworkinian language, it is the concepts as understood against a particular historical backdrop that binds a people together, rather than any particular conception of those principles (Ronald Dworkin, *Law's Empire* [Cambridge: Belknap Press, 1986]).

similarly explains in other places that "what unites a nation of citizens as opposed to a Volksnation, is not some primordial substrate but rather an intersubjectively shared context of possible mutual understanding."[28] Miller remains unconvinced, however, maintaining that such formulations seem "tantamount to admitting defeat" since "*possible* mutual understanding is surely something that exists between people everywhere."[29] This point is well taken, but Miller seems to give short shrift to the prospect that what is "*possible* mutual understanding" may ultimately become, or in some ways have already become, *actual* and, moreover, develop a distinctly European character.

To the extent that Miller does entertain the possibility of identifying a European common good as embodied in a constitution or treaty document, he is ultimately skeptical that this could inspire devotion in the common EU citizen. He joins many in arguing that EU politics suffer from a democratic deficit and do not create sufficient space for popular participation,[30] what should be a staple in any republican political community. In a way Habermas recognizes these deficiencies, too. The difference, again, is that Habermas still sees a way forward. In particular he advocates the development of a European public sphere, "created on the one hand by a European-wide civil society of voluntary groups and on the other by a European party system whose members would address European rather than national issues."[31] He accepts that European politics and citizenship will remain perfunctory and merely legal in the absence of such a public sphere. Perhaps it is this exchange

---

[28] Habermas, *The Inclusion of the Other*, 159.
[29] Miller, "Republicanism, National Identity, and Europe," 150, emphasis in original.
[30] Ibid., 153. In *A Republican Europe of States*, Richard Bellamy demonstrates how Europe might shore up its republican credentials and circumvent what some take to be its democratic deficit. Specifically, he argues that EU institutions ought to be more concerned with supporting democratic politics within Member States rather than pursue the status of political community or cultivate a *demos* at the continental level. While he does not discuss the issue of horizontal application, his prior work on courts (discussed in Chapter 2) suggests that he might view horizontality as exceeding the function he proposes for European institutions. This follows from the thrust of his book's argument that the EU should operate at the level of the Member States rather than the level of individuals. One wrinkle in thinking about his argument in general and how it applies to horizontal application comes in the fact that private actors often include immense corporations that transcend national borders (*A Republican Europe of States: Cosmopolitanism, Intergovernmentalism and Democracy in the EU* [Cambridge: Cambridge University Press, 2019]).
[31] Jürgen Habermas, *The Postnational Constellation*, ed. Max Pensky (Boston: MIT University Press, 2001), 102–103; Habermas, *The Inclusion of the Other*, 153.

that reveals the real impasse on the question of cultivating a European people. Indeed, it is at this point that we begin to see how Miller's objections are rooted in basic beliefs about the scale on which republican politics may be conducted.[32] Miller states:

> Large conglomerates such as the EU are unsuited to republican politics not just because of their size, and the physical gap that separates the central institutions from most citizens, but because they are divided in such a way that citizens' primary loyalties are inevitably directed toward their compatriots, as many empirical studies have shown.[33]

In Miller's telling, there does not seem to be much that anyone or any institution can do to foster republican politics and citizenship on the broad scale of the EU. Indeed, interests inevitably remain diverse[34] and, it would seem, centered around state, regional, and municipal divisions so that individuals simply do not have a reason to invest in politics on a continental level.

Of course, European politics can develop in any number of ways in the coming years. And although the possibility of realizing republican politics on the broad scale that is Europe is an empirical question beyond the scope of this chapter, it also depends on how we understand republican politics at all. Again, Maas illustrates in his account of multilevel citizenship that these issues of national and supranational identity need not be either–or questions.[35] Moreover, these questions are not unique to the European community, but confront virtually all federal systems and even unitary countries that are diverse. In this understanding, Europe might have more resources at its disposal to cultivate a republican politics than some scholars concede. Time alone can shed further light on these questions where the theoretical and the practical intersect.

Republican Politics, Sovereignty, and Horizontality in the EU

How do these musings on the possibility of republican politics in the EU bear on the more specific question of horizontal application in the EU?

---

[32] This is not unlike the famous debates between the American Federalists and Antifederalists about the possibility of maintaining an extended republic. See, for example, Madison's *Federalist* 10.
[33] Miller, "Republicanism, National Identity, and Europe," 154.
[34] See also Van der Walt, *The Horizontal Effect Revolution*, chap. 1 on this point.
[35] See Maas, "Multilevel Citizenship"; Besselink, "National and Constitutional Identity," 44. In a way, republican thinkers like Montesquieu might be interpreted as laying the groundwork for this kind of argument, too.

Johan van der Walt begins to answer this question when he demonstrates how the issue of horizontal application, perhaps more than any other doctrinal issue courts confront, prompts questions about sovereignty. He points to the logic of the *Lüth* case to make this point.[36] In this case, discussed in Chapters 2 and 5, the German FCC argued that the Basic Law included an "order of objective moral and legal principles" that "radiate" to affect public and private spheres alike. This sets up an understanding of the Basic Law as potentially speaking to all issues of law and life in Germany.[37] Even though Van der Walt ultimately takes issue with other aspects of *Lüth*,[38] he views this kind of power to govern all spheres of life in a polity as definitive of sovereignty. When the FCC declared that values of the Basic Law radiated to all spheres, therefore, the Court both presupposed and accrued a certain sovereignty on behalf of the Constitution and the institutions that give it effect – not least the Court itself, which exercised its ability to regulate private spaces in *Lüth*.[39] This theoretical connection between the regulation of private entities that arises from horizontal application and the concept of sovereignty is a recurring theme within arguments that are more hesitant about horizontality in EU law.[40] Indeed, when it applies EU law horizontally, the ECJ accumulates some measure of governing power to the European level of governance, probably at the expense of Member States.[41] It is for this reason that Van der Walt describes *Lüth* as having a dual destiny in Europe – while its initial instantiation in the 1958 case presupposed and bolstered the sovereignty of the German state over the private sphere, its subsequent applications in ECJ case law appropriate this same conception of sovereignty to the EU, over Germany and other Member States.[42]

---

[36] Van der Walt, *The Horizontal Effect Revolution*.
[37] Kumm, "Who Is Afraid"; Alec Stone Sweet, "The Juridical Coup d'État and the Problem of Authority," *German Law Journal* 8:10 (2007), 915–927.
[38] In particular, he identifies a kind of substantive due process in the FCC's reasoning that, he maintains, ought to be left to institutions better equipped to account for majority-minority relations and, it follows, multiple possible orders of value rather than a single objective order.
[39] Jud Mathews, *Extending Rights' Reach* (Oxford: Oxford University Press, 2018).
[40] See, for example, Van der Walt, *The Horizontal Effect Revolution*; DeMol, "The Novel Approach of the CJEU"; Bruno DeWitt, "The Crumbling Public/Private Divide: Horizontality in European Anti-discrimination Law," *Citizenship Studies* 13:5 (2009), 515–525; Stone Sweet, "The Juridical Coup d'État."
[41] *Dirk Rüffert v. Land Niedersachsen*, ECJ 346/06, ECR (2008).
[42] Van der Walt, *The Horizontal Effect Revolution*, 338–339.

Although republican political theory employs different language, its concepts convey something similar to Van der Walt's discussion of sovereignty. Moreover, the republican framework does additional work to distinguish the phenomenon of horizontal application from other claims of the ECJ to sovereignty, as in such earlier cases as *Van Gend en Loos* and *Costa*.[43] Put differently, republican theory and, specifically, the republican features this book has conceptualized as parity and duty move beyond the often imprecise language of sovereignty to uncover a thicker, more detailed account of what scholars and political actors understand to be at stake in the horizontal application of EU law.

First, Chapter 2 demonstrated how parity in the law governing both public and private spheres is a distinctive feature of horizontal application. As horizontal application rejects the strict separation of public and private spheres in favor of parity, it finds affinity in the republican idea of a common good encompassing the polity as a whole. Though government will always be in the business of regulating the private sphere, instances of horizontal application are distinct in that individual duties and duties of the state share a common origin in fundamental law. This common source of governance, of authority, implicitly recognizes a distinct "public thing," an accepted common good, that governs a particular area and a particular people understood as its own body politic. In other words, the horizontal application of rights both presupposes and reinforces borders of place and people. When the ECJ applies EU law horizontally, it is akin to declaring a European "public thing" and a European people, perhaps even prior to those of the Member States.

Secondly, and relatedly, the concept of duty introduced in Chapter 2 speaks to this set of questions. Horizontal application, by definition, derives from public commitments certain duties of individuals vis-à-vis their fellow citizens. This presumes a particular "public thing," as stated earlier, but also a particular people, charged with duties toward one another insofar as they all recognize and live under the same fundamental law. One can understand this in formal terms concerning people's legal obligations in a particular place, or in more functional terms of what people actually recognize as their duties. In either case, horizontal

---

[43] Van der Walt's account does not clearly distinguish why horizontal application constitutes a different consideration in the larger issue of sovereignty. In other words, horizontal application simply seems to be another step in the accumulation of sovereignty that began with *Van Gend en Loos* and *Costa*. My republican framework does more to distinguish these.

application presupposes a discernable citizenry that recognizes the authority of a particular fundamental law giving rise to its duties. The republican lens thus shows the significance of the question of horizontal application by revealing how it relates to more basic questions about a European "public thing" that is acknowledged and accepted by the European citizenry.

The value of employing the language of republicanism here comes into sharper relief when we consider how horizontal application has developed and is debated differently in the context of the European Court of Human Rights (ECtHR).[44] The ECJ is just one body in the panoply of EU institutions. Indeed, the EU includes institutions that correspond to the classic three branches of government and, in this sense, mirror the form and function of the national governments of the various Member States. While the scope of EU governance may be limited, its institutions comprise a fully operative government, whose ultimate aim is unity and integration. In theory, EU actors, institutions, and even individual citizens could begin to conceive of the Union as a republic or, in Van der Walt's terms, begin to attribute a measure of sovereignty to the Union. On the other hand, the ECtHR is an *international* court, belonging to no particular government and maintaining no project beyond that of addressing violations of those rights articulated in the European Convention of Human Rights. There is no associated legislative function, nor any encompassing project of unity. To this extent, the role of the ECtHR does not rival its Member States in the same sense as does the EU.[45]

In light of these differences in institutional character, horizontal application has figured into accounts of the ECtHR differently than in scholarship on and decisions of the ECJ. The question of horizontal application is less controversial for the ECtHR, perhaps because the Convention constitutes an agreement among states without any aspiration to govern the people within individual countries. And indeed, the question of horizontal application was not even raised when the Convention was drafted in 1950.[46] While some provisions of the

---

[44] Lech Garlicki, "Relations between Private Actors and the European Convention on Human Rights," in *The Constitution in Private Relations*, ed. András Sajó and Renáta Uitz (Utrecht: Eleven, 2005), 129–144.

[45] I am grateful to Victor Ferreres Comella for this insight.

[46] Pieter van Dijk, Fried van Hoof, Arjen van Rijn, and Leo Zwaak, eds., *Theory and Practice of the European Convention of Human Rights*, 5th ed. (Cambridge: Intersentia, 2018), 26–30.

Convention do amount to a charge for national governments to protect their citizens from private harms, these ultimately remain charges to the national governments and do not obligate individual citizens.[47]

To the extent that horizontal application has republican qualities, it naturally figures more prominently in debates over EU law and politics than in ECtHR discussions. The relevance of republican concepts to EU debates, however, does not mean that the EU consists of sufficiently republican elements to make those concepts work. The ability of EU institutions to count on certain republican resources, such as an acknowledged common good and a self-identifying citizenry, seems, at least on a theoretical level, to be requisite to horizontal application.[48] On the other hand, a certain endogeneity seems plausible here, as the ECJ's increasing application of horizontality may itself cultivate greater republican resources across the EU. Notwithstanding lingering theoretical issues, the ECJ has moved gradually to develop its doctrine of horizontality, as the next section explains in greater detail.

The Horizontal Application of EU Law

How, then, have judges of the ECJ developed the concept of horizontal application, and how have scholars understood this practice in the EU? The foregoing sections explained some of the theoretical questions that arise from a republican understanding of horizontal application in the context of the EU, including how the idea of the EU itself measures up against republican principles and the unique challenges of viewing horizontal application in the EU through a republican lens. This section, in turn, examines jurists' and commentators' concerns and the resources they perceive to be at their disposal in shaping the development of horizontal application in EU law. In this way, the remainder of this chapter examines discourses – how EU jurists and commentators articulate the issues surrounding horizontality, and how they propose to develop horizontal application accordingly. Of course, some of the

---

[47] Van Dijk et al., *Theory and Practice of the European Convention*. One could categorize this as a version of indirect horizontal application.

[48] Those who study and reside in national contexts largely take for granted the authority of national institutions, national borders, and national citizenship. This is not to say that such credit is always warranted. Indeed, Willem Maas raises important issues with respect to assuming the Westphalian paradigm without question or qualification ("Multilevel Citizenship"). However, as a practical matter, scholars do not debate these issues in the context of most nation-states in the same way they do in the context of Europe.

perspectives articulated in some ECJ decisions and scholarship are ambitious, viewing horizontal application as something that can be expanded, while others prove more hesitant and seek limits to this legal practice.

The initial jurisprudential development that set the stage for the debate over horizontal application came in the important *Van Gend en Loos* case (1963).[49] Following the early treaties establishing the European Community, the relationship between European and domestic law was a real question and one that could not be avoided for long. In *Van Gend*, the ECJ declared its understanding of the kind of integrated community it would have Europe become, even while, on some accounts, the Member States envisioned a future wherein greater differentiation remained among states.[50] In particular, the Court articulated the principle of direct effect, not to be confused with direct horizontal effect but rather what scholars and jurists today describe as "the capacity of a provision of EU law to be invoked before a national court."[51] With the establishment of direct effect, litigants in domestic courts could rely on provisions of EU law against national governments. The consequence of this, then and now, is that European law could be introduced into what previously might have been a purely domestic legal-political situation. Moreover, the principle necessarily enlists domestic courts for the task of enforcing Treaty provisions and directives.

Insofar as Member States did not explicitly assent to this principle of direct effect, Alec Stone Sweet goes so far as to describe *Van Gend en Loos* as a "juridical *coup d'état*."[52] On the other hand, the "teleological methodology" the Court employs in its judgment assumes an alternative, arguably republican, account of the European vision. Speaking of the Treaty establishing the European Economic Community (EEC), the Court explains that this was more than an agreement of obligations among contracting states, citing as evidence the Treaty's preamble, which refers not only to governments but also to peoples. Indeed, the Court argues, the Treaty establishes EU institutions endowed "with sovereign

---

[49] *Algemene Transporten Expeditie Onderneming van Gend en Loos v. Nederlandse Administratie der Belastingen*, ECJ 26/62, ECR (1963), 1.

[50] Paul Craig and Gráinne de Búrca, *EU Law: Text, Cases, and Materials*, 6th ed. (Oxford: Oxford University Press, 2015), 189.

[51] Ibid., 185. This is not to be confused with direct horizontal application.

[52] Stone Sweet, "The Juridical Coup d'État," 918. Stone Sweet's criticisms in this essay are sharp. He proceeds to state: "In Europe, a great deal of judicial governance proceeds on this absence of coercive authority, because it proceeds in the absence of normative authority" (926).

rights," the exercise of which affects both the Member States and their citizens.[53] In this telling, the European Community was always intended to be a political community in the full sense. In this way, the Court seized upon an opportunity to entrench a more Eurocentric vision, later cemented in the *Costa* case, that declared the primacy of European law.[54]

The establishment of the direct effect of EU law was debated alongside the additional question of *horizontal* direct effect – whether EU law could be invoked by litigants in national courts against private individuals or nonstate actors. This was, in fact, a separate question and one that needed to be answered. However, even at this high level of abstraction, it became complicated very quickly for a couple of reasons. Despite instances in European law that refer to the actual people living in Europe, as the Court in *Van Gend en Loos* finds in the EEC preamble, foundational documents of Europe by and large address the states. The 2009 Charter of Fundamental Rights, for example, specifically states in Article 51 that it obligates the Member States. While this is not necessarily the last word on the question, it has factored into the Court's reasoning on horizontal direct effect.[55]

The issue of *whom* the treaties and the Charter address, moreover, speaks directly to the questions elaborated in the previous section – namely, whether these foundational documents establish a European "public thing" sufficiently so as to hold the individuals within Member States accountable for EU commitments on the basis of their membership in that larger community. Perhaps *Van Gend* and later *Costa* gesture toward an affirmative answer here in that they are premised on the contention that European law is relevant and supreme even in the context of domestic questions.[56] Nevertheless, one would still have to make the argument that private entities are immediate participants in the European project and, therefore, that European law is equally binding on their actions. Such a step seems almost prerequisite to the argument that European commitments and values "radiate" through all spheres of life, to use the language of *Lüth*.[57]

---

[53] *Van Gend en Loos*, ECJ 26/62, *ECR* (1963). Craig and De Búrca, *EU Law*, 188; see Bambrick, "Neither Precisely National nor Precisely Federal," on "governmental authority."
[54] *Flaminio Costa v. E.N.E.L.*, ECJ 6/64, *ECR* (1964), 585; Stone Sweet, "The Juridical Coup d'État," 918.
[55] *Association de médiation sociale v. Hichem Laboubi*, Case C-176/12 (2014).
[56] Van der Walt, *The Horizontal Effect Revolution*, 334.
[57] BVerfGE 7, 198.

THE HORIZONTAL APPLICATION OF EU LAW   261

The Court first took up the issue of horizontal direct effect of EU law in *Defrenne v. Sabena* (1976).[58] This case identified the principle of equal pay for equal work[59] of the Treaty of the European Economic Community (now the Treaty on the Functioning of the European Union) as having direct horizontal application despite the fact that certain provisions of the Treaty formally addressed Member States. In this case, a woman named Gabrielle Defrenne was forced to retire from her job as an airline attendant since, under Belgian law, female flight attendants were required to retire upon turning forty. This policy, Defrenne argued, prevented her from collecting a pension equal to that of her male colleagues in retirement. The Court of Justice decided the case on the basis that the Treaty required equal treatment on grounds of gender. In particular, it argued that the prohibition of discrimination was "mandatory in nature"[60] and so must apply to both state actors and private actors. *Defrenne* ushered in a broad discussion about horizontal application. Though the decision itself only established the possibility of horizontal application for treaty law, and only "mandatory" treaty provisions for that matter, this decision was enormously consequential. Indeed, those treaties comprising the fundamental commitments of the EU would now apply to private individuals within Member States. The words of the Court make clear the significance of this step. Speaking of the equal pay principle, the Court states:

> [T]his provision forms part of the social objectives of the Community, which is not merely an economic union, but is at the same time intended, by common action, to ensure social progress and seek the constant improvement of the living and working conditions of their peoples.[61]

The Court in *Defrenne* clearly understood the project of the European Community as being to propagate a particular kind of society. More to the point, it deemed the Community's "social objectives" to be of such a nature that they necessarily impact entities beyond the state. While the Court did identify the limiting principle only to apply horizontal application for mandatory provisions, it ultimately established that the primary law of the EU has the power to create obligations for private actors within the Member States.

---

[58] *Defrenne v. Société anonyme belge de navigation aérienne*, ECJ 43/75, *ECR* (1976), 455.
[59] Then articulated in Article 119 of the Treaty of the European Economic Community, and now in Article 157 of the Treaty of the Functioning of the European Union.
[60] *Defrenne v. Société anonyme belge de navigation aérienne*, 476.
[61] Ibid., 472.

That European law comes in so many forms, as seen in *Defrenne*, complicates the question of what kinds of law may be applied horizontally to nonstate actors. EU law includes regulations, directives, treaty articles, and the Charter of Fundamental Rights. Such distinctions bear on debates over horizontal application, as scholars and jurists argue the significance of these differences – whether to limit the ECJ's extension of horizontal application or to argue the ultimate arbitrariness of these distinctions and thereby extend its reach. Insofar as EU regulations are akin to ordinary law, they do not necessarily raise the same difficult questions with respect to horizontal application. Similarly, directives are legal acts of the EU that bind Member States. Whereas regulations are self-executing, however, directives require implementation, a fact which has resulted in their further debate. Traditionally directives have not been applied horizontally because Article 228 of the Treaty of the Functioning of the European Union states that Member States are bound by a directive and bound only to the extent that the directive specifies a particular obligation.[62] Nevertheless, the ECJ has carved out some exceptions to apply directives horizontally. For example, it has broadened the very concept of "the state" to incorporate what otherwise would be categorized as private actors,[63] and allowed private individuals to hold Member States accountable when they fail to implement directives.

The fact of such distinctions suggests a general hesitance with respect to horizontal application.[64] Indeed, beginning with *Defrenne*'s distinction between "mandatory" and other provisions, a similar tendency emerged to limit the reach of horizontal application in treaty law and the Charter

---

[62] See *Marshall v. Southampton and South-West Hampshire Area Health Authority (Teaching)*, ECJ 152/84, ECR (1986). Scholars have been quick to point out that the way in which this provision obliges state actors need not preclude application to individuals and other nonstate actors (Craig and De Búrca, *EU Law*, 204–205). Moreover, scholars have persuasively demonstrated that similar textual provisions have not stopped the Court from asserting the possibility of horizontal direct effect in the case of the Charter of Fundamental Rights (Frantziou, "The Horizontal Effect of the Charter"). With such cases as *Mangold v. Rüdiger Helm* (ECJ 144/04, ECR [2005]), the Court seems to be moving away from the position that directives cannot have horizontal application. Nevertheless, *Mangold* met with much pushback from the Member States and many continue to argue for this distinction between primary law and directives (Craig and De Búrca, *EU Law*, 205). The Court thus seems to have an interest in treading lightly, as it still relies on the Member States for implementation.

[63] Craig and De Búrca, *EU Law*, 206–209. Additionally, it has insisted on a principle of "harmonious interpretation," which requires domestic courts to interpret national law "in the light of" directives (209–216).

[64] Frantziou, "The Horizontal Effect of the Charter," 663, 675.

of Fundamental Rights, areas in which the stakes are arguably even higher. Indeed, these two areas of EU law are effectively constitutional in nature. In contrast with regulations and directives, applying treaty law and the Charter horizontally would be a clearer movement (both symbolic and practical) toward increased integration and the primacy of EU commitments. It is thus unsurprising that *Defrenne*'s establishment of the horizontal application of treaty law was considered to be so groundbreaking. Indeed, even decades later, such scholars as Johann van der Walt have continued to worry about the horizontal application of treaty law.

While debates unfold in courts in terms of doctrinal technicalities, scholarship treats horizontal application as raising deeper questions as well. Even after *Defrenne*, the scholarly literature reveals disagreement about the constitutional implications of horizontal application, including the ability of the ECJ to define values and priorities for the entire Union and, more broadly, the ability of EU institutions to define values and priorities for the Member States. Johan van der Walt, for example, worries that the original formulation of horizontal application in the German FCC's *Lüth* case overlooks the possibility for disagreement over the content and prioritization of values. When this logic was appropriated from German jurisprudence by the ECJ, there was room for debate not only about which institutions were making these decisions (courts or legislatures) but also about the very government determining these values (individual countries or the EU).

Van der Walt's book focuses on the "*Laval* quartet" of cases, including the *Viking* (2007) case that determined that labor unions violated treaty provisions on freedom of establishment when they prevented the Viking shipping company from moving their legal base from Finland to Estonia.[65] Following the reasoning in *Defrenne*, the horizontal application of a treaty provision controlled the actions of the labor union in relation to the shipping company. Though, in earlier cases, the Court established criteria requiring treaty provisions to be clear and precise if they were to be applied horizontally, Van der Walt sees *Viking* as based fundamentally on judicial fiat. In the ECJ's rhetoric of "balancing" and "harmonizing" the opposing social and economic concerns at play in *Viking*, Van der Walt finds the Court making crucial and constitutive

---

[65] *International Transport Workers' Federation and Finnish Seamen's Union v. Viking Line ABP and OÜ Viking Line Eesti*, ECJ 438/05, ECR (2007); Craig and De Búrca, *EU Law*, 193.

decisions that, he argues, ought to be beyond its jurisdiction as a court and, more specifically, as a court for Europe.[66] He explains that the ECJ had no resources for balancing the right of the unions against that of the shipping company in a principled way. However, insofar as it did decide in favor of the shipping company, it yielded a "case specific prioritizing of market freedom" over bargaining rights.[67] Not only is this result not desirable policy, as far as Van der Walt is concerned, but it is not a necessary interpretation of the Treaty. In deciding *Viking*, therefore, the Court improperly assumed authority to make such a constitutional decision. He thus describes the case as a "crucial moment in the federalization"[68] of Europe, insofar as the ECJ, an EU institution, made a decision for Member States whose own institutions may have chosen, and in fact had chosen, to order and weigh these values differently.

The *Viking* case faced criticism from legal scholars when it was decided, many worrying about its apparent derogation of certain principles of labor law. However, the general practice of applying treaty law horizontally, Van der Walt's primary concern, is basically settled in ECJ jurisprudence. In Van der Walt's assessment of *Viking*, we find a Court making claims about the kind of community the EU is, as well as its status in relation to Member States. And indeed, the ECJ judgment follows what was a common line of thinking, especially early on in the Community's history, that prioritized matters of economics and transnational exchange in line with the EU's original purpose to facilitate the freedom of movement and economic cooperation.[69]

Initially, one may take this prioritization of economic concerns as a sign of humility and restraint since the EU, as represented by the Court, was not trying to be anything more than a Union committed to economic cooperation. Nevertheless, Van der Walt argues that *Viking* did more than simply prioritize economic concerns as a matter of EU law. Rather, with the development of direct effect, the Court subverted the right of collective bargaining to the right of establishment within Member States.[70] Moreover, and more specifically, with the development of *horizontal* direct effect, the Court created duties of unions (albeit

---

[66] Van der Walt, *The Horizontal Effect Revolution*, 340–341.
[67] Ibid., 344.
[68] Ibid., 338.
[69] See Maas, "Origins, Evolution, and Political Objectives of EU Citizenship," also on freedom of movement.
[70] Van der Walt, *The Horizontal Effect Revolution*, 346.

negative duties) not to obstruct companies' choices to relocate, even if such choices came at the expense of those the unions were obliged to protect. This latter result not only intervenes to limit the actions of a state but also assumes the role of government of the people within states. In establishing certain public values for Europe and arguing the relevance of these values across spheres, the Court asserts a European *res publica* or "public thing," to use the language of this book's republican framework, claiming itself as a locus of constitutive political decisions.

Van der Walt's solution to these concerns is simple in theory though more complicated in practice. He thinks that courts in general and the ECJ in particular should refrain from weighing in on these kinds of substantive value judgments. He suggests, instead, an emphasis on the procedural so that courts leave fundamentally political questions to legislatures and, moreover, to national institutions that may better appreciate any deep social and political divisions that exist within a state.[71] The key for Van der Walt, in other words, is that we continue to recognize difference, including different political communities among Member States, where it still exists. Van der Walt argues for this devolution back to national governance as helping to mitigate the feeling among political losers that they are subject to rules "foreign" to them and rules they cannot identify as "their own,"[72] a rationale admittedly in line with the priority of self-government in republican thought.

While Van der Walt was writing before the 2009 entry into force of the Charter of Fundamental Rights, his misgivings about the horizontal application of treaty provisions are largely applicable to the Charter, as well, insofar as both documents are considered primary law and constitutive for the EU. Eleni Frantziou, on the other hand, focuses on the implications of the horizontal application of the Charter specifically and follows Van der Walt in emphasizing the weightiness of the question of horizontal application for Europe. She states explicitly that "discussion of the horizontal effect of rights involves a deeper inquiry into the kind of society the EU is setting itself out to be and the values that lie in its core."[73] Moreover, Frantziou shares Van der Walt's assessment of the way the Court has faced the choice to rank values in cases concerning horizontal application. Noting the *Viking* case in particular, she describes

---

[71] Ibid., 347.
[72] Ibid., 348. For a different gloss on this question of parity in law, see Frantziou, "The Horizontal Effect of the Charter," 665–678.
[73] Frantziou, "The Horizontal Effect of the Charter," 675.

the confrontation between the values of a "*laissez-faire* market economy," on the one hand, and the "radical, inclusionary impact" of collective bargaining and equal pay (as in *Defrenne*), on the other.[74] Frantziou worries that in continuing to develop its doctrine of horizontal application, the ECJ will prioritize *laissez-faire* economic values at the cost of the EU's more inclusionary project concerned with substantive equality.[75] Nevertheless, Frantziou's solution is not to recoil from horizontal application, *pace* Van der Walt. Rather, after the adoption of the Charter, Frantziou would have the ECJ take up these defining questions for Europe even more directly.

Frantziou's amenability to horizontal application is rooted in her broader understanding of Europe as a community. Whereas Van der Walt continues to emphasize the Member States as the locus of politics and governance, Frantziou describes the EU as its own "polity" with its own common good.[76] Her qualms concern not the practice of horizontal application itself but the prospect of the Court reducing it to a technical question and thus ignoring its normative (one might say, republican) potential. And indeed, the Court's early decision on the question of horizontal application of the Charter, the 2014 *AMS* case, tended toward the technical.[77] This case concerned whether Article 27 of the Charter, guaranteeing the rights of workers to information and timely consultation, could be applied horizontally. The Court considered but ultimately did not apply this Charter provision horizontally, reasoning that the provision was not specific enough to ground a rights claim. Put differently, it was not so specific as to keep Member States from making their own exceptions with respect to the information and consultation that workers receive in their places of employment. Thus, the Court decided against horizontal application in this instance while leaving open the possibility that a Charter provision might apply horizontally, if sufficiently specific and precise.[78]

---

[74] Ibid., 675.
[75] Ibid., 663–675. This possibility Frantziou views as symptomatic of the Court's tendency to resort to mechanical approaches in making decisions.
[76] Frantziou, "The Horizontal Effect of the Charter," 666, 668.
[77] *Association de médiation sociale v. Hichem Laboubi*, Case C-176/12 (2014).
[78] Interestingly, the advocates general in this and other Charter cases were more willing to extend horizontal application, even to provisions like Article 27 that the Court deemed to be vague, if legislation such as an EU directive further narrowed and specified the principle in question. In a later case, *Kücükdeveci*, the ECJ seemed to accept this approach in the context of such rights as equality that it deemed fundamental or a "general

Although, like treaty law, the Charter rises to the level of primary or fundamental law of the EU, the *AMS* case revealed continued uncertainty on the part of the Court in giving these rights horizontal application. Scholars such as Frantziou criticized the mechanical distinctions the Court adopted from prior decisions, such as the requirement that a provision be "mandatory" or sufficiently specific. Rather than subjecting these cases to mechanical and what she views as arbitrary limiting principles, Frantziou would have the Court engage the substance of these questions, accounting for "what these claims can mean for people's lives" – for example, "seeing one's child, being able to work free from discrimination and receiving a pension."[79] A meaningful answer to cases of horizontal application, she continues, will account for such things and determine "how much a particular society values them."[80]

Frantziou thus argues that the ECJ should decide cases of horizontal application in light of these substantive values for the very reason that they contribute to "the kind of society the EU is setting itself out to be." To do anything else would be to give the important issues short shrift or even blindly decide against inclusionary rights protections. In this way, she argues that the Court should engage, proactively, the very questions Van der Walt wants the Court to avoid. Frantziou recognizes the political nature of these questions and does think there should be some limit to the scope of horizontal application.[81] Nevertheless, she takes as given a postnational context, referring to Europe as its own society.[82] In her view, taking up the horizontal application of Charter rights is necessary to building up a European society, à la Habermas. Not only is Frantziou more optimistic than Van der Walt with respect to what horizontal application can accomplish, but she is also comfortable with what horizontal application may engender. Indeed, she understands horizontal application as itself a key question, offering answers in the larger debate about the hierarchy of EU values. For Frantziou, the outlines of political community, of *res publica*, have already been drawn, and what remains to be debated is exactly how Europe, its people and institutions, understands its own common good.

---

principle" of EU law. See *Kücükdeveci v. Swedex GmbH & Co KG*, ECJ 555/07, *ECR* (2010); also *Mangold v. Rüdiger Helm*, ECJ 144/04, *ECR* (2005); Craig and De Búrca, *EU Law*, 193–195.

[79] Frantziou, "The Horizontal Effect of the Charter," 676.
[80] Ibid.
[81] Ibid., 676–677.
[82] Ibid., 675, 678.

In November 2018, nearly a decade after the adoption of the Charter, the ECJ took the decisive step to give virtually all of the Charter horizontal application.[83] The judgment in *Bauer et al.* actually concerned two separate cases, both involving women seeking compensation from their late husbands' employers in lieu of annual leave not taken before their deaths. In support of their case, they cited Article 31(2) of the Charter, which states: "[E]very worker has the right to limitation of maximum working hours, to daily and weekly rest periods and to an annual period of paid leave."[84] In line with Frantziou's own criticisms of the Court's jurisprudence on horizontal application, the advocate general invited the Court to "reconsider previous categorisations based on general principles or 'particularly important principles of EU social law' . . . and to confirm, once and for all, that the social rights enshrined in the Charter are equally individual and fundamental as its other provisions."[85] In this way, the advocate general encouraged the Court to move beyond the privileging of economic and property rights over social rights and, more to the point, to recognize the complete range of the Charter as fundamental. Upon putting aside such distinctions, the Court affirmed that the Charter was "sufficient in itself to confer on individuals a right which they may rely on as such in a dispute with another individual."[86] In other words, there was no longer any need to render provisions more specific with additional legislation before considering their horizontal application; the Charter provisions could now be applied horizontally.

Later cases bring into sharp relief the complexity Europe's legal pluralist environment poses for these questions. Specifically, the *Right to Be Forgotten* cases,[87] decided by the German FCC in 2019, illustrate how greater integration may actually come simultaneously with the

---

[83] Eleni Frantziou, "Joined Cases C-569/16 and C-570/16 Bauer et al: (Most of) the Charter of Fundamental Rights Is Horizontally Applicable," *European Law Blog*, November 19, 2018, accessed March 2019, https://europeanlawblog.eu/2018/11/19/joined-cases-c-569-16-and-c-570-16-bauer-et-al-most-of-the-charter-of-fundamental-rights-is-horizontally-applicable.

[84] Charter of Fundamental Rights, Article 31(2).

[85] Eleni Frantziou, "Joined Cases C-569/16 and C-570/16 Bauer et al: (Most of) the Charter of Fundamental Rights Is Horizontally Applicable," *European Law Blog*, November 19, 2018, accessed March 2019, https://europeanlawblog.eu/2018/11/19/joined-cases-c-569-16-and-c-570-16-bauer-et-al-most-of-the-charter-of-fundamental-rights-is-horizontallyapplicable.

[86] *Bauer et al.*, Joined Cases C-569/16 and C-570/16, (2018).

[87] *Right to Be Forgotten I*, 1 BvR 16/13; *Right to Be Forgotten II*, 1 BvR 276/17.

national institutions of Member States asserting their own authority.[88] In these two cases, the German FCC considered the fundamental right in EU law to have private information removed from internet searches. Not only does this raise the horizontality question, specifically of the duties of internet search operators vis-à-vis individuals appearing in searches, but it brings to the fore the relationship between domestic and EU law, as well. Indeed, these cases constituted the first time that a national court interpreted for itself the Charter of Fundamental Rights. On the one hand, this is a clear sign of the development of European integration and buy-in on the part of national institutions. On the other hand, in so assuming this interpretive role, the German FCC also carved out for itself space to control the terms of integration.[89] Indeed, the Court still maintained the priority of the German Basic Law in "matters not fully harmonized" with EU law.[90] Moreover, the practice of proportionality review still allows ample interpretive space for the German Court to depart from the ECJ's judgments as a practical matter, even while maintaining the appearance of accord.[91] So while these recent cases evince a republican parity of private actors with principles of higher law as well as conformity of German law with European rights commitments, one must note the complexity with which national institutions, such as the German FCC, continually engage with this development. Indeed, the FCC's willingness (nay, eagerness) to assume a role in applying the Charter of Fundamental Rights highlights both the reality of something like a European *res publica* and the power of national institutions to shape its future.

Conclusion

In this supranational context, a republican understanding of horizontality calls for some European "public thing" or common good to justify the step of holding private entities within Member States accountable to EU values. Whereas one may understand horizontal application in national contexts as relying upon preexisting relationships among compatriots,

---

[88] Jud Mathews, "Some Kind of Right," *German Law Journal* 21:S1 (2020), 40–44; see also Mathews's discussion of the early disputes between the German High Labor Court and Constitutional Court following the adoption of the Basic Law (*Extending Rights' Reach* (chaps. 2–3)).
[89] Ibid.
[90] Ibid., 43.
[91] Ibid., 43–44.

some might describe horizontality in the EU as signifying the *creation* of new relationships and even individual duties across a supranational community. The application of horizontality itself answers larger theoretical questions about the European project in a certain way. Specifically, in taking the step of applying public values to private entities at the continental level, the ECJ assumes the existence of a European common good and the priority of this European good over national commitments. While one should resist assuming that the nature of the European project is a zero-sum competition for sovereignty between Member States and EU institutions, the practice of horizontal application tends to pit nations against the Union. To the extent the horizontal application of rights may elevate the values of the EU over those of Member States in individual cases, so too might a European "public thing" be privileged in legal, if not political, life.

8

Conclusion

As horizontal rights seek to bring private individuals into accord with public values, this book has argued that horizontal application constitutes a republican vein in constitutionalism. This republican character is evinced in two specific features of horizontal application. Briefly, the parity that horizontality establishes between public and private law and obligations resembles the republican ideal that the common good should govern a wider expanse of the polity, across public and private spheres. Moreover, out of this parity grow new constitutional duties for private actors, resembling the republican idea that people possess certain duties to one another by virtue of being fellow citizens.

While private law can also yield legal obligations for individual citizens and private entities in the traditional vertical model, these obligations accrue a different status when they come from the same source that yields and entrenches the duties of the state, namely, a constitution. Indeed, when judges cite the constitution, rather than statutory law or the common law, as the source of individuals' duties, those duties become nothing less than demands of fundamental law. Thus, horizontality has, on the one hand, the symbolic or expressive effect of bringing more actors in a polity into the fold of its constitutional commitments. It also has the practical effect of entrenching individual duties as a constitutional matter. Indeed, in the same way that constitutional rights are meant to place certain questions above routine political processes, with horizontal application, individual duties come to exist and be enforced as a constitutional matter. Horizontal application thereby expands the function of a constitution and the scope of constitutional rights by altering the conceptual distinction between public and private on which constitutionalism is traditionally premised. Its novelty and power as a constitutional development should not be understated.

The Choice of Horizontality through the Republican Lens

Horizontal application may be a relatively new constitutional practice, but adjudicating the competing claims of private actors has long been an object of politics. More than a few recent episodes offer compelling illustrations of such conflicts and the tendency to invoke rights in debating them. These varied discussions reveal an inclination to employ the language of rights and duties across issues in our political (indeed, our moral) debates, regardless of the formal status of rights and duties as a legal matter. The ubiquity of such rights-and-duties talk likewise reveals the broad range of issues to which horizontality could potentially be applied as a formal matter, if it has not been already. In light of such inclinations toward this language in political discourse across the globe, the republican framework of this book offers new concepts to understand and examine the choice of whether to adopt formally a horizontal framework across these same debates.

Take the rise of Big Tech, specifically the role of these companies as gatekeepers of expression. Many users advocate for greater transparency about how social media platforms apply their community standards when monitoring user-generated content; some would even revise these private community standards altogether in favor of free speech and expression. Indeed, politicians and members of the public have sometimes invoked rights to argue that tech companies have duties under the constitution. Thus, rights and duties are clearly at play in some popular understandings of these private relationships.[1] Moreover, the sheer power of Big Tech has led some constitutional actors and scholars to consider whether these companies should, in fact, be treated more like state actors than private actors for certain purposes. In the 2019 *Right to Be Forgotten I* case, the German Constitutional Court explained that sometimes these companies "take on a position that is so dominant as to be similar to the state's position." Under such circumstances, the Court argued, "the binding effect of the fundamental right on private actors can ultimately be close, or even equal to, its binding effect on the state."[2]

Perhaps the example of Big Tech is limited, however, for the very reason that the power of these companies can surpass even that of many nation-states. To call such companies "private" seems to understate

---

[1] Giovanni De Gregorio, *Digital Constitutionalism in Europe* (Cambridge: Cambridge University Press, 2022).
[2] *Right to Be Forgotten I,* BVerfGE 1 BvR 16/13 (2019), para. 88.

important elements of their real nature and capacity. Other examples of conflict among private actors arise out of the COVID-19 pandemic. With the spread of this highly contagious disease came questions about what fellow citizens owe each other. Do individuals have a duty to stay home, even foregoing their livelihood in the process? To wear a mask in public? To get vaccinated? How would such duties stack up against rights not to wear a mask and not to get vaccinated? Are such duties contingent on the efficacy of each respective preventative measure? Again, the language of rights and duties suffused the discourse surrounding the pandemic, evincing the appropriateness of using a republican lens to consider such questions. Much controversy arose in choosing how to assign rights and duties to various actors as a practical matter. Not only individuals but also entire political communities have decided these matters differently.

The global experience of COVID-19 shows clearly our interconnectedness and brings home the inescapable need to adjudicate conflicts between private parties. More fundamentally, these examples illustrate the choices political communities must make about whether to "extend rights' reach"[3] to adjudicate disputes in certain corners of the private sphere. Should private spaces perhaps be governed by constitutional norms in some cases but not others? If a private actor might have some duty in upholding a public commitment, such as to a particular constitutional right, then we find ourselves on very different constitutional terrain than that of traditional understandings. Indeed, constitutional rights come to acquire different meanings and engender different relationships.

Horizontality is but one means among many to approach conflicts among private actors. Constitutional actors may seek to govern certain private relationships through antidiscrimination statutes or directive principles and may accomplish as much or more through these mechanisms than they would through horizontal application. The present project does not, however, concern primarily constitutional development or outcomes. Neither is the point to argue that horizontality is generally good or generally bad, or to show that horizontality is effective or ineffective on any particular issue. Instead, the republican lens helps us see how actors adopting and employing horizontal application debate an ever-broadening set of issues, offering a new and arguably fuller view of the theoretical potential of this practice. The hope is that this analysis equips scholars and constitutional actors alike to understand horizontal

---

[3] Mathews, *Extending Rights Reach*.

application better on the level of discourse and theory, as a foundation for making coherent and effective decisions.

How we choose to structure our discourses is itself a substantive moral and political choice, independent of the question of outcomes. Should conversations about the duties we have to each other be rooted in the constitution, as Indian and South African justices have argued?[4] Or ought the concept of constitutional duties be reserved to describe the obligations of state actors as in the United States?[5] Do we want to talk about the constitution as a moral yardstick for the broader polity as Sommeregger speaks of the German experience,[6] or assess the kind of community we are by our willingness to hold private actors to public standards, in keeping with Frantziou?[7] Or should civil society and federal structures enjoy space to operate as sources of value themselves and wrestle with some of these questions independently?[8] The republican lens illuminates which of these concepts and questions most accurately capture what we mean to say in our law and politics. In a word, the republican lens offers scholars and practitioners additional tools of analysis to uncover the theoretical, even moral, implications of horizontality in particular contexts.

Whither Horizontality?

When should constitutional actors consider adopting horizontal application? Of course, all the typical political factors of partisan interests, institutional capacity, and the like figure into the decision. But we might also contemplate this question within the domain of normative theory. Horizontality, understood in republican terms, reveals a shift in the way constitutional actors discuss rights – away from rights as individual claims against state actors toward rights as encompassing certain ends of the community. Constitutional actors might opt to revise the rights-

---

[4] *People's Union for Democratic Rights v. Union of India*, AIR 1982 SC 1473 (n. 35), 252–253; *Port Elizabeth Municipality v. Various Occupiers*, (CCT 53/03) [2004] ZACC, para. 29.

[5] *Civil Rights Cases*, 109 U.S. 3 (1883); *Shelley v. Kraemer*, 334 U.S. 1 (1948); *Bell v. Maryland*, 378 U.S. 226 (1964).

[6] Georg Sommeregger, "The Horizontalization of Equality: The German Attempt to Promote Non-discrimination in the Private Sphere via Legislation," in *The Constitution in Private Relations*, ed. András Sajó and Renáta Uitz (Utrecht: Eleven, 2005), 53.

[7] Eleni Frantziou, "The Horizontal Effect of the Charter of Fundamental Rights of the EU: Rediscovering the Reasons for Horizontality," *European Law Journal* 21:5 (2015), 675.

[8] *Pruneyard Shopping Center v. Robins*, 447 U.S. 74 (1980); Van der Walt, *The Horizontal Effect Revolution*.

centricity of traditional understandings in the context of commitments they deem most constitutive, least negotiable, or somehow more susceptible to private power. Rights then come to exist among a plurality of other constitutional commitments and sometimes even yield to those other commitments. Out of this understanding, the possibility of constitutional duties for more actors, even private actors, emerges naturally. Parity and duty fall more in line with interpretations of the broader constitutional project than traditional understandings. Among transformative constitutions, we should expect fewer limits to horizontality and perhaps even horizontality written into the constitution itself.

Apart from any outcomes constitutional actors seek through horizontality, the rationale for the approach may rest in a kind of symbolic or expressive value in bringing all actors and spheres of society under the same standard.[9] In some cases, constitutional actors truly want to distinguish the sources of obligation in public and private spaces and admit legislative discretion according to a vertical model; they may seek space for autonomy and license over and above any concerns for parity and without the language of duty. In other cases, certain particularities in the historical record or in constitutional aspirations are cause to pursue a tighter connection between private actors and public values.

As the preceding chapters showed, horizontal understandings have emerged as a response (even a corrective) to such major atrocities as those of the twentieth century – from genocide to deep-seated systems of racial violence. To construct a flourishing society in the wake of such social devastation may call for broad and more direct ownership of the good of the community and duties among citizens. Again, different legal structures achieve some of the same results, but the particular way that horizontality derives the duties of citizens from public commitments offers a degree of proximity to the common good in response to historical circumstances. Horizontality is not an expression of collective guilt but rather a tool wielded by actors seeking to confront a kind of diffuse social inheritance in order that their polity may outlive it. Slavery in the United States, caste and religious discrimination in India, genocide in Germany and Europe more generally, Apartheid in South Africa – each society considered here has a past that persists in the present, with which constitutional actors must grapple. As this book has shown, constitutional actors in each place have at least contemplated horizontality in

---

[9] Hershkoff, "Just Words," 1527; see also Brettschneider, *When the State Speaks*.

overcoming social disharmony and have invoked republican concepts of rights and duties, fraternity, and the common good in the process. And indeed, this book's republican lens will be continually apposite as long as constitutional actors contemplate horizontality's meaning and appropriateness in their respective contexts.

Making Horizontality More Republican

That horizontality tends to increase the understanding of freedom as nondomination and shift the larger society toward certain public values seems relatively straightforward. Horizontality aims to bring public ends to bear on private spaces. We should ask, however, whether horizontality's kinship with certain republican principles – notably, the common good and duty – calls for more thoroughgoing republican processes to accompany its establishment. Put differently, some might find in these republican aspects of horizontality a call to provide more fully for republican principles, perhaps contemplating the role different, more representative governing institutions should play in shaping horizontality.

Eoin Daly and Tom Hickey structure their book on republican constitutionalism in the Irish context around three themes: a republican understanding of freedom, republican institutions, and the cultivation of a broader republican society, as through education.[10] And indeed, we may locate horizontality among these broad strokes of republican constitutionalism. Moreover, considering how horizontality fits within these elements of republican constitutionalism uncovers possibilities for making this practice *more* republican. How to square horizontality with democratic articulations of republican freedom and representative institutions, for example, may be confounding. While horizontality might be understood as a democratizing effort in the sense that it brings the entire legal system under the will of the people as articulated in the constitution, it also tends to leave less to the jurisdiction of ordinary law and lawmaking. The very purpose of horizontality may be described as to constitutionalize duties in the same way rights are typically constitutionalized. Some might conclude on this basis that courts will necessarily play an outsized role.

This need not be the case. Although horizontality *constitutionalizes* the private sphere, legislative powers and even the general public may – and arguably must – participate in constitutional conversations. In the words

---

[10] Daly and Hickey, *Political Theory*.

of US Chief Justice John Marshall, "[W]e must never forget that it is a constitution we are expounding,"[11] which is to say that constitutions are always subject to interpretation and always involve some element of politics, albeit politics of a higher order. For these other realms to participate more actively in debates concerning the obligations of private actors may well elevate the discourse. Perhaps the new commonwealth model that Stephen Gardbaum identifies in many countries provides an answer by carving out space for both legislatures and courts.[12] Even while courts would inevitably maintain some special role in adjudicating individual cases, to have more institutions and more people participating in these constitutional conversations would certainly make this practice more consistently republican, balancing the resulting parity and duties with new levels of self-government in the practice of horizontality.

Buttressing the participation of plural government bodies and the general public in these conversations may also go some way to assuage the fears of those who worry about the "crumbling public/private divide" and the ways in which something like horizontality might be abused.[13] Indeed, as worries about homogenization have sometimes been leveled against republicanism, so such worries also rear their head in debates over horizontality. As Gary Jacobsohn explains:

> [T]he tradition of classical republicanism with which the founders were intimately acquainted was a fundamentally illiberal tradition that can serve as a model for contemporary republicans only if its problematic features are conveniently ignored ... What these critics have in mind are the exclusivist, discriminatory tendencies of republican communalism, tendencies that liberal constitutional arrangements were largely designed to overcome.[14]

While critics do not often go so far as to call horizontal application "exclusivist, discriminatory, or communalistic," their assessments track similar concerns about the homogenization of private and public, as well

---

[11] *McCulloch v. Maryland*, 17 U.S. 316 (1819), para. 62.
[12] Stephen Gardbaum, "The Case for the New Commonwealth Model of Constitutionalism," *German Law Journal* 14:12 (2013), 2229-2248; *The New Commonwealth Model of Constitutionalism* (Cambridge: Cambridge University Press, 2012).
[13] See, for example, DeWitt, "The Crumbling Public/Private Divide"; Van der Walt, *The Horizontal Effect Revolution*; DeMol, "The Novel Approach of the CJEU"; Stone Sweet, "The Juridical Coup d'État."
[14] Gary Jacobsohn, *Apple of Gold* (Princeton: Princeton University Press, 1993), 46-47; see also Isaiah Berlin, "Two Concepts of Liberty" (1958), in *Four Essays on Liberty* (Oxford: Oxford University Press, 1969), 118-172. Linda K. Kerber, "Making Republicanism Useful," *Yale Law Journal* 97 (1998), 1663.

as the prioritization of public commitments at the expense of the individual. Incorporating more voices, especially voices that republican theory typically identifies as more connected with the people, might better ensure that these decisions are carried out on the people's terms[15] and thus hedge against these darker possibilities.

In the mere act of adopting a constitution, a polity commits to certain principles and, to this extent, cannot pretend to be neutral. Although these norms may be applied in private spaces in both a vertical and a horizontal model of rights, these two models engender different narratives about the relationship between citizens and the "public thing" that is created by the constitution. The traditional vertical model permits a level of detachment so that even if legislation regulates private actors, these actors need not themselves assume constitutional duties. On the other hand, polities who pursue horizontal application do not rest content with the "light touch"[16] of the vertical model in maintaining and applying constitutional commitments. Ultimately, this comes down to prudential questions of constitutional design in meeting the goals a polity sets out for itself. How to conceive of the relationship between public and private actors – whether in more traditional or republican terms – rises to a level of high constitutional politics. In some instances, what Sommeregger calls "value monism" might be unnecessary or imprudent. In other cases, conventional understandings of rights may come up short, making necessary something like the republican logic of horizontality to enable the discourses to continue in a way that benefits each polity. Whatever the case, constitutional actors and scholars would do well to engage in such discourses with a historical and theoretical knowledge of republicanism and its echoes in the issues of their day.

---

[15] Pettit, *People's Terms*.
[16] Gary Jacobsohn, "A Lighter Touch: American Constitutional Principles in Comparative Perspective," in *Cambridge Companion to the United States Constitution*, ed. Karen Orren and John W. Compton (Cambridge: Cambridge University Press, 2018), 13–44.

BIBLIOGRAPHY

Ackermann, Laurie. *Human Dignity: Lodestar for Equality in South Africa* (Cape Town: Juta, 2012).
Adler, Emanuel, and Michael Barnett (eds.). *Security Communities* (Cambridge: Cambridge University Press, 1998).
Alexy, Robert. *A Theory of Constitutional Rights* (Oxford: Oxford University Press, 2010).
Ally, Nurina, and Daniel Linde. "*Pridwin*: Private School Contracts, the Bill of Rights and a Missed Opportunity." *Constitutional Court Review* 11 (2021), 275–300.
ANC Constitutional Committee. "A Bill of Rights for a Democratic South Africa: A Working Draft for Consultation." *African Journal of International and Comparative Law* 3 (1991), 608–620.
Aristotle. *The Nicomachean Ethics*. Translated by Terence Irwin (Indianapolis: Hackett, 1999).
  The Politics. Edited by Stephen Everson (Cambridge: Cambridge University Press, 1996).
Arkes, Hadley. *Beyond the Constitution* (Princeton: Princeton University Press, 1992).
Austin, Granville. *Working a Democratic Constitution* (Oxford: Oxford University Press, 1999).
Bailyn, Bernard. *The Ideological Origins of the American Revolution* (Cambridge, MA: Belknap Press, 1992).
Bajpai, Rochana. "Liberalisms in India: A Sketch." In Ben Jackson and Marc Stears (eds.), *Liberalism as Ideology: Essays in Honour of Michael Freeden* (Oxford: Oxford University Press, 2012), 53–76.
Balkin, Jack. *Constitutional Redemption* (Cambridge, MA: Harvard University Press, 2011).
  "Which Republican Constitution?" *Constitutional Commentary* 32 (2017), 31–59.
Balkin, Jack, and Sanford Levinson. "The Dangerous Thirteenth Amendment." *Columbia Law Review* 112:7 (2012), 1459–1499.
Bambrick, Christina. "Neither Precisely National Nor Precisely Federal: Governmental and Administrative Authority in Tocqueville's Democracy in America." *Publius: The Journal of Federalism* 48:4 (2018), 586–606.

Bamforth, Nicholas. "The Public Law–Private Law Distinction: A Comparative and Philosophical Approach." In Peter Leyland and Terry Woods (eds.), *Administrative Law Facing the Future: Old Constraints and New Horizons* (Oxford: Blackstone, 1997).

Barak, Aharon. *Human Dignity: The Constitutional Value and the Constitutional Right* (Cambridge: Cambridge University Press, 2015).

Bayly, C. A. *Recovering Liberties* (Cambridge: Cambridge University Press, 2012).

Bedi, Sonu. "The Scope of Formal Equality of Opportunity: The Horizontal Effect of Rights in a Liberal Constitution." *Political Theory* 42:6 (2014), 716–738.

Bellamy, Richard. "Democracy as Public Law: The Case of Constitutional Rights." *German Law Journal* 14:8 (2013), 1017–1037.

Political Constitutionalism (Cambridge: Cambridge University Press, 2007).

A Republican Europe of States: Cosmopolitanism, Intergovernmentalism and Democracy in the EU (Cambridge: Cambridge University Press, 2019).

Berlin, Isaiah. "Two Concepts of Liberty" (1958). In *Four Essays on Liberty* (Oxford: Oxford University Press, 1969), 118–172.

Besselink, Leonard F. M. "National and Constitutional Identity before and after Lisbon." *Utrecht Law Review* 6:3 (2010), 36–49.

Bhatia, Gautam. "Exclusionary Covenants and the Constitution – II: The Zoroastrian Co-op Case." *Indian Constitutional Law and Philosophy*, January 12, 2014. Accessed January 25, 2019 <https://indconlawphil.wordpress.com/2014/01/12/exclusionary-covenants-and-the-constitution-ii-the-zoroastrian-co-op-case>.

"Exclusionary Covenants and the Constitution – III: Zoroastrian Cooperative and Political Liberalism." *Indian Constitutional Law and Philosophy*, January 13, 2014. Accessed January 25, 2019 <https://indconlawphil.wordpress.com/2014/01/13/exclusionary-covenants-and-the-constitution-iii-zoroastrian-cooperative-and-political-liberalism>.

"Exclusionary Covenants and the Constitution – IV: Article 15(2), *IMA v. UoI*, and the Constitutional Case against Racially/Religiously Restrictive Covenants." *Indian Constitutional Law and Philosophy*, January 14, 2014. Accessed January 25, 2019 <https://indconlawphil.wordpress.com/2014/01/14/exclusionary-covenants-and-the-constitution-iv-article-152-ima-v-uoi-and-the-constitutional-case-against-raciallyreligiously-restrictive-covenants>.

The Transformative Constitution (Uttar Pradesh: HarperCollins India, 2019).

Bhuwania, Anuj. *Courting the People* (Cambridge: Cambridge University Press, 2017).

Bickel, Alexander. *The Least Dangerous Branch* (New Haven: Yale University Press, 1986).

Black, Charles L. Jr. "The Supreme Court, 1966 Term – Foreword: 'State Action,' Equal Protection, and California's Proposition 14." *Harvard Law Review* 81 (1967), 69–109.

Boonzaier, Leo. "Contractual Fairness at the Crossroads." *Constitutional Court Review* 11 (2021), 229–274.
Brandeis, Louis, and Samuel Warren. "The Right to Privacy." *Harvard Law Review* 4:5 (1890), 193–220.
Brandwein, Pamela. "A Lost Jurisprudence of the Reconstruction Amendments." *Journal of Supreme Court History* 41 (2016), 329–346.
  Rethinking the Judicial Settlement of Reconstruction (Cambridge: Cambridge University Press, 2011).
Breslin, Beau. *The Communitarian Constitution* (Baltimore: Johns Hopkins University Press, 2006).
Brettschneider, Corey. *When the State Speaks, What Should It Say?* (Princeton: Princeton University Press, 2012).
Bruggemeier, Gert, Aurelia Colombi Ciacchi, and Giovanni Comandé (eds.). *Fundamental Rights and Private Law in the European Union: Volume 1* (Cambridge: Cambridge University Press, 2010).
Brugger, Winfried. "Communitarianism as the Social and Legal Theory behind the German Constitution." *International Journal of Constitutional Law* 2:3 (2004), 431–460.
Cachalia, Firoz. "Democratic Constitutionalism in the Time of the Postcolony: Beyond Triumph and Betrayal." *South African Journal on Human Rights* 34:3 (2018), 375–397.
Caldwell, Ernest. "Horizontal Rights and Chinese Constitutionalism: Judicialization through Labor Disputes." *Chicago-Kent Law Review* 88:1 (2012), 63–92.
Calhoun, Charles. *Conceiving a New Republic* (Lawrence: Kansas University Press, 2006).
Checkel, Jeffrey. "International Institutions and Socialization in Europe: Introduction and Framework." *International Organization* 59 (2005), 801–826.
Chemerinsky, Erwin. "Rethinking State Action." *Northwestern University Law Review* 80:3 (1985), 503–557.
Chirwa, Danwood Mikenge. "The Horizontal Application of Constitutional Rights in Comparative Perspective." *Law, Democracy, and Development* 10:2 (2006), 21–48.
Chirwa, Danwood Mzikenge. "In Search of Philosophical Justifications and Theoretical Models for the Horizontal Application of Human Rights." *African Human Rights Law Journal* 8:2 (2008), 294–311.
Cicero. *On Duties*. Edited by M. T. Griffin and E. M. Atikins (Cambridge: Cambridge University Press, 1991).
Clapham, Andrew. *Human Rights Obligations of Non-state Actors* (Oxford: Oxford University Press, 2006).
Cockrell, Alfred. "Private Law and the Bill of Rights: A Threshold Issue of 'Horizontality.'" In *Bill of Rights Compendium* (Cape Town: LexisNexis South Africa), 3A1–3A20.

Cordelli, Chiara. "Democratizing Organized Religion." *Journal of Politics* 79:2 (2017), 576–590.

Cornell, Drucilla, Stu Woolman, Sam Fuller, Jason Brickhill, Michael Bishop, and Diana Dunbar (eds.). "Grootboom." In *The Dignity Jurisprudence of the Constitutional Court of South Africa: Cases and Materials* (New York: Fordham University Press, 2013), 415–430.

Corrin, Jennifer. "From Horizontal and Vertical to Lateral: Extending the Effect of Human Rights in Post Colonial Legal Systems of the South Pacific." *International and Comparative Law Quarterly* 58 (2009), 31–71.

Craig, Paul, and Gráinne de Búrca. *EU Law: Text, Cases, and Materials*, 6th ed. (Oxford: Oxford University Press, 2015).

Daly, Eoin. "Freedom as Nondomination in the Jurisprudence of Constitutional Rights." *Canadian Journal of Law and Jurisprudence* 28:2 (2015), 289–316.

Daly, Eoin, and Tom Hickey. *The Political Theory of the Irish Constitution: Republicanism and the Basic Law* (Manchester: Manchester University Press, 2015).

Davis, Dennis. "Twenty Years of Constitutional Democracy: A Preliminary Reflection." *New York Law School Law Review* 60:1 (2016), 39–54.

Davis, Dennis M. "Constitutional Borrowing: The Influence of Legal Culture and Local History in the Reconstitution of Comparative Influence – The South African Experience." *International Journal of Constitutional Law* 1:2 (2003), 181–195.

  "Is the South African Constitution an Obstacle to a Democratic Post-colonial State?" *South African Journal on Human Rights* 34:3 (2018), 359–374.

De Gregorio, Giovanni. *Digital Constitutionalism in Europe* (Cambridge: Cambridge University Press, 2022).

DeMol, Mirjam. "The Novel Approach of the CJEU on the Horizontal Direct Effect of the EU Principle of Non-discrimination: (Unbridled) Expansionism of EU Law?" *Maastricht Journal of European and Comparative Law* 18 (2011), 109–135.

Devlin, John. "Constructing an Alternative to 'State Action' as a Limit on State Constitutional Rights Guarantees: A Survey, Critique, and Proposal." *Rutgers Law Journal* 21 (1990), 819–902.

DeWitt, Bruno. "The Crumbling Public/Private Divide: Horizontality in European Anti-discrimination Law." *Citizenship Studies* 13:5 (2009), 515–525.

Dickson, Del (ed.). *The Supreme Court in Conference (1940–1985): The Private Discussions behind Nearly 300 Supreme Court Decisions* (Oxford: Oxford University Press, 2001).

Dinan, John. *The American State Constitutional Tradition* (Lawrence: University of Kansas Press, 2006).

Douglas, Stacy. "Ubuntu versus Ubuntu: Finding a Philosophy of Justice through Obligation." *Law Critique* 26 (2015), 305–312.

Du Plessis, Lourens Marthinus, and Hugh Corder. *Understanding South Africa's Transitional Bill of Rights* (Kenwyn: Juta, 1994).
Dürig, Günther. "Grundrechte und Zivilrechtsprechung." In Theodor Maunz (ed.), *Festschrift Zum 75. Geburtstag von Hans Nawiasky* (Munich: Isar Verlag, 1956), 157–190.
Dworkin, Ronald. *Law's Empire* (Cambridge: Belknap, 1986).
Dyzenhaus, David. "Critical Notice of *On the People's Terms: A Republican Theory and Model of Democracy*, by Philip Pettit, Cambridge University Press, 2012, xii + 333 pp." *Canadian Journal of Philosophy* 43:4 (2013), 494–513.
Eisenhower, Dwight D. "The President's News Conference." In *Public Papers of the Presidents of the United States: Dwight D. Eisenhower, 1960–1961* (Washington, DC: US Government Printing Office, 1961), 293–302.
Elkins, Zachary, Tom Ginsburg, and James Melton. "Constitutions." *Constitute*, 2023. Accessed September 13, 2023 <www.constituteproject.org/constitutions?lang=en&key=express&status=in_force>.
Ellmann, Stephen. "A Constitutional Confluence: American 'State Action' Law and the Application of South Africa's Socioeconomic Rights Guarantees to Private Actors." *New York Law School Law Review* 45 (2001), 21–75.
Eskridge, William N., and John Ferejohn. *A Republic of Statutes: The New American Constitution* (New Haven: Yale University Press, 2010).
The Federal. "Congress Proposes Law to Bar Entry of All Women to Sabarimala Shrine." February 7, 2021. Accessed April 25, 2021 <https://thefederal.com/states/south/kerala/congress-proposes-law-to-bar-entry-of-all-women-to-sabarimala-shrine>.
Fedtke, Jorg. "*Drittwirkung* in Germany." In Dawn Oliver and Jorg Fedtke (eds.), *Human Rights and the Private Sphere* (Oxford: Rutledge-Cavendish, 2007), 125–156.
Ferreira, Nuno. *Fundamental Rights and Private Law in Europe: The Case of Tort Law and Children* (New York: Routledge, 2011).
Ferreres Comella, Victor. "Do Constitutional Rights Bind Private Individuals?" Unpublished manuscript.
Finn, Meghan. "Befriending the Bogeyman: Direct Horizontal Application in *AB v. Pridwin*." *South African Law Journal* 137:4 (2020), 591–608.
Forbath, William. "Not So Simple Justice: Frank Michelman on Social Rights, 1969–Present." *Tulsa Law Review* 39 (2004), 597–638.
Frantziou, Eleni. "The Horizontal Effect of the Charter of Fundamental Rights of the EU: Rediscovering the Reasons for Horizontality." *European Law Journal* 21:5 (2015), 657–679.
  The Horizontal Effect of Fundamental Rights in the European Union (Oxford: Oxford University Press, 2019).
  "Joined Cases C-569/16 and C-570/16 Bauer et al: (Most of) the Charter of Fundamental Rights Is Horizontally Applicable." *European Law Blog*,

November 19, 2018. Accessed March 22, 2019 <https://europeanlawblog.eu/2018/11/19/joined-cases-c-569-16-and-c-570-16-bauer-et-al-most-of-the-charter-of-fundamental-rights-is-horizontally-applicable/>.

Friedman, Leon (ed.). *Argument: The Complete Oral Argument before the Supreme Court in Brown v. Board of Education of Topeka, 1952–1955* (New York: Chelsea House, 1969).

Friedman, Nick. "The South African Common Law and the Constitution: Revisiting Horizontality." *South African Journal on Human Rights* 30:1 (2014), 63–88.

Futch, Delisa. "*Du Plessis v. De Klerk*: South Africa's Bill of Rights and the Issue of Horizontal Application." *North Carolina Journal of International Law and Commercial Regulation* 22:3 (1997), 1009–1037.

Galanter, Marc. *Competing Equalities: Law and the Backward Classes in India* (Berkeley: University of California Press, 1984).

Galston, William. *Liberal Pluralism* (Cambridge: Cambridge University Press, 2002).

"Liberal Virtues and the Formation of Civic Character." In Mary Ann Glendon and David Blankenhorn (eds.), *Seedbeds of Virtue* (Lanham: Madison Books, 1995).

Gardbaum, Stephen. "The Case for the New Commonwealth Model of Constitutionalism." *German Law Journal* 14:12 (2013), 2229–2248.

"The 'Horizontal Effect' of Constitutional Rights." *Michigan Law Review* 102 (2003), 387–459.

"Horizontality in the Indian Constitution." In Sujit Choudhry, Madhav Khosla, and Pratap Bhanu Mehta (eds.), *The Oxford Handbook of the Indian Constitution* (Oxford: Oxford University Press, 2016), 600–613.

"Law, Politics, and the Claims of Community." *Michigan Law Review* 90:4 (1992), 685–760.

"Positive and Horizontal Rights: Proportionality's Next Frontier or a Bridge Too Far?" In Vicki Jackson and Mark Tushnet (eds.), *Proportionality: New Frontiers, New Challenges* (Cambridge: Cambridge University Press, 2017), 221–247.

"What Makes for More or Less Powerful Constitutional Courts?" *Duke Journal of Comparative & International Law* 29:1 (2018), 1–40.

Garlicki. Lech. "Relations between Private Actors and the European Convention on Human Rights." In András Sajó and Renáta Uitz (eds.), *The Constitution in Private Relations* (Utrecht: Eleven, 2005), 129–144.

Glendon, Mary Ann. *Rights Talk: The Impoverishment of Political Discourse* (New York: Free Press, 1991).

Green, Andrew, and Albert H. Yoon. "Triaging the Law: Developing the Common Law on the Supreme Court of India." *Journal of Empirical Legal Studies* 14:4 (2017), 683–715.

Green, Christopher R. "The Original Sense of the (Equal) Protection Clause: Subsequent Interpretation and Application." *George Mason University Civil Rights Law Journal* 19 (2009), 219–310.
Greene, Jamal. *How Rights Went Wrong* (Boston: Mariner Books, 2021).
Grimm, Dieter. "Integration by Constitution." *International Journal of Constitutional Law* 3 (2005), 193–208.
Habermas, Jürgen. "The Concept of Human Dignity and the Realistic Utopia of Human Rights." *Metaphilosophy* 41:4 (2010), 464–480.
  The Inclusion of the Other: Studies in Political Theory. Edited by Ciaran Cronin and Pablo de Greiff (Cambridge, MA: Polity Press, 1999).
  The Postnational Constellation. Edited by Max Pensky (Boston: MIT University Press, 2001).
Hailbronner, Michaela. "Transformative Constitutionalism: Not Only in the Global South." *American Journal of Comparative Law* 65:3 (2017), 527–565.
Hale, Robert L. "Coercion and Distribution in a Supposedly Non-coercive State." *Political Science Quarterly* 38 (1923), 470–494.
Hamilton, Alexander, James Madison, and John Jay. *The Federalist Papers*. Edited by Clinton Rossiter (New York: Signet, 2003).
Hanisch, Carol. "The Personal Is Political: The Women's Liberation Movement Classic with a New Explanatory Introduction." In Barbara A. Crow (ed.), *Radical Feminism: A Documentary Reader* (New York: NYU Press, 2000), 113–117.
Hartz, Louis. *The Liberal Tradition in America* (New York: Harvest Books, 1991).
Hattenhauer, Hans. *Die Geistesgeschichtlichen Grundlagen Des Deutschen Rechts*, 3rd ed. (Heidelberg: Müller, 1983).
Henkin, Louis. "*Shelley v. Kraemer*: Notes for a Revised Opinion." *University of Pennsylvania Law Review* 110:4 (1962), 473–505.
Henne, Thomas. "Die neue Wertordnung in Zivilrecht – speziell Familien-und Arbeitsrecht." In Michael Stolleis (ed.), *Das Bonner Grundgesetz: Altes Recht und neue Verfassung in den ernsten Jahrzehnten der Bundesrepublik Deutschland (1949-1969)* (Berlin: Berliner Wissenschafts-Verlag, 2006), 13–37.
Hershkoff, Helen. "'Just Words': Common Law and the Enforcement of State Constitutional Social and Economic Rights." *Stanford Law Review* 62 (2010), 1521–1582.
  "The New Jersey Constitution: Positive Rights, Common Law Entitlements, and State Action." *Albany Law Review* 69 (2006), 553–559.
  "The Private Life of Public Rights: State Constitutions and the Common Law." *New York University Law Review Online* 88:1 (2013), 1–23.
  "State Common Law and the Dual Enforcement of Constitutional Norms." In James A. Gardner and Jim Rossi (eds.), *New Frontiers of State Constitutional Law: Dual Enforcement of Norms* (Oxford: Oxford University Press, 2011), 151–172.

"Transforming Legal Theory in the Light of Practice: The Judicial Application of Social and Economic Rights to Private Orderings." In Varun Gauri and Daniel Brinks (eds.), *Courting Social Rights*. (Cambridge: Cambridge University Press, 2008), 268–302.

Hickey, Tom. "The Republican Core of the Case for Judicial Review." *International Journal of Constitutional Law* 17:1 (2019), 288–315.

Hirschl, Ran. *Comparative Matters* (Oxford: Oxford University Press, 2014).

Toward Juristocracy (Cambridge, MA: Harvard University Press, 2004).

Hobbes, Thomas. *Leviathan*. Edited by Richard Tuck (Cambridge: Cambridge University Press, 1996).

Holmes, Elisa. "Antidiscrimination Rights without Equality." *Modern Law Review* 68:2 (2005), 175–194.

Honohan, Iseult. "Educating Citizens: Nation-Building and Its Republican Limits." In Iseult Honohan and Jeremy Jennings (eds.), *Republicanism in Theory and Practice* (Oxfordshire: Routledge, 2006).

Horowitz, Harold W. "The Misleading Search for 'State Action' under the Fourteenth Amendment." *Southern California Law Review* 30 (1957), 208–221.

Horowitz, Morton J. "The History of the Public/Private Distinction." *University of Pennsylvania Law Review* 130 (1982), 1423–1428.

Isenberg, Nancy. "The Personal Is Political: Gender, Feminism, and the Politics of Discourse Theory." *American Quarterly* 44:3 (1992), 449–458.

Ivison, Duncan. "Republican Human Rights?" *European Journal of Political Theory* 9:1 (2010), 31–47.

Jackson, Robert H. Memorandum 11 (March 15, 1954) (on file with Library of Congress, Manuscript Division, Papers of Robert H. Jackson, Box 184).

Jacobsohn, Gary. *Apple of Gold* (Princeton: Princeton University Press, 1993).

Constitutional Identity (Cambridge, MA: Harvard University Press, 2010).

"Dramatic Jurisprudence." In William Eskridge and Sanford Levinson (eds.), *Constitutional Stupidities, Constitutional Tragedies* (New York: New York University Press, 1998), 172–179.

"A Lighter Touch: American Constitutional Principles in Comparative Perspective." In Karen Orren and John W. Compton (eds.), *The Cambridge Companion to the United States Constitution* (Cambridge: Cambridge University Press, 2018), 13–44.

Pragmatism, Statesmanship, and the Supreme Court (Ithaca: Cornell University Press, 1977).

The Wheel of Law (Princeton: Princeton University Press, 2009).

Jacobsohn, Gary, and Yaniv Roznai. *Constitutional Revolution* (New Haven: Yale University Press, 2020).

Jaffa, Harry. *Crisis of the House Divided* (Chicago: University of Chicago, 2009).

Kalyvas, Andreas, and Ira Katznelson. *Liberal Beginnings: Making a Republic for the Moderns* (Cambridge: Cambridge University Press, 2008).

Karp, David Jason. "What Is the Responsibility to Respect Human Rights? Reconsidering the 'Respect, Protect, and Fulfill' Framework." *International Theory* 12:1 (2020), 83–108.
Kennedy, John F. "Radio and Television Report to the American People on Civil Rights." In *Public Papers of the Presidents of the United States: John F. Kennedy, 1963* (Washington, DC: US Government Printing Office, 1964), 468–470.
Kerber, Linda K. "Making Republicanism Useful." *Yale Law Journal* 97:8 (1998), 1663–1672.
Khaitan, Tarunabh. "The Duty Bearers." In *A Theory of Discrimination Law* (Oxford: Oxford University Press, 2015), 195–213.
  "Equality: Legislative Review under Article 14." In Sujit Choudhry, Madhav Khosla, and Pratap Bhanu Mehta (eds.), *The Oxford Handbook of the Indian Constitution* (Oxford: Oxford University Press, 2016), 699–719.
  "Killing a Constitution with a Thousand Cuts: Executive Aggrandizement and Party-State Fusion in India." *Law and Ethics of Human Rights* 14:1 (2020), 49–95.
  "Reading *Swaraj* into Article 15: A New Deal for All Minorities." *NUJS Law Review* 2:3 (2009), 420–432.
King, Jeff. "Social Rights in Comparative Constitutional Theory." In Gary Jacobsohn and Miguel Schor (eds.), *Comparative Constitutional Theory* (Cheltenham: Edward Elgar, 2018), 144–166.
King, Martin Luther, Jr. "A Creative Protest." In Clayborne Carson, Tenisha Hart Armstrong, Adrienne Clay, and Susan Carson (eds.), *The Papers of Martin Luther King, Jr., Volume V* (Berkeley: University of California Press, 2006), 367–370.
Klug, Heinz. *Constituting Democracy: Law, Globalism, and South Africa's Political Reconstruction* (Cambridge: Cambridge University Press, 2010).
Knight, Ben. "European Court of Justice Tells German Churches to Respect EU Discrimination Law." *Deutsche Welle*, September 11, 2017. Accessed July 9, 2019 <https://p.dw.com/p/2nMsu>.
Kommers, Donald, and Russell Miller. *Constitutional Jurisprudence of the Federal Republic of Germany*, 3rd ed. (Durham: Duke University Press, 2012).
Krisch, Nico. *Beyond Constitutionalism* (Oxford: Oxford University Press, 2011).
Krishnaswamy, Sudhir. "Horizontal Application of Fundamental Rights and State Action in India." In C. Raj Kumar and K. Chockalingam (eds.), *Human Rights, Justice, & Constitutional Empowerment* (Oxford: Oxford University Press, 2007).
Kumm, Mattias. "Who Is Afraid of the Total Constitution? Constitutional Rights as Principles and the Constitutionalization of Private Law." *German Law Journal* 7:4 (2006), 341–369.
Kumm, Mattias, and Victor Ferreres Comella. "What Is So Special about Constitutional Rights in Private Litigation?" In András Sajó and Renáta

Uitz (eds.), *The Constitution in Private Relations* (Utrecht: Eleven, 2005), 241–286.

Laborde, Cécile. "Minimal Secularism: Lessons for, and from, India." *American Political Science Review* 115:1 (2021), 1–13.

Laborde, Cécile, and John Maynor. *Republicanism and Political Theory* (Hoboken: Wiley-Blackwell, 2008).

Larenz, Karl. *Methodenlehre Der Rechtswissenschaft* (Berlin: Springer Verlag, 1975).

Liebenberg, Sandra. "The Application of Socio-economic Rights to Private Law." *Journal of South African Law* 3 (2008), 464–480.

Socio-economic rights: Adjudication under a Transformative Constitution (Claremont: Juta, 2010).

"Socio-economic Rights beyond the Public Private Law Divide." In Malcolm Langford, Ben Cousins, Jackie Dugard, and Tshepo Madingozi (eds.), *Socio-economic Rights in South Africa: Symbols or Substance?* (Cambridge: Cambridge University Press, 2013), 63–91.

Locke, John. *Second Treatise of Government*. Edited by C. B. MacPherson (Indianapolis: Hackett, 1980).

Lowenthal, Tom. "*AB v. Pridwin Preparatory School*: Progress and Problems in Horizontal Human Rights Law." *South African Journal on Human Rights* 36 (2020), 261–274.

Lyons, Richard L. "Lunch 'Sitdown' a Legal Puzzler." *Washington Post*, March 27, 1960, E5.

Maas, Willem. "Multilevel Citizenship." In Ayelet Shachar, Rainer Bauboeck, Irene Bloemraad, and Maarten Vink (eds.), *Oxford Handbook of Citizenship* (Oxford: Oxford University Press, 2017), 644–668.

"The Origins, Evolution, and Political Objectives of EU Citizenship." *German Law Journal* 15:5 (2014), 797–819.

Macedo, Stephen. *Liberal Virtues* (Oxford: Oxford University Press, 1990).

Machiavelli, Niccolo. *Discourses on Livy*. Translated by Harvey C. Mansfield and Nathan Tarcov (Chicago: Chicago University Press, 1996).

Madlanga, Mbuyiseli. "The Human Rights Duties of Companies and Other Private Actors in South Africa." *Stellenbosch Human Law Review* 29:3 (2018), 359–378.

Manent, Pierre. *An Intellectual History of Liberalism* (Princeton: Princeton University Press, 1996).

Marti, Jose, and Philip Pettit. *A Political Philosophy in Public Life: Civic Republicanism in Zapatero's Spain* (Princeton: Princeton University Press, 2012).

Mathews, Jud. *Extending Rights' Reach* (Oxford: Oxford University Press, 2018).

"Some Kind of Right." *German Law Journal* 21:S1 (2020), 40–44.

Mathiba, Gaopalelwe Lesley. "Evictions and Tenure Security in South Africa." *ESR Review* 19:2 (2018), 12–15.

Merryman, John Henry. *The Civil Law Tradition*, 3rd ed. (Stanford: Stanford University Press, 2007).
Metz, Thaddeus. "Ubuntu as a Moral Theory and Human Rights in South Africa." *African Human Rights Law Journal* 11 (2011), 532–559.
Michelman, Frank. "Constitutions and the Public/Private Divide." In Michel Rosenfeld and András Sajó (eds.), *Oxford Handbook of Comparative Constitutional Law* (Oxford: Oxford University Press, 2012), 298–317.
  "The Interplay of Constitutional and Ordinary Jurisdiction." In Tom Ginsburg and Rosalind Dixon (eds.), *Comparative Constitutional Law* (Cheltenham: Edward Elgar, 2011), 278–297.
  "Law's Republic." *Yale Law Journal* 97:8 (1988), 1493–1537.
Michl, Fabian. "Wer darf wen 'diskriminieren'? Zum Nichtannahmebeschluss in Sachen Hotelverbot (1 BvR 879/12)." *VerfBlog*. Accessed October 12, 2019 <https://verfassungsblog.de/wer-darf-wen-diskriminieren/>.
Mill, John Stuart. *On Liberty*. Edited by Elizabeth Rapaport (Indianapolis: Hackett, 1978).
Miller, David. "Republicanism, National Identity, and Europe." In Cécile Laborde and John Maynor (eds.), *Republicanism and Political Theory* (Oxford: Wiley & Blackwell, 2008).
Modiri, Joel M. "Conquest and Constitutionalism: First Thoughts on an Alternative Jurisprudence." *South African Journal on Human Rights* 34:3 (2018), 300–325.
Moseneke, Dikgang. "Transformative Constitutionalism: Its Implications for the Law of Contract." *Stellenbosch Law Review* 20:1 (2009), 3–13.
Murphy, Walter. *Constitutional Democracy* (Baltimore: Johns Hopkins University Press, 2007).
Nair, Ravi. "Confronting the Violence Committed by Armed Opposition Groups." *Yale Human Rights and Development Law Journal* 1:1 (1998), 13–14.
Nolan, Aoife. "*Daniels v. Scribante*: South Africa Pushes the Boundaries of Horizontality and Social Rights." *I-CONnect: Blog of the International Journal of Constitutional Law*, June 27, 2017. Accessed December 20, 2017 <www.iconnectblog.com/2017/06/daniels-v-scribante-south-africa-pushes-the-boundaries-of-horizontality-and-social-rights>.
  "Holding Non-state Actors to Account for Constitutional Economic and Social Rights Violations: Experiences and Lessons from South Africa and Ireland." *International Journal of Constitutional Law* 12:1 (2014), 61–93.
O'Cinnede, Colm. "Irish Constitutional Law and Direct Horizontal Effect: A Successful Experiment?" In Dawn Oliver and Jorg Fedtke (eds.), *Human Rights in the Private Sphere* (Abingdon: Routledge-Cavendish, 2007), 213–251.
Oyowe, Anthony O. "Strange Bedfellows: Rethinking *Ubuntu* and Human Rights in South Africa." *African Human Rights Law Journal* 13 (2013), 103–124.

Pangle, Thomas. *The Spirit of Modern Republicanism* (Chicago: Chicago University Press, 1990).
Pettit, Philip. "Democracy, Electoral and Contestatory." In Ian Shapiro and Stephen Macedo (eds.), *Designing Democratic Institutions* (New York: NYU Press, 2000), 105–146.
  On the People's Terms (Cambridge: Cambridge University Press, 2012).
  Republicanism: A Theory of Freedom and Government (Oxford: Clarendon Press, 1997).
Pildes, Richard. "The Structural Conception of Rights and Judicial Balancing." *Review of Constitutional Studies* 6:2 (2002), 179–212.
Pocock, J. G. A. *The Machiavellian Moment* (Princeton: Princeton University Press, 2003).
Postell, Joseph. "Regulation during the American Founding: Achieving Liberalism and Republicanism." *American Political Thought* 5 (2016), 80–108.
Praeg, Leonhard. *A Report on Ubuntu* (Pietermaritzburg: University of KwaZulu-Natal Press, 2014).
Preuss, Ulrich. "The German *Drittwirkung* Doctrine and Its Socio-political Background." In András Sajó and Renáta Uitz (eds.), *The Constitution in Private Relations* (Utrecht: Eleven, 2005), 23–32.
Quint, Peter. "Free Speech and Private Law in German Constitutional Theory." *Maryland Law Review* 48:2 (1989), 247–349.
Quong, Jonathan. "The Argument from Autonomy." In Jonathan Quong (ed.), *Liberalism without Perfection* (Oxford: Oxford University Press, 2010), 45–72.
Radbruch, Gustav. *Einführung in die Rechtswissenschaft*. Edited by Konrad Zweigert (Stuttgart: Koehler, 1980).
Raj, Thulasi K. "Private Discrimination, Public Service and the Constitution." *Indian Law Review* 6:1 (2022), 17–36.
Rajagopalan, Shruti. "Constitutional Change: A Public Choice Analysis." In Sujit Choudhry, Madhav Khosla, and Pratap Bhanu Mehta (eds.), *The Oxford Handbook of the Indian Constitution* (Oxford: Oxford University Press, 2016), 127–142.
Ramgotra, Manjeet. "India's Republican Moment." In Udit Bhatia (ed.), *The Indian Constituent Assembly: Deliberations on Democracy* (New York: Routledge, 2018), 196–223.
Rao, Shiva. *The Framing of India's Constitution: Selected Documents, Vols. II and V* (Bombay: N. M. Tripathi, 1966).
Rawls, John. *A Theory of Justice* (Cambridge, MA: Harvard University Press, 1971).
Raz, Joseph. *The Morality of Freedom* (Oxford: Oxford University Press, 1986).
Richards, David A.J. "Kantian Ethics and the Harm Principle: A Reply to John Finnis." *Columbia Law Review* 87:3 (1987), 457–471.

Robertson, David. "Thick Constitutional Readings: When Classical Distinctions Are Irrelevant." *Georgia Journal of International and Comparative Law* 35 (2007), 277–331.

Robinson, Nick. "Expanding Judiciaries: India and the Rise of the Good Governance Court." *Washington University Global Studies Law Review* 8:1 (2009), 1–69.

Rodley, Nigel. "Can Armed Opposition Groups Violate Human Rights?" In K. Mahoney and P. Mahoney (eds.), *Human Rights in the Twenty-First Century: A Global Challenge* (Dordrecht: Martinus Nijhoff, 1993), 297–318.

Rosenblatt, Helena. *The Lost History of Liberalism: From Ancient Rome to the Twenty-First Century* (Princeton: Princeton University Press, 2018).

Rosenfeld, Michel. "The European Treaty: Constitution and Constitutional Identity – A View from America." *International Journal of Constitutional Law* 3 (2005), 316–331.

Rostow, Eugene. "The Democratic Character of Judicial Review." *Harvard Law Review* 66:2 (1952), 193–224.

Rousseau, Jean-Jacques. *Émile*. Translated by Allan Bloom (New York: Basic Books, 1979).

The Social Contract. Translated by Donald A. Cress (Indianapolis: Hackett, 2011).

Roux, Theunis. "The Dignity of Comparative Constitutional Law." *Acta Juridica* 1 (2008), 185–203.

The Politics of Principle (Cambridge: Cambridge University Press, 2013).

Sachs, Albie. "The Judicial Enforcement of Socio-economic Rights: The *Grootboom* Case." In András Sajó and Renáta Uitz (eds.), *The Constitution in Private Relations* (Utrecht: Eleven, 2005), 79–98.

The Strange Alchemy of Life and Law (Oxford: Oxford University Press, 2009).

Sadurski, Wojciech. "Joseph Raz on Liberal Neutrality and the Harm Principle." *Oxford Journal of Legal Studies* 10:1 (1990), 122–133.

Sager, Lawrence. *Justice in Plainclothes* (New Haven: Yale University Press, 2006).

Scheppele, Kim Lane. "Constitutional Ethnography." *Law and Society Review* 38:3 (2004), 389–406.

Schmidt, Christopher. "On Doctrinal Confusion: The Case of the State Action Doctrine." *BYU Law Review* (2016), 575–628.

The Sit-Ins: Protest and Legal Change in the Civil Rights Era (Chicago: Chicago University Press, 2018).

"The Sit-Ins and the State Action Doctrine." *William and Mary Bill of Rights Journal* 18 (2010), 767–829.

Schmitt, Gary, and Robert Webking. "Revolutionaries, Antifederalists, and Federalists: Comments on Gordon Wood's Understanding of the American Founding." *Political Science Reviewer* 9 (1979), 195–229.

Seidman, Louis, and Mark Tushnet. "The State Action Paradox." In *Remnants of Belief: Contemporary Constitutional Issues* (Oxford: Oxford University Press, 1996), 49–71.

Shalhope, Robert E. "Toward a Republican Synthesis." *William and Mary Quarterly* 29:1 (1972), 49–80.

Shue, Henry. *Basic Rights: Subsistence, Affluence and US Foreign Policy* (Princeton: Princeton University Press, 1996).

Shumer, S. M. "Machiavelli: Republican Politics and Its Corruption." *Political Theory* 7:1 (1979), 5–34.

Siegel, Reva B. "Equality Talk: Antisubordination and Anticlassification Values in Constitutional Struggles over Brown." *Harvard Law Review* 117 (2004), 1470–1547.

Singh, Mahendra. "India: Protection of Human Rights against State and Non-state Action." In Dawn Oliver and Jorg Fedtke (eds.), *Human Rights in the Private Sphere* (Abingdon: Routledge-Cavendish, 2007), 180–212.

Sitapati, Vinay. "Reservations." In Sujit Choudhry, Madhav Khosla, and Pratap Bhanu Mehta (eds.), *The Oxford Handbook of the Indian Constitution* (Oxford: Oxford University Press, 2016), 720–741.

Skinner, Quentin. "The Idea of Negative Liberty." In Richard Rorty, Jerome B Schneewind, and Quentin Skinner (eds.), *Philosophy in History* (Cambridge: Cambridge University Press, 1984), 193–222.

"The Paradoxes of Political Liberty." In Sterling McMurrin (ed.), *The Tanner Lectures on Human Values* (Cambridge: Cambridge University Press, 1985), 227–250.

Skwyiya, Zola, and ANC Constitutional Committee. "A Bill of Rights for a New South Africa: A Working Document by the ANC Constitutional Committee." *African Journal of International and Comparative Law* 3 (1991), 601–607.

Smith, Rogers. *Civic Ideals* (New Haven: Yale University Press, 1999).

Sommeregger, Georg. "The Horizontalization of Equality: The German Attempt to Promote Non-discrimination in the Private Sphere via Legislation." In András Sajó and Renáta Uitz (eds.), *The Constitution in Private Relations* (Utrecht: Eleven, 2005), 33–53.

Spitz, Richard, and Matthews Chaskalson. *The Politics of Transition: A Hidden History of South Africa's Negotiated Settlement* (Oxford: Hart, 2000).

Stone Sweet, Alec. "The Juridical Coup d'État and the Problem of Authority." *German Law Journal* 8:10 (2007), 915–927.

Stone Sweet, Alec, and Kathleen Stranz. "Rights Adjudication and Constitutional Pluralism in Germany and Europe." *Journal of European Public Policy* 19:1 (2012), 92–108.

Stopler, Gila. "The Personal Is Political: The Feminist Critique of Liberalism and the Challenge of Right-Wing Populism." *International Journal of Constitutional Law* 19:2 (2021), 393–402.

Storing, Herbert. "Slavery and the Moral Foundations of the American Republic." In Joseph Bessette (ed.), *Toward a More Perfect Union* (Washington, DC: American Enterprise Institute, 1995).
  What the Antifederalists Were For (Chicago: Chicago University Press, 1981).
Sunstein, Cass. "The Anticaste Principle." *Michigan Law Review* 92:8 (1994), 2410–2455.
  "Beyond the Republican Revival." *Yale Law Journal* 97:8 (1988), 1539–1590.
  One Case at a Time: Judicial Minimalism on the Supreme Court (Cambridge, MA: Harvard University Press, 2001).
Thomas, George. *The Founders and the Idea of a National University* (Cambridge: Cambridge University Press, 2014).
Thomas, Jean. *Public Rights, Private Relations* (Oxford: Oxford University Press, 2015).
Tomkins, Adam. *Our Republican Constitution* (Portland: Hart, 2005).
Tripathi, P. K. "Perspectives on the American Constitutional Influence on the Constitution of India." In Lawrence Beer (ed.), *Constitutionalism in Asia: Asian Views of the American Influence* (Baltimore: University of Maryland School of Law, 1988), 56–98.
Tushnet, Mark. "The Issue of State Action/Horizontal Effect in Comparative Constitutional Law." *International Journal of Constitutional Law* 1 (2003), 79–98.
  Red, White, and Blue: A Critical Analysis of Constitutional Law (Lawrence: Kansas University Press, 2015).
  Taking the Constitution away from the Courts (Princeton: Princeton University Press, 2000).
  Weak Courts, Strong Rights: Judicial Review and Social Welfare Rights in Comparative Constitutional Law (Princeton: Princeton University Press, 2008).
Uitz, Renáta. "Introduction." In András Sajó and Renáta Uitz (eds.), *The Constitution in Private Relations* (Utrecht: Eleven, 2005).
Van der Walt, Johan. *The Horizontal Effect Revolution and the Question of Sovereignty* (Berlin: De Gruyter, 2014).
van Dijk, Pieter, Fried van Hoof, Arjen van Rijn, and Leo Zwaak (eds.). *Theory and Practice of the European Convention of Human Rights*, 5th ed. (Cambridge: Intersentia, 2018).
Vanberg, Georg. *The Politics of Constitutional Review in Germany* (Cambridge: Cambridge University Press, 2005).
Viroli, Maurizio. *For Love of Country* (Oxford: Oxford University Press, 1995).
  "Which Patriotism for Europe?" *Eutopia Magazine*, August 5, 2014.
Watson, Alan. *The Making of the Civil Law* (Cambridge, MA: Harvard University Press, 1981).

Webster, McKenzie. "The Warren Court's Struggle with the Sit-In Cases and the Constitutionality of Segregation in Places of Public Accommodations." *Journal of Law and Politics* 17 (2001), 373–408.
Wechsler, Herbert. "Toward Neutral Principles of Constitutional Law." *Harvard Law Review* 73:1 (1959), 1–35.
Wieacker, Franz. *Privatrechtsgeschichte der Neuzeit*, 2nd ed. (Göttinggen: Vandenhoeck & Ruprecht, 1967).
Wood, Gordon. *The Creation of the American Republic* (Chapel Hill: North Carolina University Press, 1998).
 Empire of Liberty (Oxford: Oxford University Press, 2011).
Woodward-Burns, Robinson. *Hidden Laws: How State Constitutions Stabilize American Politics* (New Haven: Yale University Press, 2021).
Woolman, Stuart. "The Amazing Vanishing Bill of Rights." *South African Law Journal* 127 (2007), 762–794.
Woolman, Stuart, and Dennis Davis. "The Last Laugh: *Du Plessis v. De Klerk*, Classical Liberalism, Creole Liberalism and the Application of Fundamental Rights under the Interim and the Final Constitutions." *South African Journal on Human Rights* 12 (1996), 361–404.
Wrase, Michael. "Anti-discrimination Law and Legal Culture in Germany." In Barbara Havelková and Mathias Möschel (eds.), *Anti-discrimination Law in Civil Law Jurisdictions* (Oxford: Oxford University Press, 2019), 136–154.
Zackin, Emily. *Looking for Rights in All the Wrong Places: Why State Constitutions Contain America's Positive Rights* (Princeton: Princeton University Press, 2013).
Zitzke, Emile. "A Decolonial Critique of Private Law and Human Rights." *South African Journal on Human Rights* 34:3 (2018), 492–516.
Zuckert, Michael. *Natural Rights and the New Republicanism* (Princeton: Princeton University Press, 1994).
Zweigert, K., and H. Kotz. *An Introduction to Comparative Law*. Translated by Tony Weir (Oxford: Oxford University Press, 1987).

INDEX

AB v. Pridwin Preparatory School
  (2020), 194, 236–239
Ackermann, Justice Laurie, 146,
  173–174, 210, 217, 221
African National Congress (South
  Africa), 188, 190, 194–196, 200
African-Americans
  disenfranchisement of, 16–19
Afrikaaner ethnic nationalist party.
  See National Party (South Africa)
AGG (General Equal Treatment Act)
  (Germany), 163–184
Alexy, Robert, 4
Ambedkar, B. R., 101, 103, 107–108
American federalism, 65
American rights tradition, 93
ANC (African National Congress),
  188, 190, 194–196, 198, 200
antidiscrimination, 9, 13–15. *See also*
  caste system; equality and
  antidiscrimination; racism
Anti-Discrimination Act (ADG),
  175–181
Apartheid
  -era articulations of rights, 187, 201,
    240
  housing policy legacy,
    225–226
  inequalities in education under,
    230–232
  post-Apartheid horizontality,
    188–189
  post-Apartheid inequalities,
    210–211
  post-Apartheid societal
    transformation, 188–189
  privatization of, 199

Aristotle
  authentic freedom, 27–28
  common good in, 32–36
  on civic friendship bonds, 36–37
  virtue, 33
Austin, Granville, 102–103
autonomy, 28–30, 146, 234–235, 244

Balkin, Jack, 37–38
Barak, Aharon, 154–155
Barkhuizen v. Napier (2007), 236–239
Baron v. Claytile Ltd (2017), 235–236
Basic Law (Germany, 1949), 3–4,
  42–44, 148–154, 156–158,
  164–168, 170–171, 210–213,
  221–222
  contrasted with South African Final
    Constitution, 210–213, 215
Bauer, et al. case, 268
*Beadica and Others v. Trustees of
  Oregon Trust* (2020), 238–239
Bell v. Maryland (1964), 79–80, 82–83
Bellamy, Richard, 36, 52–54
Bhagwati, Justice P.N., 116, 118
Bhatia, Gautam, 117, 136–137
Big Tech, 10, 272–273
Bill of Rights for a New South Africa
  (1991), 195–196, 203–205
Black, Justice Hugo, 79–80, 83, 108
Blinkfüer case, 169
Blue Moonlight Properties case (2011),
  194, 229–230
Bommai, S. R. v. Union of India (1994),
  127–128
Bradley, Justice Joseph, 67–69, 76, 83,
  108
Brandwein, Pamela, 69

295

296 INDEX

Brennan, Jr., Justice William J., 80, 83
Brown v. Board of Education (1954), 80, 236
Brugger, Winfried, 148–149

Carmichele v. Minister of Safety and Security, 216–217
caste system. See also equality and antidiscrimination; racism
　American, 9, 19, 60–61
　Fourteenth Amendment (US) and, 66
　Indian, 60–61, 101, 108–109, 112–113, 129–131
　religion and, 133–134
　republicanism and, 38
Centrist Republicans, 61, 67, 69
Chandrachud, Justice Dhananjaya, 137
Charter of Fundamental Rights (European Union), 243, 245–247, 262, 268–269
Cheadle, Halton, 199–201, 214–215
Cicero, 27–28, 35, 37
City of Johannesburg v. Blue Moonlight Properties (2011), 194, 229–230
civic education, 35–36
　Civil Code (Germany), 151–154, 156–157, 161, 164–169, 209
civil rights (US)
　Civil Rights Cases of 1883, 64, 67–74, 79, 83
　Civil Rights Act (1964) and, 84
　Civil Rights Act of 1875, 66–67
　Civil Rights Act of 1964, 64, 79, 83–86, 140
　Civil Rights Acts of 1866 and 1875, 107–108
　Civil Rights Movement, 80–81
　public/private divide and, 86–87
　Title II (Civil Rights Act), 84–85
Civil War Amendments (US)
　commitment to equality and, 66, 75
　racial equality and, 71–73
　Supreme Court interpretation of, 67
　transformative constitutional potential of, 99–100
Commerce Clause (US Constitution), 83–85

common good
　about, 22–23
　Aristotle on, 32–36
　as baseline for parity and duties, 8, 34, 144, 176–177, 256
　community and, 28–30
　constitutional rights and, 32, 43–44
　in early American political thought, 30
　European Union and, 253, 256
　Interim Constitution (South Africa) and, 200–201
　Machiavelli and, 34
　in Modderklip case (2005), 226–229
　nondomination and, 39–40
　religion and, 134
　shared ends and, 6, 31–32, 95–96
common law (background), 11
common law (South Africa)
　in Carmichele v. Minister of Safety and Security, 216
　Constitutional Court and, 209–210
　constitutional duties under, 216–217, 219–220, 235–236
　constitutional principles applied to, 202, 204–205, 222–242
　duty to provide housing and, 235–236
　Final Constitution, horizontality and, 214
　limits on constitutional duties, 146, 205–206, 222–235
　rule of defamation in, 91, 218–220
　socio-economic rights and, 228
common law (United States)
　constitutional principles applied to, 93–97
　Harlan's dissent in Civil Rights Cases and, 69–71
　rule of defamation in, 65, 91–92
community, 21–22, 31–32
Constitution Act of 1951 (India), 113
Constitutional Court (Germany). See Federal Constitutional Court (FCC) (Germany)
Constitutional Court (South Africa), 208–210, 213

constitutional duties, 23–24
  explained, 2
  horizontal application and, 47–51
constitutional patriotism (European Union), 252–254
constitutional rights
  Stadium Ban case (2008), 181–182
  about horizontal application of, 4, 11, 19, 32, 246, 271–272
  common good and, 32, 43–44
  in Germany, 43–44, 156–157, 161–162, 173
  in Germany and South Africa contrasted, 145, 217
  horizontal application in India, 107, 115–117, 123, 126
  horizontal application in South Africa, 201–202, 205–206, 218–219, 236–237
  in India and United States contrasted, 61, 65–66, 120, 143
  in *Lüth* decision (1958), 169
  Pruneyard Shopping Center v. Robins (1980), 94–95
  public/private boundaries and, 17
  public commitments and, 21–22
  of the state, 94–95
  state action doctrine, racism and, 73–74
  traditional model of, 1
  in United States, 85, 87
constitutionalism. *See also* constitutional projects
  "thin" and "thick", 208
  about, 3
  American, 3–6, 64, 93, 99–100
  American and Indian contrasted, 121–122, 140–141
  Basic Structure Doctrine (India) and, 113–114
  common good and, 42–44
  commonwealth model of, 277
  German, 148–149, 154, 156, 167–168
  German and South African contrasted, 147, 210–213, 222–242
  global, 3–4
  horizontality as republican vein, 7–8, 16–25, 41, 55–57

horizontality in liberal, 7–8, 13, 15
  Indian, 104–105, 111–112, 118, 126–128
  Irish, 271–272
  postwar German, 44
  public/private divide and, 89–90
  republican, 271–272
  Shelley v. Kraemer (1948), 4–5, 74–79, 127–128
  South Africa, 186–187, 190, 215–223, 240
  subnational *res publica* and, 93–94
  total, 5
  traditional accounts of, 1, 10, 64, 73–74
  ubuntu and, 192–194
  vertical versus horizontal model, 8
contracts, 235–239
Corbett, Chief Justice Michael, 199–201
Costa case, 201
Court of Justice. *See* European Court of Justice (ECJ)
COVID-19 pandemic, 10
Critical Legal Studies movement, 17–18

Daly, Eoin, 33–34, 38–39, 276
Daniels v. Scribante (2017), 14, 45–50
Davis, Dennis, 206, 208, 210–212
De Klerk, Gert, 204
decolonization (South Africa), 190
Defrenne v. Sabena (1976), 261–262
Delhi Act of 2007 (India), 131–133
DeShaney v. Winnebago County (1989), 87–90, 119–121, 216
Devlin, John, 96
  dignity, 218–219
Dinan, John, 93
discrimination. *See* caste system; civil rights; equality and antidiscrimination; racism
Douglas, Justice William O., 79, 85
Drittwirkung, 3–4, 212, 222–242
Du Plessis v. De Klerk, 201, 203–210, 212, 219, 237
Dürig, Günter, 165, 174
duties of citizens, 6, 19–21

duties of private actors
  enforceability of, 61–62
  Fourteenth Amendment (US) and, 63
  horizontal application discourse and, 13–14
  indirect horizontal application and, 11–13
  New York Times v. Sullivan (1964), 92
  in public projects, 47–51
  public/private divide and, 8–10, 86–87
  shared ends and, 6, 226–229
  in South African constitutional project, 219–221, 230–232
  subnational *res publica* and, 93–94
duty
  about, 256–257
  American "rightsist" culture and, 19–20, 24, 57
  authoritarian regimes and, 7
  citizen, 120–121
  civic, 47
  common good and, 32–40
  constitutional debate about, 61
  constitutional duties (European Union), 243–245
  constitutional duties (Germany), 168, 182
  constitutional duties (South Africa), 189, 195, 213–214
  constitutional rights and, 1–2
  COVID-19 pandemic and, 273
  equality and, 40–41
  European "public thing" and, 245, 256–257, 265, 267–269
  freedom as nondomination and, 40–42, 47
  horizontal application of public commitments and, 47–51, 256–257
  horizontal application of rights and, 14, 20–21, 47–51, 117–118, 139
  liberal political thought about, 31
  new republican elements in constitutionalism and, 25
  parity effected by horizontal application and, 8, 22–25, 42, 275
  positive rights applied horizontally, 232
  to provide adequate housing (South Africa), 122–128, 225–226, 228–230, 235
  to provide basic education (South Africa), 236
  republican political thought about, 2, 7–8, 21, 31–38
  socio-economic rights applied horizontally (South Africa), 233
  vertical model of, 1, 19–21, 275
duty to protect
  in Germany, 154–155, 158
  in India, 118–122, 216–217
  in United States, 121–122
  United States and India contrasted, 121
  state's duty, 88, 119–122

ECJ (European Court of Justice), 250, 255, 257, 261, 263
education
  Brown v. Board of Education (1954), 80, 236
  civic, 35–36
  duty to provide (South Africa), 236
  horizontal application of right to, 189–190, 223
  inequalities under Apartheid, 230–232
  reservations in education (India), 127–131, 133
  right to (India), 47–48, 126–127
  right to (South Africa), 230–232
Eisenhower, Dwight, 80–81
Elizabeth Port Municipality case (2004), 192–193, 227
Equal Protection Clause (US), 82. *See also* Fourteenth Amendment (US)
equality
  Commerce Clause (US Constitution) and, 83–85
  public/private divide and, 65, 81–86
Equality Act (2000) (South Africa), 222–239

INDEX 299

equality and antidiscrimination
  Civil Rights Cases of 1883 (US), 67–74
  broadening state action and, 75–79
  Civil Rights Act (1964) (US) and, 84
  discrimination in *Shelly* and *Zoroastrian Cooperative* compared, 122–128
  in Germany, 149–150, 175–178, 180–181
  horizontal application in India and United States and, 60–62, 130–133
  horizontal application of provisions, 13–14
  in India, 62, 112–113
  Indian Supreme Court commitments to, 141
  republicanism and, 38
  rights in India, 99–100
European Convention of Human Rights, 257
European Court of Human Rights (ECtHR), 257–258
European Court of Justice (ECJ), 243, 250, 255, 257–258, 261–265
European Economic Community (EEC) Treaty, 259–260
European Union, 97–98
  common good and, 97–98
  horizontal direct effect, 260–270
  Van Gend en Loos case (1963), 250, 256, 259–260
  civic identity of, 251
  direct effect and, 259–260
  horizontality and, 10, 258–269
  political identity of, 250–251
  public/private divide in, 246
  republican aspirations and, 246–251
  republican politics and citizenship in, 252–254
  sovereignty issues, 255–256
  supranational integration of, 249–251
  types of law, 262

Federal Constitutional Court (FCC) (Germany), 149–150, 173, 221–242, 250, 268–269, 272

federal structure of United States, 97
Fedtke, Jorg, 156, 170–171
Fifteenth Amendment (US), 66
Final Constitution (South Africa)
  Bill of Rights and, 195–196, 203–205, 213–214
  contrasted with German Basic Law, 210–213
  direct horizontal application of, 211–214
  right to equality in, 213–215
Finn, Meghan, 237
Flume, Werner, 172
Fourteenth Amendment (US), 59–60, 63, 66, 68–69, 82–83
Frantziou, Eleni, 5, 265–268
fraternity, 106–108, 117, 139, 141
freedom
  in Aristotle, 27–28
  labor-republican view of, 117
  neorepublican concepts of, 41–42
  as nondomination, 33–34, 39–40, 47, 234–235
  as noninterference, 13, 234–235
  in Rousseau, Jean-Jacques, 41
freedom of expression
  background, 16
  in Germany, 14, 43, 45, 160–161, 164, 167–169, 171, 179–180, 184
  horizontal application of rights and, 19
  in India, 14, 204, 218–219
  in United States, 207
Friedman, Nick, 144, 188–189

Galanter, Marc, 103, 139–140
Galston, William, 23–24
Gardbaum, Stephen, 5, 119, 277
Garner v. Louisiana (1961), 79
General Equal Treatment Act (AGG), 163–184
general interest, *See* common good
general will, 34–35, 41–42
German Constitutional Court, 149–150, 173, 221–242, 250, 268–269, 272

Germany
  Blinkfüer case, 169
  Lüth case (1958), 42–44, 163–185, 188, 202, 209, 212
  Mangold case (2005), 180
  Mephisto case (1971), 168–169
  Soraya case (1973), 169–170
  Stadium Ban case (2018), 13–14, 181–184
  Basic Law. *See* Basic Law (Germany, 1949)
  common good, 155–156
  equality in private sphere, 173–181
  Federal Labor Court, 158–159, 161–163
  horizontal application discourse, 144–146, 157–163, 179–180
  horizontal application in, 9, 13–14, 143–144, 147–151, 170–173
  horizontal application of personality rights, 160–161
  horizontal effect of constitutional rights, 161–163
  horizontality in new constitution, 157–163, 171–173
  human dignity, constitutional commitment to, 154–157
  identity of new constitution, 159–160
  indirect horizontal application, 145
  public law, scope of, 151–153
  public priorities survey, 171
  rights-centric discourse, 167–168
  Weimar Constitution, 152–153
Glendon, Mary Ann, 19–21, 24, 121
Goldberg, Justice Arthur, 79, 85
Greene, Jamal, 19–21
Grootboom case (2005), 224–226
Grovey v. Townsend (1935), 17–18

Habermas, Jürgen, 251–254
Hailbronner, Michaela, 221–222
Hale, Robert, 17–18
Harlan II, Justice John Marshall, 79–80, 82
Harlan, Justice John Marshall, 64, 69–73, 80–81, 99
Harms, Justice Louis, 226
Hartz, Louis, 149

Heart of Atlanta Motel v. United States (1964), 84–85
Henkin, Louis, 77–78
Hershkoff, Helen, 93–98, 228–229
Hickey, Tom, 33–34, 38–39, 53–54, 276
Hobbes, Thomas, 26–27
Holomisa, Bantu, 218–220
Honohan, Iseault, 36
horizontal application
  by Indian Supreme Court, 115–119
  in common law, 235–236
  concepts of freedom and, 41–42
  direct, 11–13, 116, 119, 158–162, 168–169, 201–202, 211, 238–239, 261
  New York Times v. Sullivan (1964), 91–92
  of transformational values, 222–242
  political dimensions of, 57–58
  reach of constitutional rights, 4
  republican interpretations of (South Africa), 191–192
  republican potential of, 59–62
horizontal application of constitution
  Final Constitution (South Africa), 203–210
  German constitutional principles and, 189–190
  republican themes in (US and India), 59–62, 140
horizontal application of equality rights, 263–268, *See also* duty
  Anti-Discrimination Act (Germany) and, 175–177, 179–180
  as constitutional morality, 144
  commitment to, 143–147, 172–173
  constitutional duties (Germany), 178
  Defrenne v. Sabena (1976), 261–263
  European Union directives and, 185–186
  in Final Constitution (South Africa), 213–215
  in Germany, 150–151, 174–175, 179–180, 189–190, 211–212
  in India and United States, 130–133
  private sphere and, 146, 173–181
  republican themes in (Germany and South Africa), 189–190

republican themes in (US and India) and, 59–62, 140, 163–181
waning support for (Germany), 186
horizontal application of European Union law. *See* European Union
horizontal application of rights
  about, 1–2, 6, 272–274
  constitutional politics and, 21
  constitutional practice and, 8–10
  European Union and, 243–246
  international increase of, 4–5
  judicial power and, 25
  limitations analysis and, 20
  limits on constitutional duties, 235–237
  pros and cons of, 24–25
  prospects for, 274–276
  republican elements in, 20–21, 234–235
  Shelley v. Kraemer (1948), 4–5, 74–79, 127–128
  shift from vertical to, 4
horizontal effect. *See* horizontal application of rights
horizontal versus vertical rights paradigm, 16, 19–21, 278
horizontality,
  European Union and, 97
  in Germany, 9, 13–14, 143–144, 147–151, 170–173. *See also* Germany
  in India, 9–10, 143. *See also* Indian Supreme Court
  international instantiations of, 9
  rights-centrism and, 7, 90
  in United States, 9, 44–47, 60–62, 97–98, 130–133
housing policy (South Africa), 122–128, 225–230, 235–236
How Rights Went Wrong (Greene), 19–21
Howard, Jacob, 66
Human Rights Act (UK), 5

inaction. *See* state inaction
India
  Emergency Era (1975-1977), 115
  Hindu nationalism versus secularism and equality, 102

Indian Constituent Assembly, 62
Indian Constitution
  about, 101
  anti-exclusion principle, 101, 136–137
  Basic Structure Doctrine and, 113–114, 130
  Constitution Act of 1951, 113
  Delhi Act of 2007, 131–133
  Directive Principles and, 61–62, 102–103, 112–114, 128–131, 139–140
  duties of citizens in, 101
  horizontal application and, 9–10, 59–60, 99–100, 104–105, 114–115, 118–119, 128–141, 150
  Indian Young Lawyers' Association v. State of Kerala (2018), 135
  influence of US Constitution on, 61–62, 107–108
  Koushal v. Naz Foundation (2013), 137–138
  minimal secularism standard, 137
  Navtej Singh Johar and Others v. Union of India (2018), 137–138
  Naz Foundation v. Union of India (2009), 137–140
  nondiscrimination clauses in, 108–111
  private actors and, 101
  public discourses and constitutional line compared, 103–104
  ratification, deliberations preceding, 106–111
  religion and horizontal rights, 133–140
  Saifuddin v. State of Bombay (1962), 137
  same-sex couples, rights of, 137–140
  scope of, 102–103
  state's duty to protect, 118–122, 216–217, *See also* duty to protect
  Subcommittee on Fundamental Rights, 108–109
  traditional rights versus social revolution in, 102–103
  transformative versus conservative constitutional discourses, 105–106
Indian Medical Association v. Union of India, 127–130

Indian Supreme Court
  early conservatism, 111–115
  horizontal application by, 115–117
  indirect horizontal application by, 116
  public/private divide in, 111–112
  Indian Young Lawyers' Association v. State of Kerala (2018), 135
indirect horizontal application, 5, 11–13
  by Indian Supreme Court, 116
  in Germany, 145
  New York Times Co. v. Sullivan (1964), 90–92
  People's Union for Democratic Rights v. Union of India (1982), 117–119
  socio-economic rights and, 95–96
indirect third-party effect, 3–4
individual rights, 30–32
Inkatha Freedom Party (South Africa), 199
insulated private actors, 3, 99, 101, 150, 236–237, 240, 246
interconnectedness of public/private enterprise, 14–15
Interim Constitution (South Africa)
  common good and, 200–201
  constitutional commitments of, 216–217
  evolution of, 196–204
  state action doctrine and, 201–202
International Transport Workers' Federation and Finnish Seamen's Union v. Viking Line ABP and OÜ Viking Line Eesti (2007), 263–268

Jacobsohn, Gary, 277
  on *DeShaney v. Winnebago County* (1989), 87–90, 119–121, 216
  on horizontal application in India, 133, 150
  on Indian Constitution, 104, 113, 128
  on Indian independence, 102
  on public/private divide, 277–278
Jafta, Justice Chris, 239–240
Jefferson, Thomas, 2–3
judicial decision-making, horizontal application and, 50–51, 54–55, 221–222
Juma Musjid case (2011), 230–232

Kalyvas, Andreas, 6, 26, 56
Katzenbach v. McClung (1964), 84–85
Katznelson, Ira, 6, 26, 56
Kennedy, John F., 80–81
Kentridge, Justice Sydney, 205, 208
Kesavananda Bharati v. State of Kerala, 113–114
Khaitan, Tarunabh, 137–138
Khumalo and Others v. Holomisa, 218–221, 223, 231
King v. De Jager, 222–239
Koushal v. Naz Foundation (2013), 137
Kriegler, Justice Johann, 207–208
Krishnaswamy, Sudhir, 111–112, 116–117, 120–121
Kumm, Mattias, 5–6

Laborde, Cecile, 28, 137
Langa, Justice Pius, 227
Legal Realists, 17–18
Liberal Beginnings: Making a Republic for the Moderns (Kalyvas and Katznelson), 56
liberal constitutionalism, 4
  horizontal application and, 20–24, 55–57
  Kalyvas and Katznelson on, 56
liberal tradition, 16, 21, 25–32
liberalism, perfectionist, 28–30
Liebenberg, Sandra, 235
Lisbon Treaty case (2009), 250
Locke, John, 26–27
Lüth case (1958), 42–44, 163–185, 188, 202, 209, 212, 255–256

Maas, Willem, 250
Macedo, Stephen, 23–24
Machiavelli, 34
Madison, James, 39
Madlanga, Justice Mbuyiseli, 221
Manhattan Community Access Corp v. Halleck (2019), 18–19
Marsh v. Alabama (1946), 77
Marshall, Justice John, 96–97, 277
Masiya v. Director of Public Prosecutions (2007), 220–221

Mathews, Jud, 57, 162, 171, 173, 221–222
Maynor, John, 28
McCulloch v. Maryland (1819), 96–97
Mehta, M. C. v. State of Tamil Nadu (1996), 48
Mhlantla, Justice Nonkosi, 239–240
Michelman, Frank, 51–52, 145, 188, 209
Miller, David, 251–254
Modderklip Boerdery (Pty) Ltd. v. Modder East Squatters & Anor. (2001), 226–229
Modderklip case (2005), 193–194
Modiri, Joel, 190
Mokgoro, Justice J., 192
Moseneke, Justice Dikgang, 221

National Party (South Africa), 188. *See also* Interim Constitution (South Africa)
Navtej Singh Johar and Others v. Union of India (2018), 137–138
Naz Foundation v. Union of India (2009), 137
Nehru, Jawaharlal, 101–103, 106, 128
neighbourliness, 223–224, 227
neorepublicanism, 2
New York Times Co. v. Sullivan (1964), 65, 90–92
Nipperdey, Hans Carl, 158–163
Nolan, Aoife, 231–232

O'Regan, Justice Kate, 218–219
objective rights, 4, 45, 155–156
On Duties (Cicero), 35

parity effected by horizontal application
 about/defined, 22
 common good and, 8, 34, 144, 176–177, 256
 constitutional actors and, 150, 215
 duty and, 23–24, 42
 European Union and, 243–244, 246, 256, 269
 German law and, 157–158, 172
 new German constitutional order and, 23

between private behavior and constitutional values, 19, 162, 171–172, 176–178, 188, 211
 in public and private spaces, 8–10, 15, 51, 156
 of rights and, 42–47
 republican features of, 24–25, 42–47, 56, 148, 243–244, 246, 271
 scope of, 215, 222–242, 275
Patel, Sardar Vallabhbhai, 109
People's Union for Democratic Rights v. Union of India (1982), 115–118
Pettit, Philip, 28, 33–34, 38–42, 47, 152
politeia, 35
The Politics (Aristotle), 28
Polybius, 27–28
Port Elizabeth Municipality v. Various Occupiers (2004), 192–193, 227
Praeg, Leonhard, 192
President of South Africa v. Modderklip (2005), 193–194, 226–229
Preuss, Ulrich, 43–44
private law doctrine, 94–95
private spaces, adjudication of, 20–21, 94–95, 101. *See also* insulated private actors
Pruneyard Shopping Center v. Robins (1980), 93–94
public interest. *See* common good
public projects, 14–15, 19, 47, 137
"public thing", 22, 34–35, 44, 256–257, 260–261, 265, 269, 278. *See also res publica*
public/private divide,
 "white primary" cases (US), 16–19
 constitutional law and, 86–90
 equality and, 81–86
 in European Union, 246
 in Germany, 151–153, 162–163, 176
 homogenization and, 277
 horizontal application and, 18–21, 246
 preservation of, 63–65, 73–75, 83, 86–87, 90, 121
 state action doctrine and, 63–65, 73–75, 83, 86–87, 90, 92–94, 99, 121
 subnational narrowing of, 93–94

public/private divide (cont.)
  in United States, 61–64, 74–75, 86–87, 92
  in United States and India contrasted, 61–62

Quint, Peter, 149, 152, 158, 160

racism. *See also* caste system; civil rights; equality and antidiscrimination
  American, 7, 9, 19, 57–58
  Indian, 57–58
Radical Republicans, 61, 67, 69, 99, 103–104
Rawls, John, 28
Raz, Joseph, 24, 28–30
religious conflict, 62, 127–128, 133–137
republican constitutionalism, 276
republican interpretation of horizontality
  about, 2, 6
  application of equality rights, 59–62, 140, 163–181
  authoritarian regimes and, 7
  consideration in applicaton of, 10–12
  discourse about, 7–9, 15, 42, 163–184
  illiberal society and, 6
  liberal constitutionalism and, 7–8
  normative assessments of, 7
republican political theory
  about, 2, 7–8, 32–34
  constitutional politics and, 15
  European Union in, 246–251, 256
  horizontal application and, 22, 59–62
republicanism
  as corrective to liberalism and, 56–57
  civic, 21, 24, 31
  egalitarian, 37–38
  horizontal application in South African constitutionalism and, 215–216
  horizontal application of rights and, 10, 22–24
res publica. *See also* "public thing"
  American, 71, 93–94
  European, 245, 265, 267–269
  in Cicero, 35

Right to Be Forgotten cases, 268–269
right to property, 226–230
rights relationships, 18–19, 22
rights-centrism
  American constitutionalism and, 95, 99–100
  horizontal shift and, 2–6, 99
  horizontality contrasted with, 7, 90
Robertson, David, 205, 207–208
Rosenfeld, Michel, 249–250
Rousseau, Jean-Jacques, 34–35, 41
Roux, Theunis, 220
Roznai, Yaniv, 102, 104, 113, 128

Sachs, Justice Albie, 192–193, 198–199, 207–208, 221, 224, 227
Saifuddin v. State of Bombay (1962), 137
Scheppele, Kim Lane, 9, 59
Schmidt, Christopher, 79–80, 84
Schmitt, Gary, 30–32
Shah, K. T., 106–107
Shamdasani, PD v. Central Bank of India (1952), 111
Shelley v. Kraemer (1948), 4–5, 74–79, 127–128
Sinha, Chief Justice Bhuvaneshwar Prasad, 137
slavery. *See also* Thirteenth Amendment (US)
Smith v. Allwright (1944), 17
social contract, 34–35
social stratification. *See* caste system; equality and antidiscrimination; racism
socio-economic rights
  "total constitutionalism" and, 221–222
  common law (South Africa) and, 228
  duty applied horizontally (South Africa), 233
  goal of self-sufficiency and, 37–38
  in *Juma Musjid* (2011), 230–232
  indirect horizontal application of, 95–96
Sommeregger, Georg, 144, 180
Soobramoney v. Minister of Health, KwaZulu-Natal (1997), 224–225

INDEX

Soraya case (1973), 169–170
South African constitutional project
  common good and, 227–229
  Court's role in, 221–222
  duties of private actors in, 219–221, 230–233
  equality and housing guarantee and, 229–230
  horizontal application and, 9, 13–14, 144, 147, 188–192, 196, 218–220
  horizontal application of constitution and, 22, 188–190, 222–242
  horizontal application of equality rights and, 146–147, 187, 190
  republican interpretation of, 196, 227–229
sovereignty, 96–97, 255–256
Spitz, Richard, 199–200
Stadium Ban case (2008), 13–14, 181–184
state action doctrine
  1960s sit-ins (US) and, 78–79
  about, 64–65
  evolution of, 62, 81–82
  freedom of speech and, 92
  indirect horizontal application and, 89–90
  judicial interpretations of, 88–90
  narrowed public/private divide and, 92–94, 99
  preservation of public/private divide and, 63–65, 73–75, 83, 86–87, 90, 121
  racism and, 63–64
  Shelley v. Kraemer (1948), 4–5, 74–79, 127–128
  South Africa's Interim Constitution and, 201–202
  tragic outcomes of, 87–90
state constitutional rights, 94–95
state inaction, 3, 88, 120–121, 129, 216–217
State of Madras v. Champakam Dorairajan, 112–113
State of West Bengal v. Union of India, 115
Stone Sweet, Alec, 173, 259

Storing, Herbert, 19–21, 24, 30–31
subjective rights, 4, 155, 164
subnational constitutionalism, 93–94

Technical Committee on Fundamental Rights (South Africa), 199
testamentary decisions, 222–239
Theme Committee Four on Fundamental Rights (South Africa), 203
Theron, Justice Leona, 238
Thirteenth Amendment (US), 63, 66–68
Title II (Civil Rights Act), 84–85
total constitutionalism, 5
Treaty of Lisbon, 249–250
Treaty on the Functioning of the European Union, 261
Tribe, Laurence, 199–201
Tushnet, Mark, 5, 14–15, 17–18, 51

ubuntu (South Africa), 192–195, 229
United States,
  Amendments to constitution, 59–60, 63, 66, 68–69, 82–83
  Commerce Clause, US Constitution, 83–85
  Equal Protection Clause, 82
  federal structure of, 97–98
  Fifteenth Amendment (US), 66
  Fourteenth Amendment, 59–60, 63, 66, 68–69, 82–83
  Heart of Atlanta Motel v. United States (1964), 84–85
  horizontality in, 9, 44–47, 60–62, 97–98, 130–133
  public/private divide in, 61–64, 74–75, 86–90, 92
  Thirteenth Amendment, 63, 66–68
United States v. Cruikshank (1874), 69
Universal Declaration of Human Rights, 62

value monism, 176–177
Van der Walt, Johan, 255–256, 263–268
Van Gend en Loos case (1963), 250, 256, 259–260
Verma, Chief Justice J. S., 120–121

vertical model of rights
  Civil Rights Act of 1964 (US) and, 85–86, 140
  defined, 1–2, 8
  horizontal model contrasted, 16, 19–21, 278
  settled, 140
Victor, Justice Margie, 222–240
Vidya Verma v. Dr Shiv Narain Verma (1956), 111
Viking case (2007), 263–265
Vinson, Justice Fred M., 76
Violence Against Women Act (United States), 121
Viroli, Maurizio, 36–37
virtue, 23–24, 33–34, 36–39, 49–50, 176, 179

Warren, Chief Justice Earl, 81–82
The Washington Post, 81

Weak Courts, Strong Rights (Tushnet), 5
Webking, Robert, 30–32
Wechsler, Herbert, 77
Weimar Constitution (Germany), 152–153
welfare liberalism, 28–30
welfare states, 14–15
White, Justice Byron Raymond, 79–80
White, Morton, 2–3
"white primary" cases, 16–19
Wood, Gordon, 30–31
Woolman, Stuart, 208, 210–211, 220–221

Zackin, Emily, 93, 96
Zitzke, Emile, 190
Zölibat case (1957), 161–163
Zoroastrian Cooperative Housing Society v. District Registrar, 122–128

For EU product safety concerns, contact us at Calle de José Abascal, 56–1°,
28003 Madrid, Spain or eugpsr@cambridge.org.

www.ingramcontent.com/pod-product-compliance
Lightning Source LLC
Chambersburg PA
CBHW071941070126
37870CB00028B/780